MICHEL FABRE

From Harlem
to Paris

Black American
Writers in France,
1840–1980

UNIVERSITY OF ILLINOIS PRESS
Urbana and Chicago

This book is printed on acid-free paper.

Library of Congress Cataloging-in-Publication Data

Fabre, Michel.
  From Harlem to Paris : Black American writers in France, 1840–1980
/ Michel Fabre.
    p.   cm.
  Includes bibliographical references (p.   ) and index.
  ISBN 0–252–01684–X
  1. American literature—Afro-American authors—History and
criticism.   2. American literature—France—Paris—History and
criticism.   3. Afro-American authors—France—Paris—Biography.
4. Afro-Americans—France—Paris—History.   5. Harlem (New York,
N.Y.)—Intellectual life.   6. Paris (France)—Intellectual life.
7. Harlem Renaissance.   I. Title.
PS153.N5F34   1991
810.9′896073—dc20   90-27621
                                                             CIP

To the memory of my father and of the writer friends
who have died since this research was started,
and for Julien and Jessica

Contents

Foreword

The extended genesis of this book needs more than a few words of explanation. In the early 1960s, while I was doing research for *The Unfinished Quest of Richard Wright*, the experiences and reactions of the expatriate Afro-American writers who stayed with Wright in Paris in the 1950s attracted my attention to the very special emotional relationship those writers enjoyed with France, different from that of their white fellow citizens. Also, in my teaching of black literature at the Sorbonne Nouvelle, the close study of such diverse novels as McKay's *Banjo* and Baldwin's *Giovanni's Room* (not to mention the latter's brilliant analyses of what it means to be an American, and a black American, in Paris in *Notes of a Native Son* and *Nobody Knows My Name*) opened my eyes to the significant variations, due to time and temperament, in these cultural and personal relationships.

The relevance of a systematic panorama of such attitudes became clear after discussions with William Gardner Smith and other, notably younger writers like William Melvin Kelley, Ronald Fair, or Ted Joans. Consequently, when, in early 1972, I was invited to give a seminar at the University of Iowa and could travel around the United States, I launched into research for this project, interviewing writers like Arna Bontemps and John Matheus and exploring the resources of many libraries and manuscript repositories.

Thanks to the James Weldon Johnson collection at Yale University, I was able to go through the correspondence and unpublished manuscripts of most of the Harlem Renaissance writers and their white friends. At the Schomburg Collection of the New York Public Library, still located in the antiquated original building, Ernest Kaiser helped me find my way through the invaluable "vertical files" containing precious, but brittle and crumbling, clippings from the Afro-American press that dealt with France. At the Amistad Research Center, then at Dillard University, I went through the as-yet-uncataloged Countee Cullen papers and discovered the travel diary of Mary McLeod Bethune. The Fisk University Library provided information, scattered in his voluminous files, about Jean Toomer's stays at Avon. The library of the University of Atlanta contained correspondence between Harold Jackman and his Harlem Renaissance friends; also, Ernest Jones and Richard Long, both on the faculty at Atlanta, helped me explore the contacts between the New Negro and the negritude movements. At Howard University Dorothy Porter set me on the track of René Maran's contacts with Alain Locke; interviews with Mercer Cook completed the picture.

After I came back to France in 1972, I repeatedly organized my M.A. seminars to focus on the critical reception of the literary works by black Americans in France and their own experiences there. Since research assistants are not available in our institutions, many of my students volunteered to systematically investigate French magazines and newspapers to unearth articles and reviews dealing with Afro-American writers. A few chose to write theses on related topics: for instance, Claude Grimal mapped French critical reactions to black American writers between the two world wars; Catherine Bédouelle studied the treatment and place of black American literature in *Presence Africaine:* Aminata Diop worked on the Josephine Baker phenomenon; Janine Dove focused on the place of France in James Baldwin's fiction; Michèle Ségarame listed French reviewers' reactions to *Roots, Jubilee,* and *Sally Hemings.*

Later, with the help of Jean-Pierre Turbergue, I prepared and sent to French university students and to noted French writers questionnaires to evaluate their knowledge of black American writers and their image of jazz. Part of the findings was published in a translation by Steven Rubin. Such related activities did not, however, further my initial project; rather, they led me somewhat astray—namely, to start work on an *Annotated Bibliography of the Reception of Afro-American Literature* in France, which will be published by Greenwood Press.

In the meantime, a need to widen my literary and academic horizons, combined with pressing requests from French-speaking African and Caribbean students for me to teach a seminar in African and Caribbean literatures in English, deflected my interests toward Third World literatures in English, a field that I have been exploring in a comparative perspective for some fifteen years. Hence the enormous delay in completing this book, for which most of the research had been done by 1975.

It took the obstinate enthusiasm of my friend and editor Maurice Partouche of Editions Lieu Commun to persuade me to complete a French version of it first. It came out in 1985 under the title *La Rive Noire* and enjoyed a very favorable reception in France. Although it could have been translated and published at once in the United States,

I was not satisfied with the book as it was because it addressed the general French reader, providing explanations on the U.S. social and cultural background that would be superfluous to an American audience while taking the corresponding French background for granted.

While teaching a seminar at Harvard University in the spring of 1985, I added material on several writers and visitors, especially Amanda Smith, Jessie Fauset, and Mary Church Terrell, and benefited from exchanges with Farah Griffin and Werner Sollors. At Harvard the acquaintance and help of Michael Haggerty also enabled me to extend my panorama to many jazz musicians.

At that stage I faced a dilemma: should I *also* deal in depth with artists and musicians about whom I had collected much material, or should I eliminate them completely and stick to creative writers? To keep this volume to a manageable size I decided to discard a good deal of information that did not specifically relate to the *writers'* French experience. In the 1970s the material on artists and musicians was valuable, first-hand information, but with the publication of biographies on Toomer (by Nellie McKay and by Cynthia Kerman and Richard Eldridge), on McKay (by Wayne Cooper), and on Hughes (by Faith Berry and by Arnold Rampersad), this information was no longer so fresh and new. Consequently, with the competent and attentive help of Jane Blanshard, who edited and word-processed the manuscript and made worthwhile suggestions, I cut the some 700 pages I had reached by about half.

I thank Richard Wentworth, director of the University of Illinois Press, for accepting it immediately and Karen Hewitt and Cynthia Mitchell for helping so much with the final editing. As a result, this book is, more than is usually the case, a collective work—the result of much collaboration, including that of many authors who, like William Melvin Kelley, James Emanuel, Melvin Dixon, and Ted Joans, made remarks upon, and corrections to, the passages concerning them.

Among the scores of people to whom I am indebted, I wish to thank particularly the following writers, scholars, colleagues, students, friends, and acquaintances for their generous assistance: Louis Achille, Samuel Allen, the staff of the Amistad Research Center, Simone de Beauvoir, James Baldwin, the staff of the Beinecke Library at Yale University, Jean-Claude Boffard, Robert Bone, Alberta and Arna Bontemps, Jenny Aspenwell Bradley, Horace and Susan Cayton, Aimé Césaire, Barbara Chase-Riboud, Nina Cobb Kressner, Cyrus Colter, Mercer Cook, Schofield and Rosette Coryell, Ida Cullen, Léon-Gontran Damas, Beauford Delaney, William Demby, Alioune Diop, Melvin Dixon, Caroline Dudley Delteil, Ralph Ellison, James Emanuel,

Ronald Fair, William Ferris, the staff of the Fisk University Library, Hoyt Fuller, Donald Gallup, Henry-Louis Gates, Addison Gayle, Stanley Geist, Herbert Gentry, Richard Gibson, Harry Goldberg, Eugene Goodheart, Brion Gysin, Farah Griffin, Michael Haggerty, Ollie Harrington, Gordon Heath, Mae Henderson, Chester and Lesley Himes, LeRoy Hodges, the staff of the Howard University Library, Langston Hughes, Ted Joans, Claude Julien, Ernest Jones, LeRoi Jones, William Melvin Kelley, Keneth Kinnamon, Rayford Logan, Mrs. R. H. Laskell, Richard Long, Clarence Major, Yves and Yvonne Malartic, Claire and Edward Margolies, Camille Maran, Paule Marshall, John F. Matheus, Toni Morrison, Paulette and Jeanne Nardal, Mary Painter Garin, Michele Paolantonacci and the staff of the Bibliothèque Nationale, Arnold Rampersad, Jean-Jacques Recht, Ishmael Reed, Ida and William Gardner Smith, Douglas Schneider, the staff of the Schomburg Collection of the New York Public Library, Léopold Sedar Senghor, Werner Sollors, Martin Steins, Mme. Pierre Vogein-Rappaport, Jean and Ghislaine Wagner, John A. Williams, Poppy C. White, Ellen Wright, and Frank Yerby.

I have benefited from the support of grants provided by the American Philosophical Society (1972), the North Atlantic Treaty Organization (1973), the Fulbright Commission and the French-American Foundation (1980), and the prolonged hospitality of professors Charles Davis and Robin Winks in the colleges they directed at Yale University.

I thank my wife, Genevieve, for putting up for so many years with the presence, real or imaginary, of many black American writers and artists in our home and life, and also for sharing the same field of research while maintaining her own perspectives and interests.

From Harlem to Paris

Introduction

Traveling to Europe has always been for most educated Americans a means of getting in touch with their cultural heritage. Throughout the nineteenth century the European tour from London to Italy was a must for the elite of the New World, who came to admire the works of art in the Louvre or the Gothic cathedrals and discovered with amazement the economic backwardness of the Old Continent, much like Westerners traveling today in the Third World. They often felt that inefficiency went hand in hand with the easy morals of Parisian life. Thus was created the myth of a seductive but frivolous France—so much so that the doughboys who came to fight the Great War were sent both to save the land of Voltaire and Rousseau from the Huns and to bring about its moral regeneration.

During the first half of the nineteenth century, the overwhelming majority of black Americans were slaves. Even after emancipation, few were able to go abroad, so black travelers in Europe were scarce. Nevertheless, for many blacks France was associated with the idea of freedom. The French of the Revolutionary period and Abbé Grégoire's Société des Amis des Noirs were supporters of the first Afro-American woman poet, Phillis Wheatley, a slave. For them her writing was concrete proof that the Negro was indeed endowed with creative intelligence. Today the name of William Wells Brown, the first black American novelist and playwright, is familiar to many. More know that Paul Laurence Dunbar, who wrote forty years later, was the first black poet to earn a living from his writing. But who in America or France is aware that, even before Brown was known, the first black American literary school was created in New Orleans by free people of color or that some of the members of this French-speaking group were educated in France? One of them, Victor Séjour, enjoyed a successful career as a playwright in Paris and was as well assimilated into French society as his fellow black, Alexandre Dumas. Dumas was the symbol of Negro talent honored by France, and black visitors from across the ocean never failed to pay him tribute when they came to that country.

The first black visitors were professional entertainers, like Ira Aldridge, and abolitionists who had been invited to give lectures, like Brown and Bishop Daniel A. Payne. After slavery was abolished, black leaders came to France to visit the land of the egalitarian principles born of the Revolution as well as to partake of the splendor of a grandiose culture. Among them were Frederick Douglass; Booker T. Washington, president of Tuskegee Institute at the height of his fame; and Mary Church Terrell. But there were also artists like Blind Tom, the pianist, and Roland Hayes, the classical singer, and painters such as Henry Ossawa Tanner, who settled in Paris in 1891 and died there in 1937. When black American visitors saw his paintings, bought by the French government, hanging in the Musée du Luxembourg, they were convinced that artistic talent is always rewarded in Paris.

Until the Great War the myth of French culture and hospitality prevailed mainly among the black elite. In America the popular black press more often vaunted French racial liberalism—so much so that when the First World War broke out great numbers of blacks volunteered to defend the "land of democracy." In 1917 hundreds of thousands of them landed in France. Despite American military regulations that forbade fraternizing, these soldiers established relationships with French fighters and with local people. This was their first taste of true equality. The French supreme commander did not think it advisable to use the Senegalese infantry as anything more than cannon fodder, but the black Americans, benefiting from the prestige of their home country, were treated well. The soldiers brought over jazz, introduced in France by Jimmy Europe's orchestra in 1918. They took back home an image of the tolerance and generosity shown to blacks in France. Their social movements would use that image as an example to white American society over the years.

However, in the period between the two world wars, awareness of French colonial policy increased after NAACP leader W. E. B. Du Bois convened the first Pan-African Conference in Paris in 1919. Du Bois, studying the racial situation of the troops on the European front, had come up with a more complex analysis than the impressions the black American soldiers had brought back. Although he gave precedence to the social equality embodied in the cultural assimilation policy of the French government, he correctly identified the harmful effects of French colonization. Up to that point even Marcus Garvey, the Jamaican leader who blasted the white race in *The Negro World*, spared France. It wasn't until the ex-Communist Claude McKay wrote his novel *Banjo* that the idyllic picture began to show its darker side. Set in Marseilles, *Banjo* brings out the complexity of the cleavages within the black diaspora and points out the different forms of colonialization, of which cultural assimilation is perhaps the most harmful.

During the twenties, when there was a large group of American expatriates in Europe, black writers also spent time on the continent. Although they were generally stuck away in third class on the transatlantic steamers and they are never mentioned among the so-called "lost generation," comparatively as many black travelers as white came to the Old World. Mothers of soldiers killed in France came on pilgrimages to the battlefields from Flanders to Alsace; tourists sought culture and freedom, trying to forget the "red summer" of 1919 and the increasing number of lynchings. Black and white alike were fleeing from Prohibition and puritanism. They took advantage of the strong dollar to have a good time at little expense. The Europe they encountered was imbued with jazz and Negro art. This helped along the careers of black musicians who found work in the Montmartre cabarets. Black music flooded the European capitals, which established its reputation, in contrast to the United States, where it was considered lowbrow and vulgar. The flowering of the cultural renaissance in Harlem and the influence of African art, which the avant-garde had finally discovered, contributed indirectly to Josephine Baker's exotic Parisian triumph.

The same vitality brought to Paris nearly all the writers of the New Negro movement. Some spent just a few days, like John Matheus and Charles Johnson on their way to Liberia on a mission; others stayed several weeks. Still others stayed on for many months, like Langston Hughes, his friend the novelist Jessie Fauset, and young poet Gwendolyn Bennett. Hughes, down to his last penny in 1924, washed dishes in jazz cabarets but discovered the splendor of spring in Paris. As for the city's faithful admirers, they came back nearly every summer: francophile Countee Cullen stayed in the city often during the thirties and was frequently seen dancing the biguine at the Bal Colonial. Jean Toomer, devoted disciple of Gurdjieff, dashed off to the Priory at Avon, near Fontainebleau. Claude McKay preferred to knock about on the road to Marseilles, Bordeaux, and Brest, and filled his novels with French scenes. In 1921 he left the United States for Russia and only went back in 1933, via Morocco, after some eight years in France. By then he knew France intimately, her bums and her workers especially: in *Banjo* he describes the port of Marseilles as the gateway to Africa. All these writers mixed with the many musicians and with other artists as well: painters like Palmer Hayden and Hale Woodruff, sculptors like Augusta Savage and Elizabeth Prophet. Thus a black society formed in Paris, changed over the years, absorbed the latest innovations, and influenced French culture as surely as did the white Americans.

Even more important to the history of the black intellectuals was the number of contacts made in Paris between the representatives of the New Negro movement—Alain Locke, Cullen, Hughes, Walter White, and McKay, most of all—and the Caribbean and African students in the French universities during the years of the Colonial Exhibition. René Maran's Goncourt Prize–winning *Batouala*, with its preface criticizing the abuses of French colonialism, was quickly translated into English. Many a black American author, inspired by this "authentic" Negro novel, visited Maran in his modest salon. He attempted to publicize Afro-American works in the French-speaking press and supported the Nardal sisters, whose 1930 magazine, *La Revue du Monde Noir,* aimed to rehabilitate black genius.

Claude McKay's novel *Banjo* in turn influenced the French-speaking black writers. For the generation of Léopold Senghor and Léon-Gontran Damas, reading *Banjo* in French translation inspired pride in primitivism and led them to discover the cultural unity of the oppressed black diaspora. Aimé Césaire found in it the celebration of the "proud nigger," which he wrote about in his *Cahier d'un retour au pays natal.* After France's liberation Senghor—by then the established spokesman for negritude—translated texts by Toomer, Hughes, and Cullen in homage to the Harlem Renaissance. In an article titled "Trois poétes negro-américains," published in *Poésie 45,* the African poet found in their work the mark of a cosmic and human inspiration with a unique rhythm, "for song and poem are one and the same thing for the Negro, be he from America or elsewhere."

The Second World War put an end to the French vacation of Countee Cullen and his fellows. The common experience of oppression seemed to bring together the victims of the Nazis and the black Americans subjected to racism—at least that is what Richard Wright thought when, after liberation, Franco-American contacts started up with renewed vigor during what Claude-Edmonde Magny has called "the age of the American novel." Richard Wright was at the forefront of this, along with Faulkner, Steinbeck, and Gertrude Stein, who welcomed Wright to Paris. His decision to settle there permanently in 1947 was the beginning of the "times of the expatriates."

In fact, the political climate was changing. The cold war exacerbated the positions taken vis-à-vis the U.S., and the slightest opposition from any American citizen quickly labeled him un-American. And then it was only one step to Senator Joseph McCarthy's House Un-American Activities Committee—and a very short step at that, if one had ever belonged to a left-wing political party. Wright came to France to get away from racism and to find a humanistic answer to the questions everyone was raising in the postwar period. Paradoxically, he was denounced, along with Sartre and Camus, by the French communist press at the same time the American secret services were keeping tabs on him as a former communist. Although Wright, like his compatriots, never gave up his American citizenship, he refused to go back and live in America. France was less an inspiration for his novels than the scene of the ideological commitment that he shared with the existentialists. His exile gave him perspective on his country and opened up the realities of Africa to him. His uprooting made him more of a contemporary intellectual than most of his compatriots who had taken refuge in Paris.

James Baldwin left for Paris shortly after Wright. As yet unknown in 1948, he encountered great financial difficulties. Wright's death and the civil rights movement later gave him a turn at the role of the committed black writer. During the fifties, however, he was still feeling around. Paris was the setting for his novel *Giovanni's Room,* which deals with homosexuality and American self-discovery. There, Baldwin wrote the most discerning pages on exile and the search for cultural roots in Europe ever recorded by any American, black or white.

William Gardner Smith came to France in 1951, a short time after the publication of his novel *Last of the Conquerors,* about racism in the American forces occupying Germany. He quickly became a part of French society, worked as an editor at Agence France Presse, and married a Frenchwoman. His novel *The Stone Face* takes up the cause of Algerian liberation and treats of anti-Arab racism in France. Like Wright, he died in Paris, in 1974.

The popular novelist Frank Yerby first went into exile on the Riviera in 1957. Prejudice led him to move on to Spain, where he nevertheless wrote novels about France, such as *Speak Now,* which takes place in Paris during May 1968. Chester Himes also ended up in Spain. He had come to France in 1953 and left at the beginning of the sixties. In the meantime he had become famous, not for the racially committed novels he was known for in the United States, but as a master of the thriller. He was published in Marcel Duhamel's Série Noire detective series. France at least let him live, he says, while giving highly contradictory impressions of it in his autobiography. His exile did not stem from political harassment but from his grudge against his cruel motherland, which had, he felt, rejected him.

The writers Baldwin, Wright, Himes, and also Richard Gibson; the cartoonist Ollie Harrington; the painters Larry Potter, Beauford Delaney, Herb Gentry, and Walter Coleman; and numerous colored musicians made up a veritable black colony in the fifties. Their encounters, discussions, and confrontations brought fame to the Monaco and Tournon cafés in the Latin Quarter and to ex-GI LeRoy Haynes's soul food restaurant on the Rue Clauzel.

Nineteen sixty, the year of Richard Wright's death, also marked independence for many countries in Africa and the coming of age of the civil rights movement in the United States. Although the myth of "the land of liberty" had not died, the image of France had changed for black Americans. France still welcomed the expatriates—some of whom, like Baldwin, returned to the United States to live for a while—and in France they seldom encountered racism directly because the prestige of being American, and writers, spared them that. But the Arabs and increasingly numerous Africans were the objects of racial hatred. For a long time the image of libertarian France had hidden that of colonial France. Now the myth began to show its first cracks at the same time that frequent encounters took place in Paris between black Americans and Africans. The former aspired to a certain degree of integration, but the latter espoused nationalism and spoke out against the dangers of assimilation. These ideological differences were apparent at the first Congress of Black Writers, held at the Sorbonne in 1956. There Wright opposed Senghor's views on the usefulness of tradition in the fight for decolonization. Nevertheless, the Société Africaine de Culture and its American branch worked toward a better mutual understanding of the black diaspora.

Although in the fifties black Americans were primarily concerned with integration and civil rights, Samuel Allen and Langston Hughes, and also Mercer Cook, who had worked tirelessly to popularize the literary works of French-speaking blacks, began to spread the ideology of negritude in the United States. The rising popularity of the themes of negritude—blackness and "soul"—blotted out the French dream to some extent. Long before the huge success of Alex Haley's *Roots*, France's attraction for black America was declining in favor of Africa. The Algerian war showed that France was no stranger to racial oppression. Above all, even more powerful than the "Afro" fashion or the back-to-Africa ideology of the Black Power days, contacts between black Americans and Africans were multiplying. Organized tours, individual quests, and various conferences brought young intellectuals and professors, along with recognized writers like Arna Bontemps or Langston Hughes, to Dakar and Abidjan and the new English-speaking nations. From that point on, France was reduced to the role she had had in the eyes of Claude McKay: a gateway to Africa, one stop on the voyage toward a new black world.

The novelist William Melvin Kelley stayed in France for several months in 1968 as a sort of introduction to his projected discovery of Africa. During those years not all the black writers passing through shared that attitude. Melvin Van Peebles, the writer and film director, started his career in Paris, as did the novelists Carlene Polite and Barbara Chase-Riboud. Poets like Ted Joans and Hart LeRoy Bibbs lived there, mixing with the groups of beatniks in the Latin Quarter, while others, like James Emanuel, stayed in the provinces away from the crowds. Many novelists also stayed in Paris for a time. Because such tourism had become commonplace, France did not cease to be an exceptional host. On the one hand, while many racial obstacles had fallen in the United States, racism was on the upswing in France. On the other hand, the ease and rapidity of travel in general tended to make places interchangeable. France continued to attract black writers, but in the same way she attracted their white colleagues: Paris was a capital of culture, an international meeting place where the exchange rate for the dollar often made life cheaper than at home.

There were important exceptions, however. The poet Melvin Dixon came to France in search of his cultural ancestry just as he went to Africa to find his ethnic roots. The literary ancestors he was looking for, however, were not French or European writers but Wright and Hughes and all those who had developed their talents in France. Thus began a sort of literary pilgrimage to the places where the writers of the Harlem Renaissance or the expatriates of the fifties had lived. The poet Ted Joans is another exception: he was influenced by surrealism when he was very young and, beginning in 1960, traveled regularly to the "capital of poetry" as a disciple of Lautréamont and André Breton. But the image of Paris was overshadowed in his creative experience by that of the black world as a source of creativity and antirational vitality. In short, Joans prized the primitivism that was at the very source of surrealism. The attitudes of Dixon and Joans thus tended to present Paris as the place where certain aspects of black cultural history took root and mingled. The time had come for a fertile internationalism, a true crossroads of different cultures.

A detailed examination of the various experiences of all these black writers from across the ocean during their stays in France, with their expectations, discoveries, and disappointments, is interesting for two reasons. First of all, their multiple images of France with all their variations and differences shed light on both the changing reality of that country and the evolution or persistence of the myths created about her. And then the image of France and the use made of that image in works of literature by these writers are an essential complement to the image presented in the works of white American writers, the only

ones given serious critical attention until now. Finally, above and beyond the encounter of black America and France, Paris was becoming
more and more a meeting point for the different groups of the black
diaspora. An entire dimension of the intellectual history of the black
world was formed in France before she was left behind.

This retrospective of the black American writers in France for a century and a half is, generally speaking, chronological. It only occasionally touches on the experiences of the other artists: for instance, the
dancer Josephine Baker, the tragedian Ira Aldridge, and the painter
Beauford Delaney are mentioned only in passing as witnesses to their
times or part and parcel of the writers' world. I have chosen to emphasize the various and shifting aspects of a vast panorama that will
portray the complexity of the black dimension of the American experience in France, neglected until now, and the influence it had and
continues to have in both countries. If the tone of this book is light at
times, it is only to alleviate some of the passion, the emotion, and sometimes the suffering these people with strange or exemplary destinies
encountered as they traveled from Harlem to Paris.

1

The New Orleans Connection

Afro-Americans did not always see the land of "liberté, fraternité, égalité" as a haven of freedom for American blacks. For one thing, England had championed abolition earlier and more vigorously than France. Also, the rebellion in Santo Domingo, news of which spread quickly among the enslaved American blacks, clearly cast Napoleon as the villain in his dealings with liberator Toussaint Louverture. It took some time for the antislavery activities of French liberal intellectuals to show the more humanistic face of France. As a result, during the early decades of the nineteenth century, when transatlantic travel was reserved for a happy few, the major link between Afro-Americans and France was to be found in the New Orleans elite—free persons of color whose culture was strongly dependent on French traditions and whose literary and artistic production derived more from French romanticism than from their New World context. Although it was probably not well known by blacks in other parts of the United States, this New Orleans connection represents an early, important, and for a time the only, cultural link between American Negroes and France.

> Slaves cannot breathe in England: if their lungs
> Receive our air, that moment they are free,
> They touch our country, and their shackles fall.

Cowper's lines epitomized England's aspiration to be the champion of abolitionism. In quoting them as an epigraph to his *Running, A Thousand Miles for Freedom; or, The Escape*, fugitive slave William Craft probably expressed what England represented to his fellow black Americans. Yet France, both as the land of the Enlightenment and the Revolution and as a cradle of culture, very early vied with England for first place in their hearts. At the turn of the eighteenth century a Jesuit priest, Abbé Grégoire, with Robespierre, Lafayette, and others, had founded the Société des Amis des Noirs, whose action had led the revolutionary government to end slavery in the colonies for a time. Abbé Grégoire probably never met one of the very first black Americans to spend time in France—Sally Hemings, Thomas Jefferson's

slave, his wife's half-sister, who accompanied one of his daughters to
Paris in 1785.

"Dashing Sally" was fifteen years old when she arrived, a very handsome light-skinned mulatto with long black hair. She received a salary
and was apparently tutored in French, as was her brother James,
Jefferson's valet, who studied under the Prince de Condé's chef. In a
memoir her son Madison reported that she became Jefferson's con-
cubine in Paris and was pregnant by him in 1789. Since she was free
there by French law, she refused to return to the United States until
Jefferson promised to emancipate all her children when they reached
the age of twenty-one. But in spite of her other accomplishments, Sally
Hemings was not a woman of letters.[1] When Abbé Grégoire published
*An Enquiry Concerning the Moral Faculty and Literature of Negroes, Fol-
lowed with an Account of the Life and Works of Fifteen Negroes and Mulattoes
Distinguished in Science, Literature, and the Arts* in 1820, he significantly
selected Senegal-born but Boston-bred slave poet Phillis Wheatley as
one of the proofs that the black race could elevate itself to civilization.

That England came first as apostle and supporter of emancipation
is indisputable: London aristocrats had made Wheatley famous, and
not only did William Wilberforce and his circle loom larger than the
Société des Amis des Noirs in terms of international influence, but
slavery was abolished in the British colonies as early as 1838, while
it took another decade for Victor Schoelcher to proclaim emancipation in the French territories. After the generous emancipation de-
crees passed in 1790 had been rescinded by Bonaparte, the Bourbons
were no more liberal than he, and it took the efforts of Victor Hugo,
Alphonse de Lamartine, and other progressive intellectuals, as well as
a disastrous colonial war in Haiti, to bring about permanent emancipation in a resolution taken by the newly proclaimed 1848 republic.

As a matter of fact, many of the fugitive slaves turned antislavery
propagandists were in Canada or Great Britain: Alexander Crummel,
Jermain W. Loguen, Henry Bibb, William and Ellen Craft, Charles
Lenox Remond, Samuel Ringgold Ward, Frederick Douglass, and
William Wells Brown all sojourned extensively abroad. Of these, only
William Wells Brown was able to pursue his activities in Paris, and
there the language barrier often proved a hindrance.

Such was not the case with a score of *gens de couleur libres* from
New Orleans, all French-speaking and many of French descent, who
repaired to France from the 1830s onward in order to study and
sometimes to pursue a career there. To mention only writers, B. Valcour and presumably Armand Lanusse went to Paris to study; Victor
Séjour, Pierre Dalcour, Louis and Camille Thierry lived out their lives

in France. Neither fugitive slaves nor abolitionists, they all belonged to the light-skinned Negro elite who enjoyed considerable economic status in antebellum New Orleans.

To understand how this group of Creole intellectuals developed, it is necessary to retrace the peculiarities of race relations in French Louisiana. Although legislation passed in 1724 prohibited marriage or even cohabitation between French settlers and their female slaves, during the eighteenth century miscegenation became a way of life. The planters' mulatto concubines were soon influential enough for a Spanish governor to try, in 1786, to curb their prestige by barring them by decree from wearing jewels and feathers in their hair. After the rebellion led by Toussaint Louverture, the arrival of French refugees from Santo Domingo increased the number of persons of color, and they came to play, if not an important part in the politics of the colony, at least a preponderant role in its cultural life: for decades the quadroon and octoroon balls held in the Salle d'Orléans were the fashion, exciting the jealousy of the white belles.

Many wealthy white men bequeathed fortunes to the offspring of their illegitimate unions. Consequently, the *gens de couleur libres* formed a powerful caste, owning businesses, plantations, and slaves, but they were discriminated against by southern practice. Because almost no colored teachers were qualified and white Frenchmen rarely dared brave public opinion by accepting free colored pupils, wealthy mulattoes sent their children to complete their education at universities in France, where they could live according to their means and enjoy social equality.

Such was the case of Armand Lanusse, Victor Séjour, and their friends. Lanusse was born in 1812 and presumably studied in Paris, although his disciple Rodolphe A. Desdunes claimed that Lanusse saw France only through the eyes of imagination. The principal of a Catholic school for blacks in New Orleans from 1852 to 1866, he was light-skinned enough to pass for white; yet, convinced that the Creoles had no future apart from the blacks, he chose the side of the Negro. He deserves more recognition, however, for his literary endeavors: with the support of Jean-Louis Marciaq, a French teacher, he established *L'Album Littéraire,* "a journal for young people, amateurs of literature." It carried poetry, short stories, and editorials by New Orleans free men of color. The French heritage and outstanding position of this group led them to turn to sources outside the United States for inspiration and models. They felt closer to the French romanticists—especially Lamartine, Musset, and Béranger—than to any other school. Their imagined cultural home was "la belle France," the land of aesthetic refinement and liberty. From the short-lived magazine venture sprang the idea of an anthology of poems that Lanusse published in 1845 as *Les Cenelles, choix de poésies indigènes*. The title of this collection, a reference to the berries of the hawthorn bush, emphasized the difficulty of the authors' undertaking "in the midst of an environment so discouraging to their poetic inclinations" as well as their desire to "give a bright color to the dark face of their lot."[2]

It was probably B. Valcour who, casting himself as "an unrecognized son" of New Orleans, initiated the image of the Afro-American writer spurned by his mother country and thus driven to seek a spiritual home in France. Valcour actually sailed to France in order to acquire an education there. He moved freely in the highest literary circles of Paris; a keen student of Greek and Latin, he was especially fond of the classical French poets, but he was also an admirer of Victor Hugo and a master of alexandrine verse.

Pierre Dalcour spent most of his life in France, where he had originally been sent to study. He grew accustomed to the liberal atmosphere of Paris, and when he returned to Louisiana, he found it impossible to accept racial discrimination again and so chose exile. He and his brother died in Paris, where they had led a cultured existence, associating with such well-known literary figures as Hugo and Alexandre Dumas.

The prolific poet Adolphe Duhart, who wrote under the pseudonym of Leila in New Orleans newspapers, was likewise raised in France. Louise R. Lamothe, who taught in Paris after graduating there, became the director of a college for girls at Abbeville, in the north, where she taught for forty years, meanwhile starting a magazine in Paris and being awarded the Palmes académiques by the French ministry of education. Her publications were limited, however, to readers and school books. Antoine Marie, the very type of the distinguished and refined Creole of color, likewise set out for Paris. Incapable of bearing racial humiliation—the more so as his octoroon companion had borne a child to a white man—as he was about to take the boat in New York, he became demented with jealously concerning his mistress and shot himself.

Generally celebrating azure-eyed and fair-haired Creole ladies, these writers seldom denounced racism. Camille Thierry, however, sang of Abd-el-Kader, the leader of Arab resistance against the French in Algeria; and, seeing a black beggar who claimed to be "General Magloire d'Hoquincourt," he wondered in a poem whether he was not once "a great prince among the African sands."[3] Armand Lanusse told the story of a young colored lady who became insane when her

white lover forsook her because he could not legally marry her.[4] But
these writers denounced moral and social conventions. Thus Lanusse
questioned the celibacy of Catholic priests; and Camille Thierry, faith-
fulness in matrimony.

Camille Thierry, the second largest contributor to *Les Cenelles* after
Armand Lanusse and probably the best poet in the group, was the son
of an octoroon and a Bordeaux liquor merchant. His first piece, "Les
Idées," came out in *L'Album Littéraire* in the mid-1840s and brought
him instant recognition. He was about to go to Paris to pursue his
studies when his father's death compelled him to continue the family
business with his brother. He was more interested in writing, though,
and the latter used to say, "Camille puts spirit into verse, while I put
spirits into barrels." In spite of the sustaining friendship of white
Dr. Charles Testut, himself a man of letters, Camille suffered from
being excluded from New Orleans high society because of a few drops
of black blood. He early thought of exiling himself, as his poem "Le
Chant de l'Exilé" seems to indicate.

> Exile, my friend, I do fear
> But why should I tarry here? No.
> I shall leave before my way
> Be deserted by the sun's last rays.
>
> . . . .
> Who can hold me to these shores
> Where I only dwell among regrets?
>
> . . . .
> Take heart! There is another shore
> Where happiness can soar,
> Where my joy will be more vivid,
> Where my days will enjoy some sun.
>
> . . . .
> A foreign land will open its door to me
> And I shall know how to cross its threshold.[5]

At last Thierry could retire and realize his dream. He stayed a while
in Paris, dissipating much of his fortune. Then he settled in Bordeaux,
where he died in 1875, nearly in poverty because the New Orleans
firms with which he had invested his money had become bankrupt.
The previous year a collection of his poems came out under the title
Les Vagabondes, Poésies Américaines. Most of them had previously appeared in Louisiana newspapers, including evocations of local characters: an old Spanish woman, Mariquita La Calentura, whom Camille
had derided as a boy and now felt very close to; his friend Eugene B.,
who had committed suicide at nineteen; a French immigrant named

Haricot, etc. He added dramatic and historical pieces on Diane de Poitiers and other French sovereigns. His style, often reminiscent of Hugo and Lamartine, at times took on Baudelairian tones when dealing with orgies or debauchery. On the whole, he looked back to his Louisiana youth and had his Creole audience, rather than his new French acquaintances, in mind.

Thierry's half-brother, Michel Seligny, had traveled extensively in the French Antilles in 1858, reporting about them in New Orleans newspapers, before he fell in love with a married woman—the mother of ten children—was cast out by his family because of this liaison, and decided to flee to Paris with his lover. When he died in 1868, he left her a manuscript, "Junius to Octavius," a long discussion of the situation of the southern man of color written in perfect French and revealing a tolerant and broad-minded approach. In the Louisiana press he also published pieces like "La petite mendiante de Chambéry" and letters on the reception of Victor Séjour's *Son of the Night*, obviously inspired by his stay in France.

Born in 1817, Victor Séjour was the handsome son of a New Orleans quadroon and a free man of color from Santo Domingo. His father had served in the D'Aquin Battalion of Free Men of Color to defend New Orleans in 1814 and operated a tailor shop on Chartres Street. The family was respected and wealthy enough for Victor to attend the Sainte-Barbe Academy before being sent to Paris at nineteen to complete his education. There his grace and fortune soon gained him entrée to fashionable circles, and after graduating he started upon a literary career. His first piece, "Le Mulâtre," appeared in 1837 in *La Revue des Colonies*, published by a society of people of color directed by the militant Auguste Bissette. In this short story set in Saint-Marc, Haiti, he vented his own psychological sufferings through the character of Georges, a young mulatto who kills his master before discovering he is his father, and reflected on racism and slavery. But living in Paris must have prompted rosier thoughts; at any rate, Séjour's second published piece, an ode titled "Le Retour de Napoléon," expressed his pro-French feelings when the emperor's remains were brought from Saint Helena to Paris.

Séjour enjoyed a fascinating thirty-year career as a playwright. He made his debut on the stage of the Théâtre Français in 1844 with *Diegarias*, a historical drama in five acts set in fifteenth-century Spain. His next play, *La Chute de Séjan (The Fall of Sejanus)*, also in verse, ran at the same theater for three and a half months in 1848. Acquainted with Alexandre Dumas and friendly with French dramatist Émile Augier, Séjour was largely an epigone. His *Diegarias* recalls Hugo's *Hernani* in tone, setting, and style; *The Fall of Sejanus* was an adaptation of Ben

Jonson's work, set in somewhat pompous verse. In 1852 he preferred prose when he adapted Shakespeare's *Richard III*. In his dedication of *Richard III* to his father, he insisted that he did not translate Shakespeare: "to translate is to diminish. I thought that by standing erect at his feet I would better disclose his greatness."[6] The play was a box-office hit for a long time, and Séjour was hailed as "among the most beloved of the young literary generation."[7] He turned to melodrama with *L'Argent du diable* (*The Devil's Money*, 1854), and to a cloak-and-dagger plot in *Les Noces vénitiennes* (*Venetian Wedding*) the following year. He dedicated *Fils de la nuit* (*Son of the Night*) to his friend and supporter, the elder Dumas, in 1856. This story of a kidnapped boy who comes to recover his ducal heritage and save the city of Naples was lavishly set, with spectacular staging and elaborate effects that made up for the empty dialogue. Yet Séjour was an earnest craftsman, notorious for revising his plays up to the last minute. The final act of *Son of the Night* was rewritten during the first performance of the play; Séjour forced the actors to rehearse the new version during the intermission after act 4. This play was his most successful, playing to full houses for six months before a long tour in the provinces. After it, sometimes in collaboration with Thomas Barrière and Brésil, Séjour specialized in grandiose shows that struck the audience more than they moved it, and his subsequent career was in romantic drama.

During the Second Empire, he occasionally turned to more contemporary topics, as in *La Tireuse de cartes* (*The Fortune-Teller*), which duplicated the contemporary Edgardo Mortara affair: a dying Jewish baby, baptized by a Catholic maid, had unexpectedly recovered and been raised as a Christian; passing as a fortune-teller, his mother finally found the child, who had been adopted by a noble family. Possibly due to the fact that its co-author, J-F. Mocquard, was his secretary, Napoleon III himself attended a performance. The following year he also saw *Les Massacres de la Syrie* (*The Syrian Massacres*), which celebrated French intervention to stop the killing of Christians by Syrian Druses. Probably with a view to pleasing the sovereign, Séjour wrote *Les Volontaires de 1814* (*The Volunteers of 1814*), exalting French patriotism and reflecting Séjour's own devotion to the Bonapartes. It was staged in 1862. In the 1860s, Séjour concentrated again upon adventure.

Very much like Alexandre Dumas, to whom he was sometimes compared, Séjour espoused a French outlook, and he found the atmosphere of Paris little conducive to the airing of racial concerns. After treating race in his short story "Le Mulâtre," he worked on a full-length drama entitled "L'Esclave" ("The Slave"), but never staged or printed, the play has not come to light.[8] He wrote mostly for the French middle class, treating of religious faith, family, and love—all finally triumphant despite the pitfalls of ill fortune. Or he exalted the grandeur of Napoleonic heroes.

In his private life Séjour did not abide by the tenets of bourgeois morality any more than Dumas did: he fathered three sons out of wedlock by three different mothers. After revisiting his parents, however, he married a New Orleans octoroon, whom he took with him to France. He was a devoted son and, at the height of his success, brought his parents to Paris, where they lived out their last years.

His own career took a downward turn around 1870, when the critics' reception of *Henri de Lorraine* made him withdraw the play from the printers. These were the agitated times of the Franco-Prussian War and the Paris Commune, and Séjour himself reacted badly to the bloodshed and violent changes in his adopted country. He was tired of producing plays year after year, and his health was failing. He tried to turn to the novel with *Le Comte de Haag*. Published as a newspaper serial in the spring of 1872, it features a Prussian villain, condemns the violence of the Commune, and stresses the necessity of social reform in France. Tuberculosis prevented the completion of the story. In early September 1874 Séjour had to be taken to the municipal hospital, where for lack of funds he was supported by the Société des Auteurs et Compositeurs Dramatiques until his death on September 20.

He was buried at Père Lachaise cemetery, and in his funeral eulogy the popular novelist Paul Féval recalled the energetic bronze features of the youthful author and the melancholy musings of the sensitive older man wounded by the critics.[9] Although he never ceased to be a son of Louisiana, Victor Séjour probably became the first Afro-American who adopted French life to such a degree that when he died—after living for twenty-eight years in Paris and achieving a considerable reputation in literary and theatrical circles—he could deservedly be listed among French celebrities of the period.

Such writers as Thierry and Séjour certainly established for black Americans a tradition of traveling to Paris to enjoy the benefits of a nonracist cultural environment. *L'Album Littéraire* and *Les Cenelles* solidified an attempt on the part of educated mulattoes to react as a group to the cultural barrier engendered by discrimination. Their poetry was an escape from the brutal realities of the slaveholding South and also an implicit demand for social integration. By turning toward France, they were leaving, if only symbolically, their prejudice-ridden homeland for a place of educational and social opportunity.

Many Negro artists and professionals likewise attempted to escape the United States at a time when their color denied them the possibility of careers. George Boyer Vashon, the first black lawyer in New York State, was driven by prejudice to temporary self-exile in Haiti in 1848. He spent thirty months teaching at Collège Faustin in Port-au-Prince before returning to practice law in Syracuse, New York. His epic poem "Vincent Ogé" burns with race pride and yearning for retributive justice as it tells the story of the Haitian mulattoes inspired to rebel by the French Revolution but later captured, tortured, and slain.[10] Other black Americans established European ties. Born a slave, William G. Pennington escaped on coming of age and made his way as far as the University of Heidelberg in Germany, where he received the degree of doctor of divinity. Martin Delany, the well-known propagandist for black colonization of·Africa, had his European quarters in England. Because they spoke the language, colored artists from New Orleans more consistently turned toward France for their careers. This was the case of Daniel Warbourg, a stone engraver. He went to Paris in 1852 with his brother Eugene, a sculptor who made his reputation there and died in France at the age of thirty-six.

Musicians also turned to France. The son of Eulalie de Mandeville, an octoroon "placed" with a white man, Eugene Victor Macarthy had received the best musical education possible in New Orleans. His baritone voice and acting talent attracted the attention of Pierre Soulé, a prominent local white, who secured the help of the French ambassador to the U.S. to have Macarthy admitted to the Paris Conservatoire in 1840. He studied harmony and composition, but he did not choose exile or divorce himself from racial preoccupations. Upon his return to New Orleans he had a brief acting career, playing the leading role in *Anthony* and that of Buridan in *La Tour de Nesle*, both by the elder Dumas. Later a leading businessman, he carried much weight as a civil rights leader after Reconstruction, notably fighting discrimination in theaters. Richard Lambert, well known as a music teacher around 1850, had two sons who became composers. Growing restless under the restraints of Louisiana life, Lucien Lambert went to Paris for further study and ended up in Brazil. Among his best compositions are "La Juive," "Parisienne," and "La Rose et le bengali." His brother Sidney, a pianist, established himself in Paris, where he had much success with "Si j'étais roi," "L'Africaine," and "Murmures du soir," among other pieces.

Edmond Dédé, the New Orleans–born musician, orchestra leader, and composer, had studied with Constantin Deberque, who conducted the integrated Philharmonic Society there, but with the rise of hostile white sentiment against the free people of color in the 1830s, he went to Mexico City to pursue his studies. In 1857, with his savings from a job as cigar maker, he embarked for Paris, where he was granted entrance to the Conservatoire de Musique. Through Jacques Lavey, his teacher there, he became an intimate of the great composer Charles Gounod. He also studied the violin under Jean Alard. After graduating from the conservatory, he went to Bordeaux, where he became the orchestra leader at the Théâtre de l'Alcazar, a position he held for twenty-seven years. In 1864 he married Sylvie Leflet, daughter of a local bourgeois. A first-rate musician who achieved a successful career, Dédé remained still more famous in his native city, where in 1864 the performance of his Quasimodo Symphony before a vast audience of prominent Negroes and northern whites at the Orleans Theatre was a cultural high point of the decade. Among his orchestral works "Les Faux Mandarins" and "Le Palmier" overture were the most popular. In 1893 Dédé revisited New Orleans, and the colored elite gave him an unequaled welcome. But once his round of concerts was over, the maestro found daily life in the city intolerable and soon returned to France. He was working on a grand opera, *Le Sultan d'Ispahan,* when he died in Paris in 1903.[11]

None of the other Negro artists and entertainers who went to Europe in the nineteenth century achieved the fame of Ira Aldridge. The actor, whom contemporary critics called "the African Roscius," attained only in Europe the recognition refused him in his native land. Aldridge had planned to perform in Paris in 1854, but ill health prevented him from reaching France before 1866. He opened in *Othello* at Versailles—a performance *Le Figaro* described as rather exotic. The verdict of the French press was, however, largely favorable. As usual, Aldridge spoke in English and the other actors gave him the cue in French. Many a Paris celebrity attended, including Guizot of the French Academy, who was responsible for the translation of *Othello,* and the elder Dumas, who, upon this rare occasion, insisted on hugging Aldridge and proudly proclaiming, "My dear brother, I too am a Negro!" The following week the French poet Théophile Gautier saw Aldridge play the part of King Lear in a manner to produce every desirable illusion: "Cordelia herself would not have suspected her father of being a Negro. . . . In my opinion, he was superior in the role of the old king persecuted by his daughters to the one in which he was the blackamoor of Venice. In the former, he acted, in King Lear he was himself."[12]

Aldridge banqueted in Versailles at the residence of General Solomon, the Haitian ambassador to France, not only with the elder Dumas but with a third Negro guest, Pennsylvania-born T. Morris Chester, who had become a general after serving in Liberia from 1856 to 1862. Chester was visiting the Paris Exhibition of 1867; he recorded an evening at his hotel, a family resort for English-speaking tourists, when Aldridge was asked to give a recitation for the company, "which he did in a manner which delighted and charmed the gathering."[13]

The black tragedian stayed only a few weeks in Paris, but he toured the French provinces extensively. In cities such as Le Havre, Cherbourg, Bordeaux, Dijon, Dole, and Lyons, the aristocracy often spurned the entertainment, but ordinary people, although disconcerted at hearing him speak a foreign language, flocked to see one who so completely identified with his part. In April 1867 Aldridge toured the Midi, pleased with applause from a country where audiences were not noted for their enthusiasm. That same month, in Paris, Danish author Hans Christian Andersen noted in his travel diary the pleasure of having "Afric's gifted son hail [him] as a friend" when Mrs. Aldridge, herself a Swedish opera singer, introduced the actor, who was drawing large crowds to the Odéon, where he was playing Othello.[14] Three months later Aldridge died at Lodz, on his way from Paris to St. Petersburg.

One of the most vibrant tributes paid the great tragedian came from Théophile Gautier's pen after he saw him perform in the city of the czars prior to his appearance in Paris: "I was anticipating an energetic, loose-jointed and impetuous manner, somewhat wild in the style of Kean but the great Negro tragedian, probably to appear as cultured as a white man, possessed a style of acting which was sober, steady, classical and majestic. . . . He had more talent than genius, more finesse than inspiration."[15]

It would be hard to overestimate the magnetic appeal exerted on black Americans by the elder Dumas, even before emancipation. The grandson of the Marquis de la Pailletterie, a Santo Domingo planter, and dark-skinned Marie Césette, and the son of one of Napoleon's generals, the successful writer stood as a dazzling example of French recognition of black literary merit. Indeed, few French people considered his skin color, but in American terms he was a Negro. One of the few antebellum Afro-American visitors to France, and also one of the most distinguished, William Wells Brown testified to the reverence in which Dumas was held. Eager to meet Dumas, Brown had been given a letter of introduction to Dumas's close friend the popular French novelist Eugène Sue by 1848 revolutionary Louis Blanc, then in London. To no avail: "I had begun to suspect that Dumas felt that it would be too much of a condescension to give audience to an American slave and I began to grow indifferent myself upon the matter," Brown confessed.[16] One evening, however, attending a performance of *Norma* at the Opera, he noticed "a light-complexioned mulatto, apparently about fifty years of age,—curly hair, full face, dressed in a black coat, white vest, white kids,—who seemed to be the centre of attraction not only in his own circle but in others. Those in the pit looked up, those in the gallery looked down, while curtains were drawn aside at other boxes and stalls to get a sight at the colored man. So recently from America where caste was injurious to my race, I began to think that it was the wooly head that attracted attention when I was informed that the mulatto before me was no less a person than Alexandre Dumas. Every move, look and gesture of the celebrated romancer were watched in the closest manner by the audience."[17] Brown remarked admiringly that no writer filled a more important place in the literature of his country than this son of a Negro general. He clearly considered Dumas's success as a tribute paid to the whole race and as proof that the French rewarded artistic merit regardless of color.

Although Dumas was not a "race man" by any means, he was celebrated in Afro-American publications as one of the outstanding Negroes throughout the world—one whose achievements were proof of the capacity of his race to "rise," to contribute to the history and culture of mankind. His name would appear as often as those of Pushkin or even Toussaint Louverture, and his portrait graced the first issue of the *Anglo-African Magazine* in 1859. Even Frederick Douglass did not allow his militant race awareness to stifle his literary admiration for him, and most Afro-American visitors to France made a point of visiting his grave and honoring his memory.

NOTES

1. "Sally Hemings," entry by Fawn Brodie in *Dictionary of American Negro Biography*, ed. Rayford W. Logan and Michael R. Winston (New York: Norton, 1982), 309.

2. Rodolphe Desdunes, *Nos hommes et notre histoire*, 15, quoted by Edward Maceo Coleman, introduction to *Creole Voices* (Washington, D.C.: Associated Publishers, 1945), xxi. Information about the Creole writers group is derived mainly from the above and from Charles Hamlin Good's celebration of them in "The First American Negro Literary Movement," *Opportunity*, March 1932, 76–79.

3. Camille Thierry, "Au général Magloire d'Hoquincourt," *Courrier de la Louisiane*, April 23, 1851, quoted by August Viatte, *Les littératures de langue française* (Paris: Fernand Nathan, 1981), 30.

4. Armand Lanusse, "Un mariage de conscience," *Album littéraire*, August 15, 1843, mentioned by Viatte, *Les littératures*, 30.

5. Camille Thierry, "Le Chant de l'Exilé," *Les vagabondes, poésies américaine* (Paris: Lemerre / Bordeaux: De Laporte, 1874), 41, 42. Translation mine.

6. Victor Séjour, "A mon père," *Richard III* (Paris, Giraud et Dagneau, 1852), 3.

7. "Victor Séjour," entry by Charles O'Neill, in *Dictionary of American Negro Biography*, 551.

8. Ibid., 551.

9. Séjour even enjoyed a degree of posthumous notoriety, drama critic Victor Sarcey remarked, when his play *Cromwell*, interrupted by ill health as he was working on it, was staged at the Théâtre du Châtelet in April 1875 (Charles O'Neill, "Theatrical Censorship in France, 1844–1875: The Experience of Victor Séjour," *Harvard Library Bulletin* 26 [1978], 425–26).

10. Only a 400-line fragment of Vashon's "Vincent Ogé" remains, in *Autographs for Freedom*, ed. Julia Griffiths (Auburn, N.Y.: Aldeane, 1854), 41–60.

11. "Edmond Dédé," entry by Marcus B. Christian, in *Dictionary of American Negro Biography*, 168.

12. Théophile Gautier, quoted in W. Napoleon Rivers, "Gautier on Aldridge," *Crisis*, January 1932, 460.

13. T. Morris Chester, quoted by the Reverend William J. Simmons, in *Men of Mark* (1887; rpt. New York: Arno Press, 1968), 737.

14. Hans Christian Andersen, quoted in Herbert Marshall and Mildred Stock, *Ira Aldridge, the Negro Tragedian* (London: Rockcliff, 1958), 324.

15. Rivers, "Gautier on Aldridge," 459.

16. William Wells Brown, *The Black Man, His Antecedents, His Genius, His Achievements* (New York: Thomas Hamilton, 1863; rpt. Johnson Reprint Co., 1968), 128.

17. Ibid., 129.

2

Early Visitors:
Preachers and Abolitionists

Apart from a representative number of New Orleans Creoles of color, whose travels were made easier by their knowledge of French and their position in a wealthy segment of the free Negro population, the handful of antebellum black American writers who visited France consisted mainly of fugitive slaves who lectured in Europe to further the aims of abolitionism and of members of the Negro clergy who participated in political and social activities connected with civil and human rights. William Wells Brown himself—the first black American to produce both a full-length play, *The Escape; or, A Leap for Freedom*, and a full-length novel, *Clotel; or, The President's Daughter*, in 1853—first visited France in 1849, not as a man of letters but as a fugitive slave and militant abolitionist. He went to Paris as one of the twelve Massachusetts delegates to the Peace Congress, traveling with scores of others, including the Negro clergymen James W. C. Pennington of Hartford, Connecticut, and Alexander Crummel of New York City. They stayed in England and Ireland before reaching Boulogne on the eve of the congress.

The Peace Congress was an impressive conference indeed: over eight hundred delegates from all over the Western world gathered at the Salle Sainte-Cécile on the Rue St.-Lazare for want of a large-enough centrally located auditorium. Victor Hugo presided, with vice-presidents from every participating nation. The author of *Notre-Dame de Paris* was, in Brown's opinion, a great favorite of the congress; even those who could not understand what he said found his speech splendid. Many addresses followed, including those of the great men of the convention: the British politician and economist Richard Cobden; Anathase Coquerel, the Protestant clergyman from Paris; Abbé Duguerry; Henry Vincent; eloquent Émile de Girardin, editor of *La Presse;* and the deeply respected Edward Miall, editor of *The Nonconformist.* Brown considered the meeting a success insofar as Catholics and Protestants had, for once, forgotten their rivalries to voice feelings of international brotherhood. But he was severely critical of its actual results: "In one sense, the meeting was a glorious one; in another it was merely child's play, for the Congress had been restricted to the discussion of certain topics. They were permitted to dwell on the blessing of peace but . . . the committee permitted the Congress to be gagged before it had met. They put padlocks upon their own mouths and handed the keys to the government. . . . O, how I wished for a Massachusetts atmosphere, a New England convention platform, with Wendell Phillips as the speaker, before that assembled multitude from all parts of the world."[1]

Brown failed to mention his own warmly applauded contribution. He was not scheduled to speak, but Victor Hugo, not wanting to miss the opportunity to make an antislavery stand, asked the fugitive slave to address the conference during the final session, on August 24, 1849. Although several U.S. delegates were in favor of slavery—including a New Orleans gentleman who had muttered about Brown's presence among them while they were sailing, no one apparently dared to protest. With Coquerel translating ex tempore, Brown spoke against the war spirit by which slavery was enforced in America. He concluded, "If therefore we shall obtain the abolition of war, we shall at the same time proclaim liberty throughout the world, break into pieces the yoke of bondage and let all the oppressed go free."[2] *La Presse* praised Brown's speech, and *Galignani's Messenger* quoted it at length; consequently, he attracted attention in Paris circles.

Two days later the delegates were invited to a reception given by the minister of foreign affairs, Alexis de Tocqueville. "As my colored face and curly hair did not prevent me from getting an invitation," Brown remarked, "I was present with the rest of my peace brethren. Had I been in America where color is considered a crime, I would not have been seen at such a gathering unless as a servant" (*Sketches*, 73). Not only was Brown entertained in splendid rooms and served by white-wigged waiters, but when he was presented to Madame de Tocqueville in the center of the large drawing room and she learned that he had been an American slave, she extended her hand and gave him an especially cordial welcome, saying, "I hope you feel yourself free in Paris." Brown commented, "Having accepted an invitation to a seat by the lady's side, who seated herself on a sofa, I was soon what I most dislike, 'the observed of all observers.' I recognized among many of my countrymen who were gazing at me, the American Consul, Mr. Walsh. My position did not improve his looks" (*Sketches*, 74).

Brown, a keen observer, was duly impressed by the reception at de Tocqueville's mansion, noting the difference in dress and manners among the assembled dignitaries of many foreign countries as well as the splendor of the occasion: "delight seemed to beam on every countenance and the living stream floated from one room to another. The house and gardens were illuminated in the most gorgeous manner. Red, yellow, blue, green and many other colored lamps, suspended from the branches of the trees in the garden, gave life and animation to the whole scene out of doors" (*Sketches*, 74). He similarly evoked the breakfast offered at Versailles by the British delegates to honor their American friends, with some six hundred guests present and many who had not had an opportunity to speak at the congress trying to give the addresses intended to immortalize them. But he was first of all an eager discoverer of the moods and places of France. Even during the train ride from Boulogne, he had admired the rich countryside of Normandy: "Straggling cottages which bespeak neatness and comfort abound on every side. . . . The eye cannot but be gratified in viewing the entire country from the coast to the metropolis. Sparkling hamlets spring up, as the steam-horse speeds on his way, at almost every point, showing the progress of civilization, and the refinement of the nineteenth century" (*Sketches*, 56).

In Paris he stayed at the Hotel Bedford, close to the Place de la Concorde, and visited the church of La Madeleine even before having his first breakfast in France. Every day, before the sessions began, he would roam the boulevards, or he would skip lunch and visit some monument or gallery to which his membership at the Peace Congress gave him free access as a guest of the government. After the first day of the convention he was invited to a friend's house in Versailles, where he spent several hours walking through the grounds of the palace, among the statuary and the magnificent fountains. The day after, he started with the Louvre in the morning; upon walking the Grande Galerie, which he estimated to be a quarter of a mile long, he exclaimed that "all Christendom had been robbed that the Louvre might make a splendid appearance" (*Sketches*, 66).

After the session he revisited Versailles, admiring most the waterworks of the fountains of Neptune and Diana. The Petit Trianon, which he thought "the most republican of any of the French palaces," appealed to him more than the Grand Trianon because of the memories it contained of Marie Antoinette, "that purest of princesses and most affectionate of mothers" (*Sketches*, 77). The party then headed for Saint-Cloud, Napoleon's favorite residence, where every room was opened to them and the waterworks turned on in their honor. Brown observed, "Standing as we did, viewing Paris from St. Cloud and the setting sun reflecting upon the domes, spires, and towers of the city of fashion, made us feel that this was the place from which the monarch should watch his subjects. . . . At eight, the water-works were put in motion and the variegated lamps, with their many devices, displaying flowers, stars, and wheels, all with a brilliancy that can scarcely be described, seemed to throw everything in the shade we had seen at Versailles (*Sketches,* 79).

The following days the insatiable Brown walked all the rooms of the Tuileries and then the promenade at the Place du Carrousel before dining in a salon near the Palais Royal without arousing any prejudice. After several unsuccessful attempts he found the room where Robespierre once lived, at 396, Rue Saint-Honoré; seeing the hook on which his clothes once hung still in the wall, he could imagine the Incorruptible composing his fiery speeches. He searched for more residences of master spirits of the French Revolution and eventually found himself in the Rue de l'École de Médecine, where, at number 20, he was shown "something representing an old stain of blood" in the room where Charlotte Corday had stabbed Marat in his bath. Guidebook in hand, he stood where the guillotine once stood, admired the statue of Henry IV over the principal entrance of the Hotel de Ville, meditated in the room overlooking the Place de Grève where Robespierre had been dragged before the Committee of Public Safety, and looked out of the window where Lamartine had, only one year before, induced the 1848 revolutionaries to retain the tricolor instead of adopting the red flag.

For Brown, Paris was mainly a seat of history: he climbed to the top of the July Column on the site of the Bastille, admired the sculptures of Notre-Dame—the blessedness of saints, the rider on the red horse, Satan dragging the wicked to hell—before mixing with gowned barristers at the Palais de Justice on his way to the prison of the Conciergerie. He later devoted several pages to a description of Les Invalides, but his heart went to the boulevards: "The Boulevards may be termed the Regent Street of Paris or the New Yorker would call it Broadway. While passing a café, my German friend Faigo . . . recognized me, and I sat down and took a cup of delicious coffee for the first time on the side-walk, in sight of hundreds who were passing up and down the street every hour. From three till eleven o'clock P.M. the Boulevards are lined with men and women sitting before the doors of the saloons, drinking their coffee or wines, or both at the same time as fancy may dictate. All Paris appeared to be on the Boulevards and looking as if the great end of life was enjoyment" (*Sketches,* 88). In his eagerness William Wells Brown even asked a cabman to drive him to the Élysée Palace, which he wanted to see. The cabman drove between two lines of soldiers and left him in front of the massive doors, where a liveried servant opened the cab door and asked if he had an appointment with the president. In his best French he tried to explain to the gathering attendants that he was only a visitor: "amid the shrugs of their shoulders, the nods of their heads, and the laughter of the soldiers, I left the Élysée without even a sight of the president's moustache for my trouble. This was only one of the many mistakes I made while in Paris" (*Sketches*, 90).

Brown needed another full day to visit the king's apartments at Versailles and look at the painted ceilings until he felt dizzy. After a second visit to the Louvre he went to the Jardin des Plantes; to the Bourse, which he found one of the most superb buildings in the city; to the cemetery of Père Lachaise, where among others the grave of Marshal Ney caught his attention. He finally climbed the Arc de Triomphe, visited the tapestry workshops at the Gobelins, and while taking his last dinner at the Palais Royal, was introduced by his German host to the poet Béranger, the popular champion of political and religious freedom. They talked at length, and Béranger expressed strong antislavery views. Concluding his forty-page description of the French capital, Brown was able to assert: "Few nations are more courteous than the French. Here the stranger, let him come from what country he may and be ever so unacquainted with the people and language, is sure of a civil reply to any question he may ask. With the exception of the egregious blunder I have mentioned of the cabman driving me to the Élysée, I was not laughed at once while in France" (*Sketches*, 97).

In the eyes of William Wells Brown and many of his fellow abolitionists, France undoubtedly stood for freedom. In his speech at the Salle Sainte-Cécile he declared that he could speak freely against slavery in the French capital but that he could not do so in Washington without risking death. A few years later, when he wrote *Clotel*, he had a considerate French gentleman rescue his heroine, Mary, from slavery. Mr. Devenant had noticed her on the boat to Mobile, and when they reached New Orleans, he immediately took her with him on a Europe-bound vessel. Upon their arrival in Le Havre he married her, and they settled in Dunkirk. Then the gentleman was kind enough to die conveniently, allowing Mary to be united in holy wedlock with her beloved fellow black, George Green! But it is significant that Brown should have chosen a Frenchman as a rescuer and that, in a later version of the novel, he should have extended the narration of the heroine's stay in France into a not-unlikely evocation of what life there might be like.[3]

Just as Victor Séjour's Paris career became typical of the Afro-American artist in exile, so William Wells Brown's brief contact with Parisian life and French intellectuals epitomizes the visits of black

Americans to France in the nineteenth century. After emancipation wealthy or noted black American visitors were not infrequent in Paris. Unfortunately, they did not enjoy the privilege of traveling on an American passport. Brown reported the refusal that met the request of John S. Rock, a black Bostonian versed in French and German literature: Mr. Cass, then secretary of state, said in reply to Rock's application that "a passport has never been granted to a Negro since the formation of this government."[4] Mr. Rock did go to Paris, however, and underwent a serious operation performed by Nelaton, the celebrated French surgeon. Wishing to visit France while he was in London in 1859, Frederick Douglass likewise applied for a passport because, following attempts on the life of Napoleon III, the French authorities had tightened regulations concerning the entry of foreigners into the country. Douglass was refused a passport on the grounds that he was not a citizen of the United States. He then addressed a note to the French ambassador in London, who, without any delay, sent him a permit to visit France.

In spite of the reluctance of their government to assist them, a number of black Americans went to France during the latter part of the nineteenth century. Some were professionals, like T. McCants Stewart, a mathematics professor and lawyer from Charleston, South Carolina, on his way to Liberia, or J. W. Morris, president of Allen University, who toured France and Switzerland after attending the 1848 Ecumenical Council in London. Many of them reacted just as their white fellow citizens did. James T. Rapier of Montgomery, Alabama, remarked in his "Notes of Travel in Europe" that the stewards at the Hôtel de l'Europe in Lille only managed the most atrocious gibberish under pretense of speaking English or commented on "French street urchins turning somersaults or walking on their hands to get a centime"—a practice one later would associate with North African and Third World children.[5] At that time France frequently passed for a somewhat underdeveloped and decidedly exotic country!

Before emancipation black American visitors to Europe generally attended antislavery meetings there. James W. C. Pennington, who had been sent to the World Antislavery Convention in London in 1843, also lectured in Paris and Brussels before receiving a doctorate from the University of Heidelberg. In his *Recollections of Seventy Years*, Bishop Daniel A. Payne of the African Methodist Episcopal church reported several such journeys.

As president of Wilberforce University, Bishop Payne was sent to attend the general assembly of the Evangelical Alliance held in Amsterdam in mid-August 1857; he met the French clergyman Eugène

Bersier there and later managed to attend the meeting of the World Antislavery Conference in Paris in the company of the Reverend Sella Martin. He spent only three days in Paris. The language barrier prevented him from participating actively in the proceedings, but he enjoyed the socializing at the banquet tables set in the splendid hall of the Jardin des Plantes, the zoological garden. Indeed, one of the highlights of the trip was his discovery that Asian and African camels belong to different species.

Back in Paris in early September 1857, the Reverend Payne addressed the congregation of the Reverend Émile Cook; his oration was translated, which he found a tedious process for all concerned. He remained in the city for about a month, boarding with the Moindron family near the Palais Napoléon and enjoying the fluent English and musical talents of the lady of the house. He made friends with Dr. Valette, who was then head of the Lutheran church in France, frequently attending his services and conversing with his daughter, who was always eager to learn about American women. He also made friends with the Reverend Cook, who later visited him at Wilberforce. He returned to Paris at the end of November and this time stayed until April 1858. Traveling from Rouen to the capital, he admired the well-cultivated farms and gardens and the beautiful villages, which reminded him of his native Juniata valley. He boarded again opposite the Palais Napoléon, and whenever his work and mission in Paris left him time, he studied the language with a French teacher. He apparently learned enough French to be able to write it easily, since one of his biographers noted that he used it not only to read but to keep his diary when he wanted not to be understood by nosy readers.

He also attended lectures at the Sorbonne, where, he remarked, all lectures must be in accordance with the sentiment of the Roman Catholic church, while the Collège de France allowed its professors to speak freely. Among the eminent lecturers was Édouard Laboulaye, who spoke on Montesquieu's *L'Esprit des lois*—a dry topic—with wit and brilliance. Payne became acquainted with him and was introduced to some of his colleagues. Payne was thoroughly engrossed in anthropology, whose scientific findings were often called upon to prove the superiority of one race over the others; he had long discussions with Professor Quatrefages, the famous savant and anthropologist, who invited him to the Museum of Natural History. He also took an interest in a number of religious institutions and schools, including the suburban establishment for girls run by the misses Hooper and Cresseil, where his friend Eugène Bersier gave religious instruction. And he visited monuments and museums: "Like all Americans, I visited the noted places of interest in Paris—the Louvre, the Pantheon, the Jardin des Plantes, the Bois de Boulogne, the Palais de Luxembourg, where is located the throne of Napoleon Bonaparte, said to be the grandest in Europe, the Art Gallery of Luxembourg . . . these and various other places, of which I will mention the Hotel des Invalides at greater length.[6] To a description of the tomb of Napoleon, the "warrior emperor," he devoted a whole page.

In 1881, when Payne attended the Fifth Conference of the Evangelical Alliance in London, he quickly set out for Paris to find himself again among old friends. The reverends Valette and Cook had died, but he found Professor Quatrefages in his library. He was pleased to receive his latest ethnological volume, *L'Espèce humaine*, as he had been reading his *Rapport sur les progrès de l'anthropologie* assiduously for many years. He found time to revisit the places that had attracted him, especially the Jardin des Plantes, where his attention was drawn to a species of sheep from Abyssinia and the antelope of Senegal—possibly a half-conscious manifestation of the militant bishop's interest in the natural prodigies of Africa.

Not all black clergymen were as enlightened as Daniel Payne, but thinking of the Lord seldom prevented them from enjoying the less wicked attractions of the City of Light. In her autobiography, *The Story of the Lord's Dealings with Mrs. Amanda Smith,* the devout missionary considered it God's will that she should be allowed to visit Paris and Italy on her way to India, where she was to preach the gospel. On September 4, 1879, Mrs. Smith noted her admiration: "We got around to see something of Paris. My! the wonders; not strange perhaps to others but to me; the statuary, and parks, and buildings were lovely to behold."[7] She awoke full of praise on the following Sunday to find, to her great dismay, buildings were going up and men were hauling stones; laundries were open: everything was just like Saturday while others were going to church. She attended a service at the Wesleyan church, but she felt sad that "this fashionable, wicked Paris on which the eyes of the Christian world are turned for their first fashions and imitations" should not observe the Lord's day. She only remained one more day, sight-seeing again, probably visiting the porcelain factory at Sèvres, since she remarked: "I saw where the beautiful china is made" and meditated on how, just as the potter molded clay, the Lord fashioned the soul until it was ready to be taken to the furnace of His will. Not far from there, in a very wide avenue with beautiful trees on either side, she saw a kind of open-air festival or fair with long rows of gypsy wagons. But her party had to take the train to Turin at two in the afternoon, on the Thomas Cook tour. And this was the last she would ever see of Paris.

NOTES

1. William Wells Brown, *Sketches of Places and People Abroad* (Boston: John P. Jewett, 1855), 71–72, hereafter cited in the text as *Sketches*.

2. William Wells Brown, "Reports of the Peace Congress," quoted in William E. Garrison, *William Wells Brown, Author and Reformer* (Chicago: University of Chicago Press, 1969), 150.

3. Such an image of France as a land of equality is reflected in *Iola Leroy*, a novel Frances Ellen Harper published as late as 1892. The protagonist is a beautiful, white-skinned, and perfectly educated octoroon whom her white husband cannot impose upon his acquaintances. He plans to live in the North or, knowing well that there is prejudice in the North, go to France. Only in Europe can their children be educated "without being subjected to the depressing influence of caste feeling. Perhaps by the time their education is finished, I will be ready to wind up my affairs and take them abroad, where merit and ability will give them entrance into the best circles of art, literature and science." And Harper cites the examples of Ira Aldridge and of Alexandre Dumas, who "was not forced to conceal his origin to succeed as a novelist." Frances Ellen Harper, *Iola Leroy; or, Shadows Uplifted* (1892; rpt. Salem, N.H.: McGrath, 1969), 85, 84.

4. William Wells Brown, *Clotel; or, The President's Daughter*, (1853; rpt. Salem, N.H.: Ayer, 1969), 247–68.

5. James T. Rapier, unpublished manuscript, Yale University Library.

6. Daniel Payne, *Recollections of Seventy Years* (Nashville, Tenn.: AME Sunday School Union, 1888), 199.

7. Amanda Smith, *The Story of the Lord's Dealings with Mrs. Amanda Smith* (Chicago: Meyer and Brother, 1893), 286.

3

After Emancipation:
The "Talented Tenth" in Paris

Although emancipation gave all black Americans the legal freedom to travel as they chose, few were able to afford a transatlantic voyage. Until the 1920s the writers of "the talented tenth" did not visit Europe in significant numbers. Before the turn of the century only black leaders, like Frederick Douglass and Booker T. Washington, joined the increasing stream of their white fellow citizens on the European tour, which, as in the novels of Henry James, was now depicted as a spiritual pilgrimage to the sources of American civilization. However, a few Negro intellectuals did include a visit to France in their education, formal or informal. This was true of Mary Church Terrell, W. E. B. Du Bois, Carter Woodson, and James Weldon Johnson, who, despite their occasional criticism of French colonial policies, deeply enjoyed French culture and racial attitudes.

Frederick Douglass probably provides the most detailed and representative account of the reverence that French culture and refinement aroused in educated American visitors to Europe. Granted permission to enter France in 1859, he could not avail himself of the opportunity because news reached him in London of the critical illness of his daughter Annie, and he sailed back to New York at once. It took him nearly thirty years to satisfy his wish to see Paris. In 1886, during his second European trip, he visited the city with his wife and Theodore Stanton. In 1895, Theodore Tilton recalled in his "Sonnet to the Memory of Frederick Douglass," "He came to Paris and we paced the streets / As if the twain were truants out of school."[1] Tilton took the visitors to the tomb of Lafayette, who had fought for American independence; to the statue of Lamartine, the abolitionist poet and politician; to the site of the Bastille, which impressed Douglass so deeply that he wrote his son Lewis: "I find the people here singularly conscious of their liberty, independence and their power. They show it in their whole carriage and in the very lines of their faces, and no wonder, for they, more than any other people in Europe, have asserted all three in the face of organized oppression and power. But in no act have they done this more than in taking the Bastille."[2]

Douglass was prone to see France as the embodiment of "liberté, égalité, fraternité," the heir of the egalitarian ideals of the Enlightenment. Theodore Stanton got him tickets of admission to the French Senate, where the session seemed to him unexpectedly more "wild and tempestuous" than any in the United States. He was introduced to Victor Schoelcher, who had implemented emancipation in the French colonies and who, at the age of eighty-two, was writing a biography of Haitian liberator Toussaint Louverture. Schoelcher invited Douglass to visit him at his house, where the two men exchanged memories of antislavery activities. Significantly, Douglass's race consciousness prevented him from admiring Alexandre Dumas wholeheartedly. He wanted to see the statue by Gustave Doré as an acknowledgment of the literary genius of a colored man, but he was angry that the famous writer "had never said one word for his race" and he refused to honor the character of a man to whom, as a Negro, he had no reason to be grateful. He was more enthusiastic about the abolitionist stand of Victor Hugo and Schoelcher.

Douglass liked Paris because he did not feel any color prejudice there. The Negro was not an object of ridicule there, he believed, possibly because blacks had often been in Paris as artists or scholars rather than as slaves. This absence of prejudice Douglass credited to the influence of the Catholic church. He was delighted to discover his own *Narrative* on file in the Bibliothèque Nationale. He soon learned enough French to be able to discover things for himself. He came to realize that he was a celebrity of a sort in Paris and to consider himself an unofficial ambassador of the American Negro. He also felt ready to pass judgment on European racial attitudes: the French and the English he considered "sound in their convictions and feelings concerning the colored race," but he noted the influence of American prejudice, due partly to the stereotyped image of the black displayed by Negro "buffoons and serenaders," as he called the artists and entertainers then touring Europe, and partly to the slanders of malevolent American writers. In order to counteract such influence, he made it his duty to present a positive image of the American Negro in both public statements and private conversations.

"Aside from the great cities of London and Paris, with their varied and brilliant attractions, the American tourist will find no part of a European tour more interesting than the country lying between Paris and Rome."[3] Thus did Douglass express his enthusiastic response to the area that he considered the cradle of European culture, as well as the battleground of the historical conflict between civilization and barbarism. The southern leg of what at that time comprised the European tour fascinated him. He noted with joy "an increase in black hair, black eyes, full lips and dark complexions, a style of gayly colored dress, startling jewelry and an outdoor free and easy movement of the people" as he moved further toward the Midi (*Life*, 252).

Visiting the palace at Fontainebleau he regretted the trimming of nature by compass and square, and the too-perfect uniformity of pruning. Although a kindly woman had volunteered as a guide, he did not like Lyons because a large military display and the pealing bells of Fourvière associated in his mind the Church and the Army, oppression and slaughter, which seemed to go hand in hand. But Dijon evoked memories of St. Bernard and Bossuet, generous preachers, and of the revolutionary Mirabeau in his prison, as well as "a black image of the Virgin Mary about which one might philosophize" in one of the city's chapels (*Life*, 564). In Avignon the papal fortress moved Douglass to meditation and a diatribe against the tyranny of the Grand Inquisition, but he found the city a charming, quaint place, definitely a must for American tourists, who, incidentally, seemed to share his regard for it, especially in the 1920s. Arles, where the ruins of the Roman amphitheater and the graves at the Aliscamps fascinated Douglass, offered in his opinion "the narrowest queerest and crookedest streets" yet seen in his journey (*Life*, 567). The south of France meant not only history but also closer proximity to Africa: in the customs of carrying loads on the head, of congregating at dusk in village squares, and of sharing of agricultural tasks by both sexes, Douglass felt he found evidence of a common identity with Africans, which he welcomed as proof of human brotherhood.

Marseilles, with "its deep-blue waters sparkling under the summer sun and a half tropical sky, fanned by balmy breezes from Africa's golden sands," amounted to a true discovery, soon transformed into a symbol (*Life*, 568). The flourishing trade of the city, a mixture of the West and East, struck the visitor less than the visible influence of Africa on Mediterranean culture and the sight of the Château d'If. In Paris Douglass had grudgingly honored Alexandre Dumas as a Negro; the day after his arrival in Marseilles, however, he took his wife for a boat trip to the weird old rock from which Edmond Dantès was reportedly hurled in *The Count of Monte Cristo*, "because the genius of the Negro writer had woven around it such a network of enchantment." About thirty years later another black American, Mary McLeod Bethune, would hail Marseilles for exactly the same reasons: the presence of so many Africans and the fictional memory of the elder Dumas, whom France had feted for his talent.

Like most American tourists Douglass sojourned for a few days in

Nice, which he found to be a beautiful resort for health and pleasure but by far the most expensive place on his European trip. He then headed for Greece and Egypt via Italy. In his eyes the visit amounted to a sort of personal consecration. Thinking of the refusal of his government to grant him a passport in 1859, he wrote: "My gratification was all the more intense that I was not only permitted to visit France and see something of life in Paris, to walk the streets of that splendid city and spend days and weeks in her charming art galleries, but to extend my trip to other lands and visit other cities. . . . To think that I, once a slave on the Eastern shore of Maryland, was experiencing all this was well calculated to intensify my feeling of good fortune by reason of contrast, if nothing more. . . . Now I was enjoying what the wisest and best of the world have bestowed for the wisest and best to enjoy" (*Life*, 587–88).

Douglass's attitude toward France and Europe in general was indeed representative of perceptive black American visitors after emancipation: he was not looking for a haven, as Victor Séjour had; he appreciated the absence of racial discrimination, especially in the recognition of Negro achievement, as much as the continuing influence of the egalitarian principles of the French Revolution. France was for him a land of freedom and culture, and in undertaking his European tour Douglass was paying homage to the cradle of American culture, just like his white fellow citizens. His impressions contained, however, unambiguous reverence for his African heritage, a dimension often missing from the reports of other Afro-American visitors. What predominated was a sense of sharing the cultural heritage of mankind at its best on equal terms with men of all nations and races—proof that the black man had risen above the despised status of a slave.

Booker T. Washington, who succeeded Douglass as the recognized leader of his race, aroused more interest on the part of the French than he bestowed upon them. He received from French journalists, travelers, observers, and intellectuals more attention than was ever paid Douglass, largely because he represented a striking example of material achievement in the United States. From the late 1890s to his death in 1915, he was hailed as a splendid orator and great educator, and the only man capable of guiding the Negro toward success. Even such bigoted French authors as Charles Huard and Paul Bourget, who perpetuated the stereotypes of black laziness and bestiality, would single him out for praise. Paul Adam wrote in his 1906 *Vues d'Amérique:* "The example of his life would support all the claims of the enthusiastic negrophiles if it were not an exception. In Haiti and in Liberia, republics founded long ago by former slaves, a deplorable state of barbarism persists."[4]

Because of their alleged lack of earnestness and morality, Booker T. Washington himself did not hold the French in high esteem. He shared the perception of France—so widespread among his puritanical contemporaries—as a frivolous, femininely attractive, but somewhat reprehensible nation: "In the matter of truth and high honor, I do not believe that the average Frenchman is ahead of the American Negro; while so far as mercy and kindness to dumb animals go, I believe that my race is far ahead. In fact, when I left France, I had more faith in the future of the black man in America than I ever had possessed." Such were his conclusions in his autobiography.[5]

This belief was based on a stay of several weeks in Paris in May and June 1899, during which Washington behaved very much like the important guest he was. He traveled with Senator Sewell of New Jersey and enjoyed first-class fare on board the *Friesland*. In Paris he was welcomed by Theodore Stanton and invited to a banquet at the American University Club with Bishop Ireland and former president Benjamin Harrison—General Horace Porter, the American ambassador, presiding. He attended several receptions given by American officials, meeting justices Fuller and Harlan of the Supreme Court. Although he tried to escape attention, he was asked to speak from the pulpit of the American Chapel on a Sunday. He breakfasted with Auguste Laugel, one of the commissioners of the Paris Exposition and a personal acquaintance of Lincoln, but he mostly associated with Americans.

Washington's visit to the painter Henry Ossawa Tanner, in his studio at 51 boulevard Saint-Jacques, is indicative of his outlook. Convinced that the color of his skin would always prevent his work from getting full recognition in America, in 1891 Tanner had exiled himself to France. His paintings had attracted attention in the French capital, and some of them—notably *The Raising of Lazarus*—had been acquired by the French government and were displayed in the Musée du Luxembourg. Writing to the editor of the *Colored American*, Washington noted the painter's perseverance as well as his talent, and his success at being one of the few American artists exhibited at the Luxembourg museum: "Mr. Tanner is determined that he shall not be known as merely a successful Negro artist but that his work shall stand upon its merit alone," he commented, while acknowledging that "here in France no one judges a man by his color. The color of the face neither helps nor hinders."[6] However, in Booker T. Washington's eyes the recognition granted Tanner in France was not especially indicative of

French lack of prejudice but—as he stated in his guarded manner, always careful not to displease American whites—a reinforcement of his belief that "any man, regardless of colour, will be recognized and rewarded just in proportion as he learns to do something well" (*Up from Slavery*, 181). True to his gospel of self-help and practical education, he stressed excellence in any field, however humble, without remarking on the specificity of cultural and artistic achievement.

Washington visited most of the museums and art galleries in Paris, but he was less impressed by them than he was led to reflect on the moral inferiority of the French, struck as he was by "the love of pleasure and excitement which seems in a large measure to possess the French people" (*Up from Slavery*, 182). In a letter to the New York *Age*, printed under the title "On the Paris Boulevards," Washington began rather auspiciously: "On a beautiful, sunny day, combine the whirl of fashion and gayety of New York City, Boston and Chicago on a prominent avenue and one then has some idea of what it is to be seen here in Paris upon one of her popular boulevards."[7] He remarked that fashion seemed to sway everything in Paris, but it was merely to complain that, wanting to buy a pair of shoes, he could not find one in his size because it was "not the fashion," he judged, to wear large shoes in France. Nor could he visit the grave of Toussaint Louverture, as he had planned, because it was in the north of France and without a monument. As for the numerous Haitians studying in the capital, he deplored their apparent intention of making a career there instead of going back to develop their homeland.

Although convinced that southern blacks did not suffer from comparison with Europeans "in all that marks a lady or a gentleman," he strongly advised them against coming to France with the hope of finding employment unless they had prior contact and wealth. During his visit he had been approached for help by three race brothers, courageous and industrious people but without work. Washington noted significantly: "I have just secured passage for one of these men to the United States. His parting word to me was 'The United States is good enough for me in the future'!"[8]

Professor Othon Guerlac, who translated *Up from Slavery* in 1904, reported Washington's suggestion that his appraisal of the French as a nation of pleasure seekers be suppressed in the French version. Was this an example of the accommodationist's reluctance to offend potential readers? Was it an acknowledgment of the superficiality of his comments?[9] At any rate, his impressions of France were mixed, and it was to Denmark that he turned for an educational model.

Later, French journalist Jules Huret, a distinguished world traveler and a perspicacious mind, spent several days at Tuskegee Institute in 1904 as the guest of its president. Huret described Washington as a typical American, with clear and definite notions about ideas and things and a dislike of generalizations; he was certainly a pragmatic, utilitarian thinker. His short stay in Paris had not helped him develop either his rather unformed artistic tastes or his limited knowledge of the French past. To Huret's questions and remarks the black leader reacted as an unenlightened American businessman would have done: "He inquires," Huret recorded, "whether there have been any original inventions in France. . . . I sense in him as in all Americans an exaggerated national pride, which obviously stems from their utter ignorance of history. One of his complaints about Europe is the slowness of the people and lack of general activity. 'It seems to me,' he says, 'that in Europe one is always on vacation. There are too many holidays' " [10]

Huret considered Emerson a greater mind than Carnegie and Rockefeller, but Washington did not. Little able to share the achievements of European culture, he was not awed by them and reacted like a successful American deeply convinced of his country's superiority on all levels. In other terms, many of the stereotypes often applied to blacks—shiftlessness, dishonesty, lack of morality—he applied to Latin nations, including France, convinced as he was that, by virtue of their being Americans, his race brothers were potentially superior to the citizens of the "underdeveloped" countries of Europe.

In contrast to the reactions of Booker T. Washington—a short-time visitor convinced of his superiority as an American citizen—the impressions of Mary Church Terrell, who sojourned repeatedly in France between 1888 and 1921, were a more precise reflection of the changing racial situation as well as an expression of a greater consciousness of its manifold aspects. The daughter of Robert Church, who had amassed a fortune in Memphis real estate when the city was stricken by yellow fever epidemics in the 1870s, Mary Church had studied French for one year at Oberlin College and was teaching it at Wilberforce University when her father offered her a trip to Europe. In 1888 she went with him on a Cook's tour of England, Belgium, France, and Switzerland.

On board the *City of Berlin* Harriet Beecher Stowe's half-sister, Mrs. Hooker, provided her with introductions to some influential people in Paris, where she also chanced to meet Oberlin's dean of women. She made the most of her stay by visiting monuments and museums: "I drank everything of historic interest at great gulps—I could never see enough in one day and never grew tired. Long stairways

I climbed eagerly," she remembered, duly sending her relatives and friends letters and postcards describing the places she visited: "The priceless paintings in the Louvre opened up an entirely new world to me. It was the first time I had seen the works of the old masters or the best specimens of the modern school, and I rejoiced in the glorious opportunity of learning something about art." [11]

In September her father left her in Paris—reluctantly. Although he had promised to let her study abroad, the big city hardly seemed an appropriate setting for a well-bred young American woman of affluence. She at once moved out of their cozy hotel on the Rue de Richelieu in order to board with a French family highly recommended by Mrs. Hooker. The hostess's young niece taught Mary colloquialisms and phrases not generally found in books. She enjoyed her company, but living in Paris was expensive: "It is impossible to find board in a private family of any respectability whatever for less than forty dollars a month. If they can be found, it is beyond my powers at present to find them," she wrote her father.[12] Moreover, whenever she wanted to attend the theater, she needed a chaperon, whose ticket had to be paid for even if she expected no fee. Without waiting for her father's answer, the young lady, who insisted on being self-sufficient, arranged to stay with a family in Lausanne to avoid being exposed to the dangers of Paris. For a whole year she attended a private school, learning French but taking care to pronounce it the Parisian way when the Swiss usage differed.

In 1899 Mary's stepmother won $25,000 in a lottery and decided to attend the Paris Exhibition. They all visited Paris in grand style, but Mary seemed wary of French males, to the point that she once forced a cabman who was driving them toward the suburbs instead of taking them straight to their hotel to turn back, because she had heard that rich Americans risked being held up after nightfall. Americans thronged to the exhibition. There Mary met a "sure-enough flesh-and-blood African prince who was one of the most courteous, cultured, magnetic, and attractive personalities" she had ever encountered. "He had been educated in Paris and had acquired the manners of the French although he was dressed in oriental splendor" (*A Colored Woman*, 83). Yet the well-bred young lady did not elope with the African prince but chose to complete a year of studies in Berlin.

Later her work in the feminist movement brought her to Europe again. By then she had married Robert H. Terrell, the first black municipal judge in Washington, D.C., and she had been elected president of the National Association of Colored Women. She attended the International Congress of Women in Berlin in 1904. After the event she revisited Paris. "What joy," she noted, "what rapture to return to my old French camping grounds after an absence of fifteen years! How I love France and the French people! To be sure, they have faults like other groups, but with all their faults I love them still. . . . The country in which I was born and reared and have lived is my fatherland, of course, and I love it genuinely but my motherland is dear, broad-minded France in which people with dark complexions are not discriminated against on account of their color" (*A Colored Woman*, 209).

In Paris Mrs. Terrell met the editor of *La Revue des Revues*, Jean Finot, who had published *Le Préjugé des races*, which ridiculed the claim to superiority made by certain races and which incidentally made reference to the personality and work of Mary Terrell. They became fast friends. On this visit she expressed the wish to see Henry O. Tanner's painting *The Raising of Lazarus* in the Luxembourg museum. But the painting was no longer either there or in the reserve: it had already been taken to the Louvre. One of the guards was immediately sent there with her to show her the painting. "Thus it was that I had the rare privilege and the great pleasure of feasting my eyes upon the masterpiece of a colored man" (*A Colored Woman*, 211). Those were additional reasons for liking Paris and the French!

The next time Mrs. Terrell went to Paris, she was sent by the executive board of the Women's Peace Party as a delegate to the International Peace Congress of 1919. She sailed with Jane Addams; Jeanette Rankin, the first female member of the U.S. Congress; Dr. Alice Hamilton; and other distinguished people on the *Noordam*. The hotels were full, so they had to stay at the luxurious Hotel Continental before it was decided that the congress would convene in Zurich in May. Mrs. Terrell spent another five weeks in Paris on her way home, renewing her acquaintance with Jean Finot, who now directed *La Revue Mondiale*. She discussed prejudice with him at length: "Nothing was more exhilarating than to talk with this great French writer who believed head, heart and soul in the fine mental and spiritual endowment of the dark races" (*A Colored Woman*, 338). Finot was not afraid that the large number of Americans in France might introduce discrimination there. He had, however, been offered money by rich Americans to stop his "foolish prattle" about the equality of races. Mrs. Terrell remarked that trying to teach French people to discriminate against blacks had amounted to an obsession with some of her fellow citizens during the war, but Finot was confident that the French would have none of it. Mrs. Terrell was introduced to the commissioner in charge of colonial affairs, Blaise Diagne: "Tall, very dark (almost black), straight as an arrow, self-possessed, dignified and full of reserve power, this French African was a living, breathing illustration of the possibilities of his people under favorable conditions when given the opportunity of cultivating their brains, coupled with the chance of reaching in which their ability enables them to attain" (*A Colored Woman*, 339). Diagne made it possible for her to attend a meeting of the Chamber of Deputies, where she could observe the half-dozen Negro members exchanging views, laughing, and joking with their white colleagues. She did not fail to infer that "nobody who has a drop of African blood in his veins can fail to honor and love France on account of the way she treats her black subjects when they live on her own soil and mingle with other citizens of the great Republic" (*A Colored Woman*, 339). Suspicious, however, that France did not always treat her black subjects as she should, Mrs. Terrell undertook to question every French Negro she came across until she was satisfied by the puzzled and hurt tone of an African whose attitude and voice "were precisely what one would expect from a child who had been asked whether his mother gave him enough to eat, a bed to sleep in and decent clothes to wear" (*A Colored Woman*, 339). His faith in the Frenchman's feelings of affection toward his race convinced her that, whatever might be the practice in the colonies themselves, equality existed in France for Africans from the French colonies.

Mrs. Terrell did not fail to contrast French and American behavior toward blacks. She recounted how William Monroe Trotter, the editor of the Boston *Guardian*, had been refused a passport and had just managed to sail to France incognito as a cook on the freighter *Yarmouth* in April 1919. The delegate of the National Equal Rights League and the secretary of the Race Petitioners at the Versailles Peace Conference, Trotter was trying to carry a petition telling the true conditions under which colored Americans lived. When the *Yarmouth* docked at Le Havre, the crew was not permitted to go ashore, but Trotter managed to be sent to mail a letter. Leaving his suits and money on board, he pursued his trip to Paris looking like a tramp. An American Negro couple put him up until he could cable for money. Then, with the help of the editor of the left-wing *Journal du Peuple* and of a journalist at *L'Avenir*, he alerted the French press. Although Trotter was successful in arousing French opinion, he was refused admission as a representative of the National Race Congress at the Peace Conference, and his petitions were never discussed. President Wilson refused his request for an audience. He certainly made a greater impression on the French people than on the American delegation.[13]

Mrs. Terrell herself encountered difficulties when she tried to take the trip to the devastated regions of France that was generally offered free by the U.S. government to "citizens in good standing." Nearly all the delegates to the Peace Congress with whom she had associated had already taken it, but she had never been invited, apparently on account of her race. Only after the intervention of the French Captain Boutté, a colored man who was designated her guide, was she allowed by U.S. officials to take the trip: "Thus it was that I saw the devastated sections of France, the terrible destruction of the villages and towns, the miles upon miles of the wicked barbed wire with which the fields had been interlaced and the beautiful, age-old structures which had been shot to pieces. . . . In the Argonne forest I plucked a piece of ivy which grew near the grave of an American soldier and although I carried it about with me a long time for many miles from pillar to post, several pieces of it survived, so that in two places I have living things to remind me constantly of France. . . . I was glad I had struggled against the exhibition of race prejudice shown by my countrymen in France and finally had the opportunity to see for myself. . . . It was an object lesson in the horrors of war which I can never forget" (*A Colored Woman*, 347).

The kindhearted lady also fought a constant battle for kindness to dumb animals—a quality that, Booker T. Washington himself noted, the French did not seem to possess. The way horses were treated in Paris made her heart ache: they carried heavy loads, and the drivers plied their whips vigorously. Rarely did she spend a day without remonstrating on the street with some Frenchman about his cruelty—with such charm and tact, however, that she rarely got into trouble.

Later, in 1921, Mrs. Terrell had occasion to take a stand for the use of colonial troops to occupy the Rhineland. She refused to sign a petition, circulated by her board of education colleagues in the United States, requesting the removal of black French troops on the grounds that German women would be in danger of being raped. She was confident that black colonials could not behave worse than the white American Marines had done in Haiti, and in this she was supported by Jane Addams. She even protested to French Premier Poincaré when he sent the U.S. State Department a cable assuring them that only white soldiers would occupy the Ruhr. This was deference to race prejudice, she believed, and she wrote: "Thus for the first time in her history, France publicly places a stigma on her black citizens. Having preserved an unblemished record in this particular for centuries, France has at last publicly prostrated herself before the monster—Race Prejudice, and trailed her proud banner in the dust. . . . May the day never dawn when France will exchange her slogan of Liberty, Equality and Fra-

ternity which colored people have always enjoyed on her beloved soil
for one of discrimination, prescription and prejudice which handicap
them so seriously and from which they suffer so terribly in the United
States" (*A Colored Woman*, 366–67). Premier Poincaré never replied to
that letter.

Relating not only Mrs. Terrell's initial discovery of France in the late
nineteenth century but also her increasing sophistication in analyzing
the diverse elements of racial etiquette in the 1920s may cause us to
retrace our steps, yet it reveals that the New Negro movement was far
from being limited to the American scene and that the European, and
specifically French, experiences of its forerunners at the turn of the
century were probably instrumental in fostering this renaissance.

The case of W. E. B. Du Bois, the best-known instance of a black
intellectual leader getting an international education, will be dealt with
in a separate chapter. Yet other colleagues, collaborators, or fellow
writers of his enjoyed similar experiences, notably Carter Woodson
and James Weldon Johnson.

After working as a miner in West Virginia, Carter Goodwin Woodson studied for an M.A. at the University of Chicago and spent a whole
semester as a student at the Sorbonne before returning to obtain his
degree from Chicago in 1908. He had learned French in the United
States and soon practiced it so well that he became fluent in it, as he
was in Spanish. In Paris he did graduate work in history with professors Aulard, Diehl, Lemonnier, and Bouché-Leclerc. I have been
unable to document whether his course of studies led him to consider
the history of Africa as a prerequisite, not only for a historian of the
black diaspora but for an American historian with a truly international
perspective, and whether he was influenced by the vogue of African
art that was just starting in Paris. But seven years later Dr. Woodson
organized the Association for the Study of Negro Life and Culture,
and starting in 1916 he edited *The Journal of Negro History*.

Very possibly, the special appeal that French culture—whether in
Paris or in Port-au-Prince—held for "the elder statesman of the Harlem Renaissance" can be traced to the admiration James Weldon Johnson felt for his grandfather on his mother's side. Stephen was one of
the children a native Haitian had borne to Étienne Dillet, an officer
in the French army before the end of the eighteenth century. During
the war of Haitian independence, Étienne had sent his family to Cuba
for refuge, but their schooner was captured by a British privateer and
taken into Nassau harbor. Thanks to the help of a well-to-do citizen,

one Lamotte, Stephen was able to become not only the best tailor in town but inspector of police, postmaster, and a member of the Nassau assembly for over thirty years. He married Mary Symonette, herself descended from a former African slave and a Frenchman, Captain Simonet. Their only child, Helen Louise, was James Weldon Johnson's mother.

The summer after his graduation Johnson declined the chance to visit Europe with a tourist party of Baptist preachers. The first time he went, he accompanied his brother, composer J. Rosamond Johnson, and his brother's vaudeville partner, Bob Cole, whose operettas were booked for six weeks at the Palace Theatre in London. Following the suggestion of Brander Matthews, the three left for several months during the summer of 1905 with the intention of going first to Paris and using it as a base for further travels. They had allegedly sold a song for $13,000, which they spent during these lighthearted months. In his autobiography, *Along This Way,* James Weldon Johnson reminisced: "From the day I set foot in France I became aware of the working of a miracle within me. I became aware of a quick readjustment to life and environment. I recaptured for the first time since childhood the sense of being just a human being. I need not try to analyze this change for my colored readers: they will understand in a flash what took place. . . . I was suddenly free: free from a sense of impending discomfort, insecurity, danger; free from the conflict within the Man-Negro dualism and the innumerable maneuvers in thought and behavior that it compels; free from the problem of the many obvious or subtle adjustments to a multitude of bans and taboos; free from special scorn, special tolerance, special condescension, special commiseration; free to be merely a man."[14]

On the boat the party met a fashionable young American who advised them to put up at the Hotel Continental, where they lived in luxury for two days before looking for a pension. They saw a performance at the Marigny and, after dinner, were guided to the Olympia music hall, where the band played "Under the Bamboo Tree" and "The Congo Love Song" in their honor. Johnson spoke Spanish fluently, but his French was none too good. He made quick progress, however, by meeting the chorus girls at the Olympia regularly. The visitors attended only one American party, at the home of a singer at the Opera, but they saw of Paris all they could, pleasurably and without making a business of it. Johnson was less interested in history than in the French and the atmosphere of the city. "What I wanted most and what cannot be gotten vicariously was impressions from the life eddying around me and streaming by. I wanted to see people, people at every level, from an elite audience at the Opera House to a group of swearing fishmongers in the market" *(Along This Way,* 211).

Leaving for Belgium with few expectations, Johnson was relieved to find Brussels "un vrai petit Paris," as he put it. London gave his brother and Bob Cole an unforgettable welcome. But Paris remained for him the place he could be himself and be free to partake of the cultured, sophisticated life to which his family background had accustomed him. Shortly after this trip Johnson started his career as a song writer, helping his brother with the lyrics of the operetta *The Shoofly Regiment* in 1906. His appointment as a consul in Central American countries deprived Johnson of the opportunity to visit France again. By 1907, after working feverishly in the Republican election campaign, he expected a position as consul in Nice. After the wave of black protest aroused by the dismissal of an entire battalion of the 25th Negro Infantry following the Brownsville, Texas, riot, President Roosevelt had expressed willingness to make the appointment as an official goodwill gesture, but the secretary of state refused, and Johnson found himself trapped in Venezuela.

In Haiti, where he stayed on many occasions after his first important visit to investigate the U.S. occupation for the NAACP in 1920, Johnson had ample occasion to speak French. His stand against racist practices and brutality by the U.S. occupation force brought him the respect and friendship of Haitian patriots and writers, including Jacques Roumain. Apparently, Johnson's attraction to French culture was a lifelong affair. He related in his autobiography that on the way back from Japan in 1929 he had a French table on shipboard, with James Macdonald of the Foreign Policy Association, Adolphe Perry, and John D. Rockefeller. He was well versed in French literature: to one of his poems, written in 1899, he gave the title "Chanson pour elle"; and when Eleanor Teems wrote him in 1932, mentioning her nostalgia for Paris and quoting verse that she believed to be anonymous, Johnson replied by return mail to let her know that Alfred de Musset was the author of

> La vie est vaine,
> Un peu d'amour,
> Un peu de peine,
> Et puis bonjour.

His own *God's Trombones* was greatly praised when extracts from it appeared as outstanding examples of Negro belles lettres in French literary journals. Jean Roux-Delimal translated eight of his black sermons in verse for *Les Cahiers du Sud,* in which they appeared in October 1930 with a long introduction on Negro dialect and black literary achievements. The issue enjoyed great critical acclaim, and Walter White, who had met several French critics at the time, was convinced that *God's Trombones* would soon come out in translation, but that took another thirty years.

NOTES

1. Theodore Tilton, "Frederick Douglass in Paris," *Open Court* 2 (April 28, 1887), 151.

2. Frederick Douglass to Lewis Douglass, November 7, 1886, quoted in Philip Foner, *Frederick Douglass* (New York: Citadel Press, 1969), 324.

3. Frederick Douglass, *The Life and Times of Frederick Douglass* (1892; rpt. New York: Macmillan, 1962), 562, hereafter cited in the text as *Life*.

4. Paul Adam, *Vues d'Amérique* (Paris: Ollendorf, 1906), 158.

5. Booker T. Washington, *Up from Slavery*, in *Three Negro Classics* (New York: Avon, 1965), 182–83, hereafter cited in the text.

6. Washington, quoted in *Booker T. Washington Papers*, ed. Louis Harlan (Urbana: University of Illinois Press, 1976), 5:142

7. Washington, "On the Paris Boulevards," New York *Age*, June 8, 1899, quoted in *Booker T. Washington Papers*, 5:132

8. Ibid., 5:142.

9. See Mercer Cook, "Booker T. Washington and the French," *Journal of Negro History* 40 (1955), 318–40.

10. Jules Huret, *De New York à la Nouvelle-Orléans* (Paris: Fasquelle, 1904), 394. Translation mine.

11. Mary Church Terrell, *A Colored Woman in a White World* (Washington, D.C.: Ransdell, 1940), 67, hereafter cited in the text.

12. Terrell to Robert Church, September 24, 1888, in "Mary Church Terrell's Letters from Europe to Her Father," *Negro History Bulletin* 38 (September 1976), 615.

13. See Stephen R. Fox, *The Guardian of Boston: William Monroe Trotter* (New York: Atheneum, 1972), 226–29.

14. James Weldon Johnson, *Along This Way* (New York: Viking, 1933), 209, hereafter cited in the text.

4

W. E. B. Du Bois and World War I

William Edward Burghardt Du Bois was the proud descendant of Jacques Du Bois, a French Huguenot who emigrated to America in 1784. His middle-class upbringing in Great Barrington, Massachusetts, in part accounts for his early attraction to European culture. When he decided to pursue studies in Europe from 1892 to 1894, he planned to spend one year in Germany and one year in Paris. Once in Berlin, however, he thought it best to gain a thorough knowledge of one nation rather than a shallow exposure to two and decided to stay. Later he regretted that he had not studied in France instead, yet by economizing toward the end of his stay, he managed to spend a long-anticipated month in Paris before leaving Europe.[1] In May 1894 the suicide of General Boulanger still lingered in people's minds, and this was also the year when President Carnot was assassinated and Dreyfus condemned for high treason. But Du Bois's interests at the time lay in culture, not in politics: "Those events gained only my passing attention. I was fascinated by the glory of French culture in painting, sculpture, architecture and historical monuments. I saw Sarah Bernhardt. I haunted the Louvre," he remembered in his autobiography.[2]

An address he delivered at Wilberforce University in 1896 on "The Art and Art Galleries of Modern Europe" reflects his enthusiasm for the Louvre, whose fame outshone that of the Vatican collection and the museums of Florence, Dresden, Munich, Venice, and Vienna. Du Bois reacted with the same awe and admiration on his second visit to Paris. He went with Thomas J. Calloway, the Negro special agent who had collected the American Negro exhibit for the Exposition Universelle, and helped him install the exhibit in the large white World's Fair building on the banks of the Seine. He himself prepared the Georgia Negro section of the exhibit, for which he was awarded a gold medal—one of fifteen prizes the exhibit received. In "The American Negro in Paris" he stressed that the intention had been to show the history, present condition, education, and literature of black Americans. The two hundred books on the shelves demonstrated that the "most unique and striking" section was that of literature: "The development of Negro thought [was] of immense psychological and practical interest." Thus could "a small nation of people" honestly present its achievements to the world's most cultured opinion.[3]

Already fluent in French, Du Bois wandered "wide and deep" through Paris, and his attitude was typically the opposite of Booker T. Washington's. Upon his return Du Bois told an all-black audience in Louisville, Kentucky, about "the greatest of the world's cities—Paris":

> I say greatest advisedly, for there is not on earth a city comparable in *all* the things that make a great metropolis to the capital of France. . . . In Paris alone have we combined a vast aggregation of human beings under a modern municipal government amid historic surroundings and clothed in an outward magnificence and grandeur unparalleled in history. The sweep of that one vast avenue from the Arch of Triumph to the Louvre through the Elysian Fields—that avenue which kings and emperors have trod and Genius and fashion made famous—with the Venus of Milo at one end and the memory of Austerlitz at the other— before that avenue the streets of the world pale into insignificance. Here is the centre of the aesthetic culture of the 19th century and from the brilliant cafés of the sweeping Boulevards go forth edicts more despotic than the decrees of Caesar. . . . The vast staircase of the Grand Opera of Paris leads where no other staircase in the world leads. The crowns bestowed by the 40 Immortals rank higher than any other honors of the learned world; the editors of the great newspapers of Paris rule more people than Cyrus the Great—and the man or woman in the civilized world who has not at least a distant acquaintance with the language of the Parisian dare not claim a pretense to liberal culture.[4]

It would be difficult to find a more discerning American admirer of French culture than Du Bois. He visited Paris again in 1906 and, in all probability, went there another time, after attending the Races Conference in London in 1911. Consequently, when he was sent to France in 1918 by the board of the NAACP to investigate the condition of black troops in the American Expeditionary Force, Du Bois was returning to familiar ground.

Before the First World War black American visitors to France had represented only a chosen few—generally affluent, educated, cultured. Within a year the arrival of thousands of black American troops on French soil changed things radically; above all, it popularized the image of French racial equality among the Negro masses in an unheard-of fashion. When the war broke out, the Afro-American press was prompt in reporting the role of French colonials in it; the

December 1914 charge of the African soldiers that broke the Von Kluck offensive, for instance, received much publicity. The best indication of such interest is to be found in the monthly reports provided by the *Crisis* magazine. Du Bois, its editor, strongly advocated black American participation in the war on the grounds that victory over an avowedly racist enemy would entail some gains on the racial front at home. Page after page was devoted to the practice of mixing colored troops with the finest French regiments at Verdun while no mention was made of the little-known French practice of segregating the Senegalese and using them as cannon fodder. But mention was made of Gene Bullard, a Negro from Columbus, Ohio, who had joined the Foreign Legion and been awarded the Croix de Guerre and of the fact that the French army could boast two generals, four colonels, 150 captains, and countless lieutenants of the Negro race—this in the November 1917 issue that carried the news that seventeen black American soldiers had been hanged in retaliation for the Houston race riots. The June 1918 issue was proudly called the Soldiers' Issue since, at long last, some 200 thousand black Americans in France had been allowed not only to serve as stevedores and maintenance personnel but to fight on the front line.

Afro-American writers were among the first to sing the heartrending plight of "fair France." Jessie Fauset's sentimental verse was reprinted from *The Independent:*

> Oh little Christ, what can this mean,
> Why must this horror be,
> For fainting France, for Faithful France
> And her sweet chivalry?
> "I bled to free all men," you say.
> "France bleeds to keep men free."[5]

In June 1918 Fenton Johnson declared: "France is bowed in desolation. To her I dedicate the young men of my blood, that she might be saved from the claw of the vulture. Fear not, land that exalted Bonaparte, Toussaint hears thy call!" Gallantly, the black poet forgave Napoleon's treacherous treatment of the Haitian rebel. The caption under a full-page photograph of the officers of the Eighth Illinois Regiment in France significantly reads:

> The ebon hero writhes and fain would speak.
> Saddened the major reads his fading glance
> And kneels to hear no native rally shout
> But dying murmured: "Long live France."[6]

The June 1920 issue of the *Crisis* even carried a one-act play by the late Joseph Seamon Cotter, "On the Fields of France," in which two American officers, one white, one colored, died hand in hand, wondering why they had not lived that way at home.

Thus could writers imagine black participation in the war. Reality was sadly different, however; while the French population's congenial welcome gave them a new taste of social equality, black American soldiers generally suffered from discrimination in the U.S. Army. This is precisely what Du Bois came to investigate.

Two Negro divisions, the 92nd and 93rd infantries, were part of the American Expeditionary Force. The former had been sent complete— some 21,000 men who arrived in June 1918. Under the command of General Ballou and white company officers, they fought mostly in the Argonne. In this all-American division Jim Crow practices were the rule, and most of the Negro staff and field officers were gradually replaced under the pretext of inefficiency. The 93rd division arrived incomplete, numbering only some 12,000 men. The troops were black and so were the field officers, but except for Colonel Charles Young of the 372nd regiment, the only Negro colonel in the U.S. Army, the company officers were white. The black troops hoped that Young would be placed in command, but he was railroaded out and replaced by Colonel Tupes. The 369th regiment, consisting of black New Yorkers, landed at Brest in December 1917 and was brigaded in the 16th and 161st French infantry divisions. The French needed troops and were not inclined to discriminate between Americans. In the beginning, however, they made the mistake of using the black New Yorkers as shock troops, believing that, like the Senegalese, they could not be trained in trench warfare. Later the black American troops were trained with the white French troops and fought alongside them. The 370th U.S. regiment of the colored Illinois National Guard arrived in April 1918 under Colonel Roberts; they were likewise brigaded in the 36th French division, then with the 59th, under General Rondeau, who used them efficiently after they occupied the front line at Saint-Mihiel with the French 34th. Finally, the U.S. 371st and 372nd regiments were brigaded with General Goybet's 157th division. The brigading of these black regiments under French command made wholesale discrimination against black troops and officers by white Americans difficult, since it was continually offset by the generous appreciation of the French command. The French treated these soldiers in terms of perfect equality and brotherhood and kept up their morale when they remained under fire for 191 days in the case of the 369th, the Hell Fighters, who earned a record number of French citations and medals.

Prejudice was more comfortable in the 92nd division, which remained under the U.S. high command, and conditions were even worse among the 150,000 blacks serving as stevedores. After seeing them in Brest, Du Bois noted: "Worked like slaves, twelve or fourteen hours a day, these men were ill-fed, poorly-clad, indifferently housed, often beaten, always Jim Crowed and insulted and yet they saw the vision—they saw a nation of splendid people threatened and torn by a ruthless enemy; they saw a democracy which simply could not understand color prejudice. They received a thousand little kindnesses and half-known words of sympathy from the puzzled French and French law and custom stepped in repeatedly to protect them, so that their only regret was the average white American."[7]

Du Bois did not exaggerate. He had been sent to investigate American treatment of black troops because reports of discrimination and slander, aimed at keeping the Negro out of the regular army, were filtering out. Just as they had been accused of cowardice and incompetence by white staff officers, the black soldiers had been accused of rape by other American racists. Du Bois's careful investigation, including questionnaires sent to the mayors of all French towns where black Americans had been billeted, revealed that only a single case of rape and two attempts had taken place in the 92nd division (few units could boast of such restraint!) and that Afro-American troops got on beautifully with the local population.

Du Bois sent illuminating vignettes to the *Crisis* about his discoveries. His impressions of war-torn France are indicative of his feelings for the country. As he arrived at the Gare Montparnasse with Robert R. Moton, who had been sent by the American secretary of war to speak to the black American troops before they sailed back home, "the confusion was the worst I had ever conceived of in well-ordered France," Du Bois noted. "No one to collect tickets, no porters, no cabs and a surging crowd." Everywhere were evidences of war—"cannon, protected buildings—but most of all the women clad in silent black."[8] Although he enjoyed seeing again the crowds on the Boulevard des Italiens and the great sweep of the Champs Élysées, he did not find the city the world knew: "Paris, with its soul cut to the core—feverish, crowded, nervous, hurried; full of uniforms and mourning bands, with cafés closed at 9:30—no sugar, scarce bread, and tears so intertwined with joy that there is scant difference. Paris has been dreaming a nightmare, and though she awakes the grim terror is upon her—it lies on the sandbags covering monuments, on the closed art treasures at the Louvre."

In the same editorial he paid the city of Toul the same vibrant homage. He found it grim in the early dusk, a symbol of a half-crushed country he did not remember: "Here was France beaten to her knees yet fighting as a nation never fought before, calling in her death agony across the seas till her help came and with all their strut and careless braggadoccio saved the worthiest nation of the world." And he evoked the narrow, mud-filled streets of Maron, in Lorraine, with black soldiers from Alabama, Mississippi, and Philadelphia tramping in the cold on the banks of the Moselle. One of them was playing the trumpet: "Wild and sweet and wooing leapt the strains upon the air. French children gazed in wonder—women left their washing. Up in the window stood a black Major, a Captain, a Teacher and I—with tears behind our smiling eyes. Tim Brimm was playing by the town-pump"[9]

The May 1919 issue of the *Crisis* published devastating "Documents of the War," fully authenticated. One had been sent out by the French Military Mission stationed with the American Expeditionary Force, at the latter's request. It stated that the familiarity with which the French public treated the American Negro was a matter of grievous concern to the Americans, who considered it an affront to their national policy; such contacts, they feared, were likely to generate in blacks aspirations intolerable to the whites. Therefore, the rise of any intimacy between American Negroes and the French had to be prevented; black troops must not be commended too highly; the native population must not "spoil" the Negro, and white women, in particular, had better keep away from those whose vices were "a constant menace to the American who has to repress them sternly."[10] When this document was distributed by the Military Mission among the French préfets, the French Ministry ordered it collected and burned. French *colons* feared the familiarity of the Negro with white women, but this did not correspond to the spontaneous reactions of the population with whom black American troops were quartered.

Stories of interracial fraternization abounded. The *Crisis* printed a letter from a French woman recounting how the initial fear of the inhabitants of a small village at the arrival of black troops had soon turned into fine cooperation: "We see the little children in the arms of the huge Negroes, confidently pressing their rosy cheeks to the cheeks of ebony, with their mothers looking on in approbation. A deep sympathy is created for these men which yesterday was not even surmised. . . . Now one is honored to have them at his table. One spends hours in long talks with them, with a great supply of dictionaries. . . . Late at night the workers in the fields forget their fatigue as they hear the melancholy voices which call up to the memory of the exile his

distant country. In the lanes along the flowery hedges more than one
blond head is seen moving thoughtfully beside a curly head while the
setting sun makes blue the neighboring hills, and gently the song of
night is awakened." The lady concluded her idyllic evocation with the
unforgettable cry: "Soldiers who arrived among us one clear June day
redolent with the scent of roses, you will always live in our hearts!"[11]

Since the French newspapers had often described the Senegalese
shock troops as wild animals, even when extolling their bravery, some
French villagers were initially frightened of black troops. Afro-American soldiers did their best to make friends with the French. Moreover,
French reactions to white American troops, who sometimes behaved
as if in conquered territory and despised "the froggies," were often
less favorable than toward the blacks. William Pickens could thus recount "How Colored Soldiers Defeated the Real Enemy at Granvillars"
with the help of the townspeople: the first soldiers ever stationed in the
little town were the colored Chicago 370th, and the villagers, thinking
that color predominated in the United States, took this first sample
as representative of all Americans. These soldiers were polite, hearty,
and gentle to women, carrying water buckets or pushing baby car-
riages for them. When a white American regiment camped five miles
from Granvillars, they visited local homes but were less courteous.
They also tried to prevent the French girls from associating with their
colored friends. The girls confided this to the blacks, and a colored
lieutenant decided to address the whole town; he denounced the white
soldiers in the neighboring village and said they were not Americans
but "crackers" and "pecks." As a result doors were closed to the white
soldiers, who, when they sat in cafés and restaurants, were subjected
to a sort of quarantine or segregation.[12] An often-reported anecdote
dealt with a similar occurrence: in a remote French village the first
soldiers billeted with the populace were black, and they had made
such good friends with the French that, after they were replaced by
a contingent of white Americans who behaved with arrogance, the
mayor officially complained, requesting that "true Americans"—i.e.,
black ones—be sent.

Du Bois himself, evoking his visit to Maron and a meal in the house
of a Lorraine woman whose four sons had been killed in the war, made
elaborate literary use of bitter and sweet memories:

> It was a tiny house whose front window lipped the passage sidewalk
> where ever tramped the feet of black soldiers marching home. There
> was a cavernous wardrobe, a great fireplace invaded by a new and jaunty
> iron stove. Vast, thick piles of bed rose in yonder corner. Without was
> the crowded kitchen and up a half-stair was our bedroom that gave

upon a tiny court with arched stone staircase and green trees. We were a touching family party held together by a great sorrow and a great joy. How we laughed over the salad that got brandy instead of vinegar—how we ate the great golden pile of fried potatoes and how we pored over the post-card from the lieutenant of the Senegalese—dear little vale of crushed and risen France in the day when Negroes went "over the top" at Pont-à-Mousson.[13]

One might be tempted to believe that the editor of the *Crisis* exaggerated favorable reports of the friendliness of the French toward American black troops were not such reports to be found in the entire black press as well as in private correspondence. On August 26, 1919, a colored private, William Hewlett, wrote: "We regret that on October 1919 we will sail for our home in Petersburg, Va. United States of America where true democracy is enjoyed only by the white people. There is an air of liberty, equality and fraternity here which does not blow in the black man's face in liberty-loving, democratic America. . . . Why did black men die here in France 3300 miles from their home? Was it to make democracy safe for the white people in America, with the black race left out?"[14]

Assuredly, Du Bois was voicing such sentiments when he declared: "For bleeding France and what she means and has meant and will mean to us and humanity and against the threat of German arrogance we fought gladly and to the last drop of blood. For America and her highest ideals we fought in far-off hope. For the dominant Southern oligarchy entrenched in Washington we fought in bitter resignation."[15] Thus the experiences of thousands of Negro soldiers created the myth of racial equality in France. Stories of fraternization in "la douce France" would be told among black Americans to the point that Richard Wright recalled that French women and American Negroes' experiences in France were among the topics that southern whites did not like Negroes to discuss in the 1920s.[16]

Testimonies from black Americans about their first taste of freedom in France were numerous, yet very few among them couched their memories in touching verse or high-flown prose. When they wrote, they were moved by the need to tell the story truthfully in order to counter the lies disseminated about the black soldier's supposed cowardice or disorderly conduct. Among such efforts is W. E. B. Du Bois's research for a history of the Negro in the Great War, which he never finished. Several others appeared, however: Emmet J. Scott's *Official History of the American Negro in the World War* (1919) and Arthur W. Little's *From Harlem to the Rhine: The Story of New York Colored Volunteers*

(1936), both brimming with information about the doings and experiences of the Hell Fighters or the military bands that were "filling
France full of jazz." *The History of the American Negro in the Great World
War,* which W. Allison Sweeney, contributing editor to the *Chicago De-
fender,* completed in 1919, focused more on their splendid record in
the battle zones of Europe. More personal, and somewhat more literary, testimonies came from the Reverend Henry Hugh Proctor in his
Between Black and White and Addie Hunton and Kathryn M. Johnson
in *Two Colored Women with the American Expeditionary Forces.*

The Reverend Proctor landed in Brest in March 1919, at the request of General Pershing's headquarters, "to help sustain the morale
of the boys left behind to clean up the debris of the war." [17] In three
months he traveled four thousand miles in France, visiting all the
battlefields and speaking to nearly a hundred thousand Negro soldiers. He was accompanied by a black singer, Professor J. E. Blanton
of South Carolina, and a black pianist, Helen Hagan of New Haven,
Connecticut. They entertained the men and led them in singing before Proctor spoke to filled-to-capacity auditoriums. The sermon high-
lighted simple principles: getting an education, saving money, making
friends, getting married, joining the church—the things the doughboys would do upon their longed-for return home.

During his travels across battlefields or through nearby cities, Proctor never heard a single complaint by the natives concerning black
troops: "It was a remarkable thing that a colored person could approach a Frenchman anywhere without an introduction and almost
immediately be on terms of *bonhommie.* I believe the Negro and French
are affinities. They are both emotional, artistic, musical, fun-loving
and religious. Perhaps that is why they understand each other so
quickly" (*Between Black and White,* 160). He emphasized the fine impression made by his race brothers, and even noted that the French
appreciated the fact that the Negro had come over to fight for a
democracy he had never enjoyed at home. As a result, the French
were quick to resent injustices toward colored American soldiers by
the white Americans. The blacks "soon caught up the spirit of the
French people, and resented any discrimination on racial grounds"
(*Between Black and White,* 161). Proctor witnessed a riot in Romaigne
because the YMCA had drawn the color line in serving soldiers at their
canteen.

The Reverend Proctor reported moving stories of bravery, including this account of a last-minute rescue: a black lieutenant had been
sent to clean out a machine-gun nest and was cut off from the regiment, only a screen of smoke protecting him from the Germans.

Pinned down by a creeping barrage of fire, he calculated that he had about a quarter of an hour to live. But then he heard "the German bugle blow on one side, and on the other hand the band playing the Star Spangled Banner—and the war was over" (*Between Black and White*, 163). He also noted that, among the many chores they performed, the black American troops were left with the duty of burying the dead: "They picked up those by the roadside, scurried [*sic*] the forest for the unburied, and took up those improperly interred. They assembled the bodies in the cemeteries which are the most beautiful spots in la Belle France" (*Between Black and White,* 164). Doing what others had refused to do, the black troops were among the last to return home to the United States.

The daughter of a founder of the Negro Elks and a prominent member of the African Methodist Episcopal Church, Addie Waites had received a fine education before marrying William A. Hunton and being appointed by the national board of the YWCA to work among students. In 1907 she had gone with her children to Switzerland and Strasbourg, where she took classes at Kaiser Wilhelm University. In 1917, a widow with her children fully grown, she volunteered for YMCA service.

One of three Negro women permitted to work among the black troops, she reached France in the summer of 1918: "We entered the Gironde river and steamed slowly between vine-clad heights, over-topped by stately chateaux, between flowering meadows with picturesque villas, up to Bordeaux. It was thus we 'Answered the Call.'"[18] After such rosy impressions of the city to which the government had removed, after the pride of seeing colored soldiers guarding German prisoners, and the thrill of being among "many Colonial troops, Chinese laborers and more or less maimed French soldiers" (*Two Colored Women,* 15), they found Paris a city of darkness, its lights heavily hooded; troops crowded the stations, and shell and bomb alerts sounded nightly. The treasures of the Louvre were hidden, sandbags hugged Notre-Dame, and bread-lines and meatless days contrasted with the illuminated city Addie Hunton had visited a decade earlier.

The narrative ranges far and wide but reports mostly on segregation in the U.S. forces and on the welcome tendered the American Negroes by the French, very much in the way Du Bois did. It also evokes the atmosphere and morale in several black regiments, from Camp Pontanezen near Brest to the front lines near Verdun. Hunton's first assignment was the supply and transport center at Saint-Nazaire, where she added a literacy course and a Sunday evening discussion program to the movies and the usual canteen service. The authors write of the entertainment for the troops (the only black artist they ever saw was Helen Hagan) and especially of the leave areas—beautiful, historic places untouched by battle fire—where many black soldiers were sent and came to appreciate what French life was like: Nice, Chambéry, Challes-les-Eaux, etc. None of these was as successful as Aix-les-Bains, where Addie Hunton was transferred in January 1919. She helped organize a full program of religious, athletic, and cultural activities for the thousand Negro troops who arrived each week for a brief interval of relaxation. The black madonna at nearby Myans attracted considerable attention, as did Chambéry with the Croix du Nivolet, and the Fountain of Elephants, which was the rallying point for American soldiers taking the train to Challes, where they could use the thermal establishments free of charge in the mornings. Excursions to the Dent du Chat peak, Hautecombe Abbey, and the Lake of Bourget were organized, not to speak of vaudeville shows, weekly lectures, and receptions given by the local inhabitants, who expressed their sympathy and admiration very courteously. For many black soldiers the leave area remained a beautiful memory, a "mountain of vision and hope in France for those who reached it" (*Two Colored Women*, 174–78).

A whole chapter of the narrative is devoted to the authors' relationships with the French. Everywhere they discovered that the French had been warned about the loose morality and general incapability of American Negroes, and that the soldiers were usually forbidden to meet French civilians. This propaganda was spread "to the topmost peaks of the Alps Mountains away up among little shepherd girls who knew nothing except what others came up to tell them: *"Soldat noir— vilain!"* (*Two Colored Women*, 186). But where contacts occurred, they were friendly, and the French women, especially, took offense at the U.S. Army's attempt to control their acquaintance and morals. French people resented the white Americans' low opinion of their women, and they sometimes could be overheard saying that "if the American soldiers had on German uniforms, they could not be told from the Huns" (*Two Colored Women*, 191). Mrs. Hunton witnessed several clashes between French civilians and American white troops. At Saint-Nazaire, for instance, on April 1, 1919, a Frenchwoman having lunch with a black Frenchman was insulted by American officers present in the restaurant. Her brother, who understood English, resented it: the place was wrecked in a free-for-all fight that stopped only when a machine gun was mounted to restore order. By the end of the war white Americans were far less popular than in 1917 and were often described as "children at best, brutes at worst." In contrast, longer contact between the French and black Americans, as well as French appreciation of the Negroes' musical abilities, deepened friendships.

Both the YMCA and the French government encouraged soldiers to learn French; professors were sent to teach the rudiments of conversational French, and books were distributed free. After April 1919 the army took on the educational work: classes in French and in French history and literature were quite popular. With assistance from the French ministry of education, an American university for undergraduates was established at Beaune, Côte d'Or. Later, colored American soldiers from all parts of France applied for admission to the foreign universities, as they were entitled to do, and as many whites did. But in some camps they were told that colored were not allowed; efforts were made to get the 92nd Division out of France before they could make application. As a result, only one black officer, Captain D. K. Cherry of North Carolina Agricultural and Technical State University, was able to take courses at the University of Bordeaux. About a dozen black noncoms were admitted: four at Bordeaux, one at Toulouse, one at Marseilles, and seven in Paris, mostly in pharmacy and sciences—but George Marshall of Texas got a B.A. in literature. The number of American blacks admitted to French military schools, whether at Langres, La Courtine, or Vannes, was much larger, often due to the personal intervention of their French commanding officers.

The impact upon France of American jazz music, introduced by the 815th Pioneer Infantry band led by Lieutenant Jimmy Europe, is now history. Its fame spread as the band played in city after city. Mrs. Hunton recalled a very early performance in Paris, during the Conference of Allied Women in August 1918. It was a grand occasion at the Théâtre des Champs-Élysées, with many official addresses and a Royal Opera singer. The black musicians were invisible in the pit, but Europe stood on an elevated platform while he led the band of the 15th New York Infantry in the French national anthem as Premier Poincaré entered his box. Other popular band leaders were Sergeant-Major Bailey, Bandmaster Oliver Mead, and Sergeant Stevenson, whose coffin was strewn with flowers and wreaths by French admirers when he killed himself accidentally at Chambéry. Lieutenant "Chief" James Wheelock became popular by playing a few kilometers back of the front lines with the 808th Pioneer Infantry.

Mrs. Hunton's most arduous task began in May 1919, when she was assigned to the military cemetery at Romagne, near Verdun, where Negro soldiers were engaged in reburying other Americans killed in the Meuse-Argonne battle. She tried to assuage their resentment at being left behind to do that gruesome work. Like the Reverend Proctor, she emphasized that burying the dead fell to black soldiers because the white Americans had refused the task. After the armistice they began at Romagne, Beaumont, Belleau Wood, Fay-en-Tardenois, and Soissons. They would start at dawn to locate the dead on the battlefield and work until dusk. In the *New York Evening Post* William G. Shepherd remembered as one of the burning pictures of all the war "the sight of these Negro sexton-soldiers working on a hilltop on a rainy evening, outlined against the gloomy sky at dusk." [19] Mrs. Hunton herself noted that, the day before General Pershing reviewed the Romagne cemetery, she saw long lines of black soldiers, each carrying a white cross, walking for hours on end in order to provide for the 22,000 Americans interred there. Already, visitors to post-armistice Paris, having seen the tombs of Lafayette and Napoleon and the palaces of Versailles and Fontainebleau, would turn toward the devastated areas. Rheims, with its far-famed cathedral in ruins, superseded Chartres as a place of pilgrimage.

Addie Hunton returned to America in late 1919. In her conclusion to *Two Colored Women* she echoed Du Bois's impressions of the aftermath of black participation in the battle in France:

> Approximately 150,000 soldiers, officers and men went to France to represent the colored race in America. Many of them were brigaded with the French while other thousands had a contact and association with this people which resulted in bringing for the entire number a broader view of life; they caught the vision of a freedom that gave them new hope and new inspiration. . . . Many hundreds had the opportunity of traveling through the flowering fields of a country long-famed for its wonderful monuments, cathedrals, art galleries, palaces, chateaux, etc., that represent the highest attainment in the world of architecture and art. They looked upon the relics left by a people long gone and saw the picturesqueness of a great and wonderful country as they took their way from the port cities to the front line trenches or to the towering Alps, or through the farms and villages of quaint and thrifty people. And while they traveled, they learned that there is a fair-skinned people in the world who believe in the equality of the races, and who practice what they believe. (*Two Colored Women*, 253–54)

Du Bois's own contacts with France did not end with his investigation of the treatment of black troops in the U.S. Expeditionary Forces there. His major achievement, at the time, was the convening of the first Pan-African Congress in Paris. It took place from February 19 to 21, 1919, at the Grand Hotel. Not only was it authorized (after much hesitation) by Premier Clémenceau, but since Blaise Diagne, the high commissioner to French Colonial troops, presided, the intrinsically but covertly anticolonialist gathering was officially convened by Diagne for the protection of African natives and people of African descent. Du Bois, as secretary, managed to preserve the orientation and the militancy of the meeting, whose resolutions, worded in careful terms, represented a first important step toward improving the conditions of colonized Africa.

In 1921 the second Pan-African Congress met in summer and autumn in Brussels, London, and Paris, again with the support of Diagne, who almost controlled it. But the influence of overly pro-French blacks was strongly countered. This time a Pan-African Association was created, even duly registered with the Paris Préfecture de Police on December 8, 1921. Rayford W. Logan was appointed deputy secretary of the association.[20] Du Bois found it increasingly difficult to work with Diagne and his like. Before the fourth Pan-African Conference in Lisbon in 1923, he met with deputies Boisneuf and Isaac Béton while Diagne and Candace were out of town and "came to amicable understandings."[21] However, the liberal policy of the French government in allowing the Pan-African conferences was gradually giving way to a sterner defense of their colonial interests.

Although a strong opponent of French colonial domination, Du Bois remained a friend of France, especially during the dark hours of Nazi occupation. He began his July 6, 1940, editorial for the Pittsburgh *Courier:* "The greatness of France in her culture and people will not and cannot die." Against President Roosevelt's own preferences, he was a strong partisan of De Gaulle and claimed that "De Gaulle will be and should be the ruler of postwar France despite U.S. and British hostility."[22] Du Bois saw Paris again in April 1949, when he attended a world peace meeting, his travel financed in part by the pro-communist American Peace Committee. He landed at Orly, Shirley Graham recalled, at the very moment when Paul Robeson was making his much-discussed speech at the Salle Pleyel, stating that he wished black Americans would never join to fight the U.S.S.R. Du Bois was feted in the salons of the Claridge Hotel, and true to his distinguished and cultured self, he was loved by the waiters at Henri's because he consulted them in French, following their recommendations for a dessert of crêpes suzette. But Du Bois's political stand led the U.S. government to refuse him a passport when he was asked to be a delegate to the first conference of Negro artists and writers, organized in Paris in September 1956 by the Société Africaine de Culture. Only in 1959, when he undertook a tour of the U.S.S.R. and China, was he able to stop in France once more, on his way to Moscow.

A few black soldiers remained in France after the war: a handful pursued studies there, a few more set up businesses or made a living in the entertainment world. But some had established close relationships with French families or fellow-soldiers and kept up a correspondence with them. Also, through Army agencies or special provisions made for them by the U.S. government, some Negro veterans were able to revisit the battlefields. A handful of black veterans thus came to France with the American Legion in the fall of 1927. Out of one thousand American soldiers they were exactly eleven from the 369th Infantry, including Harry Smith, Noble Sissle, Henry Anderson, George Jones, and their families. They visited the Vosges, where they had covered themselves with glory, and they were heartily welcomed by the French population.[23] Another group of seventy participated in the Armistice tenth anniversary commemorative parade. They arrived in France with a few women auxiliaries; they visited not only the battle-fields but many other places as well. J. A. Rogers, reporting on what he called "The Second A.E.F. Invasion of France," wrote that they "went *everywhere* which means something in Paris," even attending a banquet given by the Comité de Défense de la Race Nègre at Café Turqueti.[24] The newly founded race organization was led by Georges Forgues, who delivered a speech on some of the accomplishments of the French Negroes. Yet such occurrences were rare: while the French government awarded Dr. Harriet E. Rice, a Negro woman, the Re-connaissance Française bronze medal for her services in the French military hospitals during the war,[25] it was reported that Negro and white Gold Star mothers would not be sent to France on the same ship to visit the graves of their sons.

The establishment of a lasting connection with French cultural life was left to wealthier Negro tourists, artists, and writers, and these, like white Americans, seldom visited the French provinces, with the exception of the Riviera. Although many a French soldier had come across Senegalese troops or Hell's Fighters in the trenches or hospitals, a black man was still something of a curiosity. But curiosity was not tinged with fear or hostility—on the contrary. As late as 1931 Nancy Cunard, born into the British nobility but a fiery radical, sojourned with her lover, black American musician Henry Crowder, in the Dor-dogne valley. In Paris, she remarked, no one except a few American tourists stared at an interracial couple in the elite places, the restau-rants, or the streets, but she expected more surprise from the inhabitants of the tiny village of Creysse, on the river banks: "Few foreigners come here and the old man who appeared suddenly from the tangle of bushes was most interested. 'English, aren't you,' says he in dialect, 'but yon black man's not the first; seen many in the war—my son was with them . . . magnificent fellows—vilely treated in their own country, I'm told, and as for what I've heard of Americans . . .' He worked himself up, beating his breast. So fact, it seems, would travel to the innermost regions."[26] Fond memories of black Americans apparently still lingered in the French countryside. As for the image of France in the heart of many a veteran who spoke fervently to his acquaintances back home, it had become, beyond the gay, refined entertainment of the City of Light, that of a land of freedom and fair treatment, "a paradise for American Negroes."

NOTES

1. W. E. B. Du Bois, "Reading, Writing and Real Estate," *Negro Digest* 1 (October 1943), 64.

2. Du Bois, *The Autobiography of W. E. Burghardt Du Bois* (New York: International Publishers, 1968), 177.

3. Du Bois, "The American Negro in Paris," *American Monthly Review of Reviews*, November 1900, 577.

4. Du Bois, *Against Racism: Unpublished Essays, Papers, and Addresses, 1887–1961*, ed. Herbert Aptheker (Amherst: University of Massachusetts, 1985), 57.

5. Jessie Fauset, *Crisis*, February 1919, 186.

6. Fenton Johnson, "War Profiles," *Crisis*, June 1918, 67.

7. Du Bois, in *Crisis*, June 1919, 65.

8. Du Bois, "Letters from Dr. Du Bois," *Crisis*, February 1919, 164.

9. Du Bois, editorial, *Crisis*, March 1919, 216–17.

10. "Documents of War," *Crisis*, May 1919, 227.

11. "The Colored American in France," *Crisis*, February 1919, 167–69.

12. *Crisis*, November 1919, 200–203.

13. *Crisis*, March 1919, 216.

14. William Hewlett to W. E. B. Du Bois, August 26, 1919, *The Correspondence of W. E. B. Du Bois: Selections, 1877–1934*, ed. Herbert Aptheker (Amherst: University of Massachusetts Press, 1973), 234–35.

15. Du Bois, "Opinions," *Crisis*, May 1919, 13.

16. Richard Wright, *Black Boy*, (New York: Harper, 1940), 202.

17. Henry Hugh Proctor, *Between Black and White* (Boston: Pilgrim Press, 1925), 157, hereafter cited in the text.

18. Addie Hunton and Kathryn Johnson, *Two Colored Women with the American Expeditionary Forces* (New York: Brooklyn Eagle Press, undated), 13, hereafter cited in the text. Addie Hunton wrote the larger part of the book.

19. William G. Sheperd, *New York Evening Post*, undated clipping, Schomburg Collection, vertical files.

20. A young history graduate and one of the few black veterans to have remained in Europe, he served as secretary to the third Pan-African Conference in 1923 and worked for the association until the following year. Only upon his return did he start teaching in American universities. The rest of his career was linked to his interest in French-speaking blacks.

21. Du Bois to A. Spingarn, December 2, 1923, Harvard University Library.

22. Du Bois, editorial, Pittsburgh *Courier,* July 8, 1944, 1.

23. Monroe Mason, "With the American Legion in France," New York *Amsterdam News,* September 28, 1927.

24. Joel A. Rogers, "The Second A.E.F. Invasion of France," New York *Amsterdam News,* October 21, 1927.

25. "France Pays Negro Woman Honor for War Service," New Orleans *Times-Picayune,* September 17, 1931.

26. Nancy Cunard, "Does Anyone Know Any Negroes?" *Crisis,* September 1931, 300.

5

Langston Hughes and Alain Locke: Jazz in Montmartre and African Art

Me, I always wanted to study French,
It don't make sense—
I'll never go to France,
But night schools teach French.
Now at last I've got a job
Where I get off at five,
In time to wash and dress.
So, s'il vous plaît, I'll study French.[1]

Langston Hughes's first emotional link to France, as reported in his autobiography *The Big Sea*, was the thrill of being able to understand the French of Guy de Maupassant, linked to the awakening of his desire to become a writer: "The soft snow was falling through one of his stories in the little book we used in school, and that I had worked over so long before I really felt the snow falling there. Then all of a sudden one night the beauty and the meaning of the words in which he made the snow fall, came to me. I think it was De Maupassant who made me really want to be a writer and write stories about Negroes, so true that people in far-away lands would read them—even after I was dead."[2] This was in Cleveland, Ohio, where Langston Hughes graduated from high school in 1920. Significantly, another early mention of France hints at literary achievement: when he apprised his father, a lawyer, of his ambition to become a writer, young Langston could think of only Alexandre Dumas as an example of a colored writer who had made money. His father remarked, "Yes, but he was in Paris where they don't care about color" (*Big Sea*, 62).

In Hughes's mind the image of France early evoked literary accomplishment and absence of racial prejudice. Although he dreamed of staying in France for a while, the already celebrated author of "I Have

Known Rivers" reached it only after a memorable voyage to Africa as a mess boy in 1923: there he was able to observe that French colonials in Dakar did not behave better toward the natives than other whites did. After a second transatlantic voyage, this time to Holland, Hughes met the French son-in-law of a Rotterdam dock watchman and began conversing with him in his high-school French: "The more I.talked to him about Paris, the more I wanted to go there—and not just go but *stay* long enough really to know the city. I felt sure I would fall in love with Paris once I saw it" (*Big Sea,* 140). In February 1924, at the end of yet another voyage and disgusted with the old, dangerous freighter, Hughes bravely caught the train to Paris with only seven dollars in his pocket. He was persuaded, after the thrill of crossing "la frontière," that his dream would come true. But what could an American do in Paris with so little money and no connections? Thrilled as he was to be walking across the Place Vendôme and the Place de la Concorde under the snow, before ending up at the Louvre in order to get warm while admiring the Venus de Milo, Hughes was immediately confronted with the necessity of finding a job and a place to stay.

His witty recounting of how he repaired to Montmartre and shacked up in a dingy hotel room with Sonya, an out-of-work Russian émigré ballet dancer, his reminiscing about his jobs as nightclub chasseur on the Rue Fontaine and second cook at the Grand Duc cabaret have now become anthology pieces. While writing *The Big Sea,* he could give his hotel room at 15, Rue Nollet, in the 17th arrondissement, a romantic aura: "The room was right out of a book and I began to say to myself I guess dreams do come true and sometimes life makes its own books. Because here I am, living in a Paris garret, writing poems and having champagne for breakfast (because champagne is what we had with our breakfast at the Grand Duc from the half-empty bottles left by unsuspecting guests" (*Big Sea,* 163–64).

In his first letter to his friend Countee Cullen, three weeks after his arrival, Hughes in fact conveyed less romantic impressions. For a week he had come close to starving as he tramped the city in search of work. He had fallen into the heart of Parisian nightlife, in Montmartre, because it was one of the few places where English was spoken, and due to the influx of musicians and entertainers, it was the real center of black American presence: "But about France! Kid, stay in Harlem! The French are the most franc-loving, sou-clutching, hard-faced, hard-worked, cold and half-starved set of people I've ever seen in my life. Heat unknown. Hot water, what is it? You even pay for a smile here. Nothing, absolutely nothing is given away. You even pay for water in a restaurant or the use of the toilette. And do they like

Americans *of any color?* They do not!! Paris, old and ugly and dirty. Style? Class? You see more well-dressed people in a New York subway station in five seconds than I've seen all my three weeks in Paris. Little old New York for me! But the colored people here are fine, there are lots of us."[3]

A couple of months later Hughes still advised his friend Harold Jackman, who wanted to emulate him: "Stay home! . . . Jobs in Paris are like needles in hay-stacks for everybody and especially for English-speaking foreigners." It was not a matter of racial discrimination, as the numerous French blacks apparently lived and worked under the same conditions as other Frenchmen, but the conditions were all the worse as the city was overrun with Latins who worked for next to nothing. As a result, a franc (six cents) was harder to get in Paris than a dollar in New York. The Negro jazz bands and performers were the only ones who did well. Hughes remarked that girls' wages were so low that they could not afford to live alone: "One will live with you forever if you only pay the room rent." In Montmartre, at least, one apparently never took the trouble to get married. He thought he had been unwise to expect so much from Paris without knowing much about it; but, strangely enough, he was not alone, and English-speaking people there seemed to be stuck on the city: "If you gave them all a ticket home tomorrow, I doubt if they would leave Paris."[4]

Hughes's contacts with the French—generally limited to the working class and to people he met in the street, in shops, or out of necessity—were diverse. At times he was almost chased by employees as he sought some work; a team of bricklayers shouted "dirty foreigner" at him, but he was able to explain such hostility as "anti-foreign feeling among French workers because so many Italians and Poles had come to Paris and were working for even lower wages than the underpaid Frenchmen" (*Big Sea,* 155). At least they did not shout "dirty nigger" at him! Conversely, he fondly remembered the elderly French couple who let him have a cheap room in their quiet working-folks' hotel on the Rue Nollet.

While Claude McKay, also penniless, sought work in the artists' studios of Montparnasse, Hughes's Paris was, for a long time, restricted to the Montmartre of nightclubs, the Place Pigalle, a little café on the Rue La Bruyère, and what he called the "Parisian world of color." His employers were mostly black: he worked as a doorman at the tiny nightclub of Mme. Moffat, a woman from Martinique. Then his friend Rayford Logan, a Negro lieutenant who had stayed in France after the war, came to his rescue and helped him find a job at the Grand Duc, where black aviator and legionnaire

Gene Bullard was manager. Being a second cook really meant washing dishes for Bruce, the big, brown-eyed chef. From the pantry
Hughes could hear, and sometimes see, the Negro entertainers as they
played and danced, mostly for white American patrons, among whom
were writers Robert McAlmon and Anita Loos. Hughes remembered
brown-skinned singers Florence Embry Jones and "Bricktop" and jazz
musicians Buddy Gilmore, Palmer Jones, Frank Withers, and Cricket
Smith getting ready for jam sessions. In the tiny kitchen he struggled
to fit the rhythms of jazz into the rhythm of words:

> Me an' my baby's
> Got two mo' ways
> Two mo' ways to do the buck.
>
> .   .   .   .
>
> *Da, da,*
> *Da, da, da!*
> Soft light on the tables,
> Music gay,
> Brown-skin dancers
> in a cabaret.

"Me an' My Baby" was later called "Charleston" and published in
Vanity Fair. This was the first time Hughes was ever paid for his writing—the astronomical sum of twenty-five dollars.

Later, in *Fine Clothes to the Jew,* he included yet another piece inspired by the universal appreciation of jazz music in Montmartre:

JAZZ BAND IN A PARISIAN CABARET

> Play that thing,
> Jazz band!
> Play it for the lords and ladies,
> For the dukes and counts,
> For the whores and gigolos,
> For the American millionaires,
> And the school teachers
> Out for a spree.
>
> .   .   .   .   .   .
>
> You know that tune
> That laughs and cries at the same time.
>
> .   .   .   .
>
>   May I?
>   Mais oui,
>   Mein Gott!

Parece una rumba.
Play it, jazz band![5]

The poem first appeared in the *Crisis* in December 1925.

The first syncopated poems of the jazz poet par excellence were thus inspired by the nightclubs of Paris as well as the cabarets of Harlem. But there were days of gloom, when Hughes contemplated leaving the city and wrote poems full of desperation, like "Song of a Suicide" and the short piece that began: "I am waiting for my mother. / She is Death. . . ."[6] Contemporary poems like "Lament for Dark Peoples," "The White Ones," and "Afraid" even seemed to express a rejection of the Western world by the Negro "caged in the circus of civilization."[7] Was this a very personal reaction to the coldness of the City of Light? At any rate, Hughes decided not to stay there too long and inquired, in a letter to Alain Locke, about the possibility of entering Howard University in September.[8]

With the coming of spring Hughes started to explore more of Paris, especially the Latin Quarter and the Luxembourg Gardens, which Alain Locke praised in his comforting letters to him. At the Luxembourg Langston met Anne Coussey, a sophisticated middle-class London girl of Anglo-African descent who was studying at the Raymond Duncan school. If we are to believe his correspondence and his friends' reactions, he fell in love with her: Countee Cullen, for instance, wrote him on May 11, 1924: "So you're in love at last." Later, to Harold Jackman, Hughes wrote somewhat coolly on May 26: "My 'little love' has gone back to Piccadilly and tho' our hearts may be broken, they still beat."[9] They were madly infatuated: they were in Paris in the spring, and they went to delightful tea parties at a little place on the Boulevard Saint-Michel, where Langston would eat like a wolf; they went dancing; they took long walks in Parc Monceau and at Versailles. To "Nan," Langston wrote a few passionate poems—or did he use the passion she inspired in him to try his hand at love poetry in "Fascination"?

> Her teeth are as white as the meat of an apple,
> Her lips are like dark ripe plums.
> I love her.
> Her hair is a midnight mass, a dusky aurora.
> I love her.
> And because her skin is the brown of an oak leaf
> in autumn, but a somber color,
> I want to kiss her.[10]

They would discuss his poetry, and she did not refrain from expressing criticism when she wrote him: "I see the little poem you wrote about the girl with the Oak Leaf [herself] was published in the June *Crisis.* It seemed slightly worse in print. . . . I'm afraid you are getting into a groove, there is a sameness about your things. I wonder if Paris is responsible for it, or perhaps you're not really original." [11] She was deeply in love, but being a dutiful daughter, she did not elope with Langston although she broke off her previous engagement shortly after her family shipped her back to London. She hoped he would join her, but he did not; for several years, she remained "his to a cinder" and kept writing him. Only in 1930 did she marry a barrister in Trinidad. As late as February 1927 Hughes published poems hinting of enduring memories of Anne, or was "A Letter to Anne" simply an old poem that the writer wanted to see in print? [12]

In May 1924 Hughes did not contemplate marriage; instead he was getting ready to welcome Jessie Fauset, "a woman of charm, my own brown goddess." [13] She had urged him to stay until October, when she would come for several months, as she would need him as an escort: "You can take me to all the dangerous places and I can take you to all the beautiful ones," she wrote on April 4. [14] He was beginning to know all of Paris and could boast, in May 1924, that he'd done about everything except the Louvre in detail and an airplane ride over the city. [15] Later, in *The Big Sea*, he declared that he had such a good time then that he could write only a few poems. In mid-May, however, he wrote Countee Cullen that he had a story on the nightlife of Montmartre with colored people as the characters. [16] None of his published works fits that description: his only story set in France, "The Blues of Osceola Jones," appeared in the mid-thirties and dealt with Montparnasse, not Montmartre: the heroine of the story derides the educated blacks who endlessly debate the merits of Marcus Garvey, Picasso, Oswald Spengler's *Decline of the West,* and the works of Jean Cocteau. Hughes satirizes the "niggerati," who believe that art will bring down racial barriers, prevent lynchings, and save the race.

"The Blues of Osceola Jones" in no way reflected Hughes's growing awareness of the importance of African art in the mid-twenties. In June 1924 business had begun to fall off at the Grand Duc, and he had taken to sleeping for hours to keep from eating, seized with a strong desire to go back to sea. But he remained, only in order to meet Alain Locke, who was already infatuated with his poetry. The Howard University professor of philosophy, whose anthology was soon to become the manifesto of the New Negro movement, was a Harvard B.A. and the first black American Rhodes scholar, and he had studied at Oxford and in Berlin from 1907 to 1912. Although he was as proficient in French as in German, he preferred Germany to England and France. He would usually stop in Paris for a week or two on his way to a summer in Berlin, Munich, or Oberammergau. He had already made several stays in France when, in July 1924, he visited Langston Hughes, whom he had not yet managed to meet and from whom he hoped to solicit a contribution for the Negro issue of the *Survey Graphic* he was editing. Locke knew Paul Guillaume, the connaisseur and collector of African and Negro art, and his letters to Hughes before he arrived reveal a wide-ranging acquaintance with all sorts of people and places in France. "You will be enjoying Paris but don't prejudge," he had written Hughes in May. "French people are only different—that's all. And at least you can, and will, love Paris. Be spiritually Catholic, this is the beginning of fine culture."[17] He mentioned the Parc Monceau, which he "adored," and the terraces and statues in the Luxembourg Gardens. Montmartre did not attract him much, although he often spent nights and early mornings there with his friend Léon Romano, whom he considered an embodiment of that district.

The first meeting of Locke and Hughes in Paris was truly idyllic. While, in mid-May, Hughes could hardly imagine that Paris could be a fascinating city in the summer, he was all aglow by July: "Locke's here. We are having a glorious time. I like him a great deal. I only wish we could be together all summer," he wrote Cullen, and also: "I'm enjoying my last two weeks in Paris more than any others because Mr. Locke is here."[18] Hughes was most attracted by Locke's personality: "the little brown man with spats and a cultured accent" sought him out in his new attic room on the Rue des Trois Frères, entertained him with charming conversation, took him to lunch and, later, to see *Manon* at the Opéra Comique (*Big Sea*, 184).

For Hughes his encounter with Locke in Paris was first of all an introduction to circles and concerns that had until then remained outside his own folk-oriented interests, an initiation into a more sophisticated appreciation of the role of Afro-American culture in world art. Locke introduced Hughes to Albert C. Barnes and Paul Guillaume, the famous art collectors. The special art issue of *Opportunity* in May 1924 described Dr. Barnes as a leading authority who declared that "the first and distinctly the last word is Primitive African Art."[19] The Barnes Foundation had large holdings in African art, mostly sculpture in wood and bronze. But Paul Guillaume, already famous for his collection of contemporary European painting, was the one who had most forcefully made the claim that "the modern movement in art gets its

inspiration undoubtedly from African art, and it could not be other-
wise. Thanks to that fact, France wields the artistic sceptre."[20] Hughes
later remembered he was not too impressed by Barnes, who sounded
on art like Hughes's father on business, but he greatly admired the
Guillaume collection of African sculpture, with treasures from Benin,
the Sudan, and the Congo. He already knew some of Africa, but this
convinced him even more of the importance of his African heritage.

Clearly, Hughes was interested in learning about the new trends in
writing: when, in early July, he met novelist René Maran at Cullen's
suggestion, he was quite enthusiastic about "that darn nice fellow from
the Antilles and his talk. I don't get a third of what he says. But it
is good practice in French so I'm going to see him often."[21] That
summer, Alain Locke also met René Maran, with whom he had been
corresponding ever since the latter had sent a rejoinder, rather critical of French colonialism, to Locke's pro-French article "The Black
Watch on the Rhine," in the January 1924 issue of *Opportunity.* Locke
had recently been elected a foreign member of the French Colonial
Academy and was in Paris officially under the sponsorship of that organization. He and Maran shared an interest in rehabilitating the race
and in keeping up aesthetic standards; they quickly became friends
and, in the September 1924 issue of his newly founded newspaper
Les Continents, Maran published a short article by Locke on the "New
African-American Poetry"; this was the first mention of the incipient
New Negro movement to appear in France.

Judging by Locke's own excitement, he and Hughes shared more
than literary companionship. Shortly after Hughes's departure to Italy
in August, Locke, returning from a trance-like walk up the Champs
Élysées and a long ramble in the Bois de Boulogne, wrote to his
friend: "Today, the atmosphere is like atomized gold—and last night
you know how it was—two days the equal of which atmospherically
I have never seen in a great city—days when every breath has the
soothe of a kiss and every step the thrill of an embrace." He went on:
"I needed one such day and one such night to tell you how much I love
you, in which to see soul-deep and be satisfied—for after all with all
my sensuality and sentimentality, I love sublimated things and today
nature, the only great cleanser of life, would have distilled anything.
God grant us one such day and night before America with her inhi-
bitions closes down on us."[22] Locke believed that Paris had much to
do with his happiness: in his eyes the city was a haven for aesthetic,
refined, and sensuous enjoyment of the body as well as the spirit—
a perfect blend that French freedom (so often called licentiousness

by other American visitors) allowed, liberating him not only from the constraints of Prohibition but from deeper-seated, puritanical taboos.

Although Locke clearly opened to Hughes new avenues of aesthetic enjoyment and a new appreciation of the Paris setting, Hughes wanted to see more of Europe. Without waiting for Jessie Fauset's arrival, he decided to accompany one of his fellow-employees, Romeo, when he visited his family in northern Italy while the Grand Duc was closed for the summer. After a few days near Lago di Garda, he was in love with the countryside, with the old uphill town full of simple and kind people. "I'd like to stay here forever—almost," he wrote Cullen.[23] His pleasant stay ended with a tour of Venice with Alain Locke, who had joined him, as a guide to its architectural and pictorial treasures. This time Hughes nearly suffered an indigestion of art. He intended to return to Paris by way of the Riviera in order to meet Claude McKay, but the theft of his only suitcase left him in Genoa without money or papers. He tarried there several weeks before sailing directly to New York, painting and scrubbing decks on a tramp steamer to earn his passage. His first book of poems, *The Weary Blues,* had not yet appeared, but he could boast of his first international publication—"Negro" and "A Black Pierrot" in René Maran's *Les Continents* in July 1924.

For a decade or so Hughes did not return to France. As for Alain Locke, he was in Paris again in the summer of 1926, staying at the fashionable Hotel Marigny, eagerly climbing to the top of Sacré-Coeur "in a fit of vigorous piety." In August 1927 he sent Langston Hughes a postcard from the Hotel de Ville: he was relaxing in Paris, which he found just as interesting as ever, although not so cheap; he was able to see Raquel Miller on stage before leaving for Interlaken. In the city again in August 1929 on his way back from Bad-Nauheim, he visited Countee Cullen at length. The following summer he wrote Hughes on August 6, his last day in the city before leaving for Germany: he romantically recalled the old hotel on the Rue des Trois Frères, where in 1924 he used to walk up to the fifth floor to awaken his friend. He also recorded the changes caused by the Great Depression: the reaction was being felt everywhere, and Paris was becoming lusterless, as dull as any other city. Yet practically every summer Locke returned to Europe. In 1930 and 1931 he visited Maran faithfully; through him he met younger French-speaking blacks, notably the Nardal sisters, who were busy launching the *Revue du Monde Noir,* and he spent some time at the Colonial Exhibition in 1931, getting an inkling of incipient "negritude" from talks with Louis Achille and others who were involved in cultural events connected with the exhibition. He stopped

again in Paris on his way to Vienna in 1932 and on his way to the
Salzburg music festival in 1935.

In 1931 Hughes returned to French-speaking territory, this time
to Port-au-Prince, which he found "little more than a collection of
wooden huts with tin roofs, gangs of Marines and badly lighted
streets."[24] In Haiti he visited the historical sites and sojourned in
Cap Haitien, even more provincial than the capital city, becoming engrossed in native dances that reminded him of Africa. But the major
event was his encounter with poet and ethnologist Jacques Roumain,
five years his junior, who admired his work and sent him *La Montagne
ensorcelée* and *Les Fantoches* as a New Year's gift, saying, "I see in you the
greatest Negro poet of all the Americas."[25] In 1935, when Roumain
was imprisoned for communism, Hughes was active on the Committee
for the Release of Jacques Roumain. They remained lifelong friends.

Until his return to Paris in 1937, Hughes maintained a few contacts
with France. He met a few French visitors in New York, like writer
Georges Adam, who was preparing a book on the United States in
1927. Carl Van Vechten invited him to a party he gave in honor of
novelist Paul Morand; Claire Goll approached him in 1929, wanting
to translate some of his poetry. His 1924 friends Retna and Henri
Cartier-Bresson, the latter soon to become famous as a photographer,
visited Langston in 1935, when he introduced them to Van Vechten.

In the thirties, however, Hughes became quite well known in French
progressive circles, largely because of his political commitment on the
side of the proletariat. French avant-garde magazines often printed
his poetry, and *Littérature Internationale* even boasted a translation of
it by Louis Aragon in 1933, the year the two poets met in the U.S.S.R.
In 1934 Éditions Rieder brought out *Sandy,* a translation of his novel
Not without Laughter, and when *Europe* magazine published "The Blues
of Osceola Jones" in 1937, Hughes was proudly introduced as "one of
the few black proletarian poets of the world." Meanwhile, in January
of that year Nancy Cunard had included "A Song of Spain" next to a
poem by Federico García Lorca in her pamphlet, *Les Poètes du monde
défendent le peuple espagnol.*

It was the Spanish Civil War that brought Hughes back to France
again. He had accepted an invitation to speak in July 1937 at the
Second International Writers' Congress in Paris, but he was mainly
traveling to Spain for a period of six months as a correspondent for the
Baltimore *Afro-American.* Because the state department had refused
him permission to go to Spain as a representative of the Negro press,
he had to sail directly to France, although most other delegates—including Anna Louise Strong, Malcolm Cowley, and Louis Fischer—

were able to attend the initial sessions of the congress in Spain. In his speech at the final session on July 17, he wondered, "Is it because the reactionary and fascist forces of the world know that writers like Anand and myself; leaders like Herndon and poets like Guillen and Roumain represent the great longing that is in the hearts of the darker peoples of the world to reach out their hands in friendship and brotherhood to all the white races of the earth?"[26] Hughes was no longer the unknown young black he had been in 1924, but a leading left-wing American writer whose stirring speech against fascism the international representatives warmly applauded in Paris.

Instead of going on to Spain, Hughes tarried in Paris for nearly two months. He saw old friends again: Jacques Roumain; René Maran, who gave a party for him and to whom he proudly inscribed his *Fine Clothes to the Jew;* the Cartier-Bressons; and Louis Aragon, whom he had met in Moscow in 1933 and who was instrumental in getting him papers to travel to Spain. Aragon had introduced him to his former love, Nancy Cunard. She had published Hughes in her *Negro* anthology and she now praised him in the October 1937 *Left Review,* while he appreciated her interest in simple people and her avoidance of academics. And he also met a host of writers from everywhere, including André Malraux, who had already fought in Spain, and dadaist Tristan Tzara. He found Paris "the same as ever, beautiful, inexpensive, and full of tourists."[27] He was a tourist himself, enjoying the Folies Bergères, where he met Josephine Baker after her show, visiting his old acquaintances in Pigalle. But he also worked busily on two plays, including a blues opera, and paid a visit to Mercer Cook, who acquainted him with two black French poets—Léon-Gontran Damas from Guyana and Léopold Senghor, whom he saw so briefly that he did not remember the meeting later. In the fall he was in Madrid, and from there he went to report on the fighting of the Abraham Lincoln Brigade before returning to France in December. At Christmas time he stayed in Montmartre at an Ethiopian-run hotel, trying to enjoy nightclubs, parties, even the opera. But sad news was everywhere: the fall of Teruel in Spain, the Italian occupation of Ethiopia, ominous rumors of war in Europe. The gloom of Paris in the winter contrasted with the mood of the previous summer. Although Aragon and poet Pierre Seghers encouraged him to remain, Hughes left for the United States in early January because his mother's health had worsened.

But in July 1938 he was back in France. When the Conférence Universelle contre le Bombardement des Villes et pour la Paix (an international meeting for peace and against the bombing of open cities) convened at the initiative of the Rassemblement Universel des Peuples, with a sponsoring committee presided over by socialist Léon Jouhaux, Hughes was asked to accompany Theodore Dreiser as a delegate. He did not address the Peace Congress, where not even La Pasionaria was allowed to speak, but he spoke at the Writers' Conference on July 26. The star speaker was Dreiser, and there were such British writers as Cecil Day Lewis, Stephen Spender, Rosamond Lehman, Rex Warner, and most of the left-wing French writers, under the leadership of Louis Aragon.

Before the conference Hughes had been invited to Nancy Cunard's place near La Chapelle-Réanville in Normandy. She was busy rallying support for Spanish refugees, and he met a few of them there "who knew a million songs and sang like gypsies" as they exchanged stories and songs late into the night.[28] After Dreiser's departure on August 1, he made another trip to see Cunard, whose grace in giving he admired as much as her involvement. He also revisited his friend Kay Boyle, the committed novelist, in Mégève, since, with five young children, she could hardly come to Paris. But leaving the Latin Quarter for his favorite little Ethiopian-run hotel on the Rue Fontaine, which felt more like Harlem, he saw mainly Henri Cartier-Bresson and his Javanese wife. Compelled by the hordes of American tourists to wait to get a booking on the *De Grasse*, he couldn't sail back until mid-September and spent most of his time working on a musical play.

NOTES

1. Langston Hughes, "Freedom Train," in *Montage of a Dream Deferred* (New York: Henry Holt, 1951).

2. Langston Hughes, *The Big Sea* (1940; rpt. New York: Hill and Wang, 1968), 33–34, hereafter cited in the text.

3. Hughes to Countee Cullen, March 11, 1942, Amistad Research Center.

4. Hughes to Harold Jackman, May 24, 1924, Atlanta University Library.

5. Hughes, "Jazz Band in a Parisian Caberet," in *Fine Clothes to the Jew* (New York: Knopf, 1927), 74.

6. Hughes, "Poem," *Crisis*, August 1924, 173.

7. Langston Hughes, "Lament for Dark Peoples," *Crisis*, June 1924.

8. Faith Berry, *Langston Hughes: Before and Beyond Harlem* (Westport, Conn.: Laurence Hill, 1983), 48.

9. Countee Cullen to Hughes, May 11, 1924, Hughes to Harold Jackman, May 26, 1924, JWJ Collection, Collection of American Literature, Beinecke Rare Book and Manuscript Library, Yale University, hereafter cited as Yale.

10. Hughes, "Fascination," *Crisis*, June 1924.

11. Anne Coussey to Hughes, July 26, 1924, Yale.

12. Hughes, "A Letter to Anne," *Lincoln News*, February 1927, 4.

13. Hughes to Jackman, May 26, 1924.

14. Jessie Fauset to Hughes, April 4, 1924, Yale.

15. Hughes to Jackman, May 26, 1924.

16. Hughes to Cullen, May 15, 1924, Amistad Research Center.

17. Alain Locke to Hughes, May 25, 1924, Yale.

18. Hughes to Cullen, July 27, 1924, Amistad.

19. "Dr. Barnes," *Opportunity*, May 1924, 133.

20. "African Art at the Barnes Foundation," *Opportunity*, May 1924, 140.

21. Hughes to Cullen, July 4, 1924, Amistad.

22. Locke to Hughes, undated, August 1925, Yale.

23. Hughes to Cullen, August 13, 1924, Amistad.

24. Hughes to Carl Van Vechten, May 27, 1931, Yale.

25. Jacques Roumain to Hughes, January 6, 1932, Yale.

26. Hughes, address to the Second International Writers Congress, Paris, July 1937, quoted in Langston Hughes, *Good Morning, Revolution: Uncollected Writings of Social Protest,* ed. Faith Berry (New York: Lawrence Hill, 1973), 99.

27. Hughes to A. Spingarn, September 18, 1937, Yale.

28. Hughes to Van Vechten, July 11, 1938, Yale.

6

Countee Cullen:
"The Greatest Francophile"

Countee Cullen was the greatest francophile of us all. He had won a French medal at Dewitt-Clinton High School and he early associated France with achievement as far as he was concerned.

—Arna Bontemps,
March 16, 1972

In fact, Countee Cullen never won a medal in French, although he did receive honors when he graduated; his prize was in creative writing. But Arna Bontemps's lasting impression of his friend's deep love for France was quite accurate. Cullen *was* the greatest francophile of them all, to such a degree that it is hard to determine whether this was the consequence or the cause of his electing to become a teacher of French. What is certain is that his increasingly fine command of the language and his thorough acquaintance with French culture and literature enabled him to appreciate whatever France had to offer him much more fully than any of his fellow-writers could.

As early as 1921 Cullen published a short story called "The French-man's Bath" in his school magazine, *The Magpie*. In 1924 he planned to sail to Europe with Langston Hughes, but while the latter managed to work his way across the Atlantic, Cullen remained to work as a busboy in an Atlantic City hotel to help pay his tuition at Harvard. He had to bide his time, but when he reached Paris, he was not without financial means as Hughes and Claude McKay had been. When he got there, in the summer of 1926, he was already the feted winner of two poetry prizes and had a brand new M.A. from Harvard.

Countee and his adoptive father, the Reverend Frederic A. Cullen, sailed for Le Havre on the *Ile de France* with several of Countee's friends: Alain Locke, on his way to Germany; Dorothy Peterson, who was teaching in Brooklyn; Negro folklore specialist Arthur Huff Fauset; and William Bond. The party even bribed the head steward to allow them to disembark ahead of time in order to pay a merry visit to Le Havre in the early morning of July 9 before catching the train for Paris. In the city the Cullens spent two glorious days; they visited as many monuments as they could manage, rode along the Champs-Élysées to the Bois de Boulogne, ran into Mercer Cook and his wife at American Express, attended Sunday mass at the Madeleine, explored Montmartre, where Langston Hughes had lived—all this before rushing to the Gare de Lyon just in time to catch the morning train for Marseilles, where they were to embark for Alexandria.

Indeed, in the mind of the Reverend Cullen the aim of their European trip was not Paris, where Countee would have preferred to remain, but the Holy Land. So they crossed the Mediterranean and visited Egypt, Lebanon, and Jerusalem. By August 1 they were on their way back—in Rome, where Countee stood bareheaded before the Shelley memorial and the century-old grave of John Keats, which inspired him to write "Endymion." Then, by way of Switzerland and the natural splendor of the Alps, they returned to Paris, where they spent two full weeks.

The Cullens did the regular tourist rounds: they saw *Tosca* and *Cavalleria Rusticana* at the Opéra-Comique, and they visited the Louvre—in too much haste. With a party that included Eslanda Robeson and other American visitors, Countee undertook to climb the towers of Notre-Dame for a close-range view of the gargoyles; he also climbed the Eiffel Tower and even visited the Palace at Fontainebleau—all before sailing back in the company of Alain Locke and Arthur Schomburg.[1]

Cullen did not mention having met René Maran on that trip. He had, however, read *Batouala* in 1922 and had been inspired by it to write a poem, "The Dance of Love," which appeared in *Opportunity* the following year. He even asked Hughes to buy Maran's poetry for him in 1924, and his friend was instrumental in getting Cullen's poem published in *Les Continents* at the same time as Locke's first article on the New Negro movement. By 1926 Locke had published *The New Negro* in book form, and he knew about recent events in the field of black art and literature on both sides of the Atlantic, which allowed Cullen to be well informed about them. Yet Cullen reacted much more to Paris as a capital of Old Europe than as a place where African art and the Negro were in vogue. He was decidedly enthusiastic about Paris. He wrote his friend Hale Woodruff, a painter about to leave for France on a scholarship: "While the two weeks I spent there were all too short, they were long enough to make me know how beautiful Paris can be. It is superfluous for one to say that I hope your work will have benefited by your stay there. I know it will."[2]

A winner of the Harmon Foundation Award for his volume of

poetry *Color,* in 1928 Cullen was given a $2,500 Guggenheim grant for one year of study abroad. Without hesitation, he chose Paris, planning to devote his time to writing a sequence of narrative poems and a libretto for an opera.[3] Among fashionable colored circles in New York the big event of 1928—indeed, one of the major social events of the decade among the Negro elite—was Cullen's wedding: on April 9 he married Yolande Du Bois, W. E. B. Du Bois's daughter. There were sixteen bridesmaids, twelve hundred invited guests, and three thousand filling the church. Du Bois himself devoted a romantic and emotional *Crisis* editorial to "The Girl Marries" and nearly ruined himself with the wedding expenses.

Strangely enough, when Countee sailed for Le Havre on the *Paris* on June 10, 1928, he was accompanied not by his bride but by his best man and intimate friend Harold Jackman. After dancing in the streets to celebrate Bastille Day, they left for Vienna and the Rhône Valley, heading for Marseilles in order to meet Claude McKay, who was, in fact, still in Seville. Instead they encountered Pierrespart, the classical dancer, before embarking for Algiers on July 17. Cullen's "Dark Tower" column in the September 1928 issue of *Opportunity* tells of many incidents during that voyage and of his liking for colorful North Africa: "We can see in every direction Algiers spreading out like a large white fan, its white roofs shining and flashing in the early morning sun, the entire panorama one of bewildering beauty if one could only forget the dirt and diseases which stalk the Arab population" (273). A year later he would call Algiers a "deceptive hussy of a town, a sort of whited sepulchre, beautiful with its sun-kindled roofs glimpsed from the deck of a slowly incoming steamer, but squalid and sickly under closer inspection."[4]

Cullen and Jackman returned to Paris in time to welcome Cullen's father. He arrived after they had visited the tombs of famous people at the Père Lachaise and Montparnasse cemeteries and danced the biguine at the Bal Colonial on the Rue Blomet. Eager to see black artists and unable to afford the Ambassadeurs, the most select nightclub in Paris, where Noble Sissle was conducting a band, Cullen allowed himself to be taken by a friend to the Bal Colonial, the rendezvous of the Martiniquans of Paris, of which he provided a colorful description:

> The music is probably as good as can be found in all Paris. . . . It is a weird sort of playing, a mélange or cross between modern jazz and the residue of old West Indian folk pieces. The most primitive notes of all are contributed by a player who shakes with varying modulations a leather box filled with pebbles. . . . As an American Negro we are somewhat startled to find that our dark complexion avails us nought among

these kindredly tinted people. Language must be the open sesame here, and it must be French. The Martiniquan lady whom we have had the temerity to ask to dance with us seems to sense an alien tongue in us, for she glides along amiably enough, but allows our painful attempts at conversation to languish gently. For the most part, as we survey the gliding, twisting panorama, we note that these Negroes have become Europeanized in dress and manner. The women are chic and smart in the Parisian way. . . . The dancing for the most part is harsh and slightly reprehensible, faintly suggestive of the antics of some of the New York night clubs. In the midst of it all, however, one couple, as if disdaining such modern contortion, glides slowly along in an old Martinique step. . . . These two are like strong trees in a storm; they do not bend. They are perhaps the remnants of what the Bal Colonial was before the tourists discovered it, perhaps somewhat analogous to what the Harlem clubs were before downtown New York found them amusing.[5]

The following day Cullen went to see *Rigoletto* at the Opera; he went alone because Jackman, with his superior musical education, spurned florid arias and bel canto. He passed the brilliantly arrayed guards at the Opera entrance somewhat late and apparently created a stir when he entered his box: "Three of the other seven sharers of the box are visibly disturbed and we note between them the fleeting passage of that expression of pained bewilderment always apparent when one of us intrudes upon the sacred aloofness of our fellow countrymen."[6]

Cullen and Jackman settled in a little family hotel, the Trianon on the Avenue du Maine, within walking distance of the Montparnasse Cemetery and of the Parc Montsouris, where Countee loved to stroll. He and Harold went to meet the Reverend Cullen at Le Havre, where the sight of a few prostitutes soliciting in the street inspired Countee to write a short poem, "The Street Called Crooked." The Cullens did not tarry in Paris but went to see the Passion play at Oberammergau and also visited Berlin, "an orderly, clean, regimented city as if on dress parade," on their way to Vienna.

When stopped by a prostitute in Le Havre, Countee had replied (if one is to believe his poem) that he had a "better lady" waiting for him at home. In fact, Yolande was far from waiting for him: she had stayed in New York, allegedly to assist her friend Harriet Pickens as a counselor at a YMCA summer camp. When she did arrive, shortly after the Reverend Cullen's departure for the United States, matters were somewhat strained between the newlyweds. Countee had rented an apartment for them on the Avenue du Parc Montsouris, close to painter Henry Tanner's place on the Boulevard Saint-Jacques, because he wanted to be able to visit his friend easily in case of need. The Tanners were in their summer home near Étaples at the time, and the

Cullens stayed with them for a few days, driving occasionally to Paris-Plage or Le Touquet to catch a glimpse of the brightly lit gambling tables at the Casino.

Did Yolande travel with Countee to Switzerland in October? He did not mention her presence when recalling the happy week he spent there for an international gathering arranged by Mabel Byrd. He admired the majesty of Mont Blanc seen from a mountain drive on a brisk October morning, and when confronting the snow-capped giant, in the way his beloved Keats and Coleridge had done, Cullen rather seemed to seek in natural grandeur the oblivion of a fretful conjugal life. Did their living in a foreign country, far from the secure surroundings of home, sharpen the disagreement between them? Why had they originally decided to marry?

Countee now definitely felt that Yolande was not sufficiently in love with him and did not respond to his desire for her. By September things had reached such a point that Cullen wrote his father-in-law about the situation. W. E. B. Du Bois replied with puzzlement and kind advice; had he not believed that a liking based on a strong intellectual companionship was more likely to be lasting than youthful infatuation, he would not have advised them to marry. Reminding Countee that "no man physically owns his wife—his possession is built on love," he beseeched him to make this crisis as easy as possible. He suggested that Yolande stay in Europe until Christmas, when he could afford to send Mrs. Du Bois over to live with her for a few months to "keep down unkind gossip and enable the break to come after a decent interval."[7] Countee agreed to grant a divorce on the grounds that he had "forsaken the conjugal domicile," as the French say. With the help of Maître Jean Beauvais the procedure was begun in November 1929.

This unfortunate situation was a severe blow to Countee, and many echoes of it are to be found in his French composition notebook of that period. He was filled with nostalgia for the lights and bustle of New York, he wrote, and went through crises of despair:

> Last night, at the Salle Pleyel, during the philharmonic concert directed by Wilhelm Mengelberg, while listening to Beethoven's music, I felt tears tremble over my eyes. I felt my heart heave, felt a yearning to see my own. This yearning lasted throughout the night. Back from the concert, I poured myself a glass of brandy, a large glass in order to help me forget all my sullen and childish thoughts. I only succeeded in giving myself a headache.
>
> I may be in love, but with whom, and why? For a long time, I have had enough of love and marriage; if I am wise, I shall not get caught again by eyes that burn too bright, by a well-turned shape supporting

only a straw-filled head. But it will be a struggle for the battlefield of the
body, a fight between brain and heart. One says: "Be wise, do not fall
in love. Read and write and study! All of those are worth much more
than love." But the other one advises, in a voice as sweet as the serpent's
speaking to poor Eve: "Love even if you must suffer."

But my French teacher, a very earnest young man, is going to laugh
at me.[8]

W. E. B. Du Bois insisted that Countee should by no means allow the
breakdown of his marriage to slow down his creative work, and, possibly to keep him writing, he requested that he send regular "Letters
from Paris" for publication in the *Crisis*.

It is difficult to determine how much poetry Countee composed at
that time, but he was assuredly busy as a student of French literature.
In the fall he registered at the University of Paris to attend lectures
in French literature and related subjects, and he also took language
classes at the Alliance Française. From his exercise book, begun in
September 1928, one learns much about his life in Paris: attending
concerts or going to hear Maurice Chevalier sing (there were a few
slang or risqué phrases that he did not catch, but Chevalier's voice was
so clear that Countee felt tempted to go and see Mistinguett). Did he
listen to Berlioz's *Damnation of Faust* at the Opera? A program bears
a scribbled note in his handwriting: "I don't like it. The words are
terrible. I'd rather be at the Bal."[9] The Bal, of course, was the Martiniquan dance hall on the Rue Blomet. Or he watched a performance
of Glizca's *Red Poppy* with a libretto by Koucelke, noting that the only
great thing about the Russians was their love of music. One of his
exercises in French composition is quite revealing about his feelings
for Paris:

> When I was only a little boy, I already wanted to visit Paris. I could
> not say why, because I had no logical reasons. It was only a thing of
> the heart. Paris was for me what Carcassonne had once been for the
> French peasant in the famous poem. In Paris I used to build my castles
> in the air.
> Again, when I graduated, we were all filled with dreams and hopes,
> and each had slightly different ones. But our different hopes were all
> linked by a hope which bound us together: we all wanted to go to Paris.
> Would this city, which I had clad with such seduction in my imagina-
> tion, finally fail me? I nearly wanted to go back home without seeing it.
> But no, it was everything I had dreamed of, and even more. Some-
> what like New York where I was born, Paris is a peerless city. Liberty,
> equality, fraternity are not only words. They express the spirit of which
> Paris is made. I have not been here long enough to have deep or de-

finitive impressions (more than a year is needed for those), but I love this café life, this quiet existence mixed with noise and quick motion which is attached to every large city. All my life long, I have loved big cities; the countryside never attracted me. In Paris I find everything that appeals to me: lights, noises in the night, places where one has fun according to one's liking, a sympathetic and tolerant world, in sum, a true civilization.[10]

With his teacher, M. Sudre, Cullen learned idiomatic phrases or tried to master difficult spellings, but the margins of his exercise books also bear a quotation from Rimbaud's "Le Bateau Ivre": "Je sais les cieux crevant en éclair, et les trombes / Et les ressacs et les courants; je sais le soir . . ."[11] The superb and notorious trio—Rimbaud, Verlaine, and Baudelaire—were his favorites among the French poets, and he could find in them echoes of, and solace for, his own spleen. Three important titles belonged to his library: the 1929 Mercure de France printing of Rimbaud's works; Verlaine's *Selected Poems*, published that same year by Bibliothèque Charpentier; and *Flowers of Evil* by Baudelaire, also in French, printed by Payot in 1928 with an introduction by Paul Valéry. In a French composition exercise called "Resurrection; or, A Return to the World" (was this a return to normal after his traumatic parting with Yolande?), Cullen evoked a lively French atmosphere, with red roofs, bells ringing, fishermen and washerwomen by the river along which his boat was gliding slowly, and, he added, "a symphony of Forget-me-nots, as Théophile Gautier would have said."[12] Of greater importance were Cullen's attempts to adapt poems by Baudelaire and to translate his own poems into French. The result of the latter venture was rather uneven, but the titles selected deserve attention: the poems were from *Color* and *Copper Sun* with many pieces from the yet-unpublished *Black Christ:* "The Street Called Crooked," "The Foolish Heart," "A Song No Gentleman Would Sing to Any Lady," "One Day I Told My Love My Heart," "Ghosts," "The Simple Truth," "Song in Spite of Myself," "Lesson"—most of those written after his arrival in Paris.

It is not known exactly when a visit to the grave of the Unknown Soldier under the Arc de Triomphe inspired Cullen's poem "At the Étoile," a rather conventional piece whose ending sounds strained:

> Since he was weak as other men,—or like
> Young Galahad as fair in thought and limb,
> Each bit of moving dust in France may strike
> Its breast in pride, knowing he stands for him.[13]

Thus Cullen kept writing and relied upon his friends and many acquaintances for company. Among his favorite Afro-American artist friends were the Tanners, the sculptor Augusta Savage, who was quite close to Countee, the painters Palmer Hayden and Hale Woodruff, and also the night club singer Alberta Hunter. He was visited occasionally by white Americans: Alan Tate, who like Gertrude Stein resided on the Rue de Fleurus, would meet him at La Coupole, dressed in a gray suit with yellow gloves. His close English friend Rex Littleboy visited him in the winter and asked to be taken to the Luxembourg Gallery to see Henry Tanner's masterpieces. In mid-February Cullen spent some time in Lausanne with his friend Jean Bredel. All that time Cullen apparently felt he did not have much to tell the *Crisis* readers since his March 1929 letter was devoted mainly to French courtesy, with half-witty remarks about the Parisian habits of endlessly shaking hands and of never wrapping their bread hygienically. Just as sweepingly as Langston Hughes had once decided that the French were not well dressed, Cullen endowed them with perpetual politeness that he ascribed to a "natural inherent streak, something fine and delicate, left over perhaps . . . from the days when France had kings and a court."[14]

While *The Black Christ* was awaiting publication, Cullen left the rich warmth of Paris and the bud-covered trees of Parc Montsouris, which he could see from his window and whose leaves he could hear "each night sighing and soughing in the wind," for the chillier climate of London.[15] While he was giving poetry readings, dining out, and meeting celebrities in England, Yolande journeyed to Paris, where she stayed at the Trianon Hotel. They exchanged letters across the Channel, discussing the possibility of a reconciliation. Was this simply a step in the legal proceedings? Did Yolande have second thoughts? At any rate, the petition for divorce was duly pursued.

In May American visitors returned to Paris. After advising Countee to go and see Princess Violette Murat, an open-minded socialite whom he jokingly dubbed "Princess Muskrat," Harold Jackman himself joined his friend for the summer. If one is to believe the press, Cullen attended numerous parties in June. There was one in his apartment with Gertrude Curtis, Caska Bond, Hale Woodruff, Bessie Miller, and Zaidee Jackson, among others; then the sculptor Elizabeth Prophet came for tea on July 2; then the whole group went to Dr. Curtis's place in Montmartre for dinner on the fourth; then it was Louis Coles's birthday party in Cecil Robeson's apartment, with Carl Van Vechten and several socially prominent black girls. Novelist Eric Walrond arrived the following day from a sojourn in Santo Domingo; on July 6 Zaidee Jackson gave a cocktail party before all went to dance the biguine at the ballroom on the Rue Blomet. Yolande was generally reported as being present: although a divorce was on the way, the couple were still putting up a front. Cullen was no party buff, however, and there is more truth in Wambly Bald's depiction of him in his reporting on "la vie de bohème" for the *Chicago Tribune* than in what one might infer from that exceptional week in July 1929: "Cullen is seldom seen on the Happy Highway. He prefers the seclusion and detachment of his studio at Montsouris where he has been living for the past year as the guest of Julian Green. . . . A fine fellow, this poet, with none of the grating peccadillos which usually mark a man of letters."[16]

In the fall Cullen decided to register at the Sorbonne and stay another year in France. In February 1930, to improve his fluency in the language, he took a room with a French family in the Rue Gay-Lussac, close to the Luxembourg Gardens. There he welcomed Charles S. Johnson and John F. Matheus, who were on their way to investigate forced labor in Liberia. He invited them to tea with Paul Robeson, a "dark professor of mystery," and "blues-eating ladies of royalty."[17] He even took them to the Bal Colonial. Invited by Padraic Colum to meet a few of his Irish peers and recite poetry with them, Cullen composed "After a Visit" as a thank-you poem. In March 1930 his divorce from Yolande was granted by the Tribunal Civil de la Seine.

Édouard Roditi, who was based in Paris, introduced Cullen to Pierre de Lanux, a frequent visitor to the United States, and to French poet Georgette Camille. Cullen was at ease in French circles and made fast friends, as was the case when he translated Fernand Gregh's weird piece "Negroism" for the April 1930 issue of *Opportunity*. He even resolved to meet Princess Murat at last. That summer, however, he quietly returned to New York City: he had extended his stay in France a year beyond his original plans, but this had not helped him write. As Arna Bontemps said in his obituary, "His springtime leaves had fallen and he was still waiting for a new season to bring another yield. He kept writing as a matter of habit and the little shelf of his books increased steadily, but that wasn't the real thing; that wasn't what he was waiting for."[18]

The Black Christ, which came out in July 1929, was literally born in Paris, in part out of Cullen's suffering from his broken marriage. The city enabled him to assuage his love pains, to nurse them, probably to make verse out of them, but it did not inspire Cullen markedly, and published pieces that refer to his life in France are few. Paris had become a habit, however—maybe a sort of drug—and Cullen returned there almost every summer during the 1930s. He was always eagerly awaited by the friends he had left there, and his stays were the more intense as they were short. "I want to do the biguine and play belote," wrote sculptor Augusta Savage from her little studio on the Avenue de Chatillon in 1931. "I think your week in Paris is going to be an orgy and I don't want to miss it."[19]

That year Countee left for France ahead of his father, as soon as he had completed the dramatization of *God Sends Sunday*. He enrolled in the summer course at the Sorbonne and found a cheap, wonderfully located room at the Hotel Saint-Pierre, on the Rue de l'École de Médecine in the heart of the Latin Quarter, where he would stay regularly in the following years. There he worked, not too assiduously, at his novel. As usual, many acquaintances were summering in Paris, including Harold Jackman, Harold Dingwall, and William White, the son of composer Clarence Cameron White. Countee and the group often saw Palmer Hayden and Hale Woodruff, and they went out a few times with Doris Dandridge and Pittsburgh *Courier* columnist Toni Schalk. In late July, Countee's faithful friends Steve and Sophie Greene gave a huge party in their home on the Rue du Douanier, where Americans black and white, not to mention Prince Kojo Touvalou Houenou and an Austrian count, mingled and danced to a Negro jazz orchestra.[20] A few days later Cullen was invited by J. D. Townsend, pastor of the Memorial Methodist Church on the Rue Denfert-Rochereau, to be the guest of Édouard Bernard, who played the piano for them in his studio. So it was fun again, a social whirl, and a merry, holiday atmosphere prevailed in Paris, due in part to the preparations for the Exposition Coloniale. The city was filled with colored people from all over the world—the West Indies, Africa, and Asia—all of them adding to its picturesque quality and seeming to vindicate Cullen's infatuation with the Bal Colonial.

In August 1932 *Opportunity* printed Cullen's sonnet "To France," which reflects his love for the country in which he was allowed to live so intensely. It begins somewhat like Wordsworth's celebration of the French revolutionary spirit but ends as a hymn of filial praise. Not only was "that fair city perched upon the Seine" lovelier than the greatest monuments, not only did Cullen want to be counted among the renowned admirers of France, but he turned toward her in moving thankfulness:

> As he whose eyes are gouged craves light to see,
> And he whose limbs are broken strength to run,
> So have I sought in you that alchemy
>
> That knits my bones and turns me to the sun;
> And found across a continent of foam
> What was denied my hungry heart at home.[21]

When the piece appeared, Countee was in Paris again, this time for professional reasons: the principal of a New York school had encouraged him to consider a career as a teacher, and he was thinking of choosing English and French as his two subject areas. He felt that his French was still inadequate and enrolled again at the Sorbonne, leaving to Jackman the pleasure of accompanying the Reverend Cullen to Athens. That summer Cullen extended his knowledge of Baudelaire to the point of freely translating "Death to the Poor" and composing two sonnets on cats, an animal for which both poets shared a passion. These pieces, as well as his earlier "After a Visit," were included in *The Medea and Other Poems* in 1935. It was in Paris that he entertained the idea of writing a new version of Euripides' *Medea,* with Rose McClendon in mind for the title role.

The summer of 1933 saw Cullen again at the Hotel Saint-Pierre, again an assiduous student of French. That year he met Étienne Hervier, who had reviewed his *One Way to Heaven* for *Marianne* magazine, and this was the occasion of a fruitful literary exchange. In July and August 1934 he combined his visit to Paris with a three-week stay in Barcelona. In the same year he was appointed teacher of French at the Frederick Douglass Junior High School 139. His idealism was somewhat dampened by the boys' attitude toward the mere idea of learning the language, but his enthusiasm and *first-hand* knowledge of Parisian life worked wonders.

In 1935 Cullen spent only the month of August in Paris—a relaxing vacation from which he brought back a portrait by Renan. In his red-and-white checkered shirt and scarlet tie, in a weird green felt hat, Cullen was captured in all his good-humoredness, and the portrait became his favorite. Cullen continued to be addicted to Paris, and from 1936 to 1939 spent the months of July and August there each year. In 1937 he took a trip to Bagnoles-de-l'Orne in Normandy, with Steve Greene, to visit Sophie, who was vacationing there; in the course of time he was finally getting acquainted with the French provinces too. Yet Paris was the setting of one of the most brilliant sights he had witnessed for a long time: the presentation of the Passion on a raised stage in front of the cathedral of Notre-Dame. A huge platform seated over twelve thousand spectators. "A comparison with the Oberammergau presentation was inevitable. I believe the French version was more picturesque, but I liked the German more. The French looked only like Frenchmen, while the Germans actually looked like Israelites and Romans."[22] Although the rumblings of war could be heard that summer, Cullen was happy—or nearly: "These are really what we may call halcyon days. And yet so ungrateful is the heart of man that I am not completely satisfied."[23]

The summer of 1938 was studious again, Cullen having registered at the Institut du Panthéon, a private school, for a series of forty language lessons. For a month Mme. Jeanne Alléon had him build sentences and rhyme the *Chanson de Roland.* From his top-floor room at the Hotel Saint-Pierre, he would write Ida Cullen, his new wife, about washing his clothes in the basin, locking the door lest the owner barge in and make a fuss. He met Langston Hughes, who had been sent over with Theodore Dreiser as a delegate to what Cullen called a "peace conference." He wrote Claude McKay, declaring that Paris was "lovely as ever. Oh to be rich enough to remain there!"[24] The international tensions seemed to have eased, and the mood of Paris was closer to the carefree ambiance of his early stays. Cullen was simply in love with the city, where he was dancing as he had never done—once imbibing four brandies (or was it delicious Martinique rum?) and having to be shown the way home. He had reached the city just in time for the celebration of Bastille Day, when, in addition, the king and queen of England were coming for a visit. The French were "in a fine state of fits and conniptions. . . . You have never really seen something quite as beautiful as the decorations all over the city. There was such singing and dancing in the streets! Every little corner had its own special orchestra and everybody danced with everybody else."[25]

Once more at the Hotel Saint-Pierre in 1939, Cullen made the most of his time before going back to attend a teachers' conference in New York on August 22. The Bal Nègre was still going on, but Paris was less full of Americans than usual. The war scare had kept them away, but Cullen did not believe in the imminence of war, and he was greatly shocked by the Nazi invasion. Throughout World War II, his concern for "bleeding France" never flagged. On August 29, 1943, he wrote Harold Jackman that he had completed a poem on France that day, calling it "La Belle, La Douce, La Grande," but that he was not too pleased with it. A probably-much-revised version of it appeared in the New York *Herald Tribune* on July 10, 1944. It began:

> France! How shall we call her belle again?
> Does loveliness reside
> In sunken cheeks, in bellies barren and denied?
> .   .   .   .
> Or douce? Can gentleness invade
> The frozen heart, the mind betrayed,
> Or search for refuge in the viper's den?
> .   .   .   .
> Or grande? Did greatness ever season
> The broth of shame, repudiation, treason?

Cullen lambasted the treason of Marshal Pétain and Premier Pierre Laval and went back to "the sainted soul of France called Joan" of

Arc, who had driven the invaders out centuries before, in order to
celebrate General de Gaulle:

> Nay even now, look up, see fall
> As on Elisha Elijah's shawl,
> Joan's mantle on the gaunt De Gaulle:
> New Knight of France, great paladin,
> Behold him sally forth to win
> Her place anew at freedom's hand,
> A place for France: la belle, la douce, la grande.[26]

Cullen, whose American patriotism had never expressed itself so
vibrantly, was anxiously awaiting the coming of peace to resume his
summer visits to Paris. He made plans to go there in 1946, but he
could not; death caught him in the spring of that year.

How can one evaluate the impact of French culture and Parisian life
on the works of "the greatest francophile" of the Harlem Renaissance?
Besides, how far did his presence in Paris help establish links between Afro-American writers and the French-speaking world? Clearly,
Cullen spent nearly as much time in France as Claude McKay, and
although his acquaintance was less diverse than McKay's and largely
restricted to Paris, Cullen's knowledge of the language and culture
enabled him to appreciate France far more than Hughes, and clearly
as much as McKay, did. But differences in class and ideological choice
intervened: whereas McKay was impatient with polished circles and
the literati and seemed to breathe more freely among "the folks,"
Cullen gives the impression that he felt he was slumming when he
made the rounds of working-class dance halls or tried the exotic setting of the Bal Colonial. He enjoyed these deeply, but possibly owing
to his puritanical upbringing, one side of his personality would hold
his spontaneity in check. Or, when attending a performance of *Rigoletto,* he would feel compelled to apologize for liking bel canto. He was
visibly torn: he sought refinement but craved more vital, lusty entertainment than romantic infatuation. Thus France could quench his
thirst for culture and unbridled enjoyment alike. Paris was the City
of Light, the repository of ancient traditions, and also the embodiment of a sexually free and piquantly dissolute life to which a touch
of Africa or the West Indies added spice.

Cullen also visualized France as a generous mother-country. In
America, which was his home, he felt that much was denied him because of his color. As a result he projected France as a haven, a substi-
tute mother, as he made clear in his sonnet "To France":

Among a fair and kindly foreign folk
There might I only breathe my latest days,
With those rich accents falling on my ear
That most have made me feel that freedom's rays
Still have a shrine where they may leap and soar—

Though I were palsied there, or halt, or blind,
So were I there, I think I should not mind.[27]

The place that granted him what "was denied [his] hungry heart at home" evidently was the one where he would have liked to retire and die. He was tolerant of French peccadillos and prone, for instance, to make courtesy a French characteristic. This was probably due to the fact that, unlike Hughes or McKay, he never had to face financial stress there or experience the xenophobia that results from job competition. Cullen always lived modestly, and his wildest splurges could not compare to the aristocratic style of his white counterparts of the "lost generation." But he was financially secure; he chose to reside in the 14th and 5th arrondissements, where artists and students lived, mostly because he liked the atmosphere of the Latin Quarter or the Parc Montsouris, whereas Hughes was driven by necessity to dwell in the still-less-expensive Montmartre area. Besides, he had many acquaintances among Americans of note, white and black, and as a luminary of the Harlem Renaissance and W. E. B. Du Bois's son-in-law, he consorted with the Afro-American elite, who sought him out when they visited Paris. He was a friend of many artists, from Henry Tanner to Augusta Savage, often at the center of black American life abroad, which he reported in his letters to *Opportunity* or the *Crisis*.

This made Cullen's position as a link between Afro-American and French-speaking writers important, the more so because he could speak French fluently. In the beginning he had very few French acquaintances, but he followed up any introductions, and his list of French contacts soon grew to an impressive length. There were a few high-society Parisians, like Princess Violette Murat, who was capable of genuinely appreciating James Weldon Johnson's *God's Trombones;* recognized French writers like Fernand Gregh, Blaise Cendrars (whose *Petits contes nègres pour les petits blancs* Cullen wanted to translate into English in 1930), or Claire Goll; there were academics like Dr. Alfred Métraux, director of the Ethnography Museum; there were also lesser-known friends and lovers like Roger Fay, with whom Countee remained in contact until 1935; Raymond Guilloux; Henri Lagarde; Jean Van Haeckeren, from Belgium, who would send reports from Eastern countries in the 1930s; Sylvestre Dorian; painter

Jean Hanau, who was still writing to Countee in 1945, calling him "Mon petit"; Étienne Hervier, who adapted *One Way to Heaven* for the French stage; and many others.

Cullen also knew the work of a large number of French-speaking blacks. *Batouala* impressed him greatly, and he read Maran's poetry, notably *Le Visage calme*, which was very much in the classical and symbolist tradition. Through Maran and Locke he met the group around *La Revue du Monde Noir* in 1930: not only the Nardal sisters but Haitians like Docteur Sajous, Enid Raphaël, Désiré Norbert, and Pétion Savain, who dined at the Cullens' in 1928 and was later asked to do the illustrations for Countee's "The Adventures of Monkey Baboon," which was never published. The Nardal group, an important first step toward the negritude movement, liked Cullen's polish, refinement, and discreet tastes; in their eyes he was a fine example of Negro genius, a luminary of the black race. Louis Achille later remembered Countee visiting him on the Rue Geoffroy Saint-Hilaire and his keen appreciation of the aesthetic choices to be made by blacks at the time.[28] In the 1930s Cullen corresponded with Martiniquan poet Emmanuel Flavia-Léopold, a friend of Maran, and with Haitian poet Jean-F. Brièrre throughout the war. His own library included a few titles by French authors writing on blacks: *Les Nègres* (1929) by colonial governor Maurice Delafosse; *Le Nègre*, by surrealist Philippe Soupault; and *Le Nègre Jupiter enlève Europe*, by Claire Goll, which he liked hardly more than Paul Morand's exotic and paternalistic *Black Magic*. Even more than he was influenced by them, however, he influenced French-speaking African writers; his poems appeared in translation in a number of magazines and anthologies, notably an anthology of American poetry compiled by Eugene Jolas in the 1930s, with those of McKay, Hughes, and Toomer. And Léopold Senghor made a point of including his "Heritage" among the poems by representative Afro-Americans he himself translated in *Poésie 45*.

NOTES

1. Rev. Frederic A. Cullen, *From Barefoot Town to Jerusalem* (n.p., n.d. [post-1944]), 76–77, 87–88.
2. Countee Cullen to Hale Woodruff, October 17, 1927, Amistad.
3. Cullen to Edith Brower, June 15, 1928, Yale.
4. "Countee Cullen to His Friends," *Crisis*, April 1929, 119.
5. Cullen, in *Opportunity*, September 1928, 272–73.
6. Ibid., 272.
7. W. E. B. Du Bois to Cullen, September 18, 1928, Amistad.

8. Cullen, notebook, 89–90, Yale. Translation mine.

9. Program for Berlioz, *Damnation of Faust,* undated, 15, Amistad.

10. Cullen, notebook, 1928, 109–10.

11. "I have seen the skies burst into lightning and waterspouts / and the surge of the sea, and the currents / I have known evenings. . . ." (Rimbaud, "Le Bateau Ivre").

12. Cullen, notebook, 43–44.

13. Cullen, "At the Étoile," *The Black Christ* (New York: Harper, 1929), 12.

14. "Countee Cullen on French Courtesy," *Crisis,* June 1929, 193.

15. Cullen, *Crisis,* August 1929, 270.

16. Wambly Bald, *Chicago Tribune,* November 4, 1929.

17. Charles S. Johnson to Cullen, undated, from aboard a ship bound for Africa, Yale.

18. Arna Bontemps, obituary for Countee Cullen, *Saturday Review of Literature,* March 22, 1947, 13.

19. Augusta Savage to Cullen, February 27, 1931, Amistad.

20. Blanche Ferguson, *Countee Cullen and the Negro Renaissance* (New York: Dodd, Mead, 1966), 133–34.

21. Cullen, *On These I Stand,* (New York, Harper, 1947), 147

22. Cullen to Edward Atkinson, August 15, 1937, Yale.

23. Cullen to Atkinson, August 1, 1937, Yale.

24. Cullen to Claude McKay, undated, Yale.

25. Cullen to Ida Cullen, July 24, 1938, Amistad.

26. Cullen, *On These I Stand,* 171

27. Countee Cullen, "To France," *On These I Stand,* 156.

28. Louis Achille, interview with the author, May 1974.

7

Claude McKay and the Two Faces of France

Of all the Afro-American writers who resided in France between the two world wars, Claude McKay remained there the longest and mixed most with all sorts of people—black and white, American and French, European and African—in both Paris and the provinces. He also derived inspiration from his French experience, not only in *Banjo,* in which Marseilles plays more than a background role but in a number of essays analyzing the complex class and race relations in Western Europe. If Countee Cullen and Langston Hughes also went beyond the tourist stage when they lived in Paris, because of his deeper political awareness McKay proved to be more discriminating than Cullen in his likes and dislikes, less superficial than Hughes in rendering French ways of life and the Paris atmosphere, and more sophisticated than either in his views about the colonial situation and the black diaspora.

His autobiography, *A Long Way from Home,* contains few comments about his reactions to France and his reasons for going there. One must be satisfied with his elliptical discussion of the motives of white American writers and artists for becoming expatriates. He noted that either they were lured to Europe because they believed America was too new—that life was riper, culture mellower, and artistic things considered of higher worth in France—or they were prompted to flee from the Puritan denial of sex and artistic freedom. But his problems were different from theirs: "What, then, was my main psychological problem? It was the problem of color. Color-consciousness was the fundamental of my restlessness. And it was something with which my white fellow-expatriates could sympathize but which they could not altogether understand. . . . They couldn't understand the instinctive and animal and purely physical pride of a black person resolute in being himself and yet living a simple, civilized life like themselves. Because their education in their white world had trained them to see a person of color either as an inferior or as an exotic."[1] This may explain why McKay wandered abroad for some fifteen years; it does not account for his going to Paris.

He spent a whole year in London first, in 1919, taking part in political activities with the socialists and writing poems that were gathered in *Spring in New Hampshire*. After a year in the United States, where he worked on *The Liberator* and was hailed nationally as the author of *Harlem Shadows*, he worked his way across the ocean again to attend the fourth congress of the Third Communist International in Moscow. He enjoyed a warm welcome, loved the people, and completed a volume on Negroes in America for the Russian audience. After May Day 1923, however, suffering from an unfamiliar diet and lack of hygiene, he left for Berlin to be treated, and from there he moved to Paris in the late fall.

When he first set foot in France, McKay was well aware of its politics and its role in colonizing Africa. As early as 1920 he had written the editors of the London *Daily World* to protest the bourgeois press coverage of the use of black occupation troops by the French in the Rhineland: the "black threat" had been made into a question of potential miscegenation. But, McKay thought, defending the morality of the Negro race mattered less than understanding that, by helping French capitalism to hold Germany down, the black troops were supporting France's dominion in Africa. He was also quick to denounce French racism. He was convinced that, in spite of appearances, Senegalese Blaise Diagne had undermined W. E. B. Du Bois's efforts at the 1919 Pan-African Conference in Paris: hadn't Diagne declared that French blacks should consider themselves Frenchmen, not colored internationalists, for "the position of Negro citizens in France [was] truly worthy of envy"?[2] Yet even such an active supporter of assimilation as Diagne, McKay noted, had been forced to concede that French whites denied the black man even mere physical equality: the victory of Senegalese boxer Battling Siki over native Frenchman Georges Charpentier for the world championship had created no less a scandal than that of Jack Johnson over Australian Tommy Burns. Even before seeing France, McKay could thus provide a sophisticated analysis of race prejudice there and of the pro-French attitude of the gullible Afro-American intelligentsia:

> The good treatment of individuals by those whom they meet in France is valued so highly by Negroes that they are beginning to forget about the exploitation of Africans by the French. . . . Thus the sympathy of the Negro intelligentsia is completely on the side of France. It is well-informed about the barbarous acts of the Belgians in the Congo but it knows nothing at all about the barbarous acts of the French in Sene-

gal, about the organized robbery of native workers, about the forced
enlistment of recruits, about the fact that the population is reduced to
extreme poverty and hunger, or about the total annihilation of tribes. It
is possible that the Negro intelligentsia does not want to know about all
this, inasmuch as it can loosely generalize about the differences in the
treatment of Negroes in bourgeois France and in plutocratic America.
René Maran wrote a novel which, by the way, is an indignant denunciation of the activities of the French government in Africa; but the author,
in spite of this, received the Goncourt prize and indisputably became
a desired member of writers' and artists' circles in France. Dr. Du Bois
writes a surprisingly moving work, *The Souls of Black Folk,* written in
splendid English; nevertheless, he remains up to the present an outcast
in American society.[3]

This set the tone for McKay's lasting attitude concerning the myth of
French liberalism: although he enjoyed genuine friendships with a
number of individual French people, he always refused to exonerate
French institutions and culture from responsibility for their colonial
oppression.

McKay's remarks concerning Maran and Du Bois are also illuminating. About *Batouala* he was mistaken, since only the preface, not
the novel, denounced the abuses of colonials without questioning colonialism per se; in the case of Du Bois, he shared the reactions of the
Afro-American intelligentsia in deploring America's lack of recognition of the "black titan." On the one hand, he reacted as a committed
left-winger; on the other, as an artist belonging to a race whose contributions to culture were slighted. This double perspective informed
the entire range of his reactions to France.

As soon as he arrived in Paris, McKay was confronted with health
and money problems. He was hospitalized in the fall of 1923 for syphilis at a primary, infectious stage, which frightened him more than it
really threatened his robust constitution.[4] That McKay suffered from
syphilis is substantiated. A poem he wrote at that time, "The Desolate
City," certainly evokes his own depressed mood more than Parisian
realities. Images of decay, putrescence, and poison conjure up a nightmare city of the mind:

> My spirit is a pestilential city,
> With misery triumphant everywhere,
> Glutted with baffled hopes and human pity.
> Strange agonies make quiet lodgement there:
>
> Its sewers bursting ooze up from below
> And spread their loathsome substance through its lanes,
> Flooding all areas with their evil flow.[5]

It is a place plagued by swarms of flies, putrid cloaca, vice contrasting with the purity of nature. The poem harks back to Baudelaire's topics and style, including sweet children's voices singing songs forever gone.

But McKay did survive. His only French acquaintance was Pierre Vogein, secretary to Charles Rappaport, who edited the Communist *Journal du Peuple;* they had become friends in Moscow. Vogein was a student, and not rich, but he proved helpful and devoted. Besides, one of McKay's acquaintances in the American colony, John Barber, an illustrator for *The Liberator,* found him employment as a model in artists' studios, notably with painter André Lhote.[6] However, by Christmas time his situation was critical again. He did not have enough warm clothes to stand the winter; in his badly heated room he caught a cold that developed into pneumonia; and only the arrival of a friend who paid the rent rescued him from being expelled from the room in which he lay sick. Although he had been working, he could not sell anything to the bourgeois papers: "My life here is very unsatisfactory for a propagandist—cadging a meal off people who are not at all sympathetic to my social ideas."[7] His friends' devotion—but mostly the money sent by Louise Bryant, his literary agent in the United States— helped McKay start afresh: urging him to write fine literature instead of newspaper propaganda, she sent him enough for three months' subsistence on the Riviera.

McKay did not leave until the fall, however, and a couple of chapters of his autobiography deal with his Paris life in 1924. They are the more memorable as he did not stay there again until 1929. He willingly associated with the American expatriates in the Montparnasse cafés; he found them sympathetic and more open-minded than the radical groups in Greenwich Village: "The environment was novel and elastic. It was like taking a holiday after living in the atmosphere of the high-pressure propaganda spirit of the New Russia," he reminisced. However, he was at most "a kind of sympathetic fellow-traveller in the expatriate caravan" (*A Long Way,* 243). This was due to his own refusal to reject American culture: he loved the raw vitality of the uncouth, Whitmanesque, rough rhythms of American life: "Fascinated by its titanic strength, I rejoiced in the lavishness of the engineering exploits and the architectural splendor of New York." (*A Long Way,* 224).

As a result, he was no Cullen-like pilgrim in search of his cultural roots, come to pay homage to the European tradition. Never does one find praise in his work for the age-old historical monuments of Paris. He did not find any glamour, either, in the bohemian cabarets of Montmartre and Montparnasse, which he occasionally enjoyed when a rich fellow citizen took him there: "Paris, away from Montmartre and

Montparnasse, seemed to me to be the perfect city of modern civilization. It was the only city I knew which provided quiet and comfortable
clubs in the form of cafés for all its citizens of every class. I appreciated but was not especially enamored of Paris, perhaps because I have
never had the leisure necessary to make an excellent clubman. If I
had to live in France, I would prefer to live among the fishermen of
Douarnenez, or in the city of Strassburg, or in sinister Marseilles, or
in any of the coast towns of the department of the Var" (*A Long Way*,
230). McKay's outlook was that of a Jamaican who had deliberately
moved to the United States and considered it an outpost of European
culture, not an uncivilized land by any means. His Jamaican childhood
had developed his sensual self, and he refused to become an aesthete
divorced from nature and the people. A Third World partisan before
the term existed, he proudly proclaimed his blackness. He was convinced that Americans like himself had much to gain from traveling
abroad and experiencing a variety of cultures, but he felt by no means
culturally inferior to the French.

   Probably around that time he composed a superb, poetic evocation of the city, called simply "Paris." Contrary to "those who never
see below / the depths profound upon which rests her strength," he
had not fallen for the generally cherished image of a lusty, licentious
"pagan paradise of courtesans / And cavaliers." Rather, Paris was a
cynical place, serpent-like in its fascination. But he had remained cool-
headed:

> Paris has never stormed my stubborn heart
> And rushed like champagne sparkling to my head
> Whirling me round and round till I am spent
> To fall down like a drunkard at her feet,
> Because it is a city more like bread
> Than wine and meat as solid nourishment
> To build the Frenchman and his mind complete
> And fit him for his civilizing part.

McKay made it clear that the sense of superiority he disliked in the
French stemmed from their conviction that they were called upon to
"civilize" the world. More than other cities, Paris was "a school / With
lessons priced that everyone can pay." No one was bound to learn, but
whoever failed to do so was a fool.[8]

   Although McKay seems to have restricted his incursions to the
Montparnasse and Latin Quarter area at first, he did not fail to have a
taste of the mirage, sensuality, and glow of Parisian life. In the expatriate circles, the big literary event had been the publication of *Ulysses*.

McKay eagerly visited Sylvia Beach and Adrienne Monnier at Shakespeare and Company; he was even photographed by Berenice Abbott but could afford neither that portrait nor Joyce's masterpiece. Another "sacred cow" was Gertrude Stein, but McKay kept away from the high priestess of the lost generation because he liked meeting people as persons, not divinities in temples (*A Long Way*, 248). He enjoyed the lively atmosphere of Montparnasse, where literary or aesthetic debates would start in an informal way in cafés. On the terrace of Le Dôme, Nina Hamnett pointed out Ernest Hemingway to him shortly after the publication of *In Our Time*, a copy of which McKay gladly accepted from an American who felt shocked by the modernity of his compatriot. McKay liked Hemingway's "hard-boiled contempt for and disgust with sissiness . . . a conventionalized rough attitude which is altogether un-European" (*A Long Way*, 252); he liked his revolutionary use of four-letter Anglo-Saxon words.

Besides Pierre Vogein, McKay met a few other people, including generous and picturesque Pascin, the painter from Central Europe. His acquaintance with Prince Kojo Touvalou Houenou, who inscribed his *Évolution des métamorphoses et des métempsychoses de l'univers* in highly florid complimentary fashion on November 23, 1923, was probably fortuitous, but when the prince and René Maran started *Les Continents*, they published translations of McKay's poems. By that time contacts were being established between Maran, several Afro-American poets, and Alain Locke, who was preparing a soon-to-be-famous Negro issue of *The Survey Graphic*. But by the end of January McKay had already left cold, rainy Paris for the Côte d'Azur. After a couple of months at La Ciotat, where he claimed to have existed on bread and water but kept writing in spite of the chilly weather, he settled in Toulon. At the big naval base he met Lucien, a young man from Brittany who, having failed to get into a cadet school, was serving in the navy as an able seaman. Lucien became Claude's devoted friend: he taught him conversational French and introduced him to the works of Anatole France because of the purity of his style; they spent much time partying, sometimes on board the battleship *Provence*, where Lucien was stationed. They went on excursions to the beaches of Ollioules, La Seyne, and Bandol; swam at Cap Nègre; or caroused with other sailors in dance halls and dives. On one occasion, on the day Lucien was celebrating his discharge from the navy, McKay had to answer to the police for their having sung the "Internationale" late at night in his room. He felt perfectly happy and well-adapted to French life. In remembrance of those days, he later wrote that he loved the Var country more than any part of France except Brittany.

In September 1924 he returned to Paris to try to sell some of his short stories. He met Edna St. Vincent Millay, who had recently married Eugene Boissevain; he got friendly and valuable advice about the writing of a novel from Sinclair Lewis, but he sold nothing. However, the efforts of Walter White and a few American liberals had succeeded in persuading the Garland Fund to send him a fifty-dollar monthly allowance, and he went south again on this scholarship.

In May 1925 McKay spent some time at Arles; although sad under the shadow of Roman and medieval ruins, he found its lively but natural and relaxed atmosphere made it the nicest of the smaller French towns he had struck so far. "It looks out on a wonderful valley and does not seem overshadowed by its past like so many historical places. It has a throbbing pace of its own and the river air is a marvellous thing," he wrote Max Eastman.[9] He had yet to discover other aspects of French provincial life even dearer to his heart: Lucien invited him to spend the summer with his family near Brest, and Claude left by way of Bordeaux to visit a Jamaican acquaintance there before going on to Brittany. He liked Bordeaux even more than Toulon, finding it clean though bustling—a harbor to his liking. He wrote patriotically to Langston Hughes: "This great river port, it's the most interesting I've struck yet exceptionally clean and attractive. And the townspeople are nicer than what I've met in Provence and other parts of France. Less excitement, gestures, posturing and *less spitting*. Oh, how the French can spit! Today the 4th, I went for a long walk along the docks and many French boats flew the Stars and Stripes with the tricolor but the English didn't."[10]

There he received the news that Lucien had suddenly died of tuberculosis. His friend's family, however, insisted that he visit them anyway, since that had been their son's desire. They were lower-middle-class people who welcomed him like one of their own children: this kindness, mingled with the sadness of his friend's death, endeared Brittany to McKay forever. He found in its people some of the qualities of the Jamaican peasants, noting the ethnic pride of a group who were clinging fiercely to their customs and language. He stayed in a hotel in Brest and often went to eat at Lucien's family's home, spending several months in Finistere. This inspired truly lyrical hymns to Brittany:

> Lovely are the fields and charming are the towns of Finistère: Brest, Morlaix, Camaret, Plougastel, Morgat, Quimper, Concarneau, Le Pouldu over to Lorient and back to Douarnenez *le Rouge* above all! How I loved Douarnenez with its high wall falling sheerly into the green waters and the big shipping boats with their tall masts hung with nets like blue veils against the misted gray-blue sky, and the fishermen in red dungarees and red-hearted.

I loved the quiet green and subdued grays and browns of Brittany, and although it rained a lot I did not miss the grand sun of Provence. Perhaps because I was sad and felt the need of solitude. (*A Long Way*, 264)

Years later this episode was to inspire an eleven-page story, "Dinner at Douarnenez." It is strongly autobiographical: upon his arrival in the port in Brittany, after a fishermen's strike, the colored visitor's eye is caught by the revolutionary names of the boats and the subdued blues and grays and browns of their hulls: "that was the color of my feelings then, coming straight after the brilliant blues and the bawdy reds, the sea-paint orange and the garbage rose of Marseilles." He has fallen in love with the place, including the small rain "like grains of millet showering down against the intermittent gleamings of the sun," which prompts him to quote Verlaine's nostalgic lines: "Il pleut dans mon coeur . . ." At this point the narrator meets a young sailor, back from Paris, who finds the Bretons stupid and disapproves of the fishermen's strike; that sailor, however, has a Guadeloupean friend with whose family he had stayed at Pointe-à-Pitre, and who invites the visitor to his parents' home. They feast on crêpes and lobster, drink *vin blanc ordinaire*, Calvados brandy, and rum, and the narrator spends the night there, in a closed wooden bed in the common room. This is bliss: "In the closed bed I felt as if I was once again in the heavy old-fashioned cradle of my childhood," enjoying "harmony united in a great singing to the earth." As they are taking the boat from Douarnenez to Brest, an older man remarks that most Frenchmen are far from being so outgoing as the sailor's family, and McKay concludes the story:

"That kind of thing could happen to you only among those stupid people. They are not French, but—"
"But what?" I asked.
"Oh, well, it just occurred to me from what you said about your experience that it mightn't be such a bad thing after all to be black."[11]

This piece is revealing: what McKay missed when leaving Jamaica and Harlem, what had endeared Russia to him, and what would later enthrall him in Spain and Morocco, he had finally found in Brittany: the people, the "folks." He did not approach them with the feelings of a left-wing intellectual eager to "lead the masses"; he related to them as he had to his own countrymen during his childhood and youth— emotionally. He was a man of simple tastes and friendships—hence his numerous acquaintances with peasants, sailors, workers—rather than an amateur of literary sets. After his discovery of Brittany, he was psychologically ready to immerse himself in the low life of Marseilles.

After several weeks in Paris, where the writing of his novel "Color

Scheme" did not "jell over," McKay repaired to Nice, again in search of a job. He first found employment as a butler to "a civilized cracker and his Russian wife," but twelve hours' work per day left him no time to write. After a month he quit to work as a builder's helper, but exhaustion prevented him even from thinking. Frank Harris, whose *Life and Loves* was extremely successful in Europe and whom he had not seen for seven years, was then staying at Cimiez. With him McKay went to see the Robesons, who had fled the rain in Paris, at Villefranche, where the Eastmans resided. These friends put McKay in touch with Irish film producer Rex Ingram, who happened to like McKay's poetry and hired him to write evaluations of novels being considered for screen adaptation—a near sinecure at forty francs a day and a room. But the studio folded in the spring of 1926. In the summer he probably exaggerated when he wrote gloomily to Louise Bryant: "Here I am . . . trying to write in swarms of flies and bugs and filth. . . . Marseilles is my last and cheapest stand. I don't want to be driven out of here by hunger and want as I was out of Cannes, Nice and Menton. After all, the few things I manage to turn out are the only joys I have."[12]

During that dry, hot summer McKay's first impressions of Marseilles were quite enthusiastic. He swam at the end of the great breakwater until he discovered a better beach, still unspoiled by the cement and tile industry, at L'Estaque, where he went for the rest of the season with a friend. The "Marseilles Motley" chapter of his autobiography opens with the expression of his relief at reaching Marseilles because he could at last live among a great band of black and brown humanity" (*A Long Way*, 277). There he found representatives from nearly every section of the black diaspora—West and North Africa, Nigeria, the West Indies, the United States: "Many were dockers. Some were regular hard-working sailors, who had a few days in port between debarking and embarking. Others were waiting for ships—all wedged in between the old port and the breakwater, among beachcombers, guides, procurers, prostitutes of both sexes and *bistro* bandits—all of motley-making Marseilles, swarming, scrambling and scraping sustenance from the bodies of ships and crews" (*A Long Way*, 277).

McKay revised his short stories, occasionally did light work as a docker since he had made friends with the Senegalese foreman of the Negro gang, and imbibed the many-sided life of the harbor, full of the excitement of brawls, robberies, police shootings, and prostitution. Among his acquaintances of those days, he later singled out in his autobiography only a couple: the Senegalese proprietor of a big café where all the Negroes used to congregate, and African nationalist and Marxist organizer Lamine Senghor, who gave him his pamphlet on colonialism in Africa and took him to the much-frequented Sea-men's International Building, newly opened by the French Communist party. McKay spent much of 1926 on the waterfront and in the cafés with a group of black dockers, sailors, and bums. A photograph in his papers shows a dozen of them standing in front of a bar around one who holds a banjo. Such was the group he would later immortalize in his novel *Banjo*, which he already had in mind.

He had already sent his short stories to the United States when William Aspenwell Bradley, the Paris agent of the American literary avant-garde to whom Louise Bryant had entrusted him, advised him, at Harper's request, to expand his novella *Home to Harlem* into a full-length novel. In expectation of Harper's advance, McKay moved to Antibes, a quieter place for writing, and completed the first part of the novel by March 1927. At that time he met French left-wing soci-ologist Georges Friedman, who was visiting the Eastmans. Friedman later recalled their meeting:

> I stopped in the small garden in front of the house, called, and Claude's head, his handsome, young and smiling head, appeared from a window at the side of the house. One could have said of him, in order to recom-mend him, not: "I am sending McKay, a young Negro writer to you," but "You'll love to hear McKay's laughter." I saw him again at the East-mans' or at his place, at the top of dirty and proud Antibes, near the towers, in a room which opened on an old façade covered by wistaria and, some time later, in Marseilles. . . . The entire personality of this robust youngster expressed the radiant life I have loved from the start, but mostly his surprisingly young face where the liveliest mirth turned at once into earnestness; his straightforward eyes, wide open on the world and people, his strong forehead which, I suppose, was inhabited by all the cares of the mind.[13]

McKay was never as intimate with Georges Friedman as he was with Pierre Vogein, however, because Friedman, although quite well off, always insisted that his friend pay his share when they ate together; also the left-wing French intellectual sometimes displayed some pater-nalism toward exotic negritude. Yet he appreciated McKay's specific outlook with discernment when he wrote: "What is especially admi-rable in Claude McKay is that he has reached the summit of his expres-sion and his meditative powers without losing anything of the human warmth of his people, while remaining on the same level with them, their rhythm and primitive strength, their colorful vision of the uni-verse, and while continuing to feel and hope with them."[14] Friedman introduced McKay to Léon Bazalgette, the editor of *Europe*, a pres-tigious progressive magazine, who accepted his story "Bad Boy" for publication, and later to Éditions Rieder, which published McKay's novels.

In January 1927 McKay was eager to use black life in Marseilles as literary material. To *Opportunity* he offered a series of articles on that topic: "I got to know it while I was stranded there last summer. It was terribly exciting, sad, picturesque, and cruel in many aspects. . . . Negroes from every part of the world are flung together there in the old port. . . . Living on the great breakwater, always bumming, sometimes working and spending their time between the Quartier Réservé and the piers. . . . I am planning to go back there and do a book about their life."[15] But the magazine showed no interest.

McKay remained in close touch with the Eastmans—now established in Marseilles, where Eliena liked to paint—and with the black group in the old port. But when he saw the latter again, the gang had dwindled: two had died in hospital, two black Americans had been repatriated, the banjo-player had gone on tour. Sad and broke, the remaining ones were attempting to leave by any possible means. McKay would have liked to start his novel while they were still around, but he had to complete *Home to Harlem* first. Money was still a problem, and he wasted precious time trying to get an old typewriter to save on typing costs and attempting to obtain his *carte de séjour* as a writer by way of recommendations so he could have it free instead of paying 375 francs.[16]

He left Antibes for Nice, where he completed *Home to Harlem* by May. He then settled in Marseilles, first at the Hotel Central, then at the Hotel Nautique on the Quai des Belges, where he at once started his novel, which he called *Banjo* when he sent a first chapter to William Bradley in October. His health was bothering him; he had high blood pressure and fainting spells. That winter was exceptionally cold, with water pipes freezing and bursting. Of the breakwater gang, only a few remained. Nigerian Simeon Nelson Dédé had tried to sail as a stowaway on the Fabre line and had been shipped back with his feet frozen after having been locked up in a cold brig. This story was to become the plot of "Romance in Marseilles," one of McKay's unsuccessful attempts at writing.

In order to gather material for *Banjo*, MacKay once paid a visit to an underworld boss to whom the painter Pascin had given him an introduction. At the time he found him "a rather dull wine-shop keeper" with nothing to show him except brothels, which he already knew.[17] Later, however, he made his visit to "the Corsican" one of the highlights of the Marseilles chapter of his autobiography. McKay himself acted as a guide to the red-light district when Bull-Frog, a petty gangster, and Isadora Duncan, who had danced for Claude in her studio in Nice, came to visit the old port. The following spring *Banjo* was nearly completed. McKay had steeped himself so completely in the Marseilles scene that he was later to regret that he might "have sinned . . . by being too photographic, too much under the fetid atmosphere of the bottom."[18]

He now wanted to get away from the Riviera. He refused on moral grounds to set foot in Italy because of the Ethiopian war, so he settled for Barcelona.[19] Spain was more expensive than France, but never had he encountered such joy and vitality. In Barcelona he came across a Martiniquan acquaintance and accepted his invitation to visit him in Casablanca, in a small Negro colony among the Arabs, so he left Spain at the end of August. In Casablanca his discovery of the juxtaposition of several cultures raised his enthusiasm to new heights. He stayed for six months, also visiting Fez and Marrakech but liking Tetuan best. He came back by way of the ancient Arab cities of Granada and Seville, learning legends he wanted to use as the basis for a new volume on Morocco: "I had a wonderful time of it in Africa. . . . I did not want to leave if it were not that the French are masters there and I prefer to live under the French in France where the government is more liberal bossing its own people. They do treat the Arabs badly. I was treated decently because I was a tourist and wore Egyptian clothes."[20]

Compared with the south of Spain, Madrid seemed to him a tepid, characterless imitation of Paris. Later, still busy polishing *Banjo* in Marseilles, he alluded to his encounters with the Spanish people with undisguised nostalgia: "I like them more than the French," he wrote Bradley. "My liking for the French is intellectual and therefore limited, while I like the Spaniards with all my senses."[21]

In his autobiography, McKay said half-jokingly that he had been enticed back to Paris not so much by James Weldon Johnson's invitation to return to the United States in order to participate in the Harlem Renaissance movement as by the thought that it might be "less unpleasant to meet the advance guard of the Negro intelligentsia in Paris" (*A Long Way*, 307). At first McKay's second extended stay in the city, which he compared to "the melody of larks chanting over a gray field" (*A Long Way*, 309) as he arrived from Nice in the spring of 1929, was busy and pleasant. He had some money and haunted the cabarets and cafés of Montmartre and Montparnasse with a girlfriend from the Antilles. He saw performances of *Rose Marie* and *Showboat*. He danced at the Bal Nègre on the Rue Blomet and even went once to Bricktop's expensive nightclub. The black Americans were everywhere. McKay met the all-Negro troupe of the Blackbirds, for whom

William Bradley gave a party, and the cast of *Porgy and Bess,* just arrived from London. He met black students and teachers, including
Countee Cullen. He saw Alain Locke again, "a perfect symbol of the
Afro-American rococo in his personality" (*A Long Way,* 313), now a
leading authority on African sculpture. He even lunched with President Hope of Atlanta University: "Thus I won over most of the Negro
intelligentsia in Paris," McKay concluded humorously, "excepting the
leading journalist and traveller" (*A Long Way,* 315)—J. A. Rogers he
could not bear. He also met a number of white Americans, notably
Carl Van Vechten, whom he found, contrary to his expectations, not
in the least patronizing, and his old friend Louise Bryant. She was
quite sick at the time and advised him to go and write another book:
"Go home to Harlem or back to Africa but don't stay in Paris!" (*A Long
Way,* 325).

McKay soon grew dissatisfied with his hectic life and the distrac-
tions of Paris. In June he fled to Antwerp for a few days in order to
work on a short story he expected to sell to *This Quarter* and wrote
to Bradley: "I can't work in Paris, I don't know why. . . . I feel depressed as I approach the machine and want to run away from it and
my thoughts. I was happy having the excuse of the story to get away." [22]
He had invited his wife to Paris in order to persuade her to settle for
a divorce arrangement that would not be too costly for him. He took
to the Vogeins this slim "Harlem schoolmistress" in a silk dress.[23] Was
she the cause of his unsettled mood or even of his coming up to Paris?
She does not seem to have been the partner of "a painful intimate
affair which lasted for weeks" and left him unfit for work.[24] At any
rate, he curtailed his stay in Paris to take refuge in Spain. He felt in
harmony with the quiet Spanish existence: "French life is too nervous
and sharp for my temperament. It may be that I exaggerate but as
soon as I crossed the border I felt as if I had escaped from a swarm
of wasps to find myself among people who can appreciate simple dignity when they meet with it, because dignity is a fundamental in their
social life." [25]

Apparently McKay was angry with the French because, when *Banjo*
was published in New York, Parisian critic André Lévinson had reviewed *it* very adversely in *Les Nouvelles Littéraires.* Lévinson claimed
that it was anti-French and anti-white because McKay had made his
black characters more deeply human than the people of Marseilles.
Resenting such a hasty judgment, McKay emphasized that he had
never tried to ingratiate himself with anyone. His irritation extended
over several letters to William Bradley, thus providing some interesting
insights into his attitude toward France:

Frankly, I do not like the French as social animals. I love to read them, from newspaper to classic, Proust, Gide or Barbusse; Voltaire, Maupassant or Anatole France. However different they may be, they have in common a magnificent malice that I have never met anywhere else in literature. But the French outlook on life seems to me about the narrowest of any people. They don't know the outside world and they don't care because it is not French. And I also think that intellectuals are over-influenced by politics. The French government knows too much about the literary and artistic life.[26]

McKay certainly admired much of French literature. Before coming to France he had been impressed by Victor Hugo, especially *Les Misérables*, and Guy de Maupassant, whose honest description of sensual love appealed to him far more than smirking over a woman deceiving her husband. Lucien had introduced him to the stylistic mastery of Anatole France; Pierre Vogein, to Voltaire, whom he appreciated for his wry, sardonic humor and for being part of the liberal tradition that led to the French Revolution. Proust, "the greatest writer . . . since Tolstoy"[27] and Gide, both social critics, also wrote perceptively about homosexuality. McKay remembered Barbusse for "the unforgettable glimpse of the African soldiers marching to the front line" in *Under Fire*.[28] He could have added Émile Zola, whose "J'accuse" had provided the inspiration for the title of a 1919 *Messenger* article. Later, he mentioned Pascal and *The Betrayal of the Intellectuals* by Julien Benda (arguing for the predominance of intellect over feeling in the making of a masterpiece in a letter to Max Eastman on April 25, 1932). With Friedman he had discussed Baudelaire, Rimbaud, and the French symbolist poets. He knew enough about French literature to speak of it with some sophistication, as when he remarked, "I decided for myself that, in spite of all the shouting, Verlaine was the greater poet than Rimbaud, for he stuck to poetry to the bitter end while Rimbaud ran away only to become a cult."[29]

Therefore, when he spoke of Francis Carco—whose *Jésus-la-Caille,* a novel about the Paris underworld, he admired (although he preferred the venturesome spirit of Blaise Cendrars)—he criticized Carco's *Printemps d'Espagne,* not for its writing but for its shallowness: Carco had not probed deep enough to evaluate the dignity of Spaniards:

a people who can realize happiness when the French are only gay. . . . It's that Spanish dignity that puts the 'maricones' in the bordels. You find them in the bordels of Morocco, too, extremely beautiful boys, ultra raffiné in that barbaric atmosphere, having nothing at all in common with the *petites tantes* of Paris. . . . I can't imagine any Frenchman understanding the Spaniards and their attitude toward sex. The French *pretend* to

take sex lightly, and that pretense has become part of the national consciousness. The Spaniards don't pretend; they know that sex is no simple
affair and for them it is complicated by the cult of the virgin before
marriage and the pressure of the Catholic church.[30]

McKay's literary tastes aside, apparently he looked up to the tradition of the French Enlightenment and human rights. But he was
acutely conscious of French official hypocrisy, believing the French are
the cleverest propagandists in the world. They hated colored people
yet pretended they were liberal. Although he liked the French reverence for the intellect, he detested the fashionable critics of Parisian
"salons" like Lévinson. He denounced, for instance, the pretentious-
ness of a magazine director who was supposed to do a writer a favor
by simply mentioning him. He even claimed that he preferred the
Americans' willingness to evaluate his own poetry as "written by a
Negro," although he often objected to being treated as a "black poet"
for aesthetic, not racial, reasons. He detested the intellectual smugness
of those French people whose feeling of cultural superiority made
them look down upon America as a raw country; reverence for history
he found oppressive; the use of assimilation and cultural refinement
to enforce the colonization of the mind he found diabolical: "I dislike [the French] because they are the most nationalistic people in
the world and they are never tired of saying they are the nation destined to keep the torch of civilization burning."[31] He developed these
arguments in *Banjo* and in several magazine articles. This is the main
reason he resisted pro-French propaganda so stubbornly. Such essentially intellectual reservations were compounded by the chauvinism,
xenophobia, and greed of the petty bourgeoisie McKay often had to
deal with—minor officials, police, small shopkeepers—whom he depicted in *Banjo*. Indeed, apart from the unpublished vignette about
Douarnenez and important sections devoted to Paris in his autobiography, the image of France in McKay's works has to be inferred from
his description of life in Marseilles in his story "Nigger Lover," in his
unfinished novel "Romance in Marseilles," and in *Banjo*.

Begun in 1929, "Romance in Marseilles" sheds light on McKay's
almost compulsive use of the big Mediterranean harbor as a locale,
which he describes in lyrical prose:

> Wide open in the shape of an enormous fan splashed with violent colors,
> Marseilles lay bare in the glory of the Mediterranean sun, like a fever
> consuming the senses, alluring and repelling, full of the unending pag-
> eantry of ships and of men. Magnificent Mediterranean harbor. Port of
> seamen's dreams and their nightmares. Port of the bum's delight, the
> enchanted breakwater. Port of innumerable ships, blowing out, blowing

in, riding the docks, blessing the town with sweaty activity and giving sustenance to worker and boss, peddler and prostitute, pimp and panhandler. Port of the fascinating, forbidding and tumultuous quayside against which the thick scum of life foams and bubbles and breaks in a syrup of passion and desire.[32]

In McKay's mind the whites in Marseilles were, on the whole, morally inferior to the blacks. Yet in *Banjo*, more than in "Romance in Marseilles," he was careful to analyze the reasons for such a situation. Although W. E. B. Du Bois reviewed the novel rather severely in aesthetic terms, he characterized the book's aim accurately as "on one hand, the description of a series of episodes on the docks of Marseilles, and on the other hand a sort of international philosophy of the Negro race [which] is of great interest."[33] Clearly, McKay intended to provide conflicting outlooks through the use of many characters, but the narrator Ray's sophisticated opinion is supposed not only to balance Banjo's sensual enjoyment of life but also to provide the vision of one "just crammed full of the much-touted benefits of French civilization—especially for colored people."[34] Such propaganda surrounds him daily, from newspaper articles to remarks by colored Frenchmen to even the self-conscious attitude of French prostitutes. But "Ray looked deeper than the noise for the truth and what he really found was a fundamental contempt for black people quite as pronounced as in the Anglo-Saxon lands. The common idea of the Negro did not differ from that of the civilized world in general. There was, if anything, an unveiled condescension in it that was gall to a Negro who wanted to live his life free of the demoralizing effect of being pitied and patronized" (*Banjo*, 275).

Whatever his color, an American had a higher face value than the rest in the Old Port, his passport being worth a good price to identity fabricators. Other blacks looked up to Afro-Americans because of their money. The French tended to treat them well, either because they wanted to contrast their liberalism with the discrimination and lynchings of white America or because of the fashion of jazz. When an elegantly clad soldier slumming in the Ditch encounters Banjo and his companions, he at once says: "Please play. You Americans? I like much *les nègres* play the jazz American. I heard them in Paris. *Épatant*" (*Banjo*, 57). As a result, the American black boys have a positive image of France as a country where, in contrast to "the United Snakes" (*Banjo*, 117), discrimination is not a daily occurrence. Goosey, the most idealistic of them all, feels protected from racism in the land of liberty and equality, and he worships it to the point of taking home a jar of French earth in order to remember that he was once there.

Many other characters, however, are more cautious and aware in "this white man's city" (*Banjo*, 164) of the hypocrisy of the French, who are mostly interested in their money. And on another occasion the narrator despisingly describes a middle-aged Frenchman trying to butt into a black people's party, smirking and leering, with patronizing remarks like: "It's good, here, eh? . . . You like drink fine champagne. . . . I know many blacks, I been in America. . . . You get good treatment here. Eat good, sleep good. . . . *Les filles*" (*Banjo*, 297).

McKay describes the French as expecting foreigners to accept them on their own terms and behave like "good boys" even when they are being cheated outrageously. This comes out in the novel when Ray's adequate French prevents the owner of a "tripe dump" from charging Banjo outrageous prices. She displays instant chauvinism, shouting, *"Je suis française, moi"* (*Banjo*, 64). Her attitude appears as only a cruder manifestation of the nationalism voiced by a French student: "I don't think you appreciate the benefits of French civilization. . . . We are especially tolerant to colored people. We treat them better than the Anglo-Saxons because we are the most civilized nation in the world" (*Banjo*, 274). Nothing infuriated McKay more than those "much-touted benefits of French civilization," and upon several occasions he had his characters remark that "the French are never tired of proclaiming themselves the most civilized people in the world. They think they understand Negroes because they don't discriminate against them in their brothels. They imagine the Negroes like them" (*Banjo*, 267).

Daily life in the Ditch proved that the French police, "the rottenest of the whole world" (*Banjo*, 274), were racially prejudiced. In the novel the color bar seems to be everywhere: a crime committed by a Senegalese is used by the press to testify to the typical brutality of the entire race; black-skinned natives are considered stupid children at best. However, McKay makes the relationship between capitalist exploitation and racism clear. Racism is just an extreme instance of xenophobia caused by economic competition. Ray recalls that when a black prince was thrown out of a Montmartre cabaret Premier Poincaré made a public declaration against discrimination, but "that won't prevent discrimination as long as the pound is lord, the dollar is king, and the white man exalts business above humanity" (*Banjo*, 149).

As a consequence, McKay's criticism of French ways must be interpreted as a refusal to exonerate France from being a part of Western civilization, which had done so much to dehumanize the colored world while it "transformed them to labor under its laws, and yet lacked the spirit to tolerate them within its walls" (*Banjo*, 314). From this point of view, it ensued that the blacks were made the repositories of warm instinct and generosity. To a lesser extent some members of the French working class, whom economic exploitation preserved from "civilization," could still react humanely, as did the café owner who warned black customers of imminent police raids. Because the money-grubbing French of the Ditch are also the victims of the dehumanizing process of Western civilization, they are also partly exonerated, but they can in no way be the heroes André Lévinson would have liked McKay to depict: "The Ditch people are not real heroes because every drop of idealism has been drained out of them by the hard, cruel existence that is theirs. . . . The black boys must be better because they are romantic; they are playing while the Ditch is grabbing for a living."[35]

McKay was not taking sides along racial lines; he explained that the situation was the result of economic pressure. Moreover, his characters react in idiosyncratic terms: the white taxi driver who lives off girls of all colors does not charge Ray for taking Banjo to the hospital; conversely, when a race-conscious Negro girl robs Taloufa to supply the needs of her white pimp, it is not a racial reaction. The black characters all respond individually to France: "Goosey loves France and wants to stay. Banjo is not in the least disturbed about loving or hating any country. The Senegalese opts for America. Ray is cynical about it all. He is intelligent enough to know that all human beings suffer and enjoy life in varying degrees in every country under the sun, although he is not unaware that the colored man has especial handicaps to meet with under the world-wide domination of occidental civilization."[36] McKay readily acknowledged a large degree of tolerance in France: "What is the secret of the French attraction for most strangers? Why do foreign colonies flourish so easily in France? The secret is France's aloofness; they tolerate strangers and allow them to do as they please as long as they don't meddle in French national affairs or do anything to hurt their pride."[37]

Had McKay not been so deeply attracted to life in Marseilles, the city would certainly have provided less literary inspiration. More than a backdrop or locale, it became an almost mythical element, largely because of its role as the gateway to Africa and of the international atmosphere of its harbor:

> . . . favorite port of seamen on French leave, infested with the ratty beings of the Mediterranean countries, overrun with guides, cocottes, procurers, repelling and attracting in its white-fanged vileness under its picturesqueness, the town seemed to proclaim to the world that the grandest thing about modern life was that it was bawdy. . . . Here for Ray was the veritable romance of Europe. The Europe that he had felt

through the splendid glamour of history, when at last he did touch it, its effect on him had been a negative reaction. He had to go to books and museums and sacredly-preserved sites to find the romance of it. Often in conversation he had politely pretended to a romance that he felt not. For it was America that was for him the living, hot-breathing land of romance. (*Banjo*, 68–69)

In McKay's poem "The Desolate City," the image of Paris as a shining beacon had been displaced. New York, with its "mighty business palaces, vast depots receiving and discharging hordes of humanity, immense cathedrals of pleasure, far-flung spans of steel roads and tumultuous traffic," held greater promise for romance in the modern world (*Banjo*, 68). But in Europe Marseilles remained the unchallenged Babylon, where sex and instinct flourished under the hot sun in spite of the greedy merchants. It was a refuge, "as if all the derelicts of all the seas had drifted up there to sprawl out their days in the sun" (*Banjo*, 56).

Compared with America as the land of unlimited expanses and opportunity, the century-laden European setting, where every inch of space had been apportioned long ago, could appear as a sort of prison; yet the boys find sufficient accommodation in the rat holes and deserted box cars. They feast on refuse from the ships and even share the festive French atmosphere which, in the novel, McKay renders by a spate of French references and phrases. By introducing many French expressions, he creates local color, evoking an atmosphere his American audience expected in about as many words as they could mispronounce; he also calls attention to the French language as a barrier, or an open sesame. Language and culture appear as important as color or nationality in creating cleavages in group consciousness. This is exemplified by the encounter between Banjo, who has been struggling with *prix fixe* and *à la carte* menus, and Ray, who speaks the language:

> "Hey, ain't anybody in this tripe-stinking dump can help a man with this dawggone lingo?"
> A black young man who had been sitting quietly in the back went over to Banjo and asked what he could help about.
> "Can you get a meaning, boh, out of this musical racket?" Banjo asked. (*Banjo*, 63)

It is no coincidence that most of the French terms in the novel should be related to food: eating is one of the major events—not only in French culture, according to the stereotypes, but in the lives of the poor. Even in the cheap dives, good cuisine is one of the positive sides of Marseilles; thus references abound to drinks like Cointreau, *gros rouge,* or *café au rhum* and to dishes like *gras double* or *pieds paquet marseillaise.* In similar fashion swear words and insults are easily mastered by newcomers.

Even Ray, the persona of the disenchanted intellectual who stands for McKay, appreciates whatever Marseilles grants him: "Ray had fallen for its strange enticement just as the beach boys had. . . . And the Vieux Port had offered him a haven in its frowsy, thickly-peopled heart where he could exist *en pension* proletarian of a sort" (*Banjo,* 66).

A denunciation of French prejudice and greed, *Banjo* also was a kind of homage to the quaint splendor of Marseilles, which is exalted in vignettes of lush everyday life, as in the following description of the fish market:

> Red fish and blue, silver, emerald, gold, topaz, amethyst, brown-black, steel-grey, striped fish, scaly fish, big-bellied fish, and curs and cats growling over the bowels of gutted fish. The fish-men tramped in in their long felt boots. The fish-women spread themselves broadly behind their stalls. And in bright frocks and thick mauve socks and wooden shoes, the fish-girls pattered noisily about with charming insouciant ease, two between them bearing a basket, buxom and attractive and beautiful in their environment, like lush water-lilies in a lagoon.
>
> The stuff of the groceries thick around the fish market was exposed on the sidewalk: piles of cheeses, blocks of butter, salt herrings, sauerkraut, ham, sausages, salt pork, rice, meal, beans, garlic. Stray dogs nosing by stopped near the boxes. Cats prowled around. A sleek black one leaped upon a keg of green olives, sniffing and humping up its back. A laughing boy grabbing at its tail; the cat leaped down, shooting into a dark doorway. A pregnant woman passing by popped one of the olives into her mouth, smacked her lips with fine relish, and called the grocer boy to give her one hecto. (*Banjo,* 85–86)

Here McKay celebrated the physical love of life that folks along the Mediterranean displayed with as much relish and flourish as black folks were wont to. He cast Marseilles in the role of an international city, the best-loved harbor in Europe. In so doing he relegated Paris to a symbol of the artificial, dissolute, hectic existence in big Western cities, a place of vanity and spiritual desolation.

He returned to Paris, in fact, after a six-month stay in Barcelona, which seemed a better version of Marseilles, in order to consult with his editor, Eugene Saxton, about "Romance in Marseilles" and to be treated for venereal disease. Dr. Lafourcade decided it was syphilis and needed energetic treatment, and McKay rushed to Berlin to consult Dr. Lange, who had treated him in 1923; he spent some time in the hospital there until a Wasserman test proved satisfactory and he could summer and rest in the Rhine Valley.

In early October 1930 he stopped in Marseilles for the last time on his way to Morocco. In Casablanca the French police took him firmly to the International Zone pending the visit of President Doumer because the British, having gotten on his trail after the publication of *Home to Harlem,* had reported him as a pro-Soviet propagandist. He was able to clear himself of the suspicion of political activism and was left in peace. On this occasion his feelings regarding the French were surprisingly nuanced: "Strangely too, I seem to like and understand the French here even better than in France. Except by that one police officer at Fez, I have never met with any discourteous treatment, neither during my first stay in Morocco in '28 nor at this time. I have been well-treated without people knowing that I am a poet and that is the real test of true courtesy, for people to meet one another humanly without knowing who each may be. I felt that thing very strongly in Spain, the poorest person standing simply on his dignity as a human being. In France I always felt the atmosphere more formal, that how one is treated may depend entirely on how one has been introduced."[38]

McKay had gone to Morocco mainly because he had been offered a house rent free. For two years he lived in Dar Hassani on the Tangiers road, learning some dialect, wearing a fez and burnoose for Ramadan, sharing the life around him. There he wrote *Gingertown* and *Black Bottom.* By 1933 he seemed lost to the Western world and his friends: rumors circulated of his conversion to Islam, of his advanced syphilis, of his incipient paranoia. In reality, he had not lost touch with the United States and Europe, and he enjoyed the visits of several friends. Although glad to live close to the Spanish world and the quaint architecture of small Mediterranean harbors, he was poor and tired, and became convinced that he should go back home. He sailed from Cádiz for New York early in 1934, deliberately putting an end to his fifteen-year-long expatriation, never to set foot in France again.

NOTES

1. Claude McKay, *A Long Way from Home* (New York: Lee Furman, 1937), 245, hereafter cited in the text.

2. McKay, introduction to *The Negro in America* (Port Washington, N.Y.: Kennikat Press, 1979), 49.

3. Ibid., 50–51.

4. See Wayne Cooper, ed., *The Passion of Claude McKay* (New York: Schocken, 1973), 222–23 note 60; and Claude McKay to Max Eastman, December 1, 1930, Yale.

5. McKay, "The Desolate City," *A Long Way*, 231–32.

6. Mme. Fanny Vogein-Rappaport, interview with the author, March 1980.

7. McKay to Grace Campbell, January 7, 1924, Yale.

8. McKay, "Paris," typescript copy in Jean Wagner's papers, Paris.

9. McKay to Max Eastman, May 1925, Yale.

10. McKay to Langston Hughes, July 6, 1925, Yale.

11. McKay, unpublished manuscript, Yale, 1, 10, 11.

12. McKay to Louise Bryant, June 24, 1926, Yale.

13. Georges Friedman, introduction to *Quartier Noir* (Paris: Rieder, 1930). Translation mine.

14. Ibid.

15. McKay to Charles S. Johnson, January 11, 1927, Amistad.

16. McKay to William Aspenwell Bradley, March 22, 1927, Yale.

17. McKay to Bradley, December 1, 1927.

18. McKay to the New York *Herald Tribune Books*, March 6, 1932, quoted in Cooper, *The Passion of Claude McKay*, 139.

19. McKay to Sonia Bullitt, May 1928, Yale.

20. McKay to James W. Ivy, September 20, 1929, quoted in Cooper, *The Passion of Claude McKay*, 148.

21. McKay to Bradley, March 14, 1929.

22. McKay to Bradley, July 5, 1929.

23. Mme. Vogein-Rappaport, interview with author, May 1980.

24. McKay to James Ivy, September 20, 1929.

25. McKay to Bradley, October 2, 1929.

26. McKay to Bradley, November 1, 1929.

27. McKay to Langston Hughes, April 3, 1928.

28. McKay, "Once More the Germans Face Black Troops," *Opportunity*, November 1939, 324.

29. McKay, "Dinner at Douarnenez," 1.

30. McKay to Bradley, July 5, 1929.

31. McKay to James Ivy, September 20, 1929, quoted in Cooper, *The Passion of Claude McKay*, 148.

32. McKay, "Romance in Marseilles," 36, Schomburg Collection.

33. W. E. B. Du Bois, "Banjo," *Crisis*, July 1929, 234.

34. McKay, *Banjo* (New York: Harper and Brothers, 1929), 275, hereafter cited in the text.

35. McKay to Bradley, November 1, 1929.

36. Ibid.

37. McKay to Arthur Spingarn, July 31, 1933, Yale.

38. McKay to Bradley, December 14, 1930.

8

Jessie Fauset and Gwendolyn Bennett

Many of the women writers of the Harlem Renaissance were unable to travel abroad. A few did go to France, like Dorothy Peterson and novelist Nella Larsen, but their stays were either very brief or have been difficult to document. An undated letter from Mrs. Imes (Nella Larsen) states that, while staying in Mallorca, she had been struggling in vain with the Spanish language and was about to try French instead, as she would leave for the south of France in April and then move to Paris to meet Dorothy Peterson.[1] In a July 1931 letter to Carl Van Vechten, Peterson alluded to attending a luncheon party on July 18, 1931, with Larsen and the Covarrubias, with Countee Cullen coming by and reading from his new play *God Sends Sunday.* Peterson, a great traveler and propagandist for black culture, was then staying in a "marvellous apartment" at 31 bis, Rue Campagne-Première, in the heart of Montparnasse. She described "the streets cluttered with French servant girls off for Sunday afternoon with their lovers, who with one hand clutch their funny little hats always one size too small and with the other grab the girl by the neck.[2] She later spent many years in Spain, where she had settled, repeatedly revisiting the south of France as well as her family in Switzerland, but she apparently never wrote about those countries.

The dean of American women writers in Paris at the time was undoubtedly Anna Julia Cooper. The daughter of a slave and a free woman, she married an Episcopal clergyman and teacher of Greek who died two years later. In 1881 she entered Oberlin College and obtained a B.A. After participating in the first pan-African conference in London in 1900, giving a paper on "The Negro Problem in America," she undertook graduate studies. She attended La Guilde Internationale in Paris during the summers of 1911 to 1913, then Columbia University. She was already an established writer. As early as 1892 she had published a volume of essays, *A Voice from the South by a Black Woman of the South,* revealing not only racial and feminist commitment but a profound knowledge of the Enlightenment and French liberal thought. For instance, in "Has America a Race Problem?" she alluded to Voltaire as "the great French Skeptic" and quoted Guizot and Taine on "the barbars of the North" (i.e., Anglo-Saxon supremacists) and Alexis de Toqueville on race relations in the United States.

At a time when teachers had no sabbatical leave, she dared to leave her position and go to Paris several times to pursue her research and finally earn her doctorate from the Sorbonne in 1925. Dedicated to her professor, Philippe Sagnac, one of the best historians of the French Revolution, her dissertation dealt critically with French attitudes and policies concerning slavery during the revolutionary period.[3] Cooper established that the homeland of liberty, fraternity, and equality, the cradle of "Les Amis des Noirs," had often failed to adhere to its principles and condoned "the barbarous practice and hateful trafficking in black labor." That same year the new Ph.D. recipient published another volume. *Le Pèlerinage de Charlemagne (Charlemagne's Pilgrimage)* included the text of the epic in medieval French, abundant notes by Julia Cooper, and a translation in modern French by a "learned and overly discreet friend" whom she thanked in her preface. She saw her scholarly contribution as an attempt to "help the American student by facilitating the study of an important and rather scarce text, one of the most ancient achievements of the French spirit and probably even of the Parisian mind."[4]

Novelist Jessie Redmond Fauset had visited Paris before World War I, but, she later recalled, she was too young, confused, and insecure to really enjoy France at that time. Her memories of that first trip must have been refreshed and supplemented by accounts by war veterans among her friends. In her novel, *There Is Confusion,* which antedates her second visit to Europe in 1924, she indeed made use of French settings.[5] Two American soldiers, white Dr. Merriwether Bye and his black friend Peter, are sent to fight with the American Expeditionary Force. They are stationed successively at Brest, at the camp of La Courtine in the Massif Central, and on the front line near Metz, where Peter carries his mortally wounded friend out of no-man's-land. Brest is evoked somewhat routinely as "the typical, stupid, monotonous French town with picturesquely irregular pavements, narrow, tortuous little streets, dark, nestling little shops and the inevitable public square." But Chambéry is treated differently. The description begins like a passage from a guidebook but soon becomes quite witty:

Chambéry up to a few years ago was celebrated chiefly because it was the location of the chateau of the old dukes of Savoy and the birthplace of Jean-Jacques Rousseau. Now it is known to thousands and thousands of Americans because during the Great War it was metamorphosed into a rest center for colored soldiers. To the tourist's mind it might stand out for three reasons: as a city in which it is well-nigh impossible to get a lost telegram repeated; as a place where one may procure at very little expense the most excellent of manicures and the most delicious of little cakes. And, thirdly, as the scene of a novel by Henri Bordeaux, "La Peur de Vivre," the story of a young girl who, afraid to face the perils of life, forfeited therefore its pleasures.6

Fauset used in a more genuine way the high illuminated cross erected on the utmost peak of the Mont du Nivolet, east of the city, as a symbol of hope, not only for Christians but for black soldiers disheartened by racism. Indeed, *There Is Confusion* incidentally dealt with the hardships due to segregation in the U.S. army in terms that strongly recall W. E. B. Du Bois's reports in the *Crisis*. It also reported the free socializing between Afro-Americans and French women and the pitched battle that once ensued when a white southern company stationed in nearby Lathus undertook to "put back the niggers in their place" while the French population watched in astonishment.

By 1924 Fauset entertained pleasant enough memories of her earlier visit to encourage her new friend Langston Hughes, then rather disgusted with the difficulty of surviving in Paris, to take advantage of the cultural opportunities the city offered: "I cannot think of anything lovelier than being young, healthy and a poet in Paris," she wrote.7 By that time a Phi Beta Kappa scholar and a graduate of Cornell, the former teacher of Latin and French was working as literary editor of the *Crisis*. Her excessive good breeding had made her decline an offer to translate René Maran's *Batouala* lest his crude descriptions of African life ruin her respectability, yet she gave the impression that she would enjoy nothing more than going slumming with Hughes around Paris. She planned to sail in the fall to study Romance languages there; devote a few months to writing; travel to the Riviera, Rome, and Vienna; and, finally, *"si j'ai de la chance,* take a trip to Dakar."8 She remembered heavenly spots in the Bois de Boulogne and the environs of Paris where numerous writers had found inspiration. She would indeed initiate Hughes into all the beautiful places, and he would escort her to all the naughty and dangerous ones.

When Fauset took a room at the Hotel Jeanne d'Arc on the Rue Vaneau in the respectable 7th arrondissement in October 1924, Hughes had already left for the United States. Was this the reason why, at first, Paris did not seem so wonderful? The charm of the city soon grew on her again: "The distances are magnificent, the buildings beautiful and Paris is the Paris of my first love. But I'm glad to have seen it in its workaday, prosaic form."[9] While having a vacation of a kind, she also attempted to harden herself and live in the present instead of indulging in romantic dreams. She registered as a student, but attending classes soon bored her, and she preferred socializing with her literary agents, the Bradleys, and meeting American friends of theirs. She visited René Maran, whom she found charming, yet confessed as an afterthought: "Whatever may be said against American whites, there is no question that American Negroes are the best there are."[10] What she mostly appreciated on French soil was an unusual period of freedom on many levels—social, racial, and cultural. It was "lovely just to be oneself and not bothering about color or prejudice," but she perspicaciously noted that her own writing seemed to be suffering from such freedom: "I think strangely enough that's why my book progresses so slowly, because I'm away from the pressure."[11] As for learning the language, after taking a few rather stupid courses at the Alliance Française and the Sorbonne extension for foreign students, she was doing more profitable work with a young French tutor.

In early January 1925 Fauset decided to visit the Midi: Carcassonne, Avignon, Nîmes, Arles, Marseilles—all cities that had been celebrated by American travelers. She returned somewhat disappointed, not by the landscapes or the monuments, but by the people. She used to love all of them before the war, but now they left her cold. She concluded that the war must have spoiled the French, and in her letters to Hughes she emphasized again her closeness to Americans: she met several writers in the Montparnasse cafés, she was invited to literary teas, and she would never forget New Year's Eve when she took a long walk in the snow-covered forest of Saint-Germain-en-Laye in the company of Sinclair Lewis. Her return to a snowy winter in Paris elicited surprising comments on her part about the French: "Last week, it snowed and rained, rained and snowed. Paris was a sight and Parisians in their overshoe-less condition looked miserable. But they endured. Aren't they a wonderful people when it comes to supporting their discomfort? I think they are a dying nation but it seems to me their death will be far distant."[12] Clearly, the young lady was reacting as a well-to-do American convinced of the superiority of her country.

Fauset left France that summer. After what appears to have been an extended tour of Europe she announced, in her introduction to the poems she contributed to Countee Cullen's anthology *Caroling Dusk:* "I've seen England, Scotland, France, Belgium, Switzerland, Italy,

Austria and Algeria. The Collège de France and Alliance Française
have given me some points on the difference between the French of
Stratford-atte-Bowe and that of Paris."[13] Was her sojourn in France
partly responsible for her rather snobbish delight in using such titles
for her poems as "Touché," "Rencontre," "La Vie, C'est la Vie," or
"Noblesse Oblige"? These poems refer to general situations, but the
last one deals with a specifically French maid or hairdresser:

> Lolotte who attires my hair
> Lost her lover, Lolotte weeps
> "May you never know, Mam'selle,
> Love's harsh cruelty."
> Happy Lolotte, she!
> I must jest while sorrow's knife
> Stabs in ecstasy.[14]

In *Plum Bun,* the novel she was writing in Paris, Fauset made hardly
any use of her French experience. She had her protagonist spend a
year there studying art on a scholarship but provided no details of her
stay. However, in *Comedy: American Style,* a novel published in 1933,
she drew on her visits to the provinces. She had Teresa Cary, a light-
skinned young Philadelphia mulatto who has broken off with a lover,
leave for France with her mother, Olivia. The two women enjoy the
"easy free-masonry" engendered by their voyage on the *S.S. Paris;*
they stay near the Rue de la Paix, encounter college classmates, and
pick up their mail at American Express. Good tourists so far. At this
stage Fauset takes her heroine to Toulouse on an unexpected trip.
A description of the Gare d'Orsay, with "the huge French clock that
showed the time from one to twenty-four" is followed by a mention
of "dun-colored Limoges, so much at variance with its delicate prod-
uct," china, before the travelers reach Toulouse at night: "Toulouse
appealed to her as strongly as Paris had offended her. . . . She liked
the narrow twisting streets, the chattering, clattering groups in them;
she found herself a little awed by the age of the University buildings,
the old decaying cloisters. Some day she would stroll through them."[15]
   Aristide Pailleron, her phonetics teacher, becomes strongly attracted
to Teresa, and he provides the ladies with an apartment—a whole
floor in his aunt's former pension—and acts as a devoted, delightful
guide and initiator: "He took them to see the marvellous church of
St. Sernin, which dates from the third century, and showed them the
tombs of the early counts of Toulouse, making them live again. . . .
For successive days, they drove along the Boulevard *Allée St. Étienne,*
Allée St. Michel and the *Grande Allée,* and Teresa, through the eyes of

Aristide, was able to reconstruct the old city walls whose place the splendid avenue had taken."[16] No detail attractive to the American tourist seems to be missing: the fine old Renaissance Hotel Bernouilli and Hotel d'Assézat, the tale of Isaure Clément and her rich gifts to the Académie evoked by her statue, the horse, wine, and flower markets, the famous local pastries eaten in little tea shops in the surprisingly twisting streets.

More interesting still, Fauset has her gallant Frenchman, who is always careful to have the ladies buy things "au meilleur marché" because he is poor himself, woo Teresa and marry her as quickly as French law permits. Thus, settling into uneventful domesticity, the young American discovers the tyranny of her mother-in-law, the pettiness of her self-satisfied husband, the silent mediocrity of French provincial life. Fauset excels in these satirical touches, undoubtedly deriving them from her own reactions. One of Teresa's pleasantest experiences is a sort of honeymoon trip to the Riviera. There, Aristide's nationalism is fully displayed as he takes her to visit Toulon:

> It seemed to his young wife that his very stature increased as he pointed out to them the grim arsenal on the north side of the *petite rade*. Somehow, his pride became hers too and she was as possessive as he, and as complacent, at the sight of the magnificent, protected anchorage which could shelter the huge fleet, its background bristling with forts and batteries. She would never forget Toulon.
>
> The great, black Senegalese quartered there, speaking in some instances beautiful, unaccented French, stirred her imagination. She saw her new country stretching arms across the sea to her black brothers, welcoming them, helping them to a place in the sun.[17]

Apparently Fauset had admired the same sights during her 1925 trip to the Midi. But the race-conscious writer could see through the alleged lack of prejudice among the French. Teresa soon discovers that her husband is a cold-hearted, nationalistic, calculating little man who, in fact, does not like the blacks. They were all right as cannon fodder and helpful in protecting France against Germany, but he thinks that French women like the *Américains noirs* only too well. Had Teresa not been able to "pass," he probably would not have married her.

Fauset was perspicacious about the French, but she could not help loving their country. In 1927, not without flourish, she flaunted her French experience when she taught French again in New York City schools: "Like the French, I am fond of dancing. . . . I should like to see the West Indies, South America and Tunis and live a long time on the French Riviera," she proclaimed.[18] After the publication of *Com-*

edy: American Style in 1934, she was able to revisit France, this time as Mrs. Harris. Again, she wrote her old friend Langston Hughes that in Avignon and throughout the Midi there was plenty of inspiration in store for him. She claimed that she had caught some of the enchantment herself. No further work of hers, however, was inspired by this visit to a country that in so many ways suited her prim, refined, and cultured personality.

Although Gwendolyn Bennett was not a major writer, her account of her stay in France when she was twenty-three is of special interest, not only because she was both an artist and a writer, but because her loneliness rendered her particularly sensitive to the atmosphere of Paris and to its impingement on her sense of personal and national identity. A poet published in *Opportunity* and the *Crisis,* a fine-arts teacher at Howard University, she was awarded a $1,000 scholarship by the Delta Sigma Theta sorority in December 1924 and chose to study in Paris for a full year. Although she hardly knew the language, she was well versed in modern French fiction from Flaubert to Anatole France and, like Countee Cullen, she wrote poetry under the influence of the symbolists.

She sailed for Cherbourg on June 15, 1925, with great expectations: having exciting encounters with artists and writers, going on merry sprees with friends from home, discovering art treasures in exhibitions and museums, sharing chic Parisian life. After visiting one of the art salons, riding all around the city in a taxi with her friend Alston Burleigh, son of the well-known black singer and composer Harry T. Burleigh, and seeing the Luxembourg Museum, she remarked: "There never was a more beautiful city than Paris. . . . There couldn't be! On every hand are works of art and beautiful vistas. One has the impression of looking through at fairy-worlds as one sees gorgeous buildings, arches and towers rising from among the mounds of trees from afar. And there are flowers, too, in Paris, oh, just billions of them. . . . And if it did not make me sad it would make me glad to be privileged to enjoy its beauty."[19]

Thrilled to find the Pantheon and Notre-Dame as magnificent as the stories she had read about them, she shared her enthusiasm with friends at home on illustrated postcards of the Paris monuments. But why should this beauty make her sad instead of glad? Apparently the reason was being away from home, all by herself, far from her beloved Gene, hence incapable of sharing her romantic discoveries and overly sensitive to the slightest difficulty. Missing an appointment with an art professor, being talked to as though she were a little girl, could bring her to the verge of tears. And imagine her panic on the night when, after seeing a movie with a French girl, she lost her way in the Latin Quarter and walked the streets frantically, clutching the medal Gene had given her like a talisman!

Always dreading to be alone, Gwendolyn did not, in fact, lack company. On June 27, 1925, by sheer chance she ran across Langston Hughes's sweetheart of the previous year, Anne Coussey, as she was going down the Boulevard Saint-Michel. Anne took her to Gwen Sinclair, who was studying fashion drawing, and she joined in Sinclair's quest for a studio, but in vain. They visited many museums, and Bennett loved to go shopping with Alston Burleigh and his father, but as shortage of money was her perpetual affliction, she bought only a pair of inexpensive and much-needed gloves. However, she enjoyed the congenial simplicity of the great singer when he took them to the English tearoom on the Rue de Rivoli or when he attempted, in broken French, to buy a pair of corduroys at the Louvre department store. And there were breathtaking cultural highs, as when, in the Musée des Arts Décoratifs, she could admire dozens of Monets and Manets or catch a glimpse of Corot's palette and hat and Delacroix's brush and pipe at the nineteenth-century French retrospective exhibition.

On the Fourth of July loneliness filled her with a new, strange patriotism, and she confided to her journal: "There are times I'd give half my remaining years to hear the 'Star-Spangled Banner.' And yet when I feel that way, I know it has nothing to do with the same 'home' feeling I have when I see crowds of American white people jostling each other about the American Express." Clearly, being away from home enabled her to see America in a rosier light, even though the presence of her fellow citizens reminded her from time to time of race prejudice. She had been taken with black musician Louis Jones to a tea dance at the fashionable Les Acacias in the Bois de Boulogne. There she felt like a dream girl in a dreamland until a remark nettled her: "It must have galled the Americans to death to see us there on a par with them. As Louis and I danced together, I heard a group of them saying among themselves: 'They dance nicely, don't they? You know, they have that native rhythm. Whoa!'"[20]

This was already on August 2. Gwendolyn had just returned from a trip to Marseilles when Dr. Owen Waller, a friend fresh from the United States, hauled her out of bed to help him find a room. But she was rewarded with a fine lunch, and then a shopping spree with three girlfriends, before being taken to the Bois de Boulogne with the party. At the beginning of her stay, Bennett enjoyed quite a lot of socializing. On Bastille Day the Wests, Mercer and Vashti Cook, Harold Jackman,

Edwin Morgan, and a few others took her to the Moulin Rouge, the Rat Mort, and Bricktop's cabaret. On August 6, some of them repeated the round with Mr. Jenkins. After dinner at a Chinese restaurant, they repaired at 2 A.M. to dance and drink champagne at the Royal Montmartre, where Louis Jones, who had briefly left Chez Florence, where he was then performing, danced with Gwendolyn. Then, finding the Grand Duc too crowded with black Americans, they went to Bricktop's: at Brick's, Lottie Gee on her first night in town was singing her hit from *Shuffle Along,* "I'm Just Wild about Harry." Bricktop herself sang her favorite, "Insufficient Sweetie." After hot cakes and sausages, *de rigueur* at the Grand Duc, the party stepped out into the lovely grey morning light at 6:30 A.M., the young lady proudly recorded. And there were more dances at Les Acacias, and nights at the Opera. On August 2, 1925, she was taken to a performance of *Thaïs,* "beautiful music and shades of Anatole France," and in that world of glitter and beauty, enjoyment and ease, she only regretted that lack of money kept her from so much.[21] The next day she attended Wagner's *Lohengrin,* thinking the French were perfect asses to have translated the opera from the German on the strength, she strangely figured, that they had been at war. This paradoxically led her to regret both the hatred between the two countries in the name of New World liberalism and the lack of such fierce patriotism in America!

Indeed, to many Gwendolyn Bennett's first months in Paris would have been paradise, yet by the end of August she was not sure whether she liked the place or not, as she wrote Countee Cullen: "My first impressions were of extreme loneliness and intense homesickness—this and incessant rain—now through the hazy veil of memories I see Paris is a very beautiful city and that people here are basically different from those I have always known. I feel I shall like being here bye and bye."[22]

For lack of contact with cultured French people rather than out of choice, Bennett kept very much in the company of Americans. One of her favorite companions was Harold Jackman, who did not write much himself but was refined and wonderfully able to enjoy high society life. At that time Jackman himself was discovering Paris for the first time. Staying at the Hotel Marignan on the Rue du Sommerard in the Latin Quarter, he wrote Langston Hughes: "Paris lives up to its name and I am not at all disappointed. . . . These days it is so lovely with its gaiety and there is so much of it. Love here in the springtime must be next to divine for in the summer it is a lovely sight to view two lovers on the boulevard just cooing to each other as it were. I tell you, rather I should ask you, what other place under the sun is like Paris, except somewhere in the tropics under the soft moonlight? I could stay there for ever."[23]

Jackman did not allude to Bennett, but she later reported spending wonderful hours in his company, trotting around the city making discoveries. She joined the private lending library run by Sylvia Beach and Adrienne Monnier on the Rue de l'Odéon, which featured the latest writers in English: "Harold and I have already ordered *Ulysses* from them. . . . Those of us who are akin to Croesus can also get a copy of Frank Harris's *Life and Loves* for 300 francs or 15 dollars. The *Ulysses* only cost 60 francs. I should love to have them both to add to my library of pornography."[24] At Shakespeare and Company she also enjoyed a few literary teas, timidly mixing with Joyce, Arthur Moss, Lewis Galantière, Ernest Hemingway, and composer George Antheil, and Sylvia Beach later invited her to a Thanksgiving dinner at her home. Bennett was also invited to tea at Gertrude Stein's and at Matisse's and even at a millionaire's place near the Bois de Boulogne. During the last week of August, she was glad to have the company of the Robesons: Paul had enjoyed a warm reception in London, and they were heading for the Riviera. She visited them nearly every day at their hotel, going around with them a lot before they curtailed their stay on account of the rainy weather.

In the fall she still entertained conflicting opinions about her stay. She could understand, she wrote Hughes, why he had not "got on" in Paris: "I know of no one place on earth where people are as joyous and gaiety-filled with the doing of a number of things and yet where one can be so unutterably alone. I spent during the first two weeks I was here the most miserable time imaginable. Too many times it seemed I had no right to be here." She had become somewhat reconciled to the cruel, cold rains that seemed to pierce her to the marrow of her bones, but she felt that "the authors who babble about 'sunny France' are damned fools."[25]

Bennett, who was no beginner in art, was angry when confronted with the impossibility of taking evening classes in Paris and at having everybody advise her to attend the New York School of Fine and Applied Arts, and she had not succeeded in finding a studio to share with Gwendolyn Lewis. As a *pis aller* she registered at the Académie de la Grande Chaumière, where she was working hard on her first nude in early August. She also registered at the Collège de la Guilde for French courses, but weary of learning so much and understanding so little, she gave them up so as not to waste three precious hours each morning. Later she attended the Académie Julian, the Académie Colarossi, and the École du Panthéon—all for art courses. Through artist Konrad Bercovici she met Franz Masereel, an imaginative Belgian painter and probably the boldest engraver of the time. She gave him English lessons, and the hospitality of the Masereels, who welcomed her into their home and introduced her to their friends, did much to alleviate her loneliness.

Before the end of September, however, her scholarship checks failed to arrive, and she was in financial difficulty. She decided to move to the northwest of the city and stay in a small pension in Pontoise, with Madame Raffalli. She loved the place: with the smell of grass and trees, the murmur of the river nearby, the quaint beauty of the little town, she felt she was retreating into the calm, impersonal heart of the countryside. She could go cycling, feeling the fresh invigorating air in the early morning. As she was the only guest at that time of the year, she became part of the family, and when her landlady's relatives came for the weekend, she would play tag or blindman's buff on the lawn with the aunts and uncles, listen to the children's laughter, and eat piles of food. One night she awoke full of fear, startled by the sound of people snoring in the nearby room, but as she saw the great, pale disc of the moon rising, she was nearly moved to write poetry, she confided to her journal on September 29, 1925.

On several occasions her sensitivity to a new way of life indeed brought her to the verge of creative writing. As she entered Saint-Sulpice during mass on August 23, she was surprised to find that the Chapelle de la Vierge was no ordinary altar but a grandiose niche with the madonna carved in marble between the heavens and the earth. Although by no means a Catholic, she knelt to pray with the worshipers, filled with awe by the pealing bells and majestic chords of the organ. Her eyes brimming with tears, she sat there, enveloped in the waves of music, feeling protected by the huge pillars. She summed up her experience in literary as well as religious terms: "Saint-Sulpice with its marvellous organ is a veritable stage for romance, set as it is in the very heart of the quarters of Dumas's 'Three Musketeers' and scene as it is for Massenet's 'Manon.' Surely one must be worse than stone not to thrill at the neighborhood itself! If there is one store selling church furniture—crosses, madonnas and altar ornaments— in the neighborhood, there must be a hundred! True, there is a gilded look to their displays but there is also the thought behind it all that devout, God-fearing people believe in and worship the 'something' of God, Truth that these things represent."[26] She came even closer to creative writing when, after a night in the Montmartre cabarets, she caught sight of the Sacré-Coeur at dawn: "I shall never forget the shock of beauty as we stepped out into the early morning streets. . . . up rue Pigalle, there stood the Sacred Heart . . . beautiful, pearly Sacré-Coeur, as though its silent loveliness were pointing a white finger at our night's debauchery. I wished then that so worthy an emotion as I felt might have been forever caught in a poem but somehow my muse refuses to work these days." [27]

She did write poetry, though. In contrast to her generally subdued, reflective, melancholy verse, her tribute to the author of *The Three Musketeers*, "Lines Written on the Grave of Alexandre Dumas," sounds unexpectedly solemn and grandiloquent:

> Thou, great spirit, wouldst shiver in thy granite shroud
> Should idle mirth or empty talk
> Disturb thy tranquil sleeping.
> A cemetery is a place for shattered loves
> And broken hearts . . . [28]

After the mad whirl at Christmas time and the ensuing nostalgia, Gwendolyn Bennett settled in at last, having found a suitable studio. Paris had finally gotten hold of her, and it did inspire two of her stories, both about exiled black Americans with broken hearts.

Paul Watson, the protagonist of "Wedding Day," comes to the city around 1910, giving boxing lessons and performing in special bouts arranged for him. Later he plays the banjo with the first colored jazz bands in small cafés patronized mostly by French people. He hates his white compatriots, and one day, when a drunken Kentuckian calls him first "bruther" and then "nigger," he beats up all the American customers, earning the reputation of a "black terror." After shooting and wounding two U.S. soldiers, he serves a long prison term but is pardoned to fight in the French army, where he behaves like a true hero.

Bennett's knowledge of the area allowed her to have her character shamble down the Rue Pigalle, which "in the early morning has a sombre beauty—gray as are most Paris streets and other worldish. To those who know the district it is the Harlem of Paris and rue Pigalle is its dusty Seventh Avenue. . . . He reached the corner of rue de la Bruyère and with sure instinct his feet stopped. Without thinking he turned into the Pit." Indeed, the Flea Pit bistro has a telephone, which Paul desperately wants to use, and, the narrator intervenes, "French telephones are such human faults." [29]

In a brand-new, pearl-gray suit, Paul is about to get married. Indeed, some time before, he has met on the street a white American girl without a sou to her name. His racial hatred has turned to compassion, and soon, to the astonishment of the Negro musicians, he is taking her to Gavarni's every night for supper. But on this their wedding day she has failed to come. Frantically, Paul rides the Métro to her place, lost in his anguished musings, but "the shrill whistle that is typical of the French subway pierced a way into his thoughts." With a bitter sense of irony, he realizes that he is traveling second class with a first-class ticket: "funny how these French said 'descend' when they meant 'get off'; funny how, after living here for all those years, he couldn't pick up French properly." Where did he really belong? Certainly not in "white" America, the story makes clear, since when he reaches the future bride's hotel, Paul finds only a note: Mary just could not go through with it—"white women don't marry colored men," she had written—and she only a street woman! [30]

Baffled love is again the theme of "Tokens," a vignette about the sad fate of a black musician. Jenks Barnett had first arrived in Europe with the jazz orchestra of Will Marion Cook. In Paris he falls in love with Tollie Saunders, a Negro entertainer, and when she leaves him, he starts on the headlong road downward: he becomes a drunkard; he spends two weeks in jail with a terrible pain in his back until his friends rescue him. After "endless days of splashing through the Paris rain in search of a job . . . then night upon night of blowing a trombone in a stuffy little *boîte de nuit*," he is sent to the American Hospital.[31] Finally, sick with tuberculosis, he ends up in the Saint-Cloud sanitorium. Just before dying, Jenks, faithful to the last, asks his friend Bill to send Tollie his silver picture frame and give his radium clock to a tubercular French kid who used to visit him. Bennett thus weaves her poetic dirge of the loveless black jazzman into a kind of Paris blues, framed by the ominous lines of the landscape: "High on the bluff of Saint-Cloud stands the Merlin Hospital, immaculate sentinel of Seraigne . . . Seraigne with its crazy houses and aimless streets, scrambling at the foot of Saint-Cloud's immense immutability. Row on row the bricks of the hospital take dispassionate account of lives lost and found." As a refrain, the "wanton unconcern of the Seine" (is this an echo of Apollinaire's "Pont Mirabeau"?) slowly flows past the rustic stupor of the suburban town: "The Seine . . . mute river of sorrows . . . grim concealer of forgotten secrets . . . endlessly flowing . . . touching the edges of life . . . moving purposefully along with great disdain for the empty, foolish gaiety of Seraigne or the benign dignity of the Merlin Hospital, high on the warm cliffs of Saint-Cloud."[32]

In June 1926 Bennett returned home to resume teaching design and water color at Howard University while acting as an associate editor for *Opportunity*. Later she was an educator in several states, a supervisor for the Federal Arts Teaching Project, and the initiator of a progressive school for Harlem children. Until her left-wing sympathies nearly brought her to face the Committee on Un-American Activities, she had an active and committed career. In comparison, the echoes of her French experience in her journal and in her writing seem strangely romantic. Was this due to an extraordinary sensitivity or simply to her youth? After all, after riding a bicycle over the soft earth along the Oise, with her lips whistling, "for hours on hours of heaven," or after relishing Van Vechten's *Blind Boy* or Alfred Kreymborg's *Troubadour,* was she not the girl who had wondered "if all people who are twenty-three and have loved are this melancholy?"[33]

NOTES

1. Nella Larsen to Dorothy Peterson, undated, JWJ Collection, Yale.

2. Dorothy Peterson to Carl Van Vechten, July 19, 1931, Yale.

3. Anna Julia Cooper, *L'attitude de la France à l'égard de l'esclavage pendant la révolution* (Paris: Marétheux, 1925).

4. Anna Julia Cooper, *Le Pèlerinage de Charlemagne* (Paris: A. Lahure, 1925), iii.

5. Jessie Fauset, *There Is Confusion* (Boni and Liveright, 1924), 247.

6. Ibid., 254.

7. Fauset to Langston Hughes, May 6, 1924, Yale.

8. Fauset to Hughes, April 20, 1924, Yale.

9. Fauset to Hughes, October 8, 1924, Yale.

10. Fauset to Hughes, October 8, 1924.

11. Fauset to Hughes, January 8, 1925, Yale.

12. Fauset to Hughes, March 16, 1925, Yale.

13. Fauset in *Caroling Dusk,* ed. Countee Cullen (New York: Harper, 1927), 65.

14. Fauset, "Noblesse Oblige," *Caroling Dusk,* 68–69.

15. Fauset, *Comedy: American Style* (New York: Frederick Stokes, 1937), 169.

16. Ibid., 175.

17. Ibid., 182.

18. Fauset in *Caroling Dusk,* 65.

19. Gwendolyn Bennett, unpublished journal, June 28, 1925, 8, Schomburg Collection.

20. Bennett, journal, 15–16, 20.

21. Bennett, journal, 20.

22. Bennett to Cullen, August 23, 1925, Amistad.

23. Harold Jackman to Langston Hughes, August 13, 1925, Yale.

24. Bennett to Cullen, August 23, 1925, Amistad.

25. Bennett to Hughes, September 1925, Yale.

26. Bennett, journal, 31.

27. Bennett, journal, 27.

28. Bennett, "Lines Written on the Grave of Alexandre Dumas," *Opportunity,* June 1926, 136–37.

29. Bennett, "Wedding Day," *Fire!* (November 1926), 26–27.

30. Ibid., 28.

31. Bennett, "Tokens," in *Ebony and Topaz,* ed. Charles S. Johnson (Freeport, N.Y.: Books for Libraries Press, 1971), 148.

32. Ibid., 149.

33. Bennett, journal, 38.

9

And Others Too

The 1920s and 1930s were indeed the heyday of American visitors in France, both black and white. These included not only the wealthy set but also a small number of race leaders on partly official, partly pleasure, trips; a good number of artists and even more musicians; and most of the luminaries of the New Negro movement, starting with Alain Locke. Langston Hughes came even before he was an established writer, while Claude McKay initiated the fashion of living abroad. Even more than Anna Cooper, Jessie Fauset, or Gwendolyn Bennett, Countee Cullen was such an assiduous student of French culture that he spent his summers in Paris. But others also came and stayed: the older generation of Du Bois and James Weldon Johnson, and also Jean Toomer, John F. Matheus, Walter White, Eric Walrond, and others.

Of French ancestry on his mother's side, Jean Toomer occasionally recalled his French connections with a degree of pride, as when he wrote in 1930: "I am of French and English descent. . . . I have been associated in New York and Paris with some of the men who have been trying to bring about a renaissance in American art and life."[1] Yet when the already outstanding author of *Cane* first sailed for France in July 1924, he was by no means undertaking a cultural pilgrimage. He intended to stay only at the Institute for the Harmonious Development of Man, which Gurdjieff had recently opened at the former priory of Avon on the outskirts of Fontainebleau, forty miles southeast of Paris.

In January of that year Toomer had met in New York A. R. Orage, one of the English disciples of the Russian guru. In search of spiritual certitudes, Toomer had become convinced that the cosmic view, supposed to offer the possibility of attaining higher awareness of oneself and the world, was the answer to the insecure and confused postwar Western quest. He had been moved by the dance and exercises, demonstrated on American stages, which seemed to recreate the body and shape it toward spiritual fulfillment: "Here I am in New York," he wrote frantically to Alfred Stieglitz, "working through the details of my first trip to France! I sail Saturday the 19th of July on board the *Savoie* for Le Havre. How long I'm going to stay, I don't know. For I go there not to 'stay' but to learn something."[2] Indeed, Toomer was so eager to leave that he did not wait for his friend Marjorie Glover, who was to join him later that summer in Fontainebleau.

Did his exclusive devotion to Gurdjieff deprive Toomer—who had read French authors with interest during his formative years, who quoted Baudelaire and had attended a series of lectures on Romain Rolland at the Rand school—of the pleasure of visiting Paris? In fact, Toomer was quite happy. Once in Fontainebleau, he apparently hardly left the premises. He wrote Stieglitz: "Ever since my arrival in France, I have been working with the Gurdjieff Institute. . . . My conjectures to you concerning its general significance have been confirmed. It is by all odds the best *general* instrument that I have found."[3]

That summer the score of disciples at the Institute had more on their hands than they had expected: in early July, driving his car recklessly, the guru nearly killed himself and required months to recuperate. As a result, when Toomer arrived he was somewhat at a loss, as there was little organized activity—no music, no efficient meals, and little conviviality. He was lodged, however, in the "Ritz" section of the priory on the same floor as the Gurdjieff family, not in the less prestigious "corridor of the monks." Bernard Metz, of the Ouspenski London circle, soon advised and directed him, set him to work on the chicken coops, and the new recruit became part of the routine. The disciples not only spent hours at gymnastics and spiritual exercises but also had to repair buildings, chop wood, garden, and, at times, prepare meals. At the end of his stay at Avon, he considered his training sufficient to begin teaching the method on his return to the United States.

When Toomer returned to France, from May 29 to October 16, 1926, he was less exclusively preoccupied with Gurdjieff, more willing to meet people and see places. Sailing on the *De Grasse*, he socialized with Mrs. Arthur Sachs, whose intelligence appealed to him and whom he planned to see again in Paris.[4] No details about his visits to the city and about the people he met there seem to be available, but he wrote at some length on life at the Prieuré: "Gurdjieff is at work finishing his book. And every evening he composes music and then has a musician student here play it for all who are there. It is strangely vital and moving. And every Saturday we all have something one would ordinarily call a Turkish bath. Gurdjieff has built a special bath. The steam, the heat reaches a temperature of 110 but, despite this, it is amazingly possible to breathe. There is no general work going on."[5]

Again, on his return to the United States Toomer tried to preach the gospel of Gurdjieff, this time in Chicago, again without much success. He returned to France the following summer, landing at Cherbourg on May 15 and leaving from Le Havre on July 17, 1927. This time he seems to have visited Paris frequently enough. At the Prieuré the spiritual intensity was the same, most of the day being devoted to meditation and veneration of the Master. According to Mrs. Edith Taylor, who attended that session, Gurdjieff had by then chosen Toomer as his American disciple and wanted him to be his prophet among the Negroes. In notes on a luncheon where watermelon was served for dessert, she recalled the following exchange:

> *Gurdjieff:* "Mister, you like such fruit?"
> *Toomer:* "Yes, yes, very much."
> *Gurdjieff:* "Then, eat like—how you say?—black baby, special name, ah, yes, pickaninny. You know how pickaninny eat?"
> *Toomer:* "You mean with both hands?"
> *Gurdjieff:* "Good, I see you very much know."
> Toomer picked up the piece of melon and ate in this fashion. When he finished, he put the rind down on the plate and looked around with a satisfied smile.
> *Gurdjieff:* "You finish, Mister? You not finished. Eat all, even white part."
> Toomer looked puzzled but picked up the rind and proceeded to eat down to the green, then again put the remains on the plate.
> *Gurdjieff:* "Get up, you finished, go back to garden. Work like eat. When in garden you finish I send you to America. You go special part of New York where big little pickaninny live; you show them you very special pickaninny receive it; you live there, work among them, enlighten such men how you live; and if honest you fulfill, will substantial commission give."[6]

That summer, while dutifully obeying the Master, Toomer took time to indulge in a short motor trip to the southern Alps and the city of Briançon, combining work and leisure.

In June 1929 Toomer sailed again to France by way of Toronto. In seventeen days at Fontainebleau he completed an account of his passage, titled "Transatlantic." He seems to have had a good time on board, especially at the captain's masquerade ball, at which he was disguised as a rajah. Apparently he fell in love with a teenager named Fay, whom he seriously considered marrying.[7]

At the Prieuré, Toomer, whom Gurdjieff had nicknamed "Half-an-hour Toomer" because he was so slow, was growing restless. He took to drinking heavily. But there is no indication that he led a gay life in Paris. He probably met a few French writers the year before, since seven of his poems had appeared in translation in French magazines, notably *Les Nouvelles Littéraires,* and in May 1929 he contributed a "Letter from America" to the French surrealist review *Bifur.* Yet, when he returned to the United States in the fall of 1928, Toomer had gained nothing as a writer from his French experience. Indeed, he had stopped being a writer to become a "thinker." As he put it in "Earth Being," he was ready to begin another chapter of his life, to attempt to establish a Gurdjieff group in Harlem. He failed miserably among his race brothers. Sadly, the summers he spent at the Prieuré d'Avon contributed to depriving the Harlem Renaissance of one of its first-rate writers.

John F. Matheus had already contributed to the *New Negro* anthology when he left West Virginia for Europe in the summer of 1925. A teacher of Romance languages, like Countee Cullen, he had graduated in French from Columbia University and intended to take the language course at the Sorbonne extension. Fifty years later he would remember it with pleasure: Professor Schneider taught French medieval art; Henry Chamard, medieval literature; and M. Guignebert, French history. Matheus was accompanied by his wife, and because they stayed in the well-off area around the Arc de Triomphe, the young couple found Paris rather uncongenial at first. But Pension l'Avenir in the Latin Quarter proved more attractive, since they could easily roam the Left Bank. John visited Paris like a conscientious tourist but had interesting encounters. He attended an international conference on Esperanto and even served as an impromptu interpreter for Sir Arthur Conan Doyle, who was lecturing to a convention of spiritualists on how to photograph ghosts. In the company of Doyle and the famous medium Karnac, he visited the beautiful mosque near the Jardin des Plantes, which was opened especially for them.

John Matheus also made a point of sampling the cabarets. Even though Paris welcomed Josephine Baker ecstatically, at the Folies Bergères Feral Benglia, the black-skinned Algerian who played the part of the Devil in the show, told Matheus about the Frenchman's own brand of prejudice. The audience objected to a black Arab appearing on stage with white female dancers in the nude. American tourists behaved much worse: Matheus saw a couple of his white-skinned compatriots leave the room in outrage when his new acquaintance the Devil entered among the white female cast.

Matheus had been brought up on the French classics, but he loved Émile Zola, Alphonse Daudet, Anatole France, and, above all, Guy de Maupassant, whose story of a heroic peasant woman who had been shot for burning a platoon of Prussian soldiers in her barn had moved him to tears. He had been affected just as much by reading Daudet's "The Last Class." He made a special point of visiting Maupassant's grave at the Parc de Repose but also took great interest in a performance of *Docteur Knock* by Jules Romains and the more avant-garde creations of Jean Cocteau.

The young couple did not have enough money to visit much of France, but luck was with them: an American who had been called home in haste sold them a round-trip ticket to the Riviera for only fifty dollars. Marseilles was a discovery—its deep azure seascape, a visit to the Château d'If in tribute to Alexandre Dumas's hero, and also, unexpectedly, encounters with the black Senegalese, who did not even really speak French. After Nice and the splendor of Monte-Carlo, they ventured across the Italian border, having been cautioned to refrain from comments and criticism, as Mussolini had just been voted into power. In Italy, of all places, an Englishman mistook John for an African and a native refused to believe he could be a U.S. citizen, leaving him to wonder about his national, as well as racial, identity!

Back in Paris Matheus met Alain Locke briefly in a café, and he went to the Musée du Luxembourg to admire the paintings of Henry O. Tanner. This was a pilgrimage on his part: like most black visitors he was honoring an artist who had exiled himself in order to escape racial prejudice and gain recognition. Had he known that Tanner was still alive in Paris, he would have ventured to approach him.[8]

In Matheus's mind, France was clearly the land of freedom of which Cullen sang. In a poem inspired by an encounter with a West Indian girl in Paris, he celebrated liberal, sophisticated France together with a keen sense of belonging to black world culture. "Belle Mamselle of Martinique" appeared in 1927 in *The Carolina Magazine*. With its meter strongly reminiscent of Cullen's "Heritage," it sings of Negro elegance on French soil:

> Belle Mamselle of Martinique
> Tell me why your dainty feet
> Trip along the Élysées?
> And your crimson turban lay
>
> Aureoling eyes of black,
> Sparkling answer rippling back
> To our interested query:
> "Are you homesick now or weary?"
>
> You live here? Ah, now, I see
> Why I like gay, old Paree,
> You're the Romance that we seek,
> Belle Mamselle of Martinique.

The girl is a "real Parisienne," but the poet asks her not to forget her native "tropic, foliaged shores / Where the torrid sun restores / Color to the Nordic cheek." His glorification of black beauty ends by stressing the tribute that France, among all nations, pays to blackness:

> Yes, I know they put a ban
> On crinkly hair and cheek of tan
> Where we live across the sea,
> Knowing not that Gay Paree
> Worships just such nymphs as you,
> Colored nymphs, whose eyes are dew,
> Colored faces, copper, bronze,
> Mango, olive, almond, orange.

Such feelings may account for Matheus's devotion to teaching, researching, and disseminating literature in French. After returning from France he studied for a doctorate at the University of Chicago, notably with Professor Régis Michaud, and he completed a translation of Paul Valéry's "Le Cimetière Marin"—an arduous task. In 1928 he spent a few months in Haiti, where he found material and inspiration for several works, including "Tambour," a folk comedy about Haitian peasants, and short stories dealing with folk beliefs and superstition. Through him, his colleague Clarence Cameron White, director of music at West Virginia State College, became interested in Haitian history and life and even composed incidental music, including a meringue, for "Tambour." White himself, a precocious violinist, had studied with the famous composer Samuel Coleridge-Taylor in London and had performed with him, touring Europe from 1908 to 1911. In the late twenties, White and Matheus decided to collaborate on an opera based on the story of Dessalines, the first emperor of Haiti. On a grant from Julius Rosenwald they visited the country to study its history and beliefs. The theme of *Ouanga* was Dessalines's attempt to purge the newly founded nation of voodoo beliefs and his assassination by mysterious means (*ouanga* means a spell or charm). The opera was performed in concert in Chicago in 1939 and finally staged successfully in South Bend, Indiana, ten years later.

While Clarence Cameron White studied composition in Paris with Raoul Laparra in 1930 and 1931 and had the pleasure of hearing the faculty of the École Normale de Musique perform a string quartet he composed at that time, John Matheus returned to Paris in the spring of 1930. He was acting as private secretary to Dr. Charles S. Johnson, one of the American members of the international committee entrusted with investigating the charges of forced labor practices in

Liberia. The black sociologist was already well known, and they were feted in Paris, where they enjoyed several parties in fashionable salons as the guests of Robert Duncan, whom they had met on board the *Roosevelt*. Matheus got acquainted with sculptor Augusta Savage and took her to dinner. He realized that the Negro was indeed in vogue in Paris: dolls representing Josephine Baker were in many shop windows, and hordes of pleasure-seekers in search of exoticism were now haunting the Bal Colonial on the Rue Blomet.

Although John Matheus never returned to France, he remained an untiring propagandist for French culture among black Americans. He edited several French readers, and in 1936, in collaboration with W. Napoleon Rivers, he prepared a school edition, with introduction and notes, of *Georges,* the only work signed by Alexandre Dumas that has a Negro protagonist.

When NAACP official Walter White was awarded a Guggenheim fellowship for creative writing, to be spent in a foreign country, it did not take long for Rebecca West and G. B. Stern, whom he saw at a party given by Carl Van Vechten, to persuade him that Villefranche-sur-Mer on the French Riviera would be the ideal place as well as the least expensive.

White entertained mixed feelings concerning French racial policies. A delegate to the August 1921 Pan-African Congress in London, Paris, and Geneva, he had been surprised to find in Senegalese Blaise Diagne, who had married into a prominent French family and been appointed High Commissioner to the Black Troops, a citizen so loyal to his adopted country that he was opposed to any open condemnation of French colonial policies—this at a time when *Voyage au Congo,* written by white Frenchman André Gide, denounced the country's excesses in Africa. Either the French habit of not objecting to mixed marriage and not imposing discrimination was devilishly crafty, or it corresponded to some real lack of prejudice in a nation so prone to colonize others.

In late July 1927 Caucasian-looking White and his wife, Gladys, who had just given birth to their second child in June, sailed for Le Havre. Many rich friends of Van Vechten were on board: Baird Leonard, Marjorie Worth, and Arthur Chamberlain Dodds, not to mention acquaintances like the Reverend Billy Sunday and literary critic Harry Hansen. They all traveled in style, and Gladys White passed for "everything from a Spanish grande dame to an American Indian."[9] In Paris William Aspenwell Bradley, the agent and friend of most American expatriate writers, took them to his apartment on the Ile Saint-Louis

to meet Isadora Duncan, who danced beautifully to the first recording
made by Paul Robeson, "Go Down, Moses." White also paid a visit to
René Maran, who was trying to get *The New Negro* published in France
and believed that James Weldon Johnson's *God's Trombones* also stood
a good chance of being translated, the French being so keen on Negro
art and writing.

After a week in a comfortable pension near the Pantheon, the family
set off for the south. Although close to Nice and the fashionable resorts, Villefranche had not yet attracted many foreign tourists, and
life was inexpensive there. On August 10 the Whites moved into Villa
Sweet Home on the Boulevard Emmanuel III. It was a huge house
with eight large rooms, central heating, a garage, and servants' quarters—all for $250 a year. White wrote enthusiastic letters to his friends
at home; their Italian maid, Vittoria, had asked blushingly for the
ridiculously low wage of $16 a month; a bottle of wine cost no more
than Évian or Perrier, which the family, suspicious of the local water,
had taken to drinking.[10] Their "lovely little villa, directly on the Mediterranean but high up in the Alps" received so much sun that Gladys
had nicknamed their baby "Copper Son" because of his tan. Jane, the
older child, was making rapid progress in French while her parents
still barely managed to ask their way or do the shopping. In his retreat Walter was growing a "delicately fashioned beard" and donned
a Basque beret. To his delight the few other tourists mistook him for
a Frenchman.[11]

These were carefree times, and the days passed quickly: "To be able
to sit on the terrace and look down on the lovely bay of Villefranche
and off in the distance at the constantly changing, colorful beauty of
the tiny peninsula which formed the left arm of the harbor made the
first leisure I had ever known in adult life a never-ending peace and
happiness."[12] For entertainment the Whites would go to Nice. There
they attended a recital of the Fisk Jubilee Singers, who created a sen-
sation. A month later, while trying to secure a copy of the *Mémoires* of
Josephine Baker for Carl Van Vechten, they learned of Isadora Duncan's tragic death—strangled by her scarf, which had gotten caught in
the wheel of her car.

Gladys had a fine time, sipping crème de cacao or drinking beer
in the open-air cafés while the old dandies flirted with her. This
was a paradise, far from Prohibition, with whiskey at $2.40 a bottle.
They were even blessed with French visitors, like Gaston Courty of
the *Journal des Débats* and painter Georges Joubin: both Frenchmen
had been very much impressed by Johnson's "Creation" poems, and
Courty would try to have *La Revue de Paris* publish them (*A Man Called
White*, 94).

White had received the fellowship to complete a novel about three generations of Negro life, yet he could hardly devote himself to the pursuit of belles-lettres, even in this unexpected haven. James Weldon Johnson's frequent letters and the newspaper headlines kept reminding him of racial violence and the NAACP's struggle in the United States. Did his concern turn into a kind of guilt? Instead of pursuing his plans for a novel, he was soon working eight hours a day on a book about lynchings. On October 15 he cut his beard and left for London to give a series of lectures on the question. Stopping in Paris, he paid Josephine Baker the visit he had long anticipated. Back in Villefranche by the end of the month, he worked harder than ever on the new book, and on January 19, 1928, he was able to mail the entire manuscript of *Rope and Faggot* to Arthur Spingarn.

Early in 1928 the Whites were disappointed to see hordes of British and American tourists invade "their" Villefranche: the prices skyrocketed, and they no longer felt at home. In February they moved to Avignon, where for half the price of the villa they rented a furnished apartment. It was located at 37, Rue Aubanel, just above the shop of their landlord, Jules Pochy, a dealer in Provençal furniture. Thanks to the Pochys, the Whites made interesting acquaintances, like Henri, a guide at the Palais des Papes, whose demonstration of "the best echo in the world" White recalled with emotion some twenty years later:

> He had so steeped himself in the history, folklore and beauty of Provence that for him the sum and summation of all human experience had concentrated there. . . . With a flourish, he ushered me into the hall of Clement VI. The only object in the room was the chalky sarcophagus of the long-dead pope. The late afternoon golden sunlight streaming in through tall, narrow slits of windows marked the grayish white floors and walls like the lines on a football field. Henri guided me to one of the corners of the huge room where he began to sing parts of a Mass in what had once been an excellent baritone and in which, even then, his age was noticeable only in the higher notes.
>
> Like a response from a far-off, invisible choir the sound came back to us. It was a moment of complete beauty.
>
> We trudged down the hall in silence, and no word was spoken even when we touched hands at parting. (*A Man Called White*, 98)

More matter-of-fact aspects of French life and food appealed to White as well. Avignon he found a queer mixture of the thirteenth and twentieth centuries: the rather Parisian atmosphere of the busy Rue de la République juxtaposed with the awesome mass of the ancient papal palace. He appreciated both the gentle somnolence and the genuine friendliness of the old town. The Whites toured the region—Arles and Les Baux mostly—and were tempted to acquire a thirteenth-century church in which a launderette, complete with brand-new American machines, had been installed. Having repeatedly sampled the delicious wines (Clos Saint Pierre sold for only twenty francs a bottle and Tavel for eighteen), White wrote Van Vechten on March 21: "Aside from such fleshly joys we like Avignon better than any place we've seen in France."

In this city, "the home of Mistral and Petrarch," as he made a point of telling James Weldon Johnson, he was able to write easily.[13] Indeed, he had nearly completed his novel when he was called back to New York by the NAACP: Charles Studin wanted him to attend a meeting with the governor of the state in preparation for a campaign designed to win the Negro vote for the Democrats. When he left France on April 4, 1928, White believed he would be back in a couple of weeks, but the repeated postponement of his return and the expiration of his leave of absence made travel prohibitively expensive.

Far from wealthy, but a man of sensibility, refinement, and literary talent, Walter White thus appreciated what France had to offer: its history, monuments, and traditions as well as its splendid landscapes and cuisine. He visited it under the best possible conditions during a vacation away from the struggle in the United States. Light-skinned enough to pass, he did not have to think of his own situation in terms of racial prejudice; yet his mind was not diverted from the racial situation at home, which he followed as an NAACP leader. It is ironic that his study of lynching in the United States, *Rope and Faggot,* was completed in the heavenly retreat of Villa Sweet Home in the heights of Villefranche.

After the enthusiastic public reception of his volume of short stories, *Tropic Death,* West Indian–born Eric Walrond had been given a contract by Boni and Liveright to write a history of the Panama Canal and the French role in the venture. In 1928, on a Guggenheim Fellowship, he traveled extensively in the Caribbean to do research. Then on an extension of the grant he went to London and Paris to investigate the French involvement in the scandal and conduct interviews with the De Lesseps family.

When he arrived in Paris in July 1929, Walrond at once became part of the Afro-American smart set through his connection with Countee Cullen, whose studio he shared for a while. He apparently did a lot of partying with him and their friends while French critic André Lévinson praised *Tropic Death* to the skies, the better to decry McKay's *Banjo.*[14] Soon Walrond moved to Bandol, a fishing village near Toulon, where he met the celebrated Nancy Cunard and became for a time a member of her entourage. After a visit to his parents in Brooklyn in the fall of 1931, he went back to France and settled in a small village near Avignon. There he reportedly worked on creative writing but did not make use of the setting or the people around him. The most tangible result of his research in France was a long article on the Panama scandal, which appeared in the Madrid magazine *Ahora* in August 1934. "Como se hizo el Canal de Panama" is a detailed account of the financial scandal involving engineer De Lesseps that nearly brought down the Third Republic.

Possibly through French contacts and with the help of his friend and translator Mathilde Camhi, a literary person in her own right, Walrond sold a few pieces to French magazines. The January 7, 1933, issue of *Lectures du Soir* carried his short story "Sur les chantiers de Panama." Its theme was racial conflict among the canal workers; its plot turned on an incident in which a Spanish shopkeeper shot a couple of Negroes as a threatening mob drew near. The following week the same magazine printed an interview with Walrond, whom Jacques Lebar considered "one of the most characteristic and colorful representatives of Negro literature together with Claude McKay." Walrond, who had read *Madame Bovary* repeatedly, was said to consider Flaubert a major novelist but to like Blaise Cendrars best among contemporary French writers for his "unique understanding of the world, the psychology and the art of the Negro."[15] Apparently Mathilde Camhi was to translate *Tropic Death,* but the book never saw publication in France. She translated only "Sur les chantiers de Panama" and a fine article called "Harlem." It was a colorful piece of reportage on how the smart set had invaded the Harlem cabarets and how a few Strivers' Row entrepreneurs like Jasbo Brown and Jim, the owner of the Bucket of Blood, had capitalized on that fashion.[16] A similar piece, "Harlem, la perle noire de New York," came out in *Voilà* on May 27, 1933. Evidently intended to be the first of a series, it was probably also the last. Around that time Eric Walrond decided to settle in England, where he spent much of the remainder of his life.[17]

The most comprehensive, yet still rather superficial, coverage of Negroes in France was provided for a number of years by Joel Augustus Rogers, the author of half a dozen volumes recording black cultural contributions or tracing famous people's genealogies to their authentic or imagined Negro ancestry. Although his readiness to be of service and his good humor endeared him to most, Rogers was not taken seriously by many members of the New Negro movement. Claude McKay was annoyed by Rogers's perpetual wonderment at finding the

French so nice, while he (McKay), who had been in contact with them for several years, knew better. Rogers did speak some French, loved brilliant conversation, and flattered himself that he was a gourmet— hence his attraction to Paris. He met a tremendous number of people there, mostly blacks from the Antilles bourgeoisie, and was thus enabled to get beneath the surface of things, or so he claimed. "American Writer Says French Negroes Have Responsible Jobs in Commerce But Pay Is Very Low; American Tourists Doing Everything They Can to Teach Frenchmen the Art of Segregation"—such was the title the September 10, 1925, Pittsburgh *Courier* gave one of his articles. Another article, entitled "How Fares the French Negro?" began with a retrospective of Latin treatment of blacks recalling a score of cases of individual advancement of Negroes under French rule, from General Dumas to Goncourt Prize–winner René Maran.[18]

To the French Negro population of Paris, with its apparently well-integrated individuals and celebrated places of good cheer and entertainment like the exotic Bal Nègre on the Rue Blomet, blacks from all over the world were a sizable and not unwelcome addition. However, Rogers was more interested in reporting about Afro-Americans in Paris. His comparisons of French and American customs were generally to Paris's advantage. To him, the most striking thing about France was her attitude toward the Negro: "Just reverse the Anglo-Saxon or cracker attitude and you have it." He concluded:

> I feel much more at home in Paris than in London in spite of the language. The French remind me more of colored folks. They are just as noisy, excitable, loveable, and light-hearted. They also take their own time about things. In the restaurants, a good thing to do is to take your bed with you between the courses. . . . The Frenchman is a true bohemian. At night he may be seen in hundreds of thousands sitting at the delightful little tables on the sidewalks of the great boulevards, sipping his café, wine or aperitif and taking his time to get acquainted with life. This is perhaps why the French are such an artistic people. Paris is a very beautiful city in spite of the rusty appearance of the buildings. . . . I cannot recall having experienced a greater elevation of soul than when I stepped into the magnificent and spacious Place de la Concorde. . . . Another thing that helps me feel at home in Paris is the number of colored folks one sees.[19]

Rogers was responding to the expectations of Afro-American readers who wanted to know what their experience in Paris might be if they ever managed to get there. And many did. In his autobiography Claude McKay mentioned a "mass migration" of the Harlem Renaissance smart set to France in the late 1920s.

An article entitled "Beth Prophet Hailed As Artist in Paris," in the

Afro-American, August 2, 1929, gave a chatty account of what Wallace Thurman liked to call "niggerati life." Evidently an intimate of Countee Cullen, the author started on July 1 with a small party at the poet's apartment. There was card-playing and gramophone music— especially "lowdown" recordings by Duke Ellington. Artists and entertainers attended: Gertrude Curtis, Bessie Miller and her daughter Olivette, Zaidee Jackson, Caska Bond, and painter Hale Woodruff. The following day a tea was organized in honor of sculptor Elizabeth Prophet, who had just exhibited her work in Paris. Then Independence Day was celebrated with spare ribs and cabbage at Gertrude Curtis's place in Montmartre, where Cora Gray, Mary Peek-Johnson, and Mrs. Fleming joined the group. The climax of the festive week was Louis Coles's birthday party, given in Cecil Robeson's magnificent mauve apartment near the Trocadéro, with an enormous buffet and plenty to drink: Zaidee Jackson sang intimate songs; the Berry Brothers danced; Geneva Washington moaned "Tomorrow"; Elizabeth Welch sang; and the guests had a ball while Jack Maze and George McLean played some good stomps. The crowd included the Cullens, Dagmar Godowsky, Cordelia Patterson, Margery Hubbard, Carl Van Vechten, Lydia Burke, Talmadge Wilson, Blanche Howell, Henrietta Dunn, Joseph Attley, Guy Robeson, two counts, and a princess. Novelist Eric Walrond had arrived that very afternoon from London. We are told that Zaidee Jackson topped this with a cocktail party in her Champs-Élysées apartment, with such guests as the Cullens, Walrond, and DeLoach Richardson. The author concluded: "Then on to the Martiniquan ball to complete this week of fun. Here some of our group can do a mean bout of ringing and twisting, along with the Martiniquans doing their delightful dance—the biguine." [20]

When they left Paris, wealthy Afro-American tourists would rush to the Riviera, which was gradually becoming a summer extension of the capital. Not untypical was the gay life of Eslanda Robeson, partying and socializing in 1925 with the "high class" Americans she knew or had met on the way from London to Nice, while her husband Paul was singing or performing.

Mary McLeod Bethune was president of the National Association of Colored Women when she went to France with the National Medical Association European tour in 1927. She conscientiously filled every page of her travel diary, calling the Eiffel Tower the "Alpha Tower," attending a performance by Josephine Baker, and signing many a "gold book" on a tour of the American cemeteries in Flanders and Champagne.

On July 23 she found herself in Nice, jotting down impressions about the more prosperous people at the beaches and resorts, or the scenery glimpsed between the scores of tunnels as she traversed the Alps. But the real surprise was Marseilles, with its vessels going to Africa and all over the world. "Saw many native Africans and dark Frenchmen," she noted, and "the palace where Alexandre Dumas wrote his last book"—a decidedly inaccurate description of the Château d'If! But the "wonderful rose garden" excited her as much as these, or the alleys and crowded streets of the city.[21]

The splendor of Paris, the desolation and American presence on the former battlefields, a hint of black awareness: in many ways Mary McLeod Bethune was a typical American tourist who listed only one French name among her European acquaintances and who felt glad, on July 28, after this "most successful and interesting trip," to "sail back for our beautiful America"—first class, of course, on the SS *Columbus.*

A contact with a French family could make all the difference in the black visitor's discovery of France. In many ways the chapters of *Fifty Years After* dealing with John Paynter's few weeks in Paris in 1936 read like a guide to the architectural treasures of the city, illustrating the saying, "When you have seen Paris, you have seen the world." John Paynter was race-conscious to the point of knowing that Henry Tanner's studio stood at 51, Rue Saint-Jacques, and above all he was lucky enough to stay with educators from Martinique, the Achille family with whom he found "a home radiating from every point of view the cultural influences of the arts and social graces."[22]

Not only was the Achilles' apartment on the Rue Geoffroy Saint-Hilaire facing the Jardin des Plantes (which had delighted Daniel Payne) and in sight of the minaret of the mosque, but the family numbered fascinating music lovers, including Louis Achille, who had been a teaching assistant in French at Howard University, and Paulette Nardal, one of the founders of the *Revue du Monde Noir*, perfectly fluent in English. She took John to many parts of the city, and he attended many musical occasions, including a memorable performance at the Folies Bergères. He left full of gratitude and hope: "Soon, we trust, the Statue of Liberty, gracious symbol of real fraternity, may be known to reflect the ideals and practices of our own beloved America, as indeed has been so pleasurably exemplified through our own happy experience and observation, with the government and people of France."[23]

The most thoroughgoing analysis of the emotional impact of France on a black American at that time is to be found not in contemporary reports or travel diaries but in *Long Old Road*, the autobiography of sociologist and psychologist Horace Cayton, written in the 1960s.[24]

When a Swedish classmate persuaded Cayton to accompany him to Europe, he was already a professional sociologist, had been married to a white woman, and had been published in *The Nation*. Torstein and Cayton arrived in Paris in the spring of 1936; the city was still in an uproar after the attempt by the Croix de Feu to stage a fascist coup. In an effort to consolidate the Popular Front, an international conference of writers had been convened for the "defense of culture," and the two attended it. There Cayton was asked by Mike Gold, the only American delegate he knew, to speak as *"the* American Negro" on the stage, since there was no other present. Thus an official member of the conference, Cayton was able to meet Gide, Dos Passos, and Huxley and to attend a party given by André Malraux, whose *Man's Hope* and *Man's Fate* he greatly admired.

Cayton explored the city with Torstein, one section at a time, walking the streets in the afternoon after having enjoyed not one but two breakfasts at sidewalk cafés where they read the day's newspapers. He even tested what he called the ultimate racial taboo by having his hair cut by a white barber.

Torstein was courting a young Frenchwoman. He left his sweetheart's sister in Horace's care, and Cayton immediately fell in love with her charm and elegance. His depiction of an afternoon they spent chatting outside the Café de la Paix on the Place de l'Opéra makes it clear that it was one of the high points of his stay. Juliette, who could hardly believe he was "un nègre" because of his light skin, appeared to like *café au lait* Negroes and jazz, but not ordinary white Americans; she thought that Parisian women were the most beautiful in the world but greatly admired the golden-brown girls from Martinique; she was attracted to Horace but refused to have dinner with him because it would entail more, and she did not want to complicate her life. The entire afternoon was free of racial tension, and Cayton recorded "an unusual emotion": "I realized with a start that I could compete for any of those women (in Paris) on equal terms with any other man, not just the white French girls but those of any color or culture" (*Long Old Road*, 230). After Juliette left, he experienced a new sense of elation that he linked with the city itself:

I walked down the rue de la Paix to the Madeleine and then down into the magnificent Place de la Concorde where I turned up the Champs Élysées. It was early evening and the air was soft and balmy. Crowds of people were sitting at the numerous terrace cafés on either side of the wide street. Paris was wonderful, Paris was beautiful, Paris was free. . . .

Walking up the broad Champs Élysées, I was just one of a crowd. I felt free and happy as I had never remembered feeling in the United States. (*Long Old Road*, 220–21)

He still wanted to satisfy his curiosity about the girls from the French Antilles: he wondered how a French colored girl would think and behave around white people. One night in a Montparnasse café, one of those beautiful golden-brown creatures entered and ordered a Cinzano at a nearby table. At Horace's request, Torstein, who was fluent in French, invited her for a drink. As introductions were being made, she asked Horace, "What are you?" and in his laborious French, he answered, "A Negro like yourself." To his surprise, "a mischievous expression came over her face. . . . "Non, monsieur, she said, you are wrong, I am not a Negro, I am a Frenchwoman" (*Long Old Road*, 224). Torstein was the one with whom the girl left. Cayton was bemused at having failed to establish rapport on the basis of race, which, in his experience as a black American, superseded any other experience in a colored man's existence. He reflected on the difference between the two cultures: "America had me conscious only that I was a Negro yet France had made this girl, though she was perhaps only a prostitute, feel at home, feel that she belonged" (*Long Old Road*, 225). During the ensuing conversation with Torstein, the subject of his possible expatriation from a country where he was "always a stranger" came up. He might stay in Europe and get a job as a sociologist in Sweden. Yet wouldn't he still be a foreigner? He could never enjoy the pride and assurance in country which the girl from Martinique had; yet he had no choice. "I knew even then that I would go back to America; it was my home and I was stuck with it. In a way I loved it. I was more American than most of its population" (*Long Old Road*, 227).

NOTES

1. Jean Toomer to Mrs. Beardsley, November 1, 1930, Toomer Collection, Fisk University.
2. Toomer to Alfred Stieglitz, July 17, 1924, Stieglitz Collection, Yale.
3. Toomer to Stieglitz, October 7, 1924, Stieglitz Collection.
4. Toomer, "First Ship," Toomer Collection.
5. Toomer to Stieglitz, June 7, 1926, Stieglitz Collection.
6. Edith Taylor Lasell to the author, March 23, 1971.
7. See Cynthia E. Kerman and Richard Eldridge, *The Lives of Jean Toomer* (Baton Rouge: Louisiana State University Press, 1987), 175, 186.
8. John Matheus, interview with author, spring 1972.
9. Walter White to Carl Van Vechten, July 30, 1927, Yale.

10. White to J. W. Johnson, August 16, 1927, Yale.

11. White to Van Vechten, September 17, 1927, Yale.

12. White, *A Man Called White* (New York: Viking, 1948), 94, hereafter cited in the text.

13. White to J. W. Johnson, February 23, 1928, Yale.

14. André Lévinson, "De Harlem à la Canebière," *Les Nouvelles Littéraires,* September 14, 1929.

15. Jacques Lebar, interview with Eric Walrond, in *Lectures du Soir,* January 14, 1933.

16. Eric Walrond, "Harlem," *Lectures du Soir,* February 4, 1933.

17. Many of these details were provided by Professor Robert Bone, letter to the author, December 23, 1985.

18. Joel Agustus Rogers, "How Fares the French Negro?" undated article, Schomberg vertical files, 129.

19. "J. A. Rogers Makes Comparison of French and American Customs," New York *Amsterdam News,* October 19, 1925, Schomburg vertical files, 130.

20. "Beth Prophet Hailed as Artist in Paris," unsigned clipping, Baltimore *Afro-American,* August 3, 1929, Schomburg vertical files. The author was probably J. A. Rogers.

21. Mary McLeod Bethune, diary, July 23, 1927, Amistad Research Center, Bethune file, box 2, 11–12.

22. John Paynter, *Fifty Years After* (New York: Margent Press, 1940), 64.

23. Ibid., 100.

24. Horace Cayton, *Long Old Road* (New York: Trident Press, 1965), hereafter cited in the text.

10

From the New Negro to Negritude: Encounters in the Latin Quarter

Any attempt to trace the contacts and transitions between the ideologies of the Harlem Renaissance and the French Negritude movement would be incomplete without some exploration of the influence, if not the actual presence, of Marcus Garvey among French-speaking blacks. When the Universal Negro Improvement Association was in its heyday, its founder was too busy organizing the Back-to-Africa movement in the United States to visit French-speaking countries. In the mid-1920s, however, *The Negro World,* the organ of the UNIA, attained a circulation of some 200 thousand copies and was disseminated throughout the world by eager sympathizers. Its fiery editorials understandably made European colonial powers uneasy, since pan-Africanism spelled, sooner or later, the end of their empires. As a consequence, *The Negro World* was banned in African, as well as in some West Indian, colonies.

Like most American black leaders, the French black elite opposed Garvey. Blaise Diagne had made it clear: the French natives were French first and black second, and they desired to remain French; none of them wanted to see Africa delivered over exclusively to the Africans.[1] However, Garvey did attract a number of sympathizers— not all of them uneducated or lower-class—in French-speaking countries, notably in the West Indies.

His staunchest supporter in Paris was Kojo Touvalou Houenou, a Dahomean prince who had remained in France after the Great War and established social ties in fashionable Parisian circles. Handsome and sophisticated, the author of a treatise on "The Involution of Metamorphoses and Metempsychoses in the Universe" in 1921, he saw no contradiction in advocating either "absolute autonomy or complete assimilation without frontiers or distinction of race for African colonies." In a lecture delivered in February 1924 at the École Interalliée des Hautes Études Sociales in Paris, he said that Africa should be developed for the benefit of Africans as well as Europeans. Kojo Touvalou had become disillusioned with the achievements of "civilization"—a farce that could end tragically in mud and blood as it had in 1914. In collaborating with René Maran in the establishment of *Les Continents*, he not only endorsed Maran's denunciation of the abuses of French colonization but intended to use the newspaper to rehabilitate the image of Africa. As one of the founders of the Ligue Universelle pour la Défense de la Race Noire, he emphasized the global dimension of the black diaspora.

It is difficult to determine how far Kojo Touvalou was influenced by Garvey's ideology, but he certainly became an important member of the UNIA hierarchy. He visited the United States in 1924 as a guest of the movement, served as a delegate to its big convention at Liberty Hall, and was appointed "potentate" to replace Gabriel Johnson, who had just resigned.[2] *Les Continents* carried several of his articles on Afro-American culture and politics, with reprints of Garvey's speeches and accounts of UNIA meetings. The prince must have interfered with French colonial policy: not only did he become the victim of slander and therefore was barred from fashionable Paris salons, but he was expelled from France and, upon his return to Dahomey, pressured into severing all ties with the Garvey movement.[3]

Garveyism did not especially appeal to French anticolonialists because they attacked the colonial system through the principles of the rights of man and the workers' international, which made no allowance for racial specificity. French blacks began to question colonization because they considered themselves exploited like many other peoples, not just blacks. Gradually, however, the notion of Negro solidarity emerged. In 1927 the first editorial of *La Voix des Nègres*, the left-wing organ of Lamine Senghor's Comité de Défense de la Race Nègre, was addressed "to all black people in the world" in a brotherly spirit. True, Garveyism avoided the fundamental questions of the social structure of black societies and the essentially capitalistic nature of oppression. But Garvey had raised the issue of race on an international level; by implying that Negro blood required the gathering of an African nation, he was applying the principle of self-determination to a given race. Likewise, Lamine Senghor declared that Negroes "belonged to no European nation and refused to follow the interests of any imperialism."[4] Wasn't there an echo of Garveyism in his desire to get rid of foreign oppression and to consider all blacks as the scattered children of Africa? The fact that the first manifestation of nationalism among French colonials attempted to establish race solidarity throughout the world and to transcend the national boundaries imposed by colonization may be explained by the supranational character of communism, but also by an echo of Garvey's dream. Yet as long as the ideals of political and cultural integration remained valid among French-speaking blacks, race consciousness in the Garvey style had little appeal. In his 1927 story "The Blues of Osceola Jones," Langston Hughes alluded to blacks in Paris spending countless hours discussing Garvey, Picasso, and Spengler's *Decline of the West,* with the implication that they were wasting their time.

Moreover, there would be an additional and important difference between Garvey's ideas and those of younger French West Indians like Aimé Césaire and Léon Damas: Garvey had glorified race, but he never doubted the superiority of American civilization. His doctrine of the self-made black man was not opposed to U.S. capitalism, and his aim largely consisted of redeeming Africa from primitivism. Césaire and Damas questioned Western values radically: true, both condemned cultural assimilation and asserted their blackness, but the Marxist analysis of oppression was equally important in their perspective.

Marcus Garvey himself was always lenient in his criticism of French colonization. He admired the nationalistic elan of Joan of Arc and revered Napoleon. When criticizing colonialism, he always spared the French and preferred to make Belgium the target of his attacks. After his deportation from the United States, he attempted to re-establish a European organizational network for the UNIA, but only a handful attended a meeting at the Albert Hall in London in 1928. In Paris, where he met with French Negro groups in April of the same year, he claimed that he had cemented a working plan to carry out the ideals of the UNIA.[5] He was overconfident, however; nothing came of these contacts.

René Maran, who had been sympathetic to Garvey's pan-Negro perspectives at the outset, was quick to dissociate himself from his racialism. After seeing him at the Club du Faubourg, where French intellectuals had invited Garvey to speak, Maran wrote to Alain Locke that he had met "that obscure visionary, the most illustrious Marcus Garvey." He had even risen after the lecture to contradict Garvey, who, "in spite of some applause, had not aroused much sympathy."[6] Maran, born in 1888 in Martinique and educated in France, later became a colonial service official in Oubangui-Shari, where he found the locale and the material for *Batouala.* When this "authentic Negro novel" won the prestigious Goncourt Prize in 1921, the Afro-American press devoted much talk to such outstanding black success. Although prim Jessie Fauset refused to translate it, lest her genteel family stop speaking to her after reading such coarse sensual descriptions, Knopf brought out the book in 1922, and the leading papers soon carried favorable reviews of it.

The book was discussed in *The Negro World*, the UNIA newspaper, not one but six times. Mary White Ovington and Joel A. Rogers read the novel in French, and Ovington praised its depiction of "a grossly sensuous tribe held in subjection by a brutal government" as an unrivaled description of the horrors of imperialism.[7] In the March 25, 1922, issue Hurbert Harrison emphasized Maran's strong denunciation of French colonial rule. On July 1 the newspaper carried a piece by G. M. Patterson, who saw *Batouala* as "something to awaken consciousness of the group everywhere," and on July 29 young Eric Walrond characterized the novel as "a series of poetic jungle pictures around which is built a story of dramatic interest. As for himself, J. A. Rogers lauded what he construed as Maran's pro-Negro propaganda in his bold portrayal of a heroic and magnificent African protagonist.[8] On October 28, 1922, William Ferris appreciated that "Maran's ideas of the harshness and severity of the French rule in Equatorial Africa are not consciously forced upon the reader but are revealed naturally in the course of the story.[9] Finally, Alain Locke himself dealt at some length with the book in an article on "The Colonial Literature of France"; he insisted that its genuine art was combined with a quest for veracity at all costs.[10] The praise of Maran's novel by the Garvey press was a sign of its powerful impact on the Afro-American literary scene in the early 1920s. Admittedly, Maran's journalistic association with Prince Kojo Touvalou, himself a fervent Garveyite, might have explained such partiality on the part of *The Negro World* had it taken place at a later date, but not that early; besides, many other leading Afro-American journals also carried favorable evaluations of the book.

Significantly, on March 24, 1924, Charles Waddell Chesnutt wrote Benjamin Brawley that he had read and liked *Batouala*. *He* especially enjoyed the treatment of natural objects and of animals, but he also approved of the "rather gruesome and gloomy picture" of conditions and customs that "the French domination [had] as yet hardly removed."[11] And as a race brother he felt that he shared Maran's triumph. The first piece by Maran to appear in *Opportunity* was a courteous rebuttal of Alain Locke's praise of the French command's treatment of black troops in his "Black Watch on the Rhine," a reply to the slanders disseminated by the Germans about Negro soldiers; Maran differed with Locke and exposed forced participation of African "volunteers" as well as the sellout of African deputies condoning colonial exploitation.[12] Locke had just been elected a foreign member of the French

Académie des Sciences Coloniales and his visit to Paris in the summer of 1924 sealed the friendship of the two men, who, ideologically and aesthetically, agreed far more than they differed.

After reading *Batouala* Countee Cullen was inspired to write "The Dance of Love," a poem celebrating primitive black beauty and grieving over the sufferings of Africa. He asked Langston Hughes, who was going to Paris, to get Maran's poetry for him; consequently, Hughes met the now-famous novelist and Prince Kojo Touvalou as well. They talked a great deal on several occasions, and Hughes wrote that he planned to visit Maran often, if only to practice his French. He also asked Cullen to send poems for publication in *Les Continents*.[13]

Indeed, the September 1, 1924, issue of the newspaper carried the very first hint of the program and achievements of the New Negro movement to reach a French-speaking audience—a short piece by Locke on "New African-American Poetry." It mentioned McKay, Toomer, Hughes, and Cullen and announced that the movement would deepen and expand Negro culture. Again in December 1925 in *Vient de Paraître* Maran called attention to the "Mouvement negro-littéraire aux États-Unis": this time, in addition to Cullen and Hughes, Jessie Fauset and Walter White received special notice. Several articles by Maran did appear in Afro-American magazines, but in spite of the efforts of Locke, Gwendolyn Bennett, and Mercer Cook, all the plans to translate his *Djouma* (an excellent novel with a dog as protagonist) and his later works failed. Meanwhile, Maran commended the achievements of Afro-American writers in French magazines and persuaded Plon to publish a translation of Walter White's *Fire in the Flint*. He tried repeatedly to have the *New Negro* anthology translated into French, but publishers balked at its size and only Locke's introduction to it appeared in *Europe*.

Most black American writers visiting France in the 1920s and 1930s stopped at Maran's very modest "salon"—not only Cullen, Hughes, and Locke but also Claude McKay, Walter White, Gwendolyn Bennett, Carter Woodson, Jessie Fauset, Mercer Cook, W. E. B. Du Bois, J. A. Rogers, and John F. Matheus. Maran's eminence in French literary circles placed him at the center of a small group of French-speaking black students, writers, and intellectuals. He felt it a personal duty to promote the literary works of his race brothers; he thus became an enthusiastic propagandist of the New Negro movement in its various guises and a direct link between English-speaking and French-speaking groups.[14]

Maran also supported the efforts of the Nardal sisters to carry on the commitment of the short-lived *Les Continents* and to publicize black cultural achievements in order to rehabilitate the image of Africa and the Negro. Paulette Nardal and her sister Jeanne had arrived in Paris in 1928 and—with the help of several West Indians, especially Doctor Sajous from Haiti—had been able to manifest their newly found race pride by publishing, from 1930 to 1932, the well-designed bilingual magazine *La Revue du Monde Noir (The Review of the Black World)*. While still in Martinique the Nardal sisters had espoused the assimilationist views of their middle-class mulatto environment. They saw themselves as French. But the paternalistic or ethnocentric attitudes of Parisians, who saw them as exotic females in the style of Josephine Baker, convinced them of white cultural chauvinism and intensified their own racial pride. They set out to vindicate black achievements and contributions to world civilization; at the same time a sense of solidarity deepened their diasporic perspectives. The first editorial of the magazine read:

OUR AIM

The triple aim which *La Revue du Monde Noir* will pursue will be: to create among the Negroes of the entire world, regardless of nationality, an intellectual and moral tie which will permit them to better know each other, to love one another, to defend more effectively their collective interests and to glorify their race.

By this means, the Negro race will contribute, along with thinking minds of other races and with all those who have received the light of truth, beauty and goodness, to the material, the moral and the intellectual improvement of humanity.[15]

In the last issue of *La Revue,* in a long piece entitled "The Awakening of Race Consciousness," Paulette Nardal herself went over the ground covered since its inception. She paralleled its blossoming in the United States and in France: in France, where the atmosphere was more liberal and open, black consciousness had taken more moderate forms, while black American revolt was more explicit, as exemplified by the New Negro movement: "Quite different was the situation among the American Negroes. Though they are not of pure African origin either, the deliberate scorn with which they have always been treated by white Americans, incited them to seek for social and cultural pride in their African past."[16]

She thought literature had forsaken the romantic, imitative poetics of *Les Cenelles* and become the vehicle of debate and protest; the impact of Garveyism, the first Pan-African Conference in Paris, and the launching of *Les Continents* and of Maurice Satineau's newspaper *La Dépêche Africaine* were so many steps toward a new awareness. It

was patent in the desire of West Indian and African students to com-
plete Sorbonne M.A.s on Negro topics. Louis Achille was writing on
Paul Laurence Dunbar, Senghor on Baudelaire's black mistress, and
Paulette Nardal herself on Harriet Beecher Stowe. Also, most of the
contributors to the *Revue* were French West Indians of color: René
Ménil, Madeleine Carbet, Louis Achille, René Beaudza, Jules Mon-
nerot from the Antilles; Colonel Nemours, Doctor Sajous, and Jean
Price-Mars from Haiti; Félix Eboué and Léon Damas from Guyana.
But many Afro-Americans were represented as well: Countee Cullen;
Claude McKay by an excerpt from *Banjo,* "Spring in New Hampshire,"
and "To America"; Langston Hughes by "I Too Sing America"; John
Matheus by "Fog"; Walter White by the lynching scene in *The Fire
in the Flint.* Jessie Fauset, Margaret Rose Martin, and Clara Shepard
(who translated every text with Paulette Nardal) also contributed. As
a result, young French-speaking blacks were exposed to the note of
militancy present in the Harlem Renaissance "New Negroes" and a
kind of pre-negritude perspective prevailed more and more—not only
an attempt to persuade the world of the value of black contributions
but a glorification of the specific gifts of the black folk. An article by
Louis Achille on Negro dances and artistic propensities even came
close to projecting, years before Senghor's often-quoted phrase, an
image of the "dancing Negro" somewhat opposed to the cold, rational,
body-conscious stance of the Western white.[17]

Indeed, the actual exchanges between black American writers in
Paris and French-speaking writers and students from French Africa
and the Antilles were somewhat limited; they took place mostly between the Nardals and visitors like Cullen, Mercer Cook, the Whites,
and Locke or between Louis Achille and the academics of Howard
University in 1931 and 1932. Later, Aimé Césaire was introduced to
the works of Sterling Brown by Edward Jones, while Léon Damas associated with Mercer Cook and Langston Hughes from 1937 to 1938.
As for Senghor, he met most of the Harlem Renaissance luminaries
only after the war. Literary and intellectual exchanges went mostly
one way—from Harlem to Paris, from the New Negro to negritude,
largely through the dissemination of black American works in anthologies like Eugene Jolas's *Anthologie de la poésie américaine contemporaine,*
in journals like *Maintenant, Age Nouveau, Vient de Paraître, Cahiers du
Sud, Commerce, Europe,* and *Mesures,* and through the translation of half
a dozen full-length books: White's *Fire in the Flint,* Hughes's *Not without
Laughter,* and most of McKay's fiction.

Of all the writings by Afro-Americans of the Harlem Renaissance
available to French-speaking blacks, the most influential was undoubt-

edly Claude McKay's novel *Banjo*.[18] This work not only depicted relationships between the races but analyzed in detail the disputes, as well as the solidarity, within the black diaspora. It also attempted to rehabilitate the primitive versus so-called civilization. To French West Indian and African students unsure of their identity and of their choices among the offerings of the West, it provided a path to reflection, if not always an answer. As DuBois put it, by that time McKay had become "an international Negro" and was able to philosophize about the whole thing.

One of the first illusions McKay dispelled was that of the lack of French prejudice against blacks, even though Africans intent on assimilation insisted it did not exist. The second illusion was that of race solidarity among Negroes. On the one hand, a sharp line existed between the masses and the intelligentsia, and McKay claimed that the former possessed "more potential power for racial salvation than the Negro literati" (*Banjo*, 222). On the other hand, the narrator in *Banjo* makes it clear that the colored population of Marseilles is divided into well-defined segments: at the top the natives of Martinique and Guadeloupe, "regarding themselves as constituting the dark flower of Marianne's blacks, made a little aristocracy of themselves" (*Banjo*, 45). At the bottom the West Africans, inaccurately called Senegalese, despised by all, while the natives of Madagascar and the islands of the Indian Ocean, the North African Negroes (themselves despised by the pure Arabs) fall somewhere in between. This general stereotyping of the different groups of French colonials according to geographical origin is compounded by the general belief among those colonials that they are Frenchmen first, hence superior: "On meeting a French West Indian, Ray would sometimes say he was American, and the other, like his white compatriot, would not be able to resist the temptation to be patronizing. 'We will treat you right over here. It is not like America'" (*Banjo*, 135). Some, however, like the Senegalese owner of the bar where the Vieux Port Negroes love to congregate, believe that in spite of discrimination and lynchings blacks are better off in the New World because they know exactly where they stand, while the French "had a whole lot to say, which had nothing to do with reality" (*Banjo*, 73).

What corresponds most closely to the French African's sense of his own traditional identity is McKay's attempted rehabilitation of the "noble savage," stressing primitivism in a positive manner heralding Senghor's definition of negritude as the "sum of values of the black world" (i.e., those values opposed to, or crushed by, Western culture). "Civilization" had uprooted and transported the natives, the better to exploit them, and its "general attitude towards the colored man was such as to rob him of his warm instincts and make him inhuman"

(*Banjo*, 163). Forced to choose between the rational values of the West and the spontaneous emotions ascribed to blackness, McKay tended to cast the Negro in the mythical guise of soon-to-come negritude—the dancing, feeling, soulful man. This was also a projection of the African's dilemma, since "only within the confines of his own true world could he be his true self," while the white man made him "painfully conscious of color and race" (*Banjo*, 163). McKay claimed that a black intellectual was uncomfortable standing watch over his native instincts in order to partake of Western civilization, but Ray, his mouthpiece, resolves that "civilization would not take the love of color, joy, beauty, vitality and nobility out of his life and make him like one of the poor mass of pale creatures. . . . Rather than lose his soul, let intellect go to hell and live instinct!" (*Banjo*, 164).

When the novel came out in France in 1932, in a translation by communist writer Paul Vaillant-Couturier and his wife, Ida Treat, reviews were largely favorable, in contrast to André Lévinson's indictment of the original publication in 1929. The left-wing critics commended McKay's denunciation of economic oppression and racism; some amateurs of exoticism even found some of their special perspective in the colorful descriptions of Marseilles's underworld and bawdy life. Jacques Roberti, whose *A la belle de jour* had just been published, denouncing brothels as a capitalist institution, wrote McKay to praise his "deep and wide-ranging book on the red-light district." He continued: "More than one reader of it will restrain his admiration for the Colonial Exhibition where the evil deeds and crimes and most sordid appetites of the 'great nations' are hypocritically donning the mask of civilization."[19]

The responses of French-speaking blacks, however, were far more significant. To them *Banjo* was primarily an important contribution to the political, social, and ideological analysis of their own plight, be they African or West Indian, subjects or citizens of France. To many it was an eye-opener. As early as 1930, even before the novel was considered for translation, the *Revue du Monde Noir* carried a long excerpt. The magazine had already printed "To America" and "Spring in New Hampshire," and McKay had already been hailed as a poet, notably for the force and restraint of "If We Must Die." But the impact of his questioning the right of so-called civilization to dispose of so-called primitives was enormous. Again in 1932, when a group of Afro-Caribbean students, breaking with the moderate tone of the *Revue*, violently denounced cultural assimilationism in the poetry of their elders, their reference and inspiration was the literature of the Harlem Renaissance. Étienne Léro claimed that "the wind that blows

from black America will soon manage, let us hope, to cleanse our Antilles of the aborted fruit and of an obsolete culture. Langston Hughes
and Claude McKay, two revolutionary black poets, have brought us,
marinated in red alcohol, the African love of life, the African joy of
love, the African dream of death."[20]

In June 1932, after the *Revue du Monde Noir* had folded, Étienne
Léro, René Ménil, and Jules Monnerot from Martinique published a
new review, *Légitime Défense*. Politically, they leaned toward the Third
International, and aesthetically they were interested in surrealistic experiments that glorified the primitive. The only issue of the review
carried Léro's poem "Pour une vierge noire," which read like a tribute to McKay's "Harlem Dancer," a translation of which had appeared
that same year in *Age Nouveau*. An excerpt from *Banjo* was used to
criticize those assimilated French West Indians who acted as though
they were white. The episode deals with a Martiniquan student who
refuses to enter the café kept by a Senegalese because he is afraid of
demeaning himself by associating with Africans. He approves of the
banning of *Batouala* in the colonies, because he sees it as an indictment of France's civilizing mission. Clearly, McKay's message had been
heard, and it spelled the first step toward negritude: no enduring cultural renaissance could occur unless it went back to the folk. There
may have been some ambiguity in McKay's appeal to French-speaking
blacks because the French translations of his novel exaggerated his
class perspective. For instance, "imperial conquest" was rendered as
"imperialist conquest," "the great army of our race" became "the great
army of the workers of our race," and "folks" was "the people" or "the
proletariat."[21] As a result, McKay could, somewhat inaccurately, be
included by Léro among "the revolutionary poets."

When in 1935 Léopold Senghor and Aimé Césaire founded
L'Étudiant Noir, a newspaper for black francophone students, they tried
to foster pride in what Césaire called *l'esprit de brousse* (the spirit of the
bush) in terms close to Ray's vindication of the primitive:

> Ray . . . always felt humble when he heard the Senegalese and other
> West African tribes speaking their own languages with native warmth
> and feeling.
> The Africans gave him a positive feeling of wholesome contacts with
> racial roots. They made him feel that he was not merely an unfortu-
> nate accident of birth, that he belonged definitely to a race weighed,
> tested, and poised in the universal scheme. Short of extermination by
> the Europeans, they were a safe people, protected by their own indige-
> nous culture. Even though they stood bewildered before the imposing
> bigness of white things, apparently unaware of the invaluable worth of

their own, they were naturally defended by the richness of their fundamental racial values. (*Banjo*, 320)

According to Edward A. Jones, then a student in Paris, the group of
L'Étudiant noir encouraged the emulation of Afro-American writers
like McKay. Jones recalled: "The concept of negritude . . . was influenced by black consciousness writers in the United States. It was the
rebirth of pride in color and solidarity in suffering." [22]

Half a century later Aimé Césaire remembered the message of "If
We Must Die," and he stated that he had "been struck by *Banjo* because for the first time one could see black people depicted truthfully,
without complexes or prejudice." [23] And Léon Damas chose

> Be not deceived, for every deed you do
> I could match, outmatch: Am I not Afric's son
> Black of that black land where black deeds are done

as an epigraph to his poem "Hiccups," which expressed disgust at
Western civilization.

Léopold Senghor repeatedly emphasized McKay's role as an eye-
opener to his generation. Admittedly, Senghor's version of negritude,
in contrast to Césaire's, placed the emphasis less on the people as proletariat than on "the folks," and this made him even more indebted
to McKay. One can easily see how Ray's repudiation of the mercantile
spirit, his disquisitions on white lack of emotional warmth and bodily
harmony, his glorification of the artistic gifts of the Negro as dancer
and singer may have appealed to Senghor. In addition to *Banjo*, *Home
to Harlem* and *Banana Bottom* were translated into French in the early
1930s; the last exalted the harmonious existence of the black peasant versus urban mass civilization and artificial "educated" behavior.
Such importance granted to the earth could not but comfort Senghor
in his glorification of the umbilical relationship of the African peasant to the soil. At the same time Senghor somewhat mistakenly saw
the black American as "the one who had been able to withstand all
attempts at economic enslavement and 'moral liberation.'" [24] Just like
McKay, he valued the fresh, fanciful behavior of the type represented
by the beach boys in *Banjo* as compared to the narrow-minded approach of the white bourgeois, the "square" quite unable to "dance."
Hadn't McKay written, "From these boys he could learn how to live,—
how to exist as a black boy in a white world and rid his conscience of
the used-up hussy of white morality. . . . A black man even though educated was in closer biological kinship to the swell of primitive earth life.
And maybe his apparent failing under the organization of the modern

world was the real strength that preserved him from becoming the thing that was the common white creature of it" (*Banjo*, 322).

The works of Aimé Césaire, Léopold Senghor, and Léon Damas—the founders of the negritude movement—did not reach a sizable French audience until the late 1940s. An early version of Césaire's *Cahier d'un retour au pays natal* appeared in a little magazine, *Volontés*, in 1939; another version came out during the war in the still more confidential, New-York-based *Hemispheres*, but the full-length poem became widely available only in the 1947 Bordas edition, with a glowing preface by surrealist André Breton. Senghor's own verse, *Hosties noires* and *Chants d'ombres*, came out after the liberation of France at about the same time as his anthology of Negro-African poetry introduced by Jean-Paul Sartre's famous "Black Orpheus." Only Damas, whose *Pigments* appeared in 1937, really stood a chance of becoming known before he had completed his anthology, *Poètes noirs d'expression française*, in 1947.

Those writers did not fail to acknowledge their kinship with Afro-American poets and the inspiration they derived from the New Negro movement. Damas, for instance, quoted McKay to introduce *Pigments*, and he chose the title "Blues" for his celebration of primitivism. Césaire paid tribute notably to Langston Hughes and Sterling Brown, whose strong feeling for the folk he shared, but also to Jean Toomer and James Weldon Johnson, in his impassioned "Introduction to Negro American Poetry" in the 1941 issue of *Tropiques*. He claimed they had rehabilitated "the everyday and commonplace Negro, whose grotesque appearance and exoticism an entire literary tradition is entrusted with pursuing": they "depict him earnestly, passionately . . . suggesting even the deep forces that command his destiny."[25] A few years later his poetry collection *Soleil, cou coupé* celebrated black survival in "Mississippi" or followed syncopated rhythms in "Blues de la pluie." He acknowledged that the Harlem Renaissance writers had helped him initiate the concept of negritude and understand that there existed Negro groups other than those in the French West Indies.[26]

Léopold Senghor was still more intent upon making known his reverence for the Afro-American cultural vanguard. Dedicated to Mercer Cook, his poem "To the Black American Soldiers" celebrated the Afro-American fighters in World War II and extolled the kinship of race and culture across oceans. Later, after his first visit to the United States, he would evoke Harlem and write:

Listen, New York, listen to your brazen male voice, your
vibrant oboe voice, the muted anguish of your tears
falling in great clots of blood
Listen to the far beating of your nocturnal heart, rhythm
and blood of the drum, drum and blood and drum.[27]

Just after the war Senghor made a point of translating poems by
Hughes, Toomer, and Cullen for a French-speaking audience. In his
introduction to this selection, he stressed the energy and sense of
rhythm of that "poetry of the peasant that has not lost touch with
the telluric forces."[28] He also quoted Hughes's pronouncement about
younger Negro poets intending to express their dark-skinned selves
regardless of audience expectations.

It would take another decade for the major works of the negritude movement to reach an English-speaking audience in spite of
the unflagging efforts of anthropologists Arna Bontemps and Langston Hughes, and those of Mercer Cook through translations, essays,
and reviews. In the early 1960s the action of Hughes, Cook, Samuel
Allen, and other organizers of the American Society of African Culture, founded as a result of the 1956 Paris conference of Negro artists
and writers, managed to popularize the poetry and perspectives of
negritude. Greatly inspired by the Harlem-based New Negro movement, they themselves were recognized as forerunners of the "black is
beautiful" concept.

NOTES

1. Blaise Diagne, quoted by David Cronon, *Black Moses* (Madison: University of Wisconsin Press, 1955), 72, 128.

2. Claude McKay, *Harlem: Negro Metropolis* (New York: Dutton, 1940), 168–
69.

3. Theodore Vincent, *Black Power and the Garvey Movement* (Palo Alto, Calif.:
Ramparts Press, 1975), 158; see also *Negro World*, June 4, 1927; and J. Lang-
ley, "Panafricanism in Paris, 1924–1936," *Journal of Modern African Studies*
7 (April 1, 1969).

4. Lamine Senghor, editorial, *La Voix des Nègres* (January 1927), 1.

5. Marcus Garvey in *Negro World*, August 4 and 11, 1928, quoted by J. Lang-
ley, "Panafricanism," 412.

6. René Maran to Alain Locke, October 23, 1928, Howard University
Library.

7. Mary White Ovington, in *Negro World*, March 4, 1922, quoted in Tony
Martin, *Literary Garveyism* (Dover, Miss.: Majority Press, 1982), 96.

8. G. M. Patterson, Eric Walrond, and J. A. Rogers in *Negro World*, quoted
in ibid., 97, 98.

9. William Ferris, in *Negro World,* quoted in ibid., 97.

10. Alain Locke, "The Colonial Literature of France," *Negro World,* December 15, 1923.

11. Charles Waddell Chesnutt to Benjamin Brawley, March 24, 1924, unpublished letter, Howard University Library.

12. See "More about Maran," *Opportunity,* April 1923, 30–31.

13. Langston Hughes to Countee Cullen, July 4, 1924, Amistad Center.

14. Michel Fabre, "René Maran, The New Negro and Negritude," *Phylon* 36 (1975), 340–51.

15. Paulette and Jeanne Nardal, "Our Aim," *La Revue du Monde Noir* 1 (n.d.), 4.

16. Paulette Nardal, "The Awakening of Race Consciousness," *La Revue du Monde Noir,* 6 (n.d.), 36.

17. Louis Achille, "The Negroes and Art," *La Revue du Monde Noir* 1:53–56 and 4:28–31. See my article "Autour de Maran," *Présence Africaine* 86 (2ème trimestre 1973), 165–72.

18. Claude McKay, *Banjo* (New York: Harper and Brothers, 1929), hereafter cited in the text.

19. Jacques Roberti to McKay, September 22, 1931, Yale.

20. Étienne Léro, *Légitime Défense* 1 (June 1932), 12.

21. Discrepancies in the translation of *Banjo* were pointed out by Martin Steins in his monumental dissertation, "Genèse et antécédents de la négritude senghorienne," Université Paris III, 1981.

22. Ernest Jones, "Afro-French Writers of the 1930s and the Creation of the Negritude School," *CLA Journal* 14 (September 1970), 18.

23. Aimé Césaire, inaugural speech to the Eighth Cultural Festival at Fort-de-France, July 3, 1979, quoted by Liliane Kesteloot, *Les écrivains noirs de langue française* (Brussels, 1965), 80.

24. Léopold Senghor, *Liberté,* 25.

25. Césaire, "Introduction to Negro American Poetry, *Tropiques* 3 (October 1941), 42. Translation mine.

26. See Michel Fabre, "Du mouvement nouveau noir à la négritude césairienne," in *Soleil éclaté,* ed. Jacqueline Leiner (Tubingen: Gunther Grass Verlag, 1984), 149–59.

27. Léopold Senghor, "To the Black American Soldiers," in *Selected Poems of Léopold S. Senghor,* ed. John Reed and Clive Wake (Oxford: Oxford University Press, 1954), 78.

28. Léopold Senghor, "Trois poètes négro-américains," *Poésie 45* 23:33.

11

"Making It" in Postwar France

When the United States joined the fighting after Pearl Harbor, hundreds of thousands of black Americans participated, but only a fraction of them went to France on D-Day or after. Conditions in the U.S. forces had changed by 1943; although segregation often prevailed in canteens and clubs, and clashes between black and white soldiers were frequent, the black American troops were not subjected to the same shameful treatment they had experienced in the American Expeditionary Forces in 1917. Moreover, instances of racism had increased in "the country of humanism and freedom."

Hugh Mulzac served in the U.S. navy during the war, plying the Mediterranean on a troop transport after French North Africa had been liberated. In his memoir, *A Star to Steer By*, he noted that at the Ferryville docks Jim Crow was frequent, not only in the U.S. forces but in the French army as well: "En route we saw one of the most amazing sights of the war—Algerian soldiers digging irrigation ditches under German guards! The French, colonialists to the end, knew they could trust the captured Nazis more than their own Algerian troops!"[1] This infuriated the crew of the *Booker T. Washington* (which Mulzac commanded) so much that they organized a party for the Tunisian trade unionists in Ferryville and contributed a sizable sum to the Algerian resistance movement. They also battled Jim Crow at the Red Cross canteens: when both races shared one club, whites enjoyed the facilities on alternate days from blacks. The French hostesses were absolutely free from antiblack prejudice, but Arabs were a different matter. A group of French mothers and chaperones, who were quite willing for their charges to jitterbug the night away with black Americans, once got very angry because a Negro GI brought an Arab girl to the club: "Either the girl had to leave, they insisted, or they would never come back" (*A Star*, 208).

In November 1944 Mulzac returned to Marseilles, where he had often called in the past: "Before the war it had been the second largest city of France and its second most charming. Gay, lively cafes had lined the boulevards, and in the center of the city along the old harbor, boatmen used to beg the visitor to ride out to the Chateau d'If, legendary site of Dumas' famous tale, *The Count of Monte Cristo.* Lovely restaurants beckoned, each with its special bouillabaisse, and near the city was an open-air amphitheater where on soft summer evenings it was possible to sit on a rock promenade and listen to some of the finest opera stars in Europe" (*A Star,* 213). Now Marseilles was a shattered port with over fifty hulls resting on the harbor bottom, evidence of the battle and bombing still fresh on the buildings and shattered quays: "Yet the city was already trying to recapture its prewar gaiety; flower-vendors were again selling their delicate blossoms, a few ancient but sprightly French taxis sped along the boulevards, and the restaurants were desperately trying to convert their meager commodities into the epicurean delights that had once made the city famous and would again" (*A Star,* 213). The sailors often took the train to Nice on weekends or stopped in the little villages along the Riviera.

Although Ralph Ellison did not visit France much, he shared the fascination it exerted on many black Americans. He recalls it began when he was barely four years old, on the day his favorite cousin returned, in soldier's uniform, from fighting in the Great War: "He arrived home with his duffle-bag filled with photographs and trophies and proceeded to regale everyone with vivid accounts of the broad social freedom he'd known in Paris."[2] As a teenager he too aspired to visit Europe and end up with those who shared the "moveable feast" of the Left Bank. He read French novelists, discovering *Jean-Christophe* by Romain Rolland on his own at Tuskegee Institute and, a little later, Antoine de Saint-Exupéry. André Malraux, whom he saw but once when Malraux had come to New York to raise money for the Spanish Loyalists, taught him more than many other writers by his fiction and his writings on art.

About the same time as Hugh Mulzac, Ralph Ellison was able to go to Europe and to witness the French battlefields after D Day. While working on *Invisible Man* in a Whitfield, Vermont, barn, he wrote Richard Wright about his desire to assert his independence of thinking and to speak, like him, "on the wavelengths of the human heart as a station getting its power from the mature ideological dynamo of France and the Continent."[3] He had already spent some time in Wales during the war, when he served in the merchant marine, and he movingly recalled his first glimpse of war-torn France:

> Aircraft carriers against the spires and gleaming domes, what a picture! It's part of the larger picture I saw sailing down the Seine on top of a load of ammunition in a ship armed to the teeth, and saw the wrecks

of Tiger tanks lying near the bomb-shattered walls of the cathedral of Rouen and the topsy-turvy streets near the square dedicated to Joan of Arc and bombers over the fields of Normandy such as Van Gogh painted and over the beautiful, well-tilled hills where Flaubert saw the rains and mists come down when he wrote *Madame Bovary*.

I saw the bombed buildings of London without a qualm—except, of course, for the human victims; what are the symbols and monuments of Britain to me that I should feel a sense of loss? But in France, it was different, even the negative symbols contain enough of their lost vitality to make one regret he failed to get there sooner. Certainly, it provided me a new perspective through which to look upon the U.S. and, brother, the view is frightful.

Ellison's evocation of France reflected both his reverence for her culture and his admiration for numerous writers of the great tradition. Several times after the war he hinted at revisiting France. But by 1953 his enthusiasm had cooled off, because he was getting tired of black Americans "running over for a few weeks and coming back insisting that it's paradise." "So many of them," he remarked, "talk and act like skulking children and all they can say about France with its great culture is that it's a place where they can walk into a restaurant and be served."[4] His problems were not primarily problems of race but of writing, and he could not believe that a trip overseas would magically solve them.

He stopped in Paris, however, on his way back from a trip to Madrid in October 1954, sharing his enthusiasm with Langston Hughes, to whom a postcard of the open-air bookstands on quai de la Tournelle proclaimed, "Paris is wonderful." But, Ellison pursued, so was Madrid, because it had not only great art but bullfights as well.[5] Talking with a boyhood friend of Lorca's, hearing flamenco with a small party, seeing Escudero dance had been worth the whole trip.

In 1955 Ellison accepted a fellowship to spend a year in Rome. He made it very clear to journalists that he was by no means an expatriate of the type to be encountered in the Left Bank cafés. On his way back he again stopped in Paris, visiting Wright, who took him up for lunch at LeRoy Haynes's soul-food restaurant on rue Manuel. By that time *Invisible Man* had come out in translation in Paris, but with a small publisher; it received hardly any reviews and did not attract much attention. Not until it was translated again by novelist Robert Merle and published by Grassett in 1967 did the novel reach the audience it deserved.

As a rule, black GIs were very welcome in France, and they enjoyed mixing socially with the French so much that a good many remained after the war, whether for a few years in order to pursue studies on GI Bill scholarships or to make a living there. There were many interracial marriages, and these couples found life easier in France, which remained the land of social freedom and equality while segregation still obtained in the United States.

Among the black fighters came poet Bruce McMarion Wright. He had grown up in Harlem and graduated in law from Lincoln University before being sent to Europe. He served gallantly in the infantry, earning several decorations, but this did not make an army fan of him. Remembering Normandy, where he had landed in June 1944, he wrote of a hedgerow countryside full of apple orchards brutalized by artillery fire: "Apples and the bodies of cows rotted in the sun. Bees were everywhere and flies formed dark clouds as they scavenged. Cows seemed uncertain as they browsed. Heat, cow-dung, blood, death and noise, in their harsh competition, all have a special stink. In the midst of it all, French farmers, moving as stoics, were seen trampling the huge vats of apples that would make that paralyzing potion known as Calvados. One drink helped all of us to move forwards under optimum sedation of fear, if not immunity, through the soft apple slush, the dung, and the bodies we used to know."[6] "When I Call beyond the Groping," a 1944 poem, evokes such impressions of the broken boughs of "apple-trees / where Norman cows / stumble in their flies and stink" (*Repetitions*, 51), while the poet-warrior wonders who will weave the blossoms into his own wreath. The discovery of France began at Omaha and Utah beaches but included many "diverse things from Sainte-Mère l'Église to Metz" (*Repetitions*, 58). It helped him, in "Journey to a Parallel," to strike a comparison between healthy and earthy "French facts and flesh" and the uptight, Puritan American character of Miss Upjohn, who disapproved of "certain acts." No wonder the poet dedicated his volume to a French woman, Yvette, for whom he wrote two poems, in 1958 and 1966, as a tribute to the magnificent beginnings of their love.

After his return in 1946 Bruce Wright pursued a career as a lawyer and also as a poet, publishing *From the Shaken Tower* in 1944 and co-editing the collection *Lincoln University Poets* with Langston Hughes in 1954. After the war he often revisited France, associating mostly with Louis Achille, who had become his close friend. And France continued to inspire his verse. In 1961 he declared: "I write poetry these days only in Europe where it has been my good fortune to be each year since 1958."[7]

"Paris Matins" characterizes the city as a geography lesson as the poet asks questions of each park and descends into the maze of the Métro in quest of answers and remedies. Sometimes Paris is only a backdrop for his scrutiny of the hypocrisy of the incense-laden splendors of Catholicism in order to affirm deeper, though somewhat incongruous, truths. In "I Have Two Sons; God Had But One," the bells of Saint-Germain-des-Prés pealing at Christmastime herald only the advent of dialectical reflection. But "Visitations" represents a real meditation on the black poet's relationship to France and its culture:

> Once we warmed the freezing scene along the Seine,
> Cast our shadows in the gardens of the dead kings.
>
> .   .   .   .
>
> Before we walked through the Luxembourg Gardens
> And its green patterns, just then a little white
> With shallow frost that spread upon its distance,
> And ice frozen in the formal fountain
> To Queen Marie de Médicis.
> Along the ways we read the marble epitaphs
> Hung with brittle blossoms,
> Remarking where and how resisting martyrs
> Occupied the enemies of France.
>
> *(Repetitions,* 28)

As he listens to the voices of English-speaking tourists, his knowledge of recent French history, which he had helped to make, leads Wright to wonder whether they, like him, are aware that the "tortured ashes of Jean Moulin" (the resistance hero) have recently been transferred to the Pantheon, "there to mix with other ghosts / Haunting out the glory which is France" (*Repetitions,* 29).

Samuel Allen was only a budding poet when he came to serve in Europe and remained to study in France after VE Day, occasionally publishing verse in *Présence Africaine* but best known as "Paul Vesey" through his collection *Elfenbeinzähne* (*Ivory Tusks*), which came out in both English and German.

Georgia-born Jimmy Davis was not inclined to be a writer but had studied to become an actor. During the war he had been conscripted and had declared that he would gladly serve his country in an integrated unit, not a segregated one. The selection committee had attempted to declare him unfit for medical reasons, an exemption he staunchly refused to accept. The progressive *PM* magazine decided to support his single-handed defiance of a Jim Crow army, and with the support of such writers as Langston Hughes and Richard Wright, the case of "Private James Davis" was publicized in the press. Davis spent several months in jail before being sent to France, which he saw as his only possible refuge. Meanwhile his artistic abilities were being recognized, and he was allowed to serve as a warrant officer in the position of band leader. He was at Soissons when VE Day was celebrated on May 8, 1945, and, along with a couple of other black American officers, was invited to the home of a French family. While they were feasting, white American officers attempted to teach their host how to treat Negroes—by excluding them—and were thrown out of the house. This convinced Davis that France was a land of freedom and racial equality, and he took advantage of an opportunity offered by the French government: for six months several hundred GIs were housed in French lycées, taught by university professors, and taken everywhere in Paris. In 1946, at the end of the session, Davis went back to the United States, where he studied dramatic art at the First Actors' Group, in Hollywood. He was offered parts in several films, but always those of servants. Disgusted after a few months of daily discrimination in hotels and public places, he decided to settle in Paris for good. There he started a career as performer and singer, becoming famous with the song "Lover Man," to which he owed his nickname. A friendly, soft-spoken person, he manages to live happily on little in his small apartment on the Avenue Reille, occasionally hosting American friends like Hughes on their visits to Paris.

Another black GI who remained in Paris was LeRoy Haynes. He was a student of the arts when he came with the army, and he remained to study on the GI Bill. He soon met a French girl, Gaby, whom he married. She became his partner in an American restaurant in Pigalle that specialized in soul food. The place rapidly became the haunt of many race brothers who had more stories to tell than money in their pockets. LeRoy Haynes himself became a friend of Richard Wright, whose French-American Fellowship Association he joined, becoming its president in the early 1950s. On several occasions he took part in cultural ventures, like the performance of Wright's *Daddy Goodness* by a troupe of amateurs led by Inez Cavanaugh.

The Nazi occupation did not alter the French people's love of jazz; in fact, they considered listening to that musical voice of freedom an act of defiance against the Germans. After the liberation of France, cabarets opened again, this time at Saint-Germain-des-Prés and Montparnasse more than at Montmartre, and black American musicians and entertainers introduced the French to the latest fashions of swing and be-bop. At the celebrated Tabou Club, writer and jazz critic Boris Vian sometimes played the trumpet. Not far from Saint-Germain Inez Cavanaugh, who had come to France in 1946 with Don Redman after being a member of the jazz jury of *Esquire* magazine, sang at the Club du Vieux-Columbier, near the Hotel Cristal on Rue Saint-Benoit, where she lived; later, with a group of musicians she animated the evenings at "Chez Inez" on the Rue Champollion.

As black American muscans and artists resumed their well-established habit of repairing to Paris, not only did they occasionally consort with writers, but they sometimes brought music, art, and writing closer together. Such was the case of Herbert Gentry, one of the first to arrive. Born in Pittsburgh in 1919, he had studied in the WPA art program and was eager to attend the Académie de la Grande Chaumière and the École des Beaux-Arts when he arrived in Paris in 1946, staying first at the Cité Universitaire. In 1948 he married Honey, a white American, and lived on the Rue Wirtz, in the 13th arrondissement. The following year they opened a café–art gallery on the Rue Jean Chaplain, in the heart of Montparnasse, where they displayed the works of young painters. "Chez Honey," one of the first places where American jazz musicians performed after the long break caused by the war, could soon boast many big names whenever they came through Paris: Don Byas, Kenny Clarke, James Moody, Pierre Michelot, and Zoot Simms performed there. Lena Horne made a splendid appearance after having kept her audience waiting for two months. The night Duke Ellington performed, the room was so packed that two mafioso-type toughs, who had previously hinted at payment for "protection," were so cowed at the sight of the crowds that they never reappeared. Other celebrities included singer Jimmy "Lover Man" Davis, the Peters Sisters, and Moune de Rivel, the first black French entertainer to perform in the United States after the war.

Herb Gentry was happy to welcome Richard Wright, who occasionally took Sartre and De Beauvoir "Chez Honey." But he was an artist first, feeling free in Paris, visiting museums, consorting with Romare Bearden, then an art student in the city, and his friend, photographer Gordon Parks. According to Bearden, "Gentry was among those American painters who, beginning in the early 50s, helped introduce the American concept of gesture, free invention, and the vivid dissonance of color to the European sensibilities. The style was then known in Paris as 'the school of the Pacific,' and, in this country, of course, as 'Abstract Expressionism.'"[8] Beginning in 1949 at the Galerie de Seine, Gentry exhibited in numerous shows. "Chez Honey," however, had difficulty competing with an increasing number of night clubs in the area, and in 1953 Gentry returned to the United States.

Other early postwar newcomers to Paris did manage to make careers there, however. New Yorker Gordon Heath had received a strict education from his Jamaican father and had originally trained as a violinist before turning to the theater. His performance in D'Usseau and Gow's Broadway success *Deep Are the Roots* as Brett, a black American soldier in World War II, made him famous, and he first came to London with the troupe in 1947. From there he went to Paris as the assistant and secretary of a wealthy New Englander intent upon researching the French experience of Thomas Wolfe to write a book on the southern novelist. During his first four months in Paris in 1947, Heath actually wrote parts of the text, which was never published. He had been introduced to the nightclub entertainer Moune de Rivel, who ran her club on the Rue du Sommerard, and he started a career as a singer and guitar player. He was popular at "Le Boeuf sur le Toit" and in Left Bank cabarets, but noticed that patrons were more interested in drinking and talking than in listening to the entertainers themselves. He decided to open a place where people would come to really hear him. Thus was launched the Club de l'Abbaye, near Saint-Germain-des-Prés, which was to be a landmark in the Latin Quarter from 1948 until the death of Heath's friend and associate Lee Payant in 1976.

Heath worked as as a comedian and a singer, an "international star," mostly in France and England. He wrote plays, lyrics, and essays while he continued to perform on both radio and TV and the live stage. Until the mid-1950s Heath hardly left Europe. His Left Bank hotel, then the Villa Racine, was a wonderful pension at 36, Rue de Sèvres. He went back to the United States, however, on several occasions, notably to perform in *Faust* (with Lee Payant as Mephisto) in the production by his old-time mentor, friend, and theater teacher, Owen Dodson of the Howard University drama department.

In Paris Heath mixed with black American writers, especially James Baldwin, although he did not share his liking for "La Reine Blanche" and heavy drinking. He occasionally met Wright and William Gardner Smith when they came to his club. Baldwin showed him *The Amen Corner* just after its completion, and he found it the most remarkable first play he had ever read: plans were made for a production, with Heath in the role of the blues man, but they did not materialize. He also read Wright's *Daddy Goodness*, which he did not like much, although LeRoy Haynes's "natural" performance in it was outstanding. Although he had mixed with left-wing writers, actors, and producers, like Dashiell Hammett, Paul Robeson, and Canada Lee, during his New York theater career, Heath was not political and found it somewhat surprising that his fellow blacks needed their bitterness in order to write. As for him, he was striving for human fullness according to the precepts of his mentor, Owen Dodson. He enjoyed France, however, and the fine treatment of black Americans there because of their cultural offerings.

All of these people were to be part of the expatriate group that thrived in Paris in the 1950s—a motley crowd of writers, artists, performers, students, and musicians whose paths crossed and recrossed in Paris. Most of the black American writers who sought refuge in Paris after World War II, however, came not as GIs but as visitors.

One of the very first was Richard Wright. Upon landing at Le Havre in the spring of 1946, he discovered the desolation of war-torn France: "The green-barnacled hulls of ships jutting out of the blue waters of the Le Havre harbor leave no room in any American's mind as to what the war meant to France. Indeed I felt a vague sense of guilt to have come to France when I saw the rubble and devastation of Le Havre. I became conscious of our clean, straight American streets as yet untouched by war. I remembered our complacency, our boasting, our curt dismissal of what we are perhaps too prone to call 'decadent European complexities' with a sense of shame."[9] For years rationing would continue; so did the black market, partly accounting for the coldness of Parisians, confronted with scarcity of food and staples, toward American tourists and visitors, placed in a privileged position, due to the advantageous exchange rate, even when they were not well off. Thus in the early 1950s James Baldwin could note that "Paris was a devastating shock . . . a large, inconvenient, indifferent city. . . . The concierge of the hotel did not appear to find your presence in France a reason for rejoicing; rather, she found your presence and, in particular, your ability to pay the rent, a matter for the profoundest suspicion."[10]
How fared the American Negro in the French imagination at the time? Baldwin's view was not far from the truth when he remarked that the French "consider that all Negroes arrive from America, trumpet-laden and twinkle-toed, bearing scars so unutterably painful that all the glories of the French Republic may not suffice to heal them. This indignant generosity poses problems of its own that, language and custom being what they are, are not so easily averted."[11] Richard Wright likewise noted with astonishment that, as a result of some six years of isolation as well as a "sentimental longing for reality as it once was, glamorous and thrilling," the French still retained a vision of the Negro as he was supposed to be in the Jazz Age; they believed that he possessed "some magic of primitive strength which accounts for his artistic expression, and that some of this primal strength, derived in some mysterious manner from Dark Africa, has actually communicated itself to a few white people and they have thereby become more human and more expressive."[12]

The new rhythm that the American Negro was supposed to have communicated to the whole nation was thought to stem from his being little urbanized, little "contaminated"—hardly an American. Wright ascribed such views to the impact of American movies, which depicted blacks as always laughing, dancing, telling tales, singing the blues, playing jazz music, or humming spirituals. The notion that the more primitive side of the American Negro had protected him from the corruption of white America irritated Wright, who saw himself and his race as embodiments of a bold move from the feudal South to the industrialized, modern North. He contended that the Afro-American was an American, a Westerner, not an African in disguise. In so doing, he not only opposed the hoary myth of the noble savage, but without being fully aware of it, the ideology of negritude that tended to endow the blacks with more soul and humanity than the rational Western white.

In *Return to Black America* novelist and journalist William Gardner Smith later gave several reasons for what he called a sort of exodus of black Americans to Europe after World War II.[13] First, many of them had been active in the civil rights movement but had found their work paralyzed, first by the war effort then by McCarthyism, when any criticism of the status quo provoked accusations of serving communist interests, thus destroying their belief that they could actually achieve their militant aims. Second, as time went on, integration was superseded by the growing awareness that it was perhaps not desirable to "integrate into the enemy." Third, according to Smith the possibility of an imminent nuclear apocalypse inspired some to try and live fully before the end came, mostly by going abroad.

Abroad, the expatriates learned to see the condition of Afro-Americans in general from a new perspective. "Many went in search of a racial shangri-la, a land of equality, a land of justice, where no man would be penalized for the color of his skin" (*Return*, 63). Smith granted that black Americans first found a tremendous détente, a relaxation arising from the relief of shedding the claustrophobia of the ghettos, of mixing freely with whites without feeling threatened by policemen, without wondering whether one would be accepted in a restaurant or a travel group, without anticipating the insult that heralded riot.

Such relaxation of color lines also affected white Americans who were on the defensive due to the anti-Americanism on the Continent. In fact, the American race problem was a sort of psychological godsend to the Europeans: "It permitted them to feel self-righteous and look down on white Americans whose money they envied anyway.

French people pulled black people aside and said: 'Isn't it horrible how they treat you in the United States?' (We often replied: 'Like you treat the Algerians.')" (*Return*, 14). As a result many white Americans, possibly in order to avoid being included among the "they," expressed integrationist views once they had taken up residence in Europe. Before World War II they had reportedly been uneasy—even sometimes infuriated—at the thought of sharing facilities or associating with their black fellow citizens on French soil. After D-Day, especially outside the armed forces, it appeared that white American GIs, students, and visitors, as well as artists and writers, were glad to act individually toward blacks in their new French milieu instead of having to put up a front and follow mass opinion. Most of the ex-GIs and visitors interviewed about this expressed genuine pleasure in having been able to speak with American blacks for the first time, to get to know them without fear of being called nigger lovers by prejudiced acquaintances at home. And several black Americans noted this relaxing change in interracial attitudes between Americans in the Paris setting. Baldwin said: "The Negro's white countrymen, by and large, fail to justify his fears, partly because the social climate does not encourage an outward display of bigotry, partly out of their own awareness of being ambassadors, and finally, I should think because they are themselves relieved at being no longer forced to think in terms of color."[14]

The lack of racial tension in France was due in part to the small number of colored people there, except in Paris. Also the blacks whom the French originally encountered were mostly artists, students, and the like. They were often better off than the French themselves and presented no social problems at the time, while the North African immigrants took the dirty jobs. "In addition," Smith noted, "the Europeans, particularly the French, like to think of themselves as traditionally devoid of prejudice" (*Return*, 64). Nonetheless, the black Americans, like other blacks and most foreigners, lived on the fringes of French society. The friends of the black American were usually the cosmopolitans—artists, musicians, jazz enthusiasts, students, intellectuals: "Their world was a gigantic and more subtle Greenwich Village. Beyond—hazy, distant, and somewhat mysterious—lay the 'real' Europe: the peasants, anonymous clerks and civil servants, the shopkeepers, the conservative middle-class, the hard-pressed workers and their employers. It is among these that the black man began to perceive the foggy outline of his old enemy, racism" (*Return*, 65).

The black American first had difficulty in separating paternalistic attitudes from what he might believe to be his own hypersensitivity: a Frenchman's asking a black American to sing the blues or play jazz did not mean a subtle way of "putting him back in his place" in a snobbish salon but rather a genuine admiration for the people who had brought the world jazz and the blues and a desire to share a highly valued cultural contribution. But the black American also discovered that some hotel managers refused to accommodate blacks, a practice common enough among apartment owners. He noticed that black people were seldom appointed to high positions and were rarely to be found in the middle-income range outside of the professions; they were most visible in low-paid civil service jobs, working for the post office or the hospitals, while nearly all of the garbage collectors and street cleaners were Arabs from North Africa.

Although sexual attitudes were very relaxed in Europe, the majority of parents did not want their children to marry colored people. Some French women and a good number of Latins were especially attracted to blacks, but, Smith reflected, "what was this, but a kind of racism— the vision of the black man as a virile (or passionate) animal, the seeking of erotic pleasure in the 'sin' of contact with forbidden skin? Some blacks in Europe took advantage of this situation but they were rarely duped by it" (*Return*, 57).

As the fifties rolled on, racism was spurred by the arrival of African immigrants and the tensions of the Algerian war. Not only did one find the traditional "U.S. Go Home" chalked on the walls of Paris, but "Les nègres en Afrique" or "Dirty Arabs." Clearly, with the breakup of former colonial empires, the Europeans felt a threat inherent in the rise of colored peoples: resentment combined with fear of further loss of relative status.

Yet it is a fact that black Americans continued to live in and visit Europe. Why? Smith reported a conversation between an American southerner and a French student: the American accurately described the torture of Djamila Bouhared, an Algerian resister, by the French Army after she had planted a bomb in an Algiers café frequented by the French. And the student replied, "Yes, it was terrible . . . but, you know, in your South, she would never have been allowed in that café in the first place" (*Return*, 57). And Smith concluded that the difference between European and American racism was one of degree. Though many landlords might refuse to rent to a Negro, many did not, and nobody on the block would meet the new colored tenant with violence nor would his arrival provoke a mass flight of the neighbors. Besides, the traditional politeness and strong individualism of the French made things easier. Rarely would a Frenchman tell you that he disliked you; to do that would be to show bad breeding. "As for individualism, it had to be seen to be believed. . . . No Frenchman wanted to be like other Frenchmen. . . . This meant it was hard to stampede them into adopting conformist attitudes, including racism. At any rate, there was a relative absence of tension in daily life, regardless of what people might be thinking behind polite exteriors. And the blacks in Europe did not care so much about what people were thinking; white *actions* were what exasperated us" (*Return*, 71).

French attitudes partly resulting from scarcity of staples and food often prompted satirical judgment from visitors. Chester Himes indulged in vitriolic caricatures in his autobiography, deriding the famished guests storming the buffet at the few parties given by his Paris publishers. The image of the stingy Frenchman that Claude McKay evoked in describing the Marseilles seafront or that Langston Hughes retained from his early days in Paris reappeared from the pen of a post–World War II newcomer.

Vincent Carter is one of the few who gave up the idea of settling in Paris because, he claims, of the coldness of people. His case may be seen as an exception, yet his vision of France in 1954, contrasting with the rosy memories he held from the times of Liberation, is quite revealing. Born in 1924, raised in Kansas City, he had served in the army in Europe. Upon his discharge he had pursued his university studies and worked in a Detroit automobile plant to raise enough money to establish himself in Paris, which he had visited at the close of the war. But his disappointment with it soon drove him to Amsterdam and then to Switzerland, where he settled for good and in 1957 completed an autobiographical narrative, *The Bern Book*. It is a journal of his disillusionment that, in his preface, Herbert Lottman calls "this century's *Anatomy of Melancholy*." [15]

In 1945 and 1946 Carter served with the 509th Port Battalion stationed in Barfleur and Rouen, and he had made many French friends in Normandy. He had often stopped in Paris as a layover between journeys and had stayed there days or even weeks at a time. He entertained hopes of a bohemian life in the city: "What a time I had in Paris! How friendly the people were! and the women! where else could one find such delectable creatures? And in April! . . . Was not Paris the center of art? Had not all, virtually all the great writers been there? Heine, Rilke and Hemingway? What succulent agony hadn't Balzac, Hugo, de Maupassant suffered in the Faubourg St. Germain! I'll find myself a crummy little room in the Latin Quarter, I thought, with an old bed, a writing table with a candle. There should be a fireplace gone to pot. I'll eat cheese and drink red wine, smoke hashish perhaps, and write memorable prose. And I'll have a beautiful but decadent mistress whom I shall immortalize in my stories (*Bern Book*, 11).

Upon his arrival at the Gare du Nord, he realized that "the great liberator" he had been was now only a tourist among others, with baggage to be inspected and loaded into a taxi. Finding a moderately priced room proved an insurmountable obstacle. After a good night's sleep, however, Carter decided to walk to the area around Strasbourg-Saint-Denis, where he had once enjoyed fine food and friendly street girls. It was raining, and he could find no trace of familiar establishments. Worst of all, as he trudged through the city in search of a cheap hotel, the receptionists kept him on the run. Was he deluded in believing that he was the victim of racism? He finally found a "crummy little room" in the Rue Monsieur-le-Prince; it opened onto an alcove roofed with a skylight; the whole floor reeked of the toilet; the sheets were damp; and he could not even read the only book he had, Homer's *Odyssey*, by the light of the tiny naked bulb hanging from the ceiling. There was no soap and one had to place a request two days in advance to take a bath in a half-size tub for 150 francs extra. Not to speak of the beds creaking during love-making in nearby rooms, and customers padding barefoot in the passage to and from the toilet.

Carter endured this for a month. In the daytime he walked the streets and visited museums and monuments by himself. He sat alone in restaurants and open-air cafés, speaking only with waiters and shopkeepers, feeling he was being overcharged for nearly everything he bought. He found himself unable to reconcile his disgust and the fact that French culture had played an important part in his education, as he passionately admired Rabelais, Villon, Montaigne, and Rimbaud, French painting and music, and the films of Louis Jouvet. He found the people utterly unsympathetic (though he confessed that he might have felt just as lonely in London or New York), yet in all fairness he recalled at length his only pleasant encounter with a Frenchman. He had just paid for his Pernod in a Latin Quarter bistro and, feeling he had been overcharged, asked the waitress for the price list. As she pretended not to hear, he gave up and left. A young Frenchman in uniform followed him and said he had paid too much for the drink:

> "Sir, I have been doing this since I came to your cursed city. You French are thieves and cut-throats and you ought to be hanged."
> "Oh non!" he exclaimed. "All of the French people are not like that. You really do not know the real French people, Monsieur. Not the ones in the bars and expensive restaurants." (*Bern Book*, 20)

And Corporal Henri Petit, with his arm in a sling after having been wounded in Tunisia, took him home for dinner, to the small room he and his wife shared with a teenage brother at the bottom of a smelly alley in one of the shabbiest parts of the city. They were poor people, and under the glare of the famished young brother Carter could hardly eat the awful-looking soup. Silence prevailed in spite of some attempts at conversation, and Carter talked loudly and smiled very often to hide his embarrassment:

> I think I even convinced them that I had a good time—all except the wife, who knew better. I failed to hide from her serene, moving eyes my embarrassment due to the glaring irony of my obviously prosperous condition as compared to theirs. She read the guilt on my face. As she lowered her eyes I felt the weight of those dreadful traveller's checks in my pocket (over three thousand dollars)—as I sipped the dirty soup and occupied the only chair. I might have given some of it, but I dared not. For the soldier had been right, these were the real French people. My offer could have offended them and made me feel worse than I already did. So I suffered the evening through and managed before I climbed onto the Métro to exact from them a promise that they would join me for dinner the following week. . . . "Au revoir," said the young lady with the courageous eyes, very tenderly and hardly above a whisper, as I boarded the train and sped away, never to return, and never to forget the pathetically beautiful and yet ridiculous scene in which I had played an undistinguished part. (*Bern Book*, 23–24)

NOTES

1. Hugh Mulzac, *A Star to Steer By* (East Berlin, DDR: Seven Seas Books, 1965), 206–7, hereafter cited in the text.

2. Ralph Ellison to the author, January 12, 1989.

3. Ellison to Richard Wright, August 18, 1948, Yale.

4. Ellison to Wright, January 23, 1953, Yale.

5. Ellison to Langston Hughes, October 21, 1954, Yale.

6. Bruce McMarion Wright, "When I Call Beyond the Groping," *Repetitions* (New York: Third Press, 1980), 48, hereafter cited in the text.

7. Bruce McMarion Wright, *Beyond the Blues*, ed. Rosey Pool (Lympne, Kent: Hand and Flower Press, 1962), 183.

8. Romare Bearden, *An Ocean Apart: American Artists Abroad* (New York: Studio Museum of Harlem, 1982), 9.

9. Richard Wright, "A Paris, les G.I. noirs ont appris à connaître et à aimer la liberté," *Samedi Soir*, May 2, 1946, 2.

10. James Baldwin, "The New Lost Generation," *Esquire*, July 1960, 114.

11. James Baldwin, "The Negro in Paris," *Reporter*, June 6, 1950, 35.

12. Richard Wright, untitled draft, 1947[?], Yale University Library.

13. William Gardner Smith, *Return to Black America* (Englewood Cliffs, N.J.: Prentice-Hall, 1970), 63, hereafter cited in the text.

14. James Baldwin, *Notes of a Native Son* (New York: Bantam Books, 1968), 100.

15. Herbert Lottman, preface to Vincent Carter, *The Bern Book* (New York: John Day, 1970), vii. Hereafter *The Bern Book* will be cited in the text.

12

Richard Wright:
An Intellectual in Exile

Young Richard Wright first heard about France as a land of racial equality from black World War I veterans in Mississippi, who recounted their experiences on the battlefields or with the civilian population. The fact that this was a taboo topic made it even more impressive. Later, along with this report of the absence of discrimination, came the idea that France was a cultural cradle where literary achievement was held in reverence. Not only did Alexandre Dumas rank high there, together with Balzac, Flaubert, Théophile Gautier, or De Maupassant, but from Rabelais and Voltaire to Anatole France and Romain Rolland, the French tradition of enlightenment and liberalism was well established, as Wright ascertained by reading the volumes in his own library prior to 1940. Proust he had discovered in Chicago, "stupefied by the dazzling magic, awed by the vast, delicate, intricate and psychological structure of the Frenchman's epic of death and decadence," and had bought the two-volume translation of *Remembrance of Things Past*.[1] Among the younger French writers he admired Henri Barbusse; he agreed with the anticolonialist, pro-Soviet stand of André Gide and saw in André Malraux's *Man's Fate* an outstanding instance of art in the service of the revolution. Aragon's *Red Front* inspired his long poem "Transcontinental" in 1935. It is not strange that he should have been attracted by the racial freedom and cultural creativity associated with Paris to the point of considering a visit there as soon as the success of *Native Son* made it possible. But the war compelled him to wait.

Meanwhile, during the summers of 1944 and 1945 he went to Quebec as the next best thing to Europe, tasting the leisurely ways of the Ile d'Orléans as a symbol of the Old World. In a letter to Gertrude Stein, with whom he exchanged views on life in postwar America and Europe, he contrasted the abrupt, straight lines of New York with the smooth curves of Quebec harbor: "Quebec is slow and ripe and organic and serene. . . . but when one returns to New York one is struck by the hurried, the green and the frantic. . . . In Quebec, man has found a way of living with the earth; in New York we live against the earth."[2]

Serenity and harmony were the features Wright expected to find in France, marked as it was by centuries of humanistic tradition, while Americans were mostly preoccupied with production and consumption, selling and buying—what Wright had denounced in his autobiography as the materialistic values of "cheap trash." Upon discovering Stein's verbal creativity and gift for recreating Negro language, he quickly concluded that one could live and write like that "only if one lived in Paris or in some out of the way spot where one could claim one's own soul. . . . All the more reason why I dream and dream of leaving my native land to escape the pressure of the superficial things I think I know."[3] He was prone to associate Paris with humanism, with an adequate relationship between the individual and his environment, and his expectations along these lines were certainly reinforced by his discovery of the writings of Sartre and Camus. Ralph Ellison had first called his attention to existential theater and Sartre's views of the metaphysical and moral choices implied in art and action—the writer's task "to cast light on the eternal values involved in the social and political disputes."[4] After meeting Sartre during his visit to the United States early in 1946, Wright began to associate France more with the humanistic outlook of intellectuals struggling to provide postwar Europe with a sense of purpose and values and far less with the heritage of an agrarian tradition. He was already convinced that the Old World was in fact not so old as the new.

Going to France, when one was *the* foremost black American writer, was not without implications. Well-meaning friends at first tried to dissuade Wright from making the trip; then—was this due to his having been a communist?—he found out that his passport was not forthcoming. Through the intervention of Gertrude Stein and Claude Lévi-Strauss, he was officially invited by the French government (although none of his expenses were paid by them), with the result that the U.S. officials even asked him to accompany paintings on loan for an exhibition as he sailed first class with his wife and daughter. His very first impressions were recorded by former cultural attaché Douglas Schneider, a friend of Gertrude Stein whom she had sent to meet him at the station, since taxis were scarce in May 1946:

> It was a very fine morning and I offered to drive them to their hotel on Rue de Vaugirard by "le chemin des écoliers." We drove from Saint-Lazare to the Arc of Triomphe, down the Champs Élysées, filled with sun; we drove round the Place de la Concorde and along the Rue de

Rivoli, then across the Gardens of the Tuileries, a gorgeous mosaic of sparkling geranium and gold flowers. Then along the quais, past Notre-Dame and up Boulevard Saint-Michel. Richard Wright was sitting in front by my side. Very talkative at the beginning, he had become more and more silent but I could hear him whisper: "What beauty, my God, what beauty." As we were driving around the square in front of Notre-Dame he turned towards me and said: "Can you imagine what this means to me? I never knew a city could be so beautiful. This is something I shall never forget. Thank you!"[5]

The beauty of Paris struck Wright, who was more conversant with abstract painting and photography than with Gothic architecture, as a quality brought to environment by history and age, a tangible although indefinable proof of a successful civilization. He associated it immediately with culture, with intellectual vitality, and also with the absence of racial pressure: "The city is so wonderful," he wrote at that time, "its intellectual life so vital that I don't think I'll return again soon. I do want to see how these people go about things. It is so good to be somewhere where your color is the least important thing about you."[6] When he confided to his editor, Ed Aswell, that Paris was all he had ever hoped it would be, from beautiful buildings to friendly and confident people, he hardly exaggerated, and his appreciation was wholehearted when he remarked: "There is such an absence of race hate that it seems a little unreal. Above all, Paris strikes me as being a truly gentle city, with gentle manners."[7]

Indeed, Wright was welcomed as befitted one of the leading American writers, since among the French intelligentsia his name was uttered in the same breath as those of Faulkner, Hemingway, Dos Passos, Farrell, and Steinbeck. He was grandly made a "citizen of honor" at the town hall and invited to countless literary cocktail parties, dinners in his honor, meetings of the Société des Écrivains, and publishers' parties. He was introduced to many an intellectual he admired, like André Gide and Albert Camus; he saw Sartre again and met Simone de Beauvoir, as well as Léopold Senghor and Aimé Césaire. Admittedly, the press tended to make each one of his declarations to journalists into a political pronouncement, with the result that he was both attacked by the French communist press as a renegade and used by anti-American propaganda as living proof that the racial question was still a thorn in America's side; he was often quoted as saying that there was more freedom in one block of Paris than in the whole of the United States and accordingly criticized by American nationalists. He was interviewed on the racial situation but even more often on the state of letters and culture in the United States. In short, although

the French press at the time tended to cast him in the role of spokesman for his race, a representative *black* American, he functioned more
often as a committed *Western* intellectual.

His own interests lay in finding out how France, a country less industrialized than the United States, free from the burden of a race
problem and with a tradition of vigorous affirmation of human rights,
could provide an answer to the problem of individual freedom—a
question that, according to him, no group in postwar America had
enough insight to answer, largely because the sufferings and discontent of the masses were kept hidden or left unexplored: "My hopes
for France may very well be wrong. But if such a call, an appeal, a
definition, is not made from here, then I really don't know where it
is coming from in the near future. . . . Before anyone [in the United
States] can even take the attitude that something can be done, he must
sense how the problem is reflected in the hearts of men, how indi-
visible is that problem. The French have a phrase for it: the Human
Condition."[8]

In short, as an intellectual Wright expected nothing less than guide-
lines for the restoration of humanism to a materialism-ridden world.
He felt, or imagined, that the French, more than any other European
nation, realized—possibly on account of the traumas of Nazi occupation—what would be lost in spirit if certain political or social choices
were made. No wonder he could express some disappointment in finding that "everybody [had] a program for everything except the welfare
of the man in the street."[9] French political parties were many, yet they
did not stand for people; institutions and society had hardened into
"corals of stances, statues of ideology, calcifications of intellect,"[10] and
the assembly line was overwhelming individual feelings and relationships. Certainly Wright wanted to hold up a caveat to the American
reader in this magnified image of the ills of his own nation. But to
contend, as he did, that the only spontaneous responses he had found
were in the black market was an exaggerated rendering of even the
gloomiest fears of the French existentialists.

True, Wright arrived in the middle of a difficult economic situation
and a confused political climate: food was rationed, gas was scarce,
and power was turned off for several hours every day; unity against
the Nazi occupation had become an egotistical struggle for survival,
leaving room for little sympathetic feeling for the oppressed anywhere.
However, a vital interest in cultural renewal and in spiritual values
existed among the intellectuals and writers Wright consorted with at
Saint-Germain-des-Prés. With its blend of individualism and tradition, and its search for humanistic answers to the dilemma of having to
choose between the two blocs, the United States and the U.S.S.R., the

general atmosphere was challenging and stimulating. But Wright did not really know the language, and a few months were too brief a time for him to analyze the situation in depth. He was better at reporting American GIs' reactions to the city or the absence of racial discrimination, or at evoking the sights of buildings destroyed and ships sunk in Atlantic harbors. It would take him years to really get deeper into French civilization.

During his first seven-month sojourn there in 1946, Wright's reports on France were more frequently the considerations of an intellectual than the impressions of either a tourist or a resident. When he decided to go back and settle there, his concerns as a future inhabitant tended to focus more on the details of everyday life.

Why did Wright decide, in July 1947, to exile himself and live in Paris? It was assuredly less "to claim his soul," as he had hoped to do in 1946, than to escape the daily humiliations and irritations caused by racism in the United States. Upon his return from Paris several incidents had convinced him that, even though he might be a first-rank American writer and the best-known black novelist, he would remain a nigger for most of his compatriots. In New York discrimination existed to such a degree that Italian neighbors complained about a black man buying a house in Greenwich Village; he was forbidden to use the elevator to visit Sinclair Lewis, who had invited him to lunch at his hotel; and little Julia was barred from using the toilets at the Bergdorf Goodman store on Fifth Avenue. After being feted as an equal by French writers and treated cordially by all the Parisians he had to deal with, he found it no longer possible to have to wonder, each time he made a move, how his white fellow citizens would take it. He decided to exile himself, he said, first to spare his children the humiliations he had undergone, then to be able to write on whatever he might choose without necessarily responding either to the racial situation or to the expectations of others. France he saw at that time as a place where he would feel free—not necessarily as a second home, still less as a mother country, as the dedication of *The Outsider* to "Rachel, my daughter who was born on *alien* soil" made clear. Going to Paris decidedly was an uprooting, as he pondered on July 30, 1947: "I'm leaving my native land with no place to stay that I can call Home; I really have no roof to come back to at all," but coming back there only a week later, on August 8, was a comforting experience: "Coming again into Paris! The sun was just setting and the pale light shone upon the old buildings and revealed their age. How earthy a people are the French! How squat the buildings sit upon the ground! It was like a dream to be riding one's own car into these beautiful Paris streets."[11]

The Wrights had money, friends, a score of trunks laden with their belongings and staples and items unlikely to be available in France. After staying with a friend in the 7th arrondissement, they managed to find an apartment in Neuilly. On the whole, they fared better than many French people and foreign visitors. Yet Wright's personal impressions at the beginning of his exile are a fascinating welter of conflicting responses to a society whose mores at once excited and baffled him as much as Mexico had done in 1940. His impression changed from one day to the next:

> August 13—No hot water yet; it is getting on my nerves. I've not had a bath since I left England [six days ago] except the kind you take with heating water and lugging it up to the bathroom and washing with a rag. And Odette [their French friend and landlady] seems to think that that is not important.
>
> August 14—The Paris sunlight falls sharp and clear outside of my hotel window. How softly it strikes the buildings though the sun is very strong! How these old walls stand the test of time and age, how used and human they look!
>
> August 15—I ate a melon and drank wine and bottled water. My French friends seemed scared because I like to drink water. One told me that it was not too good for me to drink water like that. How queer the French are! We walked home and talked about the political state of the world.
>
> August 18—How calm I've felt here in Paris! No more of that tension that grips so hard. . . . I walk down a street and feel my legs swinging free. I'm much at home this time in Paris; the last time I had to adjust myself. But this time I accept Paris and its quiet charm.[12]

In fact, Wright continued being surprised, at least for a couple of years. We find him by turns appalled by the traffic and careless drivers, by the way adults treat children, by the unbelievable tricks the black market thrives on, but especially by the routine closing of stores and shops for several hours at lunchtime, not counting the whole day on Mondays. He reacts like a hard-working puritan when he remarks that leisure should come only after you have made yourself secure. Sometimes conflicting emotions are registered in the same breath, as after a visit to the open-air market on Avenue de Neuilly: "What a riot of rich life, what people are these French; how unashamed they are to sell and buy; and frank and dirty and frank and woobly are French housewives; how the women went with their breasts trembling and with not a thought of a brassiere. I wandered slowly through it and came out with a keen sense of having been fed at the pap of life itself! What smells! What sights of vegetables, jars, bottles, etc."[13]

One senses delight in his noting how a cultured nation can relish things of the body without hypocrisy, like a primitive people. Yet Wright did not look for the still-more-backward life in the provinces. Although he was to live in France until his death in 1960, he never toured the country extensively: he spent a few days on the Riviera and on the Basque coast; later, several weeks in Corsica, in Corrèze, and a month vacationing in the Alps. The closest he came to going back to the land was in the late fifties when he bought an abandoned farmhouse at Ailly, in Normandy, and not only had it remodeled as a country house but delighted in cultivating vegetables in his garden. However, he remained for the most part a Parisian who needed the intellectual atmosphere of the city.

As soon as he had settled again, he pursued his activities as a committed writer. Starting with "Big Boy Leaves Home," which had appeared in a 1944 issue of the underground review *L'Arbalète*, his works came out quickly in French, notably with Albin Michel and Gallimard publishers but also in the prominent left-wing magazine *Les Temps Modernes*, due to the interest evinced by Jean-Paul Sartre, who wrote passionately about *Black Boy* in "What Is Literature?" He saw Wright as a writer loyal to both his southern origins and his race and yet compelled to address liberal whites—a perfect embodiment of a sort of alienation that allowed him to stand both inside and outside; his autobiography was thus born from "tension between satire and prophetic lamentation. . . . Writing for a split audience, Wright had been able to preserve the split, transcend it and make it the reason for his works of art."[14]

The two men saw much of each other in the late forties: they had dinner together and with Simone de Beauvoir; they attended the same literary and political events; they sometimes stayed up all night talking. On one such occasion Wright remarked that they were of the same opinion regarding the possibility of human action, "that it is up to the individual to do what he can to uphold the concept of what it means to be human."[15] Somewhat disappointed in not finding in France, recently liberated from the Nazis, more sympathy for oppressed and colonized peoples, Wright also noted that Sartre was the only Frenchman he had met who had voluntarily identified that French experience with the rest of mankind. Although he bought *Existentialism, Age of Reason,* and *The Reprieve* when they came out in translation, Wright had to wait for several years before touching the more metaphysical aspects of the existentialist philosophy. The same went for his reading of Beauvoir and Camus. He read the former's *Ethics of Ambiguity* in 1949 and Camus's *Caligula, Cross Purposes, The Plague,* and *The Stranger* long before he got hold of *The Rebel* in 1953. As a result, French existentialism certainly appealed to him more as an outlook on social commitment based on an ethic than as a metaphysical world vision. When Wright prepared the tenth anniversary issue of *Twice a Year,* a liberal magazine edited by Dorothy Norman, he read for inclusion in it "We Too Are Murderers" by Camus, a rather despondent appreciation of a political situation bent upon crushing individual freedom. Yet, like Wright, Camus stressed solidarity as well as individual freedom. In the same issue of *Twice a Year,* Sartre's play *The Respectful Prostitute,* focusing on the moral dilemma of one of the girls who had accused the Scottsboro Boys of rape, was included. Not only did Wright check, at his friend's request, the accuracy of the background details in the play, but he introduced the piece as a balanced approach to the race question.

Sartre was well known at the time for his antiracist stand in *Antisemite and Jew,* and among black circles for his supportive analysis of the negritude movement in "Black Orpheus," his introduction to Léopold Senghor's anthology of Negro poetry. Wright made him and Gide the French spokesmen of racial equality when he remarked, in "Why I Choose Exile," that after weeks of Parisian public politeness he had found out that the more civilized a man, the less he feared people who differed from him. The French felt so secure culturally that they were not afraid of diversity in any domain, which made Paris a truly international scene: "The French have imbibed through their education a universal scheme of reference which imputes to the alien a level of humanity different from his own in outward guise but not in intrinsic substance. . . . A rigorously competitive system of education . . . discourages pragmatic attitudes and exalts the sheer capacity for absorption of knowledge, thereby creating characters uninhibited in their quick absorption of alien facts, fostering humanistic emotions and forging personalities of wide availability of interest."[16]

By insisting upon the emphasis laid on universality in French education, Wright stressed criteria for self- and social definition other than those of economic status and race. Curiously, the strong class hierarchy of Europe allowed for more recognition of individual achievement because such achievement was measured in terms of intellectual or artistic development, not of money. Wright was attracted by the recognition granted to creations of the mind and the imagination by the French just as his fellow writers of the lost generation or the Harlem Renaissance had been, but unlike Claude McKay, for instance, he did not consider the price placed on intellect a threat to the dignity of the uneducated individual: "I was naturally attracted to a hierarchy of values that did not condemn those who are poor, even by implication, to a sub-human status. . . . In France the human ideal to be striven for is placed at the apex of a carefully graded scale of values, the prototypes of which are the priest, the soldier, the scientist, the savant . . . as an American Negro, I felt, amidst such a milieu, safe from my neighbor for the first time in my life" ("Exile," 12).

Not only were some of the most humane Frenchmen he met poor and not ashamed to be, but France made no pretense of being a welfare state in her definition of civilization in cultural terms: a black foreigner, Wright felt he could be allowed to become a Frenchman, in contrast to the reluctance of WASP America to accept him as an equal. As a result of this emotional closeness to the intellectuals of the existentialist and personalist persuasion with whom he associated, Wright was led to participate in their political activities, not only as a representative of black America but as a Western Marxist writer.

At the beginning of the cold war he proclaimed with progressive French intellectuals the right of Europe and the rest of the world to refuse to choose one of the two blocs. Although he was conscious of the communist threat and vehemently anti-Stalinist, he opposed on principle the political strings attached to the Marshall Plan and the implications of the NATO organization. When noncommunist left-wing journalists and leaders like David Rousset and Georges Altman founded the "Rassemblement Démocratique Révolutionnaire," enlisting the support of most of the existentialists, Wright himself appeared at the December 1948 rally at Salle Pleyel to speak on "Internationalism and the Human Spirit." In the name of individual freedom he denounced both American and Soviet imperialist moves: he accused both superpowers of debasing the human personality and the culture of our time by replacing qualitative values with quantitative ones. When the movement split under the pressure of choosing camps, with David Rousset condoning U.S. policy, Wright took his stand with Sartre, who opposed it, at the April 30, 1949, International Day against War and Dictatorship organized by the RDR.

Wright was therefore comforted in his vision of himself as a responsible, committed writer, regardless of race and nationality, by the then-prevailing French conception of a writer's role as embodied mostly by the existentialists. The contents of his writings themselves were influenced by his exile in France. Admittedly, his major vein of inspiration continued to come from his American life. He remarked: "I took my subject matter with me in the baggage of my memory when I left America and I'm distressingly confident that race relations will not alter to the degree that will render invalid these memories" ("Exile," 13). Yet many of his nonfiction works were concerned with interpreting French realities or American reactions to France. The French press published not only interviews with him on "the white problem" in the United States but also full-length articles like "In Paris, Black GIs Have Learned to Know and Like Freedom."[17] "A Personal Report from Paris" and especially "I Choose Exile," a long piece contrasting French and American cultures that *Ebony* refused to print in 1950, are evidence of an attempt at interpreting national differences for different audiences. Even a light vignette like "There Is Always Another Café," written in 1953, goes beyond the tourist's impressions to analyze the elements of the black man's sense of freedom in Paris. And the more fully documented "American Negroes Living in France," which was printed by the *Crisis* in June 1951, tells of job discrimination in American firms in Paris and of Wright's attempt to investigate and fight it by establishing the French-American Fellowship.

This latter move by Wright to adapt to a new environment the committed approach he had displayed in New York was short-lived and somewhat unrealistic, if one is to believe James Baldwin's account of it in "Alas, Poor Richard." Although much was made by the French press of the refusal of the American Hospital in Neuilly to hire black nurse Margaret Cleveland, the association, which numbered at best a score of black Americans, functioned more as a cultural meeting place than a pressure group, with a few prominent French intellectuals giving lectures or attending meetings.

After his trip to Chicago and Buenos Aires in 1949 and 1950 for the filming of *Native Son,* Wright settled into a more Parisian routine in his Latin Quarter apartment at 14, Rue Monsieur-le-Prince. But he also became increasingly interested in non-European countries, notably African ones, and in the presence of blacks on the French scene. As a result, *The Outsider* remains the book that coincides most with what could be called existentialist writing. He began the novel in 1947, before sailing to France. Although he gave Cross Damon, the protagonist, the possibility of enjoying a radically new identity and existence after a traffic accident, just like Sartre's hero in *The Chips Are Down,* this device probably predated Wright's reading of the play. Camus undoubtedly exerted a deeper influence. Wright read *The Stranger* in August 1947, admiring "the strong narrative prose," the delineation of the protagonist, and the deft use of fiction to express a philosophical view. Oddly enough, he found the book "a neat job but devoid of passion,"[18] but contemplated for a time rewriting *The Outsider* in the first person to bring in more immediacy and emotion, as in *The Stranger.* The existentialist trio did not contribute to the shaping of Wright's novel, but his association with them helped him solve, however clumsily, problems of the thesis novel he had attempted. Camus, however, he viewed, not inaccurately, as more of an artist or aesthete than Sartre and Beauvoir, hence further removed from his own perspectives.

In *The Outsider* Wright made timid use of his own impressions of the culture of Paris by attributing them to Eva, a white American artist, whose journal was quoted to show her soulful appreciation:

> I'm at last in Paris, city of my dreams. . . . I do manage to see it for myself, the art exhibits, the artists' studios, the sense of leisure, the love of beauty—will I ever be myself again after all this?
> Notre Dame! Rising nobly in the warm summer night like a floodlit dream—the tourist bus is crawling away, taking from me the vision of beauty, remote, fragile, infused with the mood of eternity. At the next stop, I got off the bus and walked back to Notre Dame. I could not keep to the schedule of a tourist bus! I sat on a bench and gazed at Notre Dame till almost dawn! How quiet the city is. A lonely shabby man is pushing a handcart through the city streets. Lines, space, harmony softened by dark mists. . . . Dusk of dawn kissing the pavements with tenderness. . . . Mine is the glory of those angels against the background of that pearly, infinite sky.[19]

One aspect of French culture Wright could not fail to react to—its deeply entrenched sense of superiority, expressed by the notion of a "civilizing mission" and embodied in the colonial policy of assimilation. When meeting French-speaking African intellectuals and students, he was not a little surprised to find out that they generally considered themselves Frenchmen first. He remarked, like many before him: "The French deal so subtly in assimilating the best minds from their African colonies that, should you rise to denounce colonization, the processed, educated blacks would rise to denounce you before any Frenchman would need to."[20] In the mind of an American black fighting for civil rights, integration, and full acceptance, this was bound to evoke mixed reactions. In one of the rare interviews he gave on the Algerian war (one must remember that open pronouncements about French politics by a foreigner might mean expulsion), Wright showed that he could distinguish between racism and French nationalism. He believed the Algerian war had nothing to do with race but with the awakening of French nationalism "now being employed to forcibly convert Muslims, who are religious fanatics, to Western civilization": "My feelings in such circumstances are ambiguous. Frenchmen tell the Muslims at the point of their submachine guns 'You are French.' We, American Negroes, might wish to be forced in a similar way to consider ourselves as American."[21]

In the early 1950s Wright was hopeful that France, although psychologically ill-prepared to hear the voices of the colonized Third World, could play a meaningful liberating role: "When France is equated not to England, America or Russia, but to the one and one-half billion or so people in the world who are not yet industrialized, and when the French genius of giving voice to the hopes of mankind is realized . . . France seems destined to play a role which perhaps she does not want to play, and the refusal of which will spell historical oblivion for her."[22]

As the Algerian liberation movement resorted to terrorism and as French repression spread, exacerbating anti-Arab racism on French soil, Wright sadly realized that even a socialist government like that of Guy Mollet could wage a colonialist war. When General de Gaulle's bold policy opened the way to African independence, he rejoiced: "The most important events affecting Africa . . . were born from France's decision. . . . One should not underestimate the long-range effects of France forsaking her cherished 'mission.'"[23] He clearly saw that the government had transferred the burden onto the well-trained corps of the black elite, the church, and the educators through well-understood self-interest in the race for the raw materials of the cold war.

Although he would not openly take stands on French international or colonial politics for fear of being accused of interfering in the affairs of his host country, Wright did not refrain from doing so through such cultural associations as the Société de Culture Africaine, founded by French-speaking African intellectuals around the magazine *Présence Africaine;* and his role as a link between this group and their Afro-American counterparts on such occasions as the 1956 conference of Negro writers and intellectuals at the Sorbonne was important. Also, he often used France as a privileged vantage point from which to comment upon the situation in the United States. On his first visit to France he was already convinced of the benefit of stepping back and looking at one's country from a "double" perspective: "I have learned more about America in one month in Paris than I could in one year in New York. Looking at it from this country makes all the unimportant phases of the AMERICAN problem fade somewhat and renders the true problems more vivid."[24]

During the McCarthy period France provided the ex-communist a refuge away from FBI investigations and hearing committees. Yet he was not protected from the pressures and attacks of red-baiting American nationalism on the black American expatriates whose presence in the Left Bank cafés was in itself a political statement about U.S. racism and was eagerly seized upon by pro-Soviet propaganda. Not only did the French press get into the habit of measuring black, or racially concerned, literary and artistic achievements by the yardstick of Wright's phenomenal success, but many stories circulated depicting him as a living reproach to his white countrymen's discrimination. For instance, Gregory Peck had allegedly refused to sit at the Deux Magots because Richard Wright was there, amid a circle of admirers. Or, as *Combat* reported on December 17, 1948, Wright had lunched with Mrs. Roosevelt during the United Nations session in Paris. To the first lady's question about why he had chosen to live in France, he had allegedly answered: "Well, just in order to enjoy the possibility of sitting at the same table as you." Needless to say, the anecdotes were false. But Wright could not avoid being used in such a way by critics of the American system, just as he could not avoid being the butt of French Communist party attacks, also directed against the existentialists.

Wright willingly lent his voice to antiracist groups and campaigns in support of civil rights in the United States. For instance, when the news broke of the lynching of Emmett Till or the Willie McGhee case, his opinion and pronouncements were eagerly sought. He was inclined to see himself as a conscience and a voice, warning that the American image abroad did not coincide with the best American intentions at home. He was not wrong in supposing that such criticism of America, even directed from inside by one who accepted America while rejecting its faults, would entail attacks on the part of nationalists. In 1956, for example, in his "Café Society" article about the black American circle in Paris, Ben Burns reported that "Wright's venom, retailed constantly by expatriates at sidewalk cafés plus years of headlines about Dixie lynching has succeeded in poisoning European thinking about racial problems in America. . . . Wright enjoys a good audience on the Left Bank for his hate school of literature."[25]

In spite of FBI or CIA spying on his activities, in spite of overt and covert attacks against him in American publications like *Time* magazine, Wright indeed remained a loyal citizen, even though, toward the end of his life, he was tempted to give up his citizenship. He constantly redefined what being an American meant under those circumstances, always from a humanistic, libertarian, and egalitarian perspective. It is revealing that he never thought of France, which he definitely liked, as a mother country that would have balanced his image of his fatherland in the way Mary Church Terrell or Countee Cullen, for instance, used those terms. Within his family circle he called Paris "my sweet slum," which carried some of the unbridgeable difference contained in his frequent use of the epithet "alien" to speak of France. It was not a matter of language, since he gradually learned enough French to understand it fluently and give interviews in it. It was not a matter of refusing, like Chester Himes, to get deep into French reality: he had enough French acquaintances and friends—from members of the government like Michel Bokanowski to his farmer neighbors in Normandy—and enough interpreters of France's ways and complex politics to get his intellectual bearings there better than William Gardner Smith himself. He simply had never gone to Paris as to a second home, and his emotional commitments were to his American roots and, later, to his questioning search for new ties with Third World countries, not to white Europe, whose intellectualism he respected as a Westerner but whose problems he did not really identify with.

When, in the middle fifties, Sartre and Wright drifted somewhat apart, it was due on the one hand to Sartre's moving closer to the French Communist party line, as he became persuaded that no efficient action could be taken without the support of a strongly organized group and that the Soviets really wanted peace. Yet, on the other hand, Wright felt that he differed as profoundly from Sartre as a black man would from a European: he once came to ask Sartre's support for some movement working for decolonization in Africa. Sartre was supportive, but he did not feel it was a priority—what with all the things to be done in Central Europe! Subsequently, Wright stayed away from French progressive intellectuals because he felt that the Third World would have to count on non-Europeans first. He accordingly devoted more time and attention to Africa, where he spent several months on the Gold Coast prior to writing *Black Power* in 1954, and to Asia, since he reported on the Bandung Conference the following year before addressing the problems of decolonization in the lectures and essays collected in *White Man, Listen* in 1959.

Although he was convinced that French progressives shared the same humanistic passion to defend the interests of man or advocate equality among peoples that he had found in Sartre, he rarely associated with them once the days of the Rassemblement Démocratique Révolutionnaire were over. At publishers' cocktail parties and cultural events he would meet Gide, Roger Martin du Gard, Raymond Queneau, Jean-Jacques Mayoux, and Boris Vian, among scores of others, but he shunned the crowd of pseudo-existentialists in the Saint-Germain-des-Prés cafés. For a time, after publishing in *Les Temps Modernes* and *Présence Africaine*, he associated with the group around *Preuves* and the Congress for Cultural Freedom, which financed his trip to Bandung. But his major contacts were with English-speaking writers, whether close friends like George Padmore, Peter Abrahams, and Carson McCullers or acquaintances like George Lamming and Truman Capote as they visited Paris, not to speak of the black American group of writers and artists he regularly met at the Monaco or the Tournon.

Wright's imaginative writing reveals that these were indeed his center of interest in Paris. The short story "Man, God Ain't Like That" paints a somewhat exotic French background for the detective plot of a white man's murder by his too-literal-minded African protégé. "Island of Hallucinations" remains the work in which he focuses on his own Paris experiences. This unpublished novel is a sequel to *The Long Dream,* at the end of which Fishbelly, the black Mississippi protagonist, is depicted fleeing to Paris to escape retaliation from the corrupt police chief he has exposed. It was written in 1958 and 1959, more than a decade after Wright's departure from the United States, and somewhat like *The Stone Face* by William Gardner Smith, it retraces the psychological and ideological evolution of several blacks established in Europe.

Judging from the "Five Episodes" that appeared in *Soon, One Morning,* the emphasis seems to be on the discovery of individual and racial freedom in France by American blacks:

> Slowly, things were happening to him. He could now eat in cafés surrounded by white Frenchmen, Americans, Germans without tension. And he marvelled at how good it felt to relax. "I've been toting a hundred pound sack of potatoes on my back all my life and it's goddamned good to get rid of it," he told himself. What elated him about Paris was the number of Africans, Chinese, and Indonesians swarming the streets. After he had learned the names of a few *apéritifs* he sat for long hours at café terraces covertly eyeing black Africans escorting blondes on their arms, and he would steal glances at white Americans, wondering at their degree of fury. "Jesus, if Africans can do that, I ought to be able to go to town," he told himself. Yet he did nothing. Exiled, he lived on his silent island, moping about cafés, speaking only to waiters. Fishbelly was crushed, scared, lost. Lacking words to make known even his needs he went to bed that Saturday night full of tense doubt. Were there other American Negroes in Paris? "No reason to be scared," he told himself. "I can do what I want, go where I please." Yet anxiety quivered at the core of him.[26]

Dressed to kill, Fishbelly then walks to the Boulevard Saint-Michel, hoping to pick up a girl, but he comes across a student demonstration against NATO and General Ridgeway. His felt hat, sporting a red feather in its orange and black band, attracts the attention of the student crowd, who start shouting "Quel chapeau américain!" and follow him to his hotel. This is no lynch mob, yet his heart pounds and he panics, until he yields his hat to the laughing crowd.

The next episodes are diminutive case histories in the fashion of
the vignettes of different types of blacks in *Banjo*. One meets Woodie,
a thorough bum who claims the Egyptians were black and the white
people have recently altered the earth's gravitation. Fishbelly's friend
Ned explains that Woodie is becoming crazy because the U.S. embassy
is sending him home, and he is scared of facing racism again. Then
comes a sort of black female scarecrow, Irene Stout; she turns out to
be an artistic beggar who practices her craft among rich white Americans by playing the "faithful darky" role and is probably the wealthiest
black in Paris. Later Wright is less interested in evoking the city's atmosphere, although he does so in passing, than in introducing Jimmy
Whitfield, a specialist in "steaming" white women (i.e., becoming their
lover in order to get their money), who has thrown a brick into a jew-
eler's shop window so as to be arrested by the police, thus escaping
being sent back to the United States, where charges have been brought
against him. Ned reveals that "until he had committed that crime, he
was outside of the pale of French law. But when he shattered that window, French law stepped in, placed him under its scrutiny and in a way
under its negative protection; in short, Jimmy was brought within the
scope of French civilization."[27] Under his attorney's guidance, Jimmy
becomes a minor offender and claims he wants to remain in France because he loves it; racial organizations rush to his aid, and after serving
a six-months' sentence he is freed and given an identity card!

The overall plot of "Island of Hallucinations" takes Fishbelly from
his initial bewilderment and conditioning to avenues of free choice
and positive racial consciousness until, at the end of the third volume
of the series, Wright planned to take him to Algeria and back to the
United States as a civil rights militant.

Soon after settling in Paris in 1947, Richard Wright himself had become involved in establishing links with French-speaking black writers
and, being regarded there for over a decade as *the* spokesman for
Afro-Americans, he definitely influenced the French vision of racial
matters in the United States through his statements and essays as well
as his creative writing. When Wright arrived in France, he knew more
about existentialism than about negritude. In June 1946 Léopold Senghor sought him out and shortly thereafter introduced him to Césaire.
He later met René Maran. A staunch agnostic who considered that
Christianity had been an instrument of colonization and that primitive
religion made for backwardness, Wright was, in spite of his esteem
for Senghor, very far from sharing his deeply Catholic and tradition-
alist views of negritude. He had more in common ideologically with
Césaire's Marxism, but Césaire belonged to the French Communist

party, which was attacking Wright as a renegade. It was through Jean-Paul Sartre, therefore, that Wright became one of the sponsors of the magazine *Présence Africaine*, along with leading French progressives and the negritude group. He contributed some material and was responsible for the publication of works by Samuel Allen, Gwendolyn Brooks, E. Franklin Frazier, Horace Cayton, and others. He became close to Senegalese Alioune Diop, the editor of the magazine, after the latter made efforts to deepen their understanding in 1949: Diop looked up to Wright to explain the racial situation in the United States to him and to "shed light upon that world across the Atlantic which fascinates my imagination as much as it surprises and puzzles my mind."[28] Although he largely rejected the Christian outlook, Diop himself had been unable to explain colonization in strictly Marxist terms; he stressed that perhaps the African world view, which insisted on vital forces and ancestor worship, could account for the African's cult of authority, for his valuing happiness, "the succulence of life," more than freedom, for his considering history as fate even though Diop thought it essential that Africans should acquire the conceptual and material tools of the West in order to counter its domination.

Wright's works also influenced Frantz Fanon's analysis of the psychological and social plight of the Negro in the New World. In *Black Skins, White Masks*, which he published in 1953, Fanon repeatedly referred to Wright's *Black Boy* and *Native Son* as well as to Chester Himes's *If He Hollers Let Him Go*. He even wrote Wright at that time, expressing his admiration for his work and his desire to do an in-depth study of it, requesting the titles he might have missed although his holdings were nearly complete.[29]

In 1954 Wright visited the Gold Coast, which was on its way to independence, and in April 1955 he attended the Bandung Conference, the first meeting to bring together the free nations of the Third World. As a result, when he participated, together with Senghor, Diop, Maran, and Césaire, in the organizational committee that prepared the First Congress of Negro Artists and Writers, held at the Sorbonne in September 1956, his personal views were based on first-hand observations. Eric Williams discussed the cultural situation in the Americas; the negritude intellectuals covered autonomous and nonautonomous French-speaking countries; Wright preferred to report on industrialization and nationalism in Africa.

When the conference convened, divergences between the Afro-American delegation and a majority of the other delegates began to surface. Wright's own paper, in fact, strongly opposed retaining the African cultural heritage, or at least its more religious and nonrational

implications. He felt cut off from Africa, deprived of the "instincts
that enable me to understand and latch onto this culture. . . . I cannot
accept Africa because of mere blackness and on trust." He believed,
moreover, that the beautiful culture described by Senghor had been
"a fifth column, a corps of saboteurs and spies of Europe." He posed
the question: "Must he leave it [this culture] intact, with all the manifold political implications involved in that, or must this culture suffer
the fate of all cultures of a poetic and indigenous kind and 'go by the
board'? . . . I want to be free and I question this culture, not in its
humane scope but in relationship to the Western world as it meets the
Western world."[30]

Significantly, Senghor advised Afro-Americans to rediscover and
study their African heritage, especially in their folk culture, because
it was a component of their temperament; they should seek classics
in Africa rather than in Greece. And in his paper on "Culture and
Colonization" Césaire himself proposed a less clear-cut dilemma than
Wright's: one could no more reject indigenous tradition as inadequate
than one could refuse European civilization, and the destruction of
religious taboos had also proved a form of cultural subversion that
had aided colonizers through missionary effort. Wright's formal contribution, "Tradition and Industrialization," reflected his Marxist perspectives when he equated freedom with the secular orientation of
the African elites. In fact, like E. Franklin Frazier, he also minimized
the importance of African survivals and carryover in Afro-American
culture. On such points Wright saw eye to eye with the American
delegation. With them, he also believed that in America the fight was
more a question of civil rights and desegregation than one of cultural
independence and black nationalism.

However, as far as politics was concerned, Wright and the U.S. delegates differed profoundly. He was a Marxist, and they were liberals
at best. During the September 24 debate Mercer Cook had wondered
what they were all doing in this political boat when Diop had spoken of a "cultural" conference. Also, Césaire had defined the Afro-
Americans as a semicolonized people, and John A. Davis, in a letter to
Wright, wondered: "What does he mean when he says the situation of
the Negro in America is best understood in terms of colonialism? If he
means in terms of races, I could understand that. . . . What American
Negroes want . . . is complete equal status as citizens. . . . We do not
look forward to any self-determination in the black belts if this is what
Mr. Césaire had in mind."[31]

The relationship between the American delegates and the French-
speaking representatives was far from clear or close; there was mutual

distrust and misunderstanding, and at that stage Wright played an important part as a mediator, since he was one of the few who could understand the importance of black nationalism, with the political implications of culture, in Africa and the West Indies while still favoring the civil rights struggle for desegregation in the United States.

Wright did not attend the second international conference of black writers and intellectuals in Rome in 1959. When he died in November 1960, most former French colonies had become independent, and he was seeking financial means to start on an extended trip in French West Africa to record the changes there and report on the conditions for future independent development. Clearly, in his mind the scene was no longer reconstructed France, or even emerging Europe, but already the increasingly larger group of nonaligned Third World nations.

NOTES

1. Richard Wright, *American Hunger* (New York: Harper and Row, 1977), 24.

2. Wright to Gertrude Stein, October 29, 1945, in Michel Fabre, *The Unfinished Quest of Richard Wright* (New York: William Morrow, 1973), 287.

3. Wright, unpublished journal, January 28, 1945, quoted in Michel Fabre, *The World of Richard Wright* (Jackson: University Press of Mississippi, 1985), 145.

4. Jean-Paul Sartre, quoted in Ralph Ellison to Wright, July 22, 1945, Yale.

5. Douglas Schneider to the author, December 12, 1964.

6. Wright to M. Scanton, June 15, 1946, quoted in Fabre, *World,* 156.

7. Wright to Ed Aswell, May 15, 1946, in Fabre, *Unfinished Quest,* 306.

8. Wright to M. Scanton, June 1946.

9. Wright, "A Personal Report from Paris," unpublished article, 1, in Fabre, *World,* 148.

10. Ibid.

11. Wright, journal, quoted in Fabre, *World,* 146, 147.

12. Ibid., 146–49.

13. Ibid., 150.

14. Jean-Paul Sartre, "Qu'est-ce que la littérature?" *Les Temps Modernes,* March 1947, 969.

15. Wright, journal, September 7, 1947, in Fabre, *World,* 150.

16. Wright, "I Choose Exile," unpublished typescript, 1950, quoted in Fabre, *World,* 149, hereafter cited in the text.

17. Wright, "In Paris, Black GIs Have Learned to Know and Like Freedom," *Samedi Soir,* May 25, 1946, 2.

18. Wright, journal, August 7, 1947, in Fabre, *World,* 168.

19. Wright, *The Outsider* (New York: Harper and Row, 1953), 192.

20. Wright, "I Choose Exile," 13, quoted in Fabre, *World*, 183.

21. Wright, interview in *Folket i Bild*, undated clipping, 1959.

22. Wright, "France Must March," unpublished draft, quoted in Fabre, *World*, 183.

23. Wright, introduction to the French edition of *White Man, Listen* (Paris: Calmann-Lévy, 1959), xviii. Translation mine.

24. Wright to M. Scanton, n.d., 1946, Yale; see Fabre, *World*, 189.

25. Ben Burns, "They're Not Uncle Tom's Children," *Reporter*, March 8, 1956, 22.

26. Wright, *Soon, One Morning*, ed. Herbert Hill (New York: Knopf, 1962), 141.

27. Ibid., 163.

28. Alioune Diop to Wright, undated, 1949.

29. See Michel Fabre, "Frantz Fanon et Richard Wright," in *L'Actualité de Frantz Fanon*, ed. Elo Dacy (Paris: Karthala, 1986), 169–80.

30. Wright, "Débats, 21 septembre à 21h," *Le 1er congrès des écrivains et artistes noirs*, Paris-Sorbonne, September 19–22, 1956, in *Présence Africaine* 8–10 (June-November 1956), 63.

31. John A. Davis to Wright, undated, 1956, Yale.

13

James Baldwin in Paris:
Love and Self-Discovery

Countee Cullen's student James Baldwin sailed for Paris on Armistice Day, November 11, 1948. In contrast to Richard Wright, he was "only a kid," and he had no more than forty dollars in his pocket. At twenty-one he had done enough of a novel to obtain a Saxton Fellowship; his second book (on store-front churches) had brought him no sales but earned him a Rosenwald Fellowship. For some time he had thought of leaving the United States. When he first met Richard Wright, his literary mentor who had recommended him for the Saxton Fellow-ship, Wright had seemed to him to be "sailing into the most splendid of futures, for he was going, of all places! to France."[1] And in 1946 Baldwin had written Wright in Paris: "It's a wonderful thing to have happened and the only other person I would have liked it to happen to is myself."[2]

Baldwin's reasons for fleeing from the United States were racial as well as literary. "By the time I was twenty-four, I had decided to stop reviewing books about the Negro problem—which by this time was only slightly less horrible in print than it was in real life—and I packed my bags and went to Paris," he reminisced.[3] When his most intimate friend, a young black of his own age despondent about his future in America, jumped from the George Washington Bridge, Baldwin re-solved to leave, absolutely certain that if he stayed he would come to a similar end. He had only one way to support his family—writing—and he felt that he could not become a writer in the United States; he was tired of the country and had to find another way to think about himself and live. Thus Baldwin did not go to Paris to see Wright; he did not even go *to* Paris but simply away from America. Yet he had ruled out many countries; he seriously considered only Israel, where he had American friends (but they had already left), and Paris, where he had a few acquaintances.

Of France he knew just enough to envy Wright when he was invited there. He did not know the language but had read the classics and enough of André Gide to dislike his Protestant guilt over his homosexuality, and had learned from the movies of Marcel Carné that the romantic settings of *Hôtel du Nord* and *Quai des Brumes* could correspond to a sordid reality. Indeed, Baldwin later made a point of emphasizing how limited his expectations regarding the French had been: "I would certainly have been demoralized if I had ever made the error of considering Paris the most civilized of cities and the French as the least primitive of peoples. I knew too much about the French revolution for that, I had read too much of Balzac for that."[4] He was convinced, however, that Paris offered "a refuge from American madness," a place where he could learn that it was possible for him to thrive as a writer regardless of his color.[5] Not that he wanted to forsake his black heritage, but being a Negro writer meant that one was expected to be "folkloric according to the white American standards, and that was unacceptable to me because I knew more than I could deal with in white America's terms. . . . My stay in Europe liberated me from certain American preconceptions."[6]

In the numerous essays he wrote in the 1950s on the theme of expatriation and the discovery of their American identity in Europe by black and white Americans alike, Baldwin repeatedly insisted on the legend of Paris: "The city where everyone loses his head, and his morals, lives through at least one *histoire d'amour*, ceases, quite, to arrive anywhere on time, and thumbs his nose at the puritans—the city, in brief, where all become drunken on the fine, old air of freedom. The legend operates to place all the inconveniences endured by the foreigner, to say nothing of the downright misery which is the lot of many of the natives, in the gentle glow of the picturesque, and the absurd; so that, finally, it is perfectly possible to be enamored of Paris while remaining totally indifferent or even hostile to the French" (*Notes*, 108). His essay "A Question of Identity" (1954) drew heavily on his experience and that of American students, mostly ex-GIs, with whom he associated during the first years of his stay: the American student, he remarked, lived there in a kind of social limbo, in utter irresponsibility, whether he embraced the United States or the Continent, until he was so stunned with freedom that he began to long for "the prison of home." To a certain extent Baldwin's initial stay reflected this dilemma, yet his will to become a writer and his own financial situation made his experience different from that of most of his acquaintances.

When Baldwin arrived in 1948, France was still suffering from the destruction and scarcity imposed by the war. Bread, cheese, meat, bicycles, cars, and gas were still rationed. Modern conveniences and facilities did not exist in small Left Bank hotels, and the *vie de bohème* was at first the painful experience of having to manage in an under-developed country. A refuge from American madness, some four thousand miles from home, Paris was also a very inconvenient city: "It contained—in those days—no doughnuts, no milk shakes, no Coca Cola, no dry Martinis; nothing resembling, for people on our economic level, an American toilet; as for toilet paper, it was yesterday's newspaper. . . . Paris hotels had never heard of central heating, or hot baths or showers, or clean towels and sheets and ham and eggs; their attitude towards electricity was demonic . . . and it soon became clear that Paris hospitals had never heard of Pasteur. Once, in short, one found himself divested of all the things that one had fled, one wondered how people, meaning above all oneself, could possibly do without them."[7]

Baldwin spoke next to no French, and besides Wright he had few acquaintances. He visited the elder writer shortly after his arrival and, through him, met Sartre and Simone de Beauvoir briefly, in a café; but he was too ignorant of the French cultural scene, so there was no real contact between them. There were many American blacks in Paris, the more closely knit group being the jazz musicians around Kenny Clarke, but they seldom met on the Left Bank, where at the time the black writers had not yet started gathering in cafés. As a result, Baldwin found himself very much on his own, associating mostly with white American students and artists and only occasionally with French friends and lovers. For several months he stayed in a cheap hotel on the Rue de Verneuil, where he met Marty Weissman, who wanted to become a photographer. He also associated with Yvonne Rubington and her artist husband, who lived at Malakoff on the southern edge of Paris. He visited them there a number of times, often talking about his literary endeavors. He would not follow in Wright's footsteps: both *Black Boy* and the good Negro were over; one should put an end to the folklore about blacks and start writing about them from completely different premises.[8]

The group of American bohemians the Rubingtons belonged to were mostly Jews, studying in Paris on the GI Bill. They would meet in Latin Quarter cafés or at Les Halles and often invited Baldwin, who was poorer than they. As a result, he frequently refused invitations in order not to be beholden, and concentrated on writing for hours with obstinate regularity. Yet one finds echoes of happy explorations of Paris in his articles: "The days when we walked through Les Halles, singing, loving every inch of France and loving each other . . . the jam sessions at Pigalle, and our stories about the whores there; . . . the nights spent smoking hashish in the Arab cafés . . . the mornings which found us telling dirty stories, true stories, sad and earnest stories, in grey, workingmen's cafés."[9]

Another acquaintance of young Baldwin was Stanley Geist, who had been living on the Rue de Verneuil since 1947, doing research on Stendhal and Flaubert, and who had been published in *Les Temps Modernes*. Because Baldwin had brought with him only the Bible and Shakespeare, Geist had the impression that Baldwin's literary background was limited. However, Baldwin had studied Balzac and Henry James in high school, and at the time he read James, especially *The Ambassadors* and *The Wings of the Dove*, he was clearly looking for a definition of literature as more than commitment. This was the gist of the argument he developed in "Everybody's Protest Novel." The very day he arrived in Paris, he was taken to the Deux Magots, where Wright was sitting with the editors of *Zéro*, the little magazine which published Baldwin's essay. To Baldwin's dismay Wright took him to task for attacking him and the idea of protest literature: "I had mentioned Richard's *Native Son* . . . and Richard thought that I was trying to destroy his novel and his reputation. . . . I was wrong to have hurt him. He saw clearly enough, far more clearly than I had dared to allow myself to see, what I had done: I had used his work as a kind of springboard into my own . . . for me, he had been an idol. And idols are created in order to be destroyed" (*Nobody Knows*, 157). The estrangement that ensued was never patched up.

Baldwin had met Geist at a party given by Harold Kaplan in his apartment on the Boulevard Montparnasse. The first American academic to arrive in France on the heels of the U.S. army, Kaplan was in close contact with such French intellectuals as Albert Camus, Raymond Queneau, and David Rousset, and he had been appointed director of the U.S. Information Service at the embassy. He was active in literature, and his salon had become one of the favorite meeting places of the American colony. The most meaningful acquaintance Baldwin made at the time was that of Gidske Anderson, a beautiful Norwegian girl who wanted to become a journalist. She found him intense, deep, and earnest, in his black sweater, black pants, and black coat, always slowly reading the Bible or Shakespeare. He was not in quest of adventure but of himself; like him, she was at the end of an unhappy love affair, and she often came to talk with him in his room, sometimes arriving just as he was coming back from a sleepless night spent wandering the city.

Gidske later met a couple of Americans who planned to live in Tangiers, and she persuaded Jimmy to join them in search of sun and a place where he could write in peace, away from his own emotional problems and the chilly autumn weather. When they reached Marseilles, the boat for Tangiers had just left, and they decided to wait for the next one in Aix-en-Provence. They enjoyed the October sun in the old city. The proprietor of the Hotel Mirabeau was fighting death in the next room while Jimmy typed assiduously, busy on the start of a novel. He was asked to stop, but they could not leave because a check Gidske was expecting had not arrived. Finally the hotelkeeper died, and Jimmy could work without constraint. He would talk a great deal with Gidske about his life as they ate in a small restaurant where the waitress had taken a liking to them, serving them extra portions, after her initial surprise at the blonde-and-black couple who were not even lovers. As the cold mistral began to blow, Jimmy fell ill and had to be treated at the city hospital, which was rather badly kept, with unprepossessing nurses.[10] When the check finally came, they returned to Paris. Gidske took a room at the Hotel Idéal and Jimmy stayed on the top floor of the Grand Hotel du Bac, which he described in Balzacian terms as

> one of those enormous, dark, cold and hideous establishments in which Paris abounds that seem to breathe forth, in their airless, humid, stone-cold halls, the weak light, scurrying chambermaids and creaking stairs, an odor of gentility long, long dead. The place was run by an ancient Frenchman dressed in an elegant black suit which was green with age, who cannot be properly described as bewildered or even in a state of shock, since he had really stopped breathing around 1910. There he sat at his desk in the weirdly lit, fantastically furnished lobby, day in and day out, greeting each of his extremely impoverished and *louche* lodgers with a stately inclination of the head that he had no doubt been taught in some impossibly remote time was the proper way for a proprietaire to greet his guests. If it had not been for his daughter—a hard headed *tricoteuse*—the inclination of her head was chilling and abrupt, like the downbeat of an ax—the hotel would certainly have gone bankrupt long before. (*Notes*, 117)

Gidske and Jimmy had decided to take a trip together for Christmas 1949, but she did not find him home and learned only a couple of weeks later that he had been arrested and jailed as a receiver of stolen goods. He would humorously make use of this episode in "Equal in Paris" in 1955. At the time, however, he was more than a little disturbed when police inspectors, finding in his room a bedsheet that an American friend of his had brought there, took him to the Commissariat, from which he was sent to the Fresnes prison on December 19. When the trial took place, two days after Christmas, the case was dismissed. The story of the *drap de lit* caused great merriment in the courtroom, but after days in a fetid cell with outcasts, Algerians, and other poor people, Baldwin was not warmed by this laughter—"the laughter of those who consider themselves to be at safe remove from all the wretched. . . . I had heard it so often in my native land that I had resolved to find a place where I would never hear it any more. In some deep, stony, and liberating way, my life, in my own eyes, began during that first year in Paris, when it was borne on me that this laughter is universal and never can be stilled" (*Notes,* 134).

If the legend of Paris had ever taken hold of Baldwin, it was wearing off. Paris was just a city like many others, and French institutions were no better than American: hotelkeepers were mostly interested in getting their rent paid; policemen, with their revolvers and weighted capes, were strict about passports and three-month visas. "After the first street riot one witnessed in Paris, one took a new attitude towards the Paris paving stones, and towards the café tables and chairs, and towards the Parisians, indeed, who showed no signs, at such moments, of being among the earth's most cerebral and civilized people." [11]

In France Baldwin did not consider himself a victim of xenophobia, still less of racism, but only of the illusions inevitably brought abroad by previous American writers whose experiences in Europe were similar to his. He had been liberated in Paris from becoming merely a Negro writer, but he realized that he was inescapably American. Even though his fellow Americans were no more at home in Europe than he, Europe was to a greater degree part of their inheritance. Yet he and white Americans had more in common with each other than with the French. As a writer, however, Baldwin needed a breakthrough, a necessity so important that American writers often had to go abroad in order to achieve it; in France he had encountered no need to prove that he was a "regular guy," no suspicion as an artist. This was due to the French reverence for intellectual effort, but also to the individual Frenchman's lack of fear of losing a status long defined by class divisions. What Baldwin called "a lack of social paranoia" gradually enabled him to feel that he could reach out to people, be accessible and open. He moved freely in all parts of the city, coming into contact with all sorts of people, from the Pigalle pimps and prostitutes to the well-to-do residents of Neuilly, people whose sense of reality was entirely different from his own.

Outside the circle of his American acquaintances, Baldwin associated with a number of African students from the French colonies. Baldwin's essay "Encounter on the Seine" (1950) is based on those early meetings, when he was both fascinated by, and somewhat afraid of, the dark strangers. They spoke freely of their customs and tribal traditions, their deep-rooted sense of identity, and of the literary movement of negritude. Their attitude would compel him to define himself as an American, a Westerner, even though his skin was black. More than the language barrier, they were separated by preconceptions about the fabled country of open opportunity and the exotic dark continent. But Baldwin realized the depth of his own alienation as a black American, which the Africans had never endured: "They face each other, the Negro and the African, over a gulf of three hundred years—an alienation too vast to be conquered in an evening's good-will, too heavy and too double-edged ever to be trapped in speech. . . . The American Negro can not explain to the African what surely seems in himself to be a want of manliness, of racial pride, a maudlin ability to forgive" (*Notes*, 104). Later he insisted on the inadequacy of these encounters for meaningful exchange: they were all too young to be able to define the meaning of their different backgrounds. Differences were not a matter of economics: the tremendous gap in living standards existed between American and French as well as between black Americans and Africans. It was more a matter of psychology, the necessity for the American Negro to recognize that he was a hybrid, that "this depthless alienation from oneself and from one's people is, in sum, the American experience."[12] Baldwin was tolerant, however. One day, as an African acquaintance was visiting him in his hotel room on the Rue Saint-Sulpice, where he had moved after his imprisonment, he was called downstairs to answer the phone at the booth in the lobby. He was not a little astonished to see his visitor leave, while he was still on the phone, with his own brand-new shoes on his feet. In his room he found the African's shoes with a note explaining that since they were "brothers," he had made an exchange.

Those shoes were part of the first set of clothes Baldwin proudly went to buy on the Champs Élysées when he received the check for an essay inspired by his new situation, "The Negro in Paris," which appeared in *The Reporter* in June 1950. By that time he was making some money writing articles but nearly despaired of ever becoming a novelist. Several friends had helped him: lawyer Tom Michaelis had found him an office job before defending him in court in the bed-sheet case. Mary Painter, whose help and affection were invaluable, had discussed "Many Thousand Gone" with him, encouraging him to persevere. Then employed as an economist at the American Embassy, she lived on the Rue Bonaparte, and he saw her quite often. He later inscribed *Notes of a Native Son* to her, "remembering a grim night in Paris when she alone was certain that the second essay in the book was good and would be sold."[13]

Typing furiously away in his passage-like, windowless little room near Saint-Sulpice or drinking too many coffees and cognacs in the second-floor room of the Café de Flore in order to keep warm while writing, Baldwin was rewriting *Go Tell It on the Mountain*, without being satisfied with it. For a change he would spend nights out with lovers or friends. He saw a good deal of *Zéro* editor Themistocles Hoetis before he moved to Tangiers and of Jamaican short-story writer Alston Anderson before he left for Mallorca. Bernard Hassell, a black understudy at the Folies Bergères, remained his close friend for life. His lover, white American painter Richard Olney, did his portrait at that time, and he also associated with artists Charles Marks and Jean Hélion. Other American writers passed through Paris too, like Saul Bellow and Lionel Abel, whom Baldwin met at a party given by Harold Kaplan; also Jo Frank, who gave up writing for teaching literature, and Peter Matthiessen, one of the few among his literary acquaintances with whom he remained friends.

His essays "Everybody's Protest Novel" and "Many Thousand Gone" appeared in *Partisan Review*. The former was reprinted in USIS-sponsored *Perspectives* together with "A No to Nothing" by Richard Gibson, also attacking protest literature. Baldwin was so sorely in need of money that he agreed to write an article on "Le Problème noir en Amérique" for *Rapports France–États-Unis*. The U.S. government propaganda magazine introduced him as the oldest of nine children, one who had labored as a skilled worker in weapons factories and whose "several jobs acquainted him in depth with urban and rural life in the U.S." Baldwin expressed moderate views on the "Negro problem": it was not comparable to the plight of the Jews and other minorities, nor with the condition of colonial peoples, "because the American Negro is no exploited native in a primitive country, he is an American citizen and one of the oldest inhabitants." He espoused the view of E. Franklin Frazier that the slave in America had been a broken man, compelled to immerse himself in American culture or die. He concluded that "the Negro problem exposes the struggle of a country to remain faithful to its principles and acquire the maturity necessary in order to *live* by them." The men working toward its solution were not perfect. However, "only totalitarian regimes ask more from men, and this is what their lies consist in." By countering Richard Wright's statements on the "white problem," Baldwin was on his way to becoming the darling of the American liberals.[14]

Around that time he made friends with Lucien Happersberger from Lausanne—the beginning of a long, stable relationship. Also, other blacks were coming to Paris. A former actor in the successful Broadway war play *Deep Are the Roots,* singer and poet Gordon Heath had opened a night club on the Rue de l'Abbaye with his compatriot Lee Payant. And there was Chez Inez—another Latin Quarter nightclub, run by black singer Inez Cavanaugh—that specialized in fried chicken and jazz; among the musicians who played there was pianist Art Simmons, starting a career in Paris, and he and Jimmy became friends. But the novel in progress did not jell, and in the fall Baldwin completely changed the sequence of its chapters; he rewrote it during an agonizing stay at Loèche-les-Bains, where Lucien sent him during the winter of 1951 and 1952.

When Marlon Brando helped him with the fare, Baldwin was able to travel to New York to sell his novel. He arrived there in 1952 at the height of "the national convulsion called McCarthyism." He found it threatening because he realized he was saved from public exposure only by his obscurity and comparative youth, although at thirteen he had been a convinced fellow traveler marching in a May Day parade. When his novel was finally accepted, he picked up his advance and booked passage for France at the end of the summer.

Back in Paris he found the city changed. After the fall of Dien Bien Phu, which signaled the crumbling of the French colonial empire, the attitude of the police toward the Arabs had become more vindictive, as though challenged authority was taking revenge on any colonials at hand. Most of the Arab cafés Baldwin used to haunt had been closed: tales circulated of Algerians being corralled in special camps, jailed, killed in the streets as the revolutionary movement spread, and each Algerian was forced to take sides for or against the FLN.

That year Jimmy spent much time with Gidske Anderson at Gallardon, a village not far from Chartres. In his essay "Stranger in the Village," he used his numerous visits to Chartres to emphasize the differences between the Afro-American and the European heritage. The passage on Chartres must be read as a response to the reverence expressed by Henry Adams in *Mont-Saint-Michel and Chartres* for the European sources of American culture. It indicates that, with time, Baldwin dissociated himself more and more from his white compatriots, to pose as "the black man": "The cathedral of Chartres, I have said, says something to the people of this village which it cannot say to me; but it is important to understand that this cathedral says something to me which it cannot say to them. Perhaps, they are struck by the power of the spires, the glory of the windows; but they have known God, after all, longer than I have known him, and in a different way, and I am terrified by the slippery bottomless well to be found in the crypt, down which heretics were hurled to death, and by the obscene, inescapable gargoyles jutting out of the stone and seeming to say that

God and the devil can never be divorced. I doubt that the villagers think of the devil when they face a cathedral because they have never been identified with the devil" (*Notes,* 148).

Baldwin's clear concern with the definition of his identity as a writer and as a black American was the theme of his essays of the early fifties: "The Negro in Paris," "A Question of Identity," and "Equal in Paris." More important to him, *Go Tell It on the Mountain* was published by Knopf in May 1953, and the reviews were favorable, sometimes excellent. But no royalties were forthcoming yet, and he had to go back to Loèche, where he completed "Stranger in the Village" that summer. He then visited several friends near Paris. He associated with Bill Wellburn, a southern writer who had become a bum, and with Terry Southern, who was to make good with *Candy.* Chester Himes arrived in Paris that year, and this was the occasion for renewing literary debates: "'Roots!' Richard Wright would snort when I had finally worked my way around to this dreary subject, 'What—roots! Next thing you'll be telling me that all colored folks have rhythm!' Once, one evening, we managed to throw the whole terrifying subject to the winds and Richard, Chester Himes and myself went out and got drunk. It was a good night, perhaps the best I remember in all the time I knew Richard. For he and Chester were friends, they brought out the best in each other, and the atmosphere they created brought out the best in me. Three absolutely tense, unrelentingly egotistical and driven people, free in Paris but far from home, with so much to be said and so little time in which to say it!" (*Nobody Knows,* 158). In his autobiography Himes himself remembered the occasion as a dispute between Wright and Baldwin in a bar at Saint-Germain-des-Prés.

In 1953 the black American painter Beauford Delaney arrived in Paris. Just after his stepfather's death, when he had moved to Greenwich Village, Jimmy had gone through a difficult period; he had been on the verge of a breakdown when Beauford took him under his wing and welcomed him in his studio. He not only helped him to believe in himself but, Baldwin later wrote, he helped him see the world with new eyes. When Delaney settled at Clamart, on the southern edge of Paris, Baldwin went to stay with him. The tiny apartment had one big window, in front of which grew an enormous tree. They loved to sit on the ledge and chat, looking out at the garden: "Everything one saw from this window, then, was filtered through these leaves, and this window was a kind of universe, moaning and wailing when it rained, black and bitter when it thundered, hesitant and delicate with the first light of the morning, and as blue as the blues when the last light of the sun departed. Well, that life, that light, that miracle, are what I began to see in Beauford's paintings, and this light began to stretch back for me over all the time we had known each other, and over much more time than that, and this light held the power to illuminate, even to redeem and reconcile and heal."[15]

Baldwin had entertained few expectations regarding French people; he was reacting to black Americans' proneness to cherish rather exaggerated hopes about them. He was no tourist, and the glories of the Louvre or the panorama from the Eiffel Tower did not enthrall him. With time, however, he reached a profitable modus vivendi with the hard city: "The French, you see, didn't see me; on the other hand, they watched me. Some people took good care of me, else I would have died. But the French left me alone. . . . I was freed of the crutches of race."[16]

And now he could even use France in fiction. One of his French friends, Jacques Vollet, lived near the Porte de Vincennes in a ground-floor room that Jimmy recreated in *Giovanni's Room*. He started the novel in the winter of 1953, when he left Clamart for several months at Magnanosc in the southern Alps. He drew from his own experience, but not explicitly, since he cast David, the homosexual American protagonist, as a white youngster to make him more representative of mainstream American history. David almost becomes engaged to a fellow American, Hella, who has come to study painting in Paris, but when she travels to Spain to think over his marriage proposal, he falls in love, or so he believes, with Giovanni, an Italian bartender. Not only does David's concentration on his own self-image entail a tragic end for the young European, but Giovanni's room comes to symbolize the part of his own psyche that David both rejects and feels trapped by. The description of the place, although based on Jacques Vollet's actual room, is done in evocative, rather than naturalistic, terms, with the table loaded with empty bottles, yellowing newspapers, and a single wrinkled potato, and the air laden with the smell of spilled wine. The Anglo-Saxon puritan thus refuses "the stink of love," but his "innocence" is an equivalent of corruption because of his inability to accept emotional involvement and what experience may entail. In this story of Americans abroad, Baldwin inverts the Jamesian paradigm of American innocence and European experience. The American is symbolically blond and the European dark, but the former is clearly evil and the latter basically innocent in his primitiveness—i.e., his refusal to dissociate nature and culture.

It is easy to translate Giovanni's image into a symbol of the Negro, thus making of David the puritan face of Baldwin himself as an American. In this sense the novel is autobiographical. In *No Name in the Street*,

Baldwin states, "I starved in Paris for a while but I learned something; for one thing, I fell in love. Or, more accurately, I realized for the first time that love . . . was among my possibilities. Not merely the key to my life, but to life itself. . . . It began to pry open for me the trap of color" (22–23). In contrast to David he thus equated expatriation with liberation, with shattering assumptions and crossing boundaries, and his blackness (the Giovanni side) held his Americanness (the David side) in check. Allowing himself to fall in love meant shedding self-protective strategies necessary to a black person in a white world. But Baldwin was sufficiently nurtured and enriched by these love relationships with young Frenchmen to see himself as defined in other terms than color and race.

According to Mary Painter, the first real change in Baldwin's fortunes occurred with the English publication of *Go Tell It on the Mountain*. She went with him to London on that occasion and remembered that, as they visited the British Museum, an African guard started a conversation with them and became furious because he thought Jimmy was lying when he claimed he didn't know where his black ancestors came from. The British edition of the book carried a big photograph of the author on the dust jacket, and this saved Baldwin from trouble: one evening when the French police were checking papers as usual, Baldwin found he had forgotten his *carte de séjour*. But he had a copy of his book and hesitantly showed it to the *agent;* it was accepted as proof of his identity, and the policeman said respectfully: "Oh, vous êtes écrivain, monsieur!" Not only was Baldwin not treated patronizingly, as the Arabs and Africans were, but he sensed that in France the man in the street revered artists and, far from being vindictive or jealous of the eggheads like his American counterpart, he held literary achievement as proof of personal worth and social status. This greatly endeared France to him.

Baldwin did not return to the United States for several years, except very briefly in 1952 and again when he was invited to attend the premiere of his play *The Amen Corner* at Howard University. Upon his return to Paris seven months later, he found that he had acquired prestige, not only among the black expatriates who haunted the Café Tournon but among the entire American colony. He was invited to parties and met novelists William Styron and James Jones. In 1956 he got to know Norman Mailer and his wife Adele, who were visiting Jean Malaquais, the translator of *The Naked and the Dead*. Baldwin himself had acquired more assurance; he could afford to disagree with the famous white writer on certain claims made in "The White Negro": they respected each other and went out together several times during the few weeks before the Mailers left Paris and Baldwin himself went to Corsica.

Giovanni's Room had been completed in early April 1956, but Baldwin was uncertain about its reception. And he was struggling with the same theme—love, homosexuality, and heterosexuality—in a new novel that would become *Another Country* six years later. In mid-September 1956 he attended the first conference of black writers and artists, which was held at the Sorbonne and which he covered for *Encounter* magazine. "Princes and Powers" is a detailed report of his own mixed impressions of that "cultural Bandung," as Richard Wright and others called it. He evoked the proceedings as a kind of vast parenthesis in the routine of the city: the autumn sun, the people on the café terraces, the bicycles racing on urgent errands, even the queues in front of the bakeries because of a bread strike helped him compose a backdrop against which he set up the ideological and literary debates between French-speaking Africans and the U.S. Negro delegation.

By that time Baldwin had become conscious of the necessity of a moral choice on his part. France, his host country, treated American blacks with some deference: "I was told with a generous smile that I was different: le Noir américain est très évolué, voyons! But the Arabs were not like me, they were not 'civilized' like me" (*No Name*, 27). And the police were becoming unbearably brutal: "I had watched the police, one sunny afternoon, beat an old, one-armed peanut vendor senseless in the streets, and I had watched the unconcerned faces of the French on the café terraces, and the congested faces of the Arabs" (*No Name*, 28–29). As terrorism plagued Paris, the law became increasingly repressive. In 1955, when Albert Camus directed his adaptation of Faulkner's *Requiem for a Nun* at the Théâtre des Mathurins, Baldwin had been asked to review the play. He had found out that the Mississippi novelist and the writer from Oran had in common at least the unfounded hope that victims of the white West would have the generosity to "go slow." He had never admired Camus very much, but he now felt that his own history as a black brought him closer to the Arabs than to the Europeans. Again, he had no reason to bow down to Descartes and Chartres any more than the Muslims did. The consciousness that he should take sides grew at the time of the conference of black writers—or rather with his realization that others were fighting for civil rights while they were talking in Paris. Going to lunch after one session, the group of black delegates came across a newspaper kiosk with a picture of teenager Dorothy Counts being spat upon by a white mob as she made her way into a desegregated school in North Carolina: "It filled me with both hatred and pity, and it made me ashamed. Some of us should have been there with her! I dawdled in Europe for nearly yet another year, held by my private life and my attempt to finish a novel, but it was on that bright afternoon that I knew I was leaving France. I could, simply, no longer sit around in Paris discussing the Algerian and the black American problem. Everybody else was paying their dues and it was time I went home and paid mine" (*No Name*, 50).

Shortly after the conference Jimmy and his friend Arnold left for Italy. Their destination was Ischia, near Capri, but they stopped in Corsica on the way, and when Arnold returned to pursue his studies in late October 1956, Baldwin remained alone at l'Ile Rousse, working steadily on his novel. He stayed there almost nine months, only revisiting Paris briefly at Christmastime, feeling very homesick in near isolation, in spite of the splendid scenery and warm climate.

He sailed for the United States in the summer of 1957, when he was asked to work on a production of *Job* with Elia Kazan. He intended to go South but had to work in New York for several months, coming to terms with a city with which he had long felt at odds and also gathering material on the entertainment world, which he would use in *Tell Me How Long the Train's Been Gone*. But he had made a new choice, and he started writing essays on the new black militancy in the United States, like "The Hard Kind of Courage" for *Harper's* in 1958 and "A Letter from the South" in 1959, after his stay in Atlanta and a visit to Charlotte, North Carolina, to check on school integration. Now although Baldwin was to return to France and stay there on many occasions, in his mind and heart he had left it. He was assuming the role of civil rights spokesman, appealing to the conscience of the nation in fiery, eager rhetoric. But he also went back to his early days in Paris and his inquiry into national and cultural identity in "The Discovery of What It Means To Be an American."

Back in France he remained hidden at Delaney's place in Clamart, working on his forthcoming novel. Early in 1960 he rushed to the United States to fulfill a commission from *Esquire* to write on Harlem. "Fifth Avenue Uptown: A Letter from Harlem" appeared in July 1960, while its author was becoming famous as a public speaker. When Richard Wright died unexpectedly in late November, Baldwin was not only shocked to lose the idol he had wanted to destroy in order to become himself, but was ready to take his place as a spokesman for his people. Baldwin was becoming increasingly vocal and better able to analyze diverse forms of oppression on the international scene. The Algerian rebellion and the ensuing war, terrorism, and repression whose echoes were daily heard in the Paris streets had played a part in convincing him of the importance of commitment. His fiction itself bears traces of his emotional involvement with the oppressed Arabs, notably in his short story set in Paris, "This Morning, This Evening, So Soon."

Baldwin had become a literary and political star. In the United States he was asked to give more lectures on the racial question than he could manage; after the publication of *The Fire Next Time* and *Another Country* in 1962, magazines and newspapers vied for interviews. He supported freedom rides, sit-ins, and the demonstrations like the Washington march that black organizations everywhere were busy preparing. An announcement in the August 17, 1963, Paris edition of the *New York Herald Tribune* read: "If you are an American and/ or interested in the Civil Rights march on Washington on August 28, *James Baldwin* will be at 25, Rue du Colisée at 3 P.M. on Saturday, August 17." Baldwin was joined by blues singer Memphis Slim, pianist Art Simmons, entertainers Hazel Scott and Mae Mercer, and many other concerned Americans. The following day he spoke to a capacity audience at the American Church in Paris. After his appeal a petition was signed by some eighty American citizens, including Anthony Quinn, and taken to the U.S. Embassy on August 21 by a group of 500 supporters, with French TV reporters and journalists attending. Baldwin and Bill Coleman handed the petition to the Embassy officials, and Baldwin flew to Washington on August 26, in time for the march.

After the 1960s Baldwin resided in the United States and other, mostly European, countries as much as in France, where he kept an apartment in Neuilly for a long time and where he lived for several months every year near Saint-Paul-de-Vence on the Riviera, in a renovated farmhouse that he bought after having rented it for a time. It was rather luxurious—a brown stucco house with a garden, overlooking the valley. Baldwin's own two rooms were furnished simply, however; there he retired to pound out his books after long, enjoyable dinners and animated conversation with friends. He worked mostly at night, often until dawn.

For some twenty years Baldwin was a familiar, although irregular, presence on the Paris intellectual scene, occasionally appearing at cultural events and political meetings. In 1970, for instance, he was the star of an "hommage" organized by the American Cultural Center to celebrate his friend, painter Beauford Delaney. In October of the same year he was the main speaker at a meeting organized at the American Artists and Students Center on the Boulevard Raspail to protest the persecution of the Soledad brothers by the U.S. police. The center was one of the favorite haunts of Vietnam War resisters and anti-establishment youth. Organized by the Radical Actions Projects Group, the meeting was also addressed by John Thorne and Jean Genet. Was Baldwin becoming political? At any rate, a pamphlet was circulated that quoted him as saying: "You may not be interested in politics but politics is fascinated by you."

When Henry-Louis Gates interviewed him in the company of Josephine Baker at his Riviera residence in 1973, Baldwin looked back on his twenty-year relationship with France from a perspective hardly present in his early essays. For instance, he insisted the term "expatriate," which had been applied to him, was a misnomer: "I am in 'exile' and was; one can never be an expatriate, really. One cannot possibly leave where he came from. You always carry home with you." [17] He pinpointed changes in French feeling toward all blacks since the fall of Dien Bien Phu and the Algerian rebellion. He stressed the importance of George Jackson, Malcolm X, and others in letting "the secret" out— that the prosperity of the West was standing on the back of colored peoples, including the South African miner.

In France, more than in the United States, James Baldwin continued to be regarded as a representative Afro-American. Not that he sought publicity, but journalists liked to quote his pronouncements when some world event involving blacks took place. And he increasingly performed as a spokesman for Africa too, since he tended to include all oppressed blacks under the generic "I" he used. His French career continued to flourish: nearly all his books appeared in translation and, while in the United States *The Evidence of Things Not Seen* was dismissed as being out of touch with the situation, the French-speaking press considered it an accurate analysis of the mood created in America by deep-rooted racial divisions. After *The Amen Corner* was performed at the Paris Théâtre des Nations in a production directed by Lloyd Richards in 1965, Baldwin repeatedly attempted to launch joint French and American entertainment ventures. In 1973 he announced a new film company, based in New York and Paris, with private and independent financing. He and Bernard Bos, a Frenchman of twenty-six, would work together. They planned to start with *Giovanni's Room* and then do "The Inheritance," an original scenario Baldwin had just completed. However, nothing came of those plans.

In *No Name in the Street* Baldwin remarked that his flight to Paris had been inspired by the hope that he would be treated more humanely there than he was at home. By leaving him completely alone, Paris did this for him. For a long time he did not make a single French friend, and still more time passed before he was invited to a French home: "This total indifference came as a great relief and, even, as a

mark of respect. . . . I didn't want any help and the French certainly
did not give me any—they let me do it myself; and for that reason,
even knowing what I know, and unromantic as I am, there will always
be a kind of love story between myself and that odd, unpredictable
collection of bourgeois chauvinists who call themselves *la France*" (*No
Name,* 40). Baldwin blasted French nationalism, but he grew far more
nuanced concerning France. For one thing, his command of the language increased considerably. So did his appreciation of the French
situation, although the major growth in his approach to world issues
resulted from a wider historical perspective. While Baldwin mellowed
with age, he retained a vitality that enabled him to bridge the Atlantic,
in his last years dividing his time nearly equally between Amherst and
Saint-Paul-de-Vence. As he no longer needed to establish his reputation, living in France helped him get rid of tensions and approach life
in a more leisurely fashion in the Midi. But success did not diminish
his commitment, and French intellectual life contributed to making
Baldwin more closely attuned to non-American attitudes and perspectives all over the world. Meanwhile, in his fiction he kept returning
to the emotionally charged image of Paris as the place where, due to
the fresh love of a European youth, the young American trapped in
the network of guilt about sex and race can be reborn to a healthier
enjoyment of life.

The title of the novel *Another Country* may refer to France, to which
Eric Jones, a white American actor, has escaped in order to forget a
tragic love affair with Rufus, a young black jazz drummer. In Paris
he falls in love with Yves, and their love story is related over forty
pages as it flourishes in the City of Light, under the imposing spires
of Chartres cathedral, and in a villa on the Riviera, where they live the
only interlude of calm and happiness to be found in the novel. Only
there does a couple form, free from the pressure of social forces—the
only outside character being the cook, benevolent Madame Belet. The
name "Yves" (phonetically: Eve) is symbolic, as is the fact that this episode is placed at the very heart of the book: the French youth actually
provides Eric with enough courage to return to America and try his
luck on Broadway.

Even though the short story "This Morning, This Evening, So Soon"
highlights French anti-Arab racism, Paris appears there as the setting
in which the narrator, a black American actor, has met his Swedish
wife and has lived happily for ten years, having been enabled in France
to achieve international fame.

In *Tell Me How Long the Train's Been Gone,* another black actor, Leo
Proudhammer, longs to carry his jazz records with him to the south of

France "to sit in a borrowed villa and think" over his life after a heart attack.[18] Here again, France is presented as a haven where the protagonist takes shelter in order to be restored. The same process is repeated in Baldwin's last novel, *Just above My Head*. Gospel singer Arthur Montana's career is evoked by his brother in unmistakable terms. In his small hotel on the Quai Saint-Michel, "It is his first time in France and he speaks no French and yet, strangely, he feels more at ease in Paris than he had felt in London."[19] Arthur's early impressions duplicate Baldwin's, as evoked in some of the essays of *Nobody Knows My Name:*

> He watches the lights in the dark and gleaming waters, the orderly procession of lights on the farther bank. It is a chilly night yet the people walk at a more deliberate pace than is common in New York. In Paris, one feels free to be an outsider, to watch; nothing in Paris really reminds him of home in spite of the disastrous French attempts to imitate the American scene. . . . Here he feels free, more free than he has ever been, anywhere; and, though he has yet to realize it consciously, this freedom is very largely due to the fact that he moves in almost total silence. His vocabulary exists almost entirely in his fingers and in his eyes; he is forced to throw himself on the good nature of the French and he will never, luckily, live here long enough to be forced to put this good nature to any test. . . . In the resulting silence he drops his guard.
> He could never have done that in New York, where all his senses were always alert for danger, or in London. . . .
> But nothing is demanded of him in Paris. In Paris, he is practically invisible, practically free.[20]

At Saint-Germain-des-Prés Arthur orders cognac at the Deux Magots, then Chez Lipp, where a redheaded giant befriends him. Guy Lazar, who has an uneasy conscience for having fought in the French army in Algeria, plies Arthur with Gitane cigarettes and takes him to his studio on the Rue des Saint-Pères, where they make love beautifully, in a real give-and-take fashion, like real people and not types of those social categories called "Frenchman" or "American black." Their relationship lasts as long as Arthur remains in the city; intellectual exchange is part of it, including mutual analysis of the European bewilderment concerning the black American's connections.

One could argue that, in his last fictional treatment of the "Paris idyll," Baldwin had grown far more careful to balance his appreciation for France with a few guarded insights. Yet, when it came to the emotional impact of the Paris experience, his characters were as romantic as ever:

> If, in addition to being young and seeing the Champs-Élysées for the first time at night with a lover, that lover happens, furthermore, to

be French, one is in a rare and exalted category indeed, and might as well take the vow of silence, for if your story is ever believed it can only poison your relationships. . . .

Anyway, if one has seen it [Paris] for the first time at night when one was young and one was happy, the memory comes back from time to time and the memory stings, but it causes you to remember that you have not always been happy and need not always be. (*Nobody Knows,* 500–501)

The sweet memory brings out the bitterness of other memories, while it cannot be salvaged in any other fashion than as a glowing memory. This is what the presence of Sonny Carr, singing the blues in the Latin Quarter, seems to symbolize.

In *No Name in the Street* Baldwin explicitly claimed that in Paris he starved for a while but learned something: "I realized or accepted for the first time, that love . . . was among *my* possibilities, for here it was, breathing and belching beside me, and it was the key to life" (22–23). Love began to pry open for him the "trap of color" because he found that, even when quarreling, the two real lovers would not use color as a weapon.

What made it impossible for Baldwin to dislike France, in spite of everything, was the fact that he owed to that country his own spiritual growth, through the existential discovery of love as a key to life. Whatever his reservations, a positive image springs out, and behind the mask of the fictional narrator in "This Morning, This Evening, So Soon," one can feel the presence of Baldwin himself in the statement "But I could not hate the French, because they left me alone. And I love Paris, I will always love it; it is the city which saved my life. It saved my life by allowing me to find out who I am."[21]

That the French had accepted Baldwin as one of theirs was shown not only by his being awarded the Legion of Honor in 1985 (it had been bestowed only upon Henry O. Tanner and Josephine Baker before him) but by their expecting him to have his say about current political and racial issues like prominent French intellectuals. Although he had mellowed at the end of his life, a gentle humility having superseded the fiery outrage of the earlier civil rights activist, he remained a committed writer who, among other things, would speak against apartheid as he did at one of his last public appearances, at the 1987 UNESCO International Day against Racial Segregation. When he died, the French press and TV treated him very much like Marguerite Yourcenar of the French Academy in their obituaries, as an honorary citizen of the country he had never wanted to call home.[22]

NOTES

1. James Baldwin, *Nobody Knows My Name* (New York: Dell, 1963), 155, hereafter cited in the text as *Nobody Knows*.

2. Baldwin to Richard Wright, undated, 1946, Wright Archive, Yale University.

3. Baldwin, *Notes of a Native Son* (New York: Bantam Books, 1971), 2, hereafter cited in the text as *Notes*.

4. Baldwin, *No Name in the Street* (New York: Dial Press, 1972), 39, hereafter cited in the text as *No Name*.

5. Baldwin, interview with Henry-Louis Gates, September 5, 1973, in *Afro-American Writing Today*, ed. James Olney (Baton Rouge: Louisiana State University Press, 1989), 14.

6. Baldwin, interview with the author, April 1974.

7. Baldwin, "The New Lost Generation," *Esquire*, July 1961, 113–14.

8. Yvonne Rubington, interview with the author, December 1971.

9. Baldwin, "The New Lost Generation," 113.

10. Gidske Anderson, *Mennesker i Paris* (Oslo: Ascheborg, 1964), 108–29.

11. Baldwin, "The New Lost Generation," 115.

12. Baldwin, interview with author.

13. Mary Painter Garin, interview with the author, November 16, 1971.

14. Baldwin, "Le problème noir en Amèrique," *Rapports France–États-Unis*, September 1951, quotes on 39, 47.

15. Baldwin, "Introduction to an Exhibition of Beauford Delaney, Opening December 4, 1964, at the Gallery Lambert," in Richard Long, *Beauford Delaney, A Retrospective* (New York: Studio Museum in Harlem, 1978), 19.

16. Baldwin, interview with Gates, 2.

17. Ibid., 6.

18. Baldwin, *Tell Me How Long the Train's Been Gone* (New York: Dell, 1970), 243.

19. Baldwin, *Just above My Head* (New York: Dial Press, 1979), 467.

20. Ibid., 468.

21. Baldwin, *Going to Meet the Man* (London: Corgi Books, 1967), 137.

22. Baldwin died on November 30, U.S. time, December 1, French time, in 1987.

14

Chester Himes's Ambivalent Triumph

Of the fifteen years Chester Himes lived mostly in France, he spent about seven in Paris and three in the provinces, mainly in the south— about as much as Richard Wright's total exile. Although Himes made his reputation as an author of detective fiction in Paris, his work is not as clearly linked with this French setting as James Baldwin's because Himes rarely referred to his French experiences in his fiction, preferring to recount his years of exile in his autobiography, and also because of his ambiguous attitude toward Europe and his claim that, although he had elected to live there, he remained an American first.

It is difficult to piece together Himes's image of France from his fleeting accounts of people and places he liked or from his reactions to slights real or imagined and praise enjoyed. Asked toward the end of his life to evaluate what France had meant to his career, he considered it mostly from a black writer's point of view:

> For me France was the opportunity to write without the barriers imposed by race, politics, my state of health, finances, or my appearance. The color of a person's skin holds no advantage in France; most French people never notice it, unless it is beautiful. The French will support any person who works at his or her profession unless it is injurious to themselves or others. . . .
>
> I am a writer of fiction. I came to Europe in the Spring of 1953 and stayed briefly in Paris, then went to southwestern France, London, the Balearic Islands of Spain, back to Paris and went back to the U.S. broke and without hope. . . . During my eleven-month residence in New York, I learned that the U.S. offered me no future. . . . Richard Wright was then having his turn. But France had attributed fame and fortune to Alexandre Dumas and his son and many other blacks.
>
> In Paris, I found many ways to feed myself without disastrous effects. I gathered throwaway scraps in the markets, old bread, stale wine, and hotel proprietors let me live in rooms until I could afford to pay. Girls contributed love and sometimes encouragement, and I was permitted

to use all public reference sources. France did not support me; it let me live and grow strong enough to concentrate on my work, which was writing. . . . I became famous. My detective stories, along with other books published in France, sold to other countries. Eventually my books were picked up by the U.S.[1]

Admittedly, *The Quality of Hurt* and *My Life of Absurdity* contain more carping remarks on French people than favorable impressions. Instead, he stresses the hurts he suffered and the absurd behavior he encountered. Conversely, one finds in his correspondence more praise of French surroundings and some heartfelt appreciation of French acquaintances. On the whole, when balancing contradictory impressions and allowing for passing irritation, Paris appears to have been the place where Himes managed to achieve international fame as a writer although it took him over a decade to realize how important the city had been to him.

When he went to Europe in 1953, Chester Himes had forty-four well-filled years behind him—years of achievement but also of frustration. Born in 1909 to a respectable southern family, he had been more influenced by his mother, a mulatto with literary and social pretensions, than by his darker father, a teacher of blacksmithing. His fall down an elevator shaft, the ensuing disability, and the desire to compensate may help explain why this promising student was sentenced to up to twenty-five years for armed robbery in 1928. While serving seven years in the Ohio state penitentiary, Himes became a short-story writer published in *Esquire* magazine. He discovered in writing a means of achieving respect and a sense of identity: "The world can deny me all other employment . . . but as long as I write, whether it is published or not, I'm a writer and no one can take that away."[2]

Fostered by racial discrimination, Himes's disillusionment with the United States grew with his inability to maintain the pride that had accompanied his marriage. Menial and temporary jobs, Jim Crow employment in Los Angeles plants, and the impossibility of supporting his wife properly partly explain his divorce. He vented his frustration in a fine first novel, *If He Hollers Let Him Go*, which did well in 1945, and again in *Lonely Crusade*, an all-encompassing indictment of the American system, labor unions, and communist organizations. The book met with adverse criticism, and Himes despaired of ever being able to affirm his vision against such odds. It is significant that, thirty years later, he should remember the mixed critical response to his second novel as a devastating blast: "Of all the hurts I had suffered before, . . . the rejection of *Lonely Crusade* hurt me most. . . . The whites rejected me, the blacks did not want me. I felt like a man without a country, which in fact I was" (*Hurt*, 102–3). What he construed as an all-out campaign to silence him in America prompted him to look for a refuge in France, where *Lonely Crusade* was scheduled to appear in translation, with a glowing preface by Richard Wright.

In May 1946 Himes had already thought of following Wright to Paris within a year, at least for a visit. Again in 1951 he wrote his French translator, Yves Malartic, of his desire to go. A novelist in his own right, Malartic had published *Au pays du bon dieu*, dealing with the experiences of a black GI in France, and the two men quickly became friends. Himes soon confided his difficulties with American publishers, his divorce, and how his new companion, Vandi Haygood, wanted "the money to start pouring."

His failure to make a living from his writing in the United States had convinced Himes that he had to live elsewhere. Now forty-four, an ex-convict, without a university degree, he could support himself only by working at menial jobs or by writing. He had made countless applications to publishers of newspapers, books, and magazines, and the novels he had published did not bring in enough to support him, while his ideas for new books were unacceptable. As he told Malartic repeatedly, and later wrote to John A. Williams, "I suppose I could say that was my main reason for leaving America—just to keep alive."[3]

By May 1952 he had postponed his trip because of his financial situation and because he wanted to write *Cast the First Stone* before visiting Europe with Vandi. By October, flattered to see the French edition of *La Croisade de Lee Gordon*, he claimed that he had not gotten over "the real head-whipping" for that book in the United States, and if he made a little money, he would come over next spring. Although his passport had not yet been granted, he made a third-class reservation on the *Ile de France* for April 2, 1953, and for weeks, practicing with Vandi's Linguaphone records, he studied French with great zeal. He intended to stay in France for six months and work on a new novel, *The Third Generation*, for which he had received a $2,500 advance.

Little did Himes expect to encounter on shipboard a New Englander, Willa Trierweiler, who told him everything about her unhappy marriage to a Dutch dentist and the breakdown that had sent her to an institution. He felt for her as never before for a woman. Was it love? At any rate, Willa was on her way to get a divorce; she promised to join him in Paris in May. As a result, Himes was probably too much a prisoner of his own emotions to approach Paris objectively. *The Quality of Hurt* evokes his arrival in humorous or grotesque vignettes: expensive porters at Le Havre, crowded compartments on the boat train, finicky and rude customs officers, and the irritating inability to make himself understood when he mumbled Wright's address to a taxi driver. Himes had taken the precaution of asking Malartic, Wright, and another American friend, Dan Levine, to make hotel reservations for him and to meet him at the station. He managed to miss all three of them, and when he was driven to the Latin Quarter through dimly lit streets, he fumbled with the "minuterie" at Wright's place just long enough to be thrown out by the ferocious concierge. After another trip to the Gare Saint-Lazare and back, he miraculously landed at the Hotel Delavigne, to discover that Wright had reserved a room for him there, while his friends were giving him up for lost at the station. Spiced with a portrait of the concierge as some antediluvian mammal, such errors and coincidences became a purple passage in his autobiography.

Should one trust contemporary accounts of Himes's discovery of Paris more than his own remembrances of it, fifteen years later? In a March 1954 article intended for *Ebony* magazine, he sounded quite positive: "I found Paris very pleasant in April; the chestnut-trees were in bloom, the weather was balmy, the cafés crowded along St. Germain, the students out in all their many-national glory on Saint Michel, the book stalls on the quais, fishermen on the Seine—just as everyone has read about it. No surprises, no discoveries. There was an abundance of food, both cooked and raw. I had brought an alcohol stove from America and I cooked my breakfast in my room, the good smell of Nescafé and jambon and oeufs brouillés permeating the waxed corridors, watering the mouths of hungry lovers and early-rising clerks." Getting beyond the expected clichés after a disquisition on the surprisingly tame Parisian taxi drivers and a portrait of a black-market money changer, he focused at once on the "expatriates": "The American colony in the Quartier Latin is dominated by the bustling, confident personality of the 'new' Richard Wright who holds court for his neophytes in a little café, The Monaco, just back from the Odéon on St. Germain and down from the Rue Monsieur-le-Prince, a block where he lives with his wife and two lovely daughters. . . . Wright stops by once or twice a day and talks loudly of world politics, the American dilemma, the nature of Communism and the pitfalls of creative writing. Most listen, and perhaps a few agree."[4] Himes stayed close to the Luxembourg Gardens, up the street where novelist William Gardner Smith lived, who maintained his individuality by holding his own court, smaller but perhaps better-informed than Wright's, in the café Tournon.

Wright had gone out of his way to welcome Himes, taking him around, introducing him to the brothers, eating out with him and Ben Zevin of World Publishers, inviting him to his home or to friends' on several occasions, interpreting for him the situation of the Paris intellectual. But Himes felt estranged from the novelist who had made it: he described him as a kind of bourgeois Frenchman who had taken to driving a Citroën and whose children, he claimed, were cared for by an efficient French governess while Ellen conducted a literary agency. Was Himes resentful of Wright's success and security? Was he resentful of the latter's disregard for Willa when she came to join him? At any rate, Himes clearly played up William Gardner Smith as the younger, more committed, and better-informed talent against the well-established intellectual he found patronizing: "I don't know what I expected to get from Paris, but whatever it was I didn't get it. I don't think that is due entirely to the city. It seems now, looking back, that Dick Wright might have been blocking me off from meeting people and getting to know the city; he spent a great deal of time with me but it was all pointless."[5]

Himes made new acquaintances, notably the cartoonist Ollie Harrington and the black painter Walter Coleman and his startling Swedish wife, Torun; he consorted with the Monaco crowd—English-speaking, student-artist types, Americans mostly, some British, a few Scandinavians, a few African colonials. He was even present when Wright and James Baldwin had a heated argument about their literary father-son relationship. He attended dinners with publishers, notably with Mrs. Putnam in a Rabelaisian Montmartre restaurant, or cocktail parties, including one at Buchet-Chastel in celebration of Henry Miller; he was interviewed by journalists like well-informed and friendly Annie Brièrre of *France-USA*. In sum, he was taken care of and decently welcomed. Yet he was convinced he was not being sufficiently honored. When his faithful friend Yves Malartic attempted to make him meet French people by inviting him to dinner with several friends of his, Himes remembered mostly a dull evening with people "whose efforts seemed to be to belittle Americans" and of having been made fun of at the Deux Magots on account of his faulty French.

Vandi Haygood came from New York within a week of his own arrival, and he was proud of such a good-looking, sexy companion, who was a big hit with the brothers and the French. They threw notorious parties at Harrington's apartment and dined in splendor at Maxim's and the Tour d'Argent. Willa had been writing steadily; she arrived at last from Holland, ready to share his room at the Hotel Michelet, which he now found too cheap for such a special woman. Busy with sentimental affairs, far from fluent in French, disappointed with his fellow black Americans' alleged lack of attention, highly critical of the Parisian circles, Himes cast himself in his autobiography as one apart, although he did in fact seldom remain alone: "I didn't fit in, I wasn't an intellectual, and I didn't have a title," he noted in describing a reception at the home of friends of the Wrights (*Hurt*, 211).

Seeing that Chester needed a quiet place to write and be alone with Willa, the Malartics suggested that they spend some time at their family home in Arcachon. On May 6, 1953, the couple set off for Villa Madiana, and the following week Chester wrote in glowing appreciation: "We have done little except enjoy the charm of your villa and the quiet exquisite enchantment of the shore and the fishing boats and the busy fishermen repairing and painting their boats. The weather has been beautiful. Last night was the first chilly night and we built a fire in the fireplace and drank a bottle of champagne and had dinner inside. . . . We love your home and the warm wonderful feeling of being surrounded by books. It is all so very nice. Everyone is very kind and friendly and helpful. It is peaceful and warm and friendly—the way one hopes the world would be."[6] Himes did little writing during the month they spent there, except to bring all the loose ends of *The Third Generation* together in one long dramatic incident. He started a new novel—later *The Primitive*—making many false starts on it while reading *The Brothers Karamazov*. When they left in early July, he concluded: "All in all, our two months there had been exquisitely happy and satisfying" (*Hurt*, 243). This was largely due to their complete involvement in each other and their isolation from the race problem.

In his 1954 article for *Ebony* magazine Himes devoted four pages to sketching the distinct atmosphere of Arcachon, its natural beauty, the ways of the fishermen and their colorful wives, with an American audience in mind; yet his portrait, among others, of the buxom washerwoman across the street was more a tribute to her courage and family sense than a caricature. He contrasted the fashionable villas of actors Charles Boyer and Annabella or of French Communist party leader Maurice Thorez at the other end of the town with the simple ways of the oyster farmers and fishermen who walked barefoot and got tipsy and quarrelsome on the red wine in the dim cafés. His piece was almost a celebration of the wives who kept the picturesque houses spotlessly clean and cooked the lovely-smelling Gallic food—"good women who valiantly served their menfolk in home and bed and never once thought of bathing in the bay for the fun of it."[7]

At his poetic best, which is rare in his writing, Himes was capable of evocations of the seaside landscape and the Aiguillon oyster shoals in terms reminiscent of Claude McKay's "Dinner at Douarnenez": "Standing at the end of a street where it runs down into the water, especially at sunset when the tiny shell-fish frantically crawl over the pebbled bottom near the shore in search of food, there is ofttimes a peace and silence profound, it seems, like another world; the ships silhouetted along the ragged shoreline, the lights of the downtown promenade in the distance, the half-dozen or so derelict rotting hulls of wrecked fishing schooners emerging from the water like dead, decaying skeletons, like 'Shadow' coming out of the East River in a shroud of seaweed with six forty-five slugs in his body—it is so weird, so lonely and forsaken you get the feeling that the oyster farmers got their seed mixed and planted bits of rotten sail and this was the harvest." [8]

Later, in *The Quality of Hurt,* Himes did not record such splendid landscapes or local reactions to his presence. He noted that the natives were very curious, stopping to stare at him. Yet, although there was much anti-Americanism, with the walls of the Latin Quarter chalked with the inscription US GO HOME, Himes did not find racial prejudice as such—only strict class lines among the old families, which automatically relegated many Negroes to the lower classes.

After the idyllic stay at Arcachon, Chester and Willa went to London, where they collaborated on a novel based on her experiences in a hospital in Switzerland. However, six months of bad weather, unheated rooms, and blatant racial discrimination were all they could take, and in late January 1954 they fled to Mallorca. Himes's impressions of Puerto de Pollensa and Deya, which touched his emotions more than any other place that he had known before or since, were about as contradictory as those of France. He did not consider remaining in Europe after completing his novel: "For my part, judging from what I have seen so far (and I don't think anything I'll see henceforth will change it) I like America best; I like it despite its faults and there are many; perhaps I like it because of them. I am what America made me and the longer I stay the more I discover how much of America is in me and how much of me is in America. I have a notion, grown out of the little I have seen, that America offers practically everything but antiquity to be found in the rest of the world. The tragedy for me is I can share only a small part of its great offerings." [9] Such high-sounding patriotism is partly due to his writing for a U.S. audience at the height of the McCarthy era; yet Himes's discovery of his Americanness as a black American, unable to share a large part of his country's offerings because of discrimination, corresponds to Baldwin's realization of his heritage at the same time.

While Himes enjoyed the Mallorca setting and bustling Spanish life, he realized how much he missed the cultured atmosphere of Paris: "I am weary of Spain and this primitive and un-intellectual life," he wrote the Malartics on July 7, 1954. Now he viewed Paris more positively: "I wish very much to get back to Paris and live there and learn the city. It seems so much closer to me now than it did when I was there, and I will get much more out of it when I go back than I did when I was first there. Looking back, it seems to me that when I first came from America, I was in a condition of petrification, or what is better known as hardening of the brain, a common illness in America."[10]

Using a bogus check, Chester secured tickets back to Arcachon, hoping to find shelter there, but the Villa Madiana had just been sold. The couple arrived in Paris on a gloomy October day, just in time to find Correa's rejection slip for his novel. To survive, they pawned Willa's ring and one of their typewriters before she found a job as proofreader. This was barely enough to buy food in the Buci market and cook it in their room at the Hotel Jeanne d'Arc. Due to the influx of Arabs and blacks, small hotelkeepers were introducing discrimination, and Chester was refused a room that Willa obtained shortly afterwards. As a result, he found Paris "profoundly hostile to American Negroes."[11] He was desperate by the time a contract for *The Primitive* and an advance from The American Library enabled him to pay off his debts and send Willa to New York on December 1. Alone in Paris Himes did not try to "learn the city"; he moved to London to work on a new fiction project, then sailed for the United States around Christmas. At the Albert Hotel in Greenwich Village, again utterly disillusioned with New York, he wrote Malartic: "After having been away from New York for a couple of years it seems like a sort of second-rate place, perhaps not so much second-rate as robot-matic."[12] In the fall he was expecting the royalties for the paperback edition of *If He Hollers* to enable him to flee immediately for Paris. In fact, he needed to flee from himself as much as from his country: the news of Vandi Haygood's suicide had shocked him all the more as he was "killing" her in his latest novel; his relationship with Willa had dwindled to masochistic weekend bouts until she had finally returned to Holland in July. Chester had to work as a busboy in Manhattan luncheonettes in order to eat. When he sailed on the *Ryndam* on December 14, 1955, he claimed in his autobiography: "My last thought before losing sight of the mainland was that the best thing that ever happened to me was to lose Alva . . . and sever all my ties with the United States."[13]

After a spree with prostitutes around the Gare Saint-Lazare, Himes settled at the Hotel Royer-Collard in the Latin Quarter. He went back to the routine of endless talks at the Café Tournon with the black expatriates, of picking up younger girls (some French but mostly foreigners) curious about black sex to share his meals, his bed, his solitude after he had done a steady morning's work on "Mamie Mason" at the Café Au Départ.

At the Tournon, the blacks "performed," exchanging jokes in front of a large audience, with Chester following Ollie Harrington's lead: "The absurdity of the other blacks was ofttimes hurting. But ours never, it was only entertaining. During that Spring, the café Tournon became the most celebrated café in all of Europe. All of us vocal blacks collected there to choose our white woman for the night" (*My Life*, 37). During those months Himes associated with William Gardner Smith; Richard Gibson; the painters Herb Gentry, Bertel, and Larry Potter; the reporter Frank Van Brackle; the mathematician Josh Leslie; Ollie Harrington; and Wright, who "came every afternoon after lunch to play the pinball machine" (*My Life*, 35). However, he now felt removed from Wright, whose popularity was declining since he had "become a middle-class French-type political analyst," Himes thought, paradoxically the lonelier as he wanted to escape aloneness. If we are to believe his April 26, 1956, letter to Van Vechten, Himes had rejected committed literature as much as discussions of politics and race:

> From here "the Negro problem" in America seems very strange and I think I will never be able to write about it seriously. . . . It's just that it doesn't make sense any more on either side. There is a line in your letter which no doubt put the finger exactly on what I mean: "Perhaps the Negro can no longer bear to see himself treated seriously in fiction or on stage." I believe that applies to all circumstances about American Negro life. . . . Anyway, I'm glad I don't think about it any more. I've got my life almost down to fundamentals and it's pleasant. I don't even think about the Algerian problem about which the French are going crazy. (Quoted in *My Life*, 39)

In Paris Plon had accepted *The Third Generation*, and Gallimard was about to publish *La Fin d'un primitif*. Himes managed to live on that advance, but he had to complete "Mamie Mason," and he availed himself of Daniel Guérin's invitation to stay at his villa in La Ciotat in June 1956. He loved the picturesque little town, the big house, and the large terraced garden dropping down to the sea, which he had all to himself. By the end of the month he was able to mail the manuscript to the United States.

A few weeks before his departure for La Ciotat, Himes had met a German girl, Regine Fischer, at a party at Bertel's. She was in her twenties and Harrington's girlfriend, but they had fallen for each other, and now she was deluging him with letters while he displayed her photograph on his writing table. Upon his return to Paris he stayed

at her place on the Rue Mazarine, and then they got a housekeep-
ing room at the Hotel Rachou on the nearby Rue Gît-le-Coeur. She
attended drama classes at the Vieux Colombier and spoke French
well. He who had never bothered much about French culture now not
only accompanied her to the theater to see Gérard Philippe or Jeanne
Moreau but learned the language with her as a teacher while she introduced him to student circles and interests. He saw less of the race
brothers, except for Walter Coleman, who was still painting; Torun
was making jewelry.

When Chester went to Bielefeld to meet Regine's family, Otto
Fischer, a respectable bookseller, talked him into leaving his daughter
alone for a year to try the strength of their love. She remained in Germany while he returned to a solitary routine of cheap food, cooked
in his hotel room, with a liter of red wine to get him started typing away. Himes was not invited to speak at the conference of Negro
writers held in September at the Sorbonne, but on that occasion he
saw Baldwin and George Lamming again and met the members of the
Afro-American delegation.

In spite of his claims that he was no longer dealing with the Negro
problem, he was busy that same month on *A Case of Rape*, a book set
in Paris, which he described as a "story about four American Negroes
convicted in a French court of raping and murdering an American
white woman." [14] It focuses on the implications of the verdict rendered
by a French court. A French couple has seen Elizabeth Brissaud apparently fighting with four black men in front of the window of a small
hotel room before she is found dead, her clothes undone. Some of the
men's faces are scratched. The autopsy reveals that her death was due
to a heart attack caused by repeated sexual intercourse under the influence of an aphrodisiac. Not being able to imagine that the deceased
could have come to Scott Hamilton's room and made love with the defendants of her own free will, the court has consequently pronounced
a verdict of guilty. Yet, just like Mrs. Brissaud, the black men are intelligent, cosmopolitan, and seemingly well-adjusted people. This totally
imaginary case was derived from actual people and events: Himes's
love affair with Willa; his expatriate friends Bertel, Harrington, Leslie,
and Smith, of whom the other defendants are composite portraits.
As for Roger Garrison—the self-styled investigator, a southern-born
black novelist who has married a white woman, been catapulted into
fame by his autobiography, and sought freedom in France—who else
could it be but Richard Wright?

Himes definitely felt the need to strike back at people and attitudes
that had infuriated him. A letter to Walter Freeman, with whom he

was trying to place *A Case of Rape,* makes clear his willingness to change the characterization of Elizabeth if necessary to ensure U.S. publication. He was denouncing France, not America, he claimed: "The book is essentially a condemnation of French racial attitudes and was written and conceived before the French fiasco in Suez."[15] He reported that Malartic had shown the typescript to several French lawyers, who had been infuriated by it, but Himes wanted to strike at "those bastard European countries" where he said he had been refused service and hotel rooms more often than in New York City.

He characterized official France as hypocritical and increasingly racist as it experienced setbacks in trying to maintain its colonial empire. Also, insofar as he identified with Scott Hamilton, Himes was also settling accounts with a Paris he did not like: "What Scott disliked most about Paris was what it did to the dreamers who gravitated there. It was not the manner in which it destroyed the young and foolish dreams hourly placed on its altar. It was the manner of destroying the capacity for dreaming. All meanings were changed and distorted or perhaps they were given their true definition and shape, which was equally destructive. Love became sexuality; aspirations became ambition. Achievement was limited to a single day, culminating in bed, yours or someone else's, where everything Parisian was reputedly made. One traded in a dream of happiness for a night of love."[16]

In a letter to Walter Freeman, written December 10, 1956, Himes alluded to his "trying desperately to write a detective story to get a little money." This new venture had been prompted by Marcel Duhamel, who had translated *If He Hollers, Let Him Go* into French in 1948 and was now director of the Série Noire thrillers at Gallimard. With a 50,000-franc advance against a total of one thousand dollars (a large sum then), Himes had embarked on a story he had heard Walter Coleman tell, about suckers being taken in by tricksters who claimed they could multiply money chemically. He completed it in January 1957, in a period of intense emotional frustration, as Regine had not returned to Paris. Though it did not turn his head, the money Himes received from his Série Noire deal changed his mind about France. He went back to a less drastic diet, bought fancy clothes, and had his *carte de séjour* renewed: "I didn't want to leave Paris at the very time I was beginning to be successful. . . . Now I was a French writer and the United States could kiss my ass" (*My Life,* 112–13).

Regine came back from Germany still bent upon marrying him. At her insistence Chester registered at the Alliance Française. For some time he attended classes dutifully every morning and worked afternoons on "A Jealous Man Can't Win" at the Café Select on the Boule-

vard Montparnasse. By February 1957 he could boast of a contract
for eight Série Noire titles, all set in Harlem, to be written at the rate
of one every two months. *My Life of Absurdity* emphasized the sense of
fulfillment brought to Himes by financial ease:

> I did not speak French and I had no intention of learning. Except
> for a tiny minority of intellectuals, I thought all the French were racists,
> or at least they did not think well of anyone else on earth. . . . Even if
> the Americans had not tried to kill me as I thought, they had certainly
> ignored me. . . . Every other American black living abroad was at least
> recognized if not helped. But as far as Americans were concerned, I
> was dead.
>
> I had become completely free. I had a German girl, a German car.
> I was making my living from French publishers, and I had no reason
> whatsoever to put foot in America. I had gotten myself as free as possible
> and I was contented if not happy. (*My Life,* 145)

Wasn't this a very illusory way of dissociating himself from race
brothers who were certainly no more dependent upon the United
States than he was?

In early July 1957 Himes went to Stuttgart and Copenhagen. September in Paris was marked by a big meal with the Duhamels, the
Colemans, and Harrington at LeRoy Haynes's restaurant, and also by
a celebration at Plon's to mark the two-hundredth volume of the "Feux
Croisés" series, for which Chester was chosen to represent American
authors. He met Rebecca West, Nikos Kazantzakis, and others at the
eulogies and cocktail party. Chester and Regine were off to Mallorca
shortly after. Again, it proved hard to write there, and he was glad
to be back in April 1958. Going back to Paris meant living in another
hotel room, this time on the Rue Saint-André-des-Arts, and facing
Duhamel without a completed manuscript. But a contract with an advance came from Plon for *Mamie Mason,* and it seemed possible to go
and live on the Riviera. Himes wanted to stay near Antibes, where
the Colemans lived, and on Duhamel's advice he visited Jean Giono
on the way, delighted to find him so interested in his work. He loved
the south of France: "I realized immediately I had entered another
world. It was not at all like Mallorca; the people were more alive, more
intelligent. I was not just another half-ass tourist . . . I was a person
even if the people didn't like me" (*My Life,* 179). Chester and Regine
visited the Verdon canyon and ended in Vence, where they found an
apartment in July 1958.

In the fall *La Reine des pommes* was awarded the Grand Prix de
la Littérature Policière, and in November Himes duly attended the
televised cocktail party at which the prize was officially awarded. He

was now a celebrity, and reporters from *Nice-Matin* were waiting for him when he returned to Vence. Although he later emphasized the absurdity of success, he enjoyed a sense of his own importance: "I became a person not to be thrown away; I became a person comparable to Richard Wright, and the French didn't know what to do with me because I wasn't attacking America but looking at blacks with their extreme absurdity. The students read me for relaxation; there is nothing more relaxing than an absurd nigger" (*My Life*, 181–82). Himes may have exaggerated the absurdity of his situation, but he certainly had a point when he spoke of baffling French critics only too eager to see any black writer as an embattled militant, the better to use him to condemn racism in America while pretending it did not exist in France.

In Vence Himes worked on more books, until Regine's mother came to stay with them in March 1959. When the two women left for Germany, he stayed at Guérin's place in La Ciotat again with Mickey, the first of his dogs, but soon left for Paris to settle in Lesley Packard's apartment on Rue Grégoire de Tours.

Himes had known Lesley for some time: she worked in the photographic section of the *New York Herald Tribune* and wrote a column for its Paris edition; he was coming back to her devotion and her attractive personality. He returned to the Café Tournon too, to bask in his friends' praise or in strangers' admiration. When he handed in the outline and a portion of a novel titled "Don't Play with Death," he received another half-million francs from Gallimard. He felt rich and was happy with Lesley, who took a personal interest in his welfare. From the Hotel Welcome he moved to Harrington's apartment while his friend was in Berlin in April 1959, then to the apartment of a reporter friend of Lesley's on the southern edge of the city. The second half of 1959 was hard for him psychologically, however: he wanted more and more to live with Lesley, and he dreaded Regine's return. Meanwhile, he was working steadily on "Imbroglio Negro" (later *All Shot Up*) and on a movie scenario. In *My Life of Absurdity*, Himes confessed: "I was losing contact with reality, I . . . felt that everyone was imposing on me . . . I was becoming resentful of the way the Americans were treating me and resentful of the French who read my books and couldn't understand them" (195).

Around Christmas 1959 Regine came back. Jealous of Lesley, she began fighting with Chester. She slashed her wrists, was treated in a psychiatric clinic in Nogent-sur-Marne, and then sent to the south of France to convalesce while Chester tried to write "Be Calm" (later *The Heat Is On*). Before Regine could come back, Chester and Lesley drove to Italy in their vintage 1934 Fiat roadster and then stayed at Cagnes on the Riviera before moving to Lesley's place in Paris. In March 1960 Regine was back, and fleeing from her, Chester moved to Biot, where he stayed all spring at the Colemans'. Then he decided to take Regine with him to Kitzbühel, where he wanted to complete *The Heat Is On*, which he managed to do in two months. At this point he and Regine separated.

On October 12, 1960, he wrote to Van Vechten of his plans: "I hope to get to Tunis in the middle of December and from there to Ghana and begin an extemporaneous journey through the more settled of the new nations. However, from here I can't say and might end up in a pot of cannibal stew." Himes did not undertake this African trip. After a stay in Italy he drove to Saint-Tropez, where the news of Richard Wright's sudden death on November 30 reached him and brought him back to Paris. He had not seen much of Wright after the latter had heard that he was using him as a character in *A Case of Rape*. Wright had also moved to the Rue Régis, outside the Latin Quarter. Himes attended the cremation at Père Lachaise and helped Harrington write "The Last Days of Richard Wright," a long piece that *Ebony* magazine had requested. Back on the Riviera Himes confessed: "My brain seemed to whirl without purpose. I had never realized before how much influence Dick had over me . . . over my life, not that I wanted to live like Dick [but] I didn't consider anyone else. . . . And now my brain was stale. All I could think was about those two beat-up wrecks" (*My Life*, 216–17).

Visiting the Colemans helped, especially at Christmastime. Walter's portraits of jazz musicians were soon to be exhibited at the Gallery Moutet in Paris, and a leaflet was prepared with color reproductions and short captions quoting Afro-American authors. Himes felt slighted, however, because he was not asked to contribute. He was depressed because he saw himself "broke, outcast, put down by the American publishers, ignored by the English publishers, nibbled on by the German publishers, only honored by the French for almost free" (*My Life*, 220). Again, when he visited Mougins in the summer of 1961 and was feted by the owner of the famous Hotel de France, he remarked: "I was amazed daily to discover how well I was known in France. I was famous but almost broke" (*My Life*, 321).

Back on the Riviera in the summer of 1961, Himes stayed with the Colemans; he visited Duhamel at Mouans-Sartoux, and also the Picassos. Unimpressed, he wrote to Lesley: "Duhamel and Germaine took me to have lunch with Picasso and all the Little Picassos . . . and all the sycophants of Picasso and then afterwards we had to go to Picasso's 'castle' and all this lasted from 12:30 until almost 8 P.M. and by then my nerves were jumping out of my skin."[17]

On October 23, he had a car accident near Sens, having fallen asleep while attempting to drive to Paris and back without stopping; everyone was in an uproar, but his fracture of the pelvis was tiny. At the American Hospital in Paris he was contacted by Pierre Gaisseau and Arthur Cohn to write a scenario on Harlem life, for which he accepted an advance of 12,000 new francs. At Marianne Greenwood's place at Antibes, during the hurricane-ridden winter of 1962, he lost himself in the story for several weeks until the script came out as "Baby Sister," a sort of black Greek tragedy. At Christmastime he was partying in a Paris nightclub when his legs suddenly gave way under him. It was a false alarm: he rested in Antibes until February while completing another scenario, which he had copyrighted by the Association des Auteurs de Films on March 2, 1962, as "An American Negro in Black Africa." Nothing came of it, and meanwhile seven major American studios turned down "Baby Sister."

Mamie Mason was a success in France, and its author was celebrated everywhere. Himes was asked to supervise a television film for ORTF, starting July 1, 1962, and to write a report for the Lazareff press on the situation in Harlem. For a few weeks he worked with the crew in New York, and they completed a film for the "Cinq Colonnes à la Une" news show; but when he saw it edited down to forty-five minutes, Himes did not like it. He wanted the report he wrote for Lazareff to be a rebuttal to the film. "Harlem, an American Cancer" was bitter and anti-American and told it like it was (*My Life*, 251), but *France-Soir* never printed it. Later Himes gave it to *Présence Africaine* and *Die Welt*.

After a vacation in Corsica with Lesley, Himes stopped in Marseilles to visit his friend Roger Luccioni, the jazz drummer and band leader. He was honored on the front page of the communist daily, *La Marseillaise*. Back in Paris he agreed to write an article comparing the racial situation in America with the Algerian problem in France for the tabloid *Candide*. Shortly after, he wrote Van Vechten: "Now I am in trouble with the OAS—the terrorist group—and I will have to leave France for a time. I wrote a small piece for a newspaper here in which I compared the racists in Mississippi to the OAS and I have been seriously warned that it is dangerous for me to be here."[18] Indeed, Himes was exaggerating. At any rate, he only "fled" from Paris in order to join the Colemans at Biot.

He was then contacted by novelist John A. Williams, whose *Night Song* he liked very much and who requested biographical material from him for a literary project, later *The Angry Black*. This may have

set Himes thinking about writing about his expatriate experience: "I
know I will use my European experience for material; but what I must
decide is whether to write a straight autobiographical account or fic-
tionalize it. I would very much like to write this account of my years in
Europe as a straight autobiography in three books; each book with my
life with a woman, all three completely different. The first an American socialite (Boston—Smith College, etc.), married, divorced, three
daughters; the second an infantile, immature, very crazy German in
her twenties; the third English, good family, in her thirties, a member
of the right people." [19] Clearly Regine now belonged to the past, and
Europe, the place where he had experienced the relationships and
ceaseless travels that had filled ten years of his life, was little more than
a setting, with somewhat strange people who, he claimed, misunder-
stood him even when they read his works and did not cheat him out
of his money.

   After a mix-up between Gallimard and Plon, due to Himes's signing
contracts for detective stories with both of them, and a big celebration
at Les Halles with record producers Eddie and Nicole Barclay, Himes
suddenly flew to New York. He was on his way to Mexico, eager to
stay with Marianne Greenwood and write a new novel during the winter. There a mild stroke sent him to the Mérida hospital, whence Van
Vechten's money bailed him out in February 1963. At the New York
Neurological Institute the tests proved satisfactory, and he returned
to Paris.

   During the summer of 1963 *Une Affaire de viol* was published by Les
Yeux Ouverts, a small concern that went bankrupt. So Himes got only
1,500 francs for the first publication, in French, of *A Case of Rape*. The
book got some publicity, however, largely because well-known novelist
Christiane Rochefort had written a preface to it. According to Himes
the French press was incensed that "a black writer who knew all of the
black suspects [should] set out to prove that rape was always a political
crime and that the government itself was racist" (*My Life*, 268). Himes
contended that he had written the novel "to emphasize the preconceptions and humiliations that black Americans were subjected to in
Paris during the Algerian war." [20] When he declared that "at the height
of the racist Algerian war, all the Parisian press claimed that I was
calling the French racists," Himes was not wrong about the nature of
the accusations leveled against him, but he was certainly exaggerating
the impact of a single *Paris-Presse* article with the headline "Etes-vous
raciste, monsieur?" to the point of concluding: "I became very much
disliked" (*My Life*, 269). On the one hand, *A Case of Rape* did not sell,
and few readers could really know Himes's antiracist stand; on the

other hand, he himself had adopted a nonpolitical, nonracial attitude. To most French people who knew of him, he remained simply a writer of great detective stories.

Around that time Himes went to the Riviera again—to Biot, where he visited the Colemans, and to Cannes, where, thanks to Christiane Rochefort, who was the secretary of the film festival, he attended many showings, basking in his celebrity: "My name had become a byword . . . at last, I felt recognized. I felt I had become more famous in Paris than any black American writer who ever lived" (*My Life*, 270). During Lesley's summer vacation Himes spent a whole month in Antibes. Then, after three months in Paris he took off again for Saint-Laurent-du-Var, near Nice, in mid-December. His novel "Back to Africa" (later published as *Cotton Goes to Harlem*) was to be translated into French, and he rewrote it for three weeks running until he was satisfied it was probably the best of his detective stories.

Himes returned to Paris on January 15, 1964, to a lovely apartment into which Lesley had already moved, on Rue Bourbon-le-Château near the Buci market: "It was a fantastic location with the market at one end of the block and a clear view of Saint-Germain-des-Prés on the other side with a small park just beneath the windows—Place Furstenberg. But the difficulty was one had to climb seven flights of stairs. . . . It had a big ornate bath with many mirrors inside the door, then a medium-sized bar . . . in front of which was a large expanse of living-room with a window and a big dining-room table built around the central beam . . . a bedroom upstairs with large double doors opening into a large railed balcony" (*My Life*, 276). This was indeed the first place Himes could call home in Paris, a place fit for entertaining friends at dinner and giving parties. There were many visitors: black photographer Emil Cadoo; Art Simmons, pianist of the Living Room; novelist John A. Williams on a European trip; activist Carlos Moore, whose denunciations of Cuban racism Himes was ready to believe and who once brought Malcolm X. Himes had met the Muslim leader in Harlem, he agreed with his perspectives except about religion, and he was glad to see him again when he visited Paris to speak at a rally at the Mutualité.

Violence was exploding in America, and Himes was sought for a long interview in the Jewish magazine *L'Arche* on the strained relations between blacks and Jews in the United States. In the summer he prepared an ambitious project on the growth and present state of the Harlem ghetto for *Paris-Match*, but the deal fell through. Himes was interviewed for a special issue of *Adam*, which printed a series of articles on Harlem. The cover displayed a superb color portrait of him

by John Taylor, so striking that many people now got to know him by
sight, and he truly was, as he boasted, "the best-known black in Paris"
(*My Life,* 291). Many of his novels were being reprinted in paperback
in the United States, and he was making "a little money; a step ahead
of poverty" (*My Life,* 291). He recommended Melvin Van Peebles to
write the text for Wolinski's comic strip of *La Reine des pommes* for
Hara-Kiri, a progressive avant-garde magazine. Van Peebles was also
working on a scenario for *A Case of Rape,* which he did not complete;
instead, the following year he won a French prize to shoot his own
film, "La Permission," his first feature-length movie.

Lesley and Chester had to move out of their apartment when the
lease expired, and while Lesley settled on the Rue d'Assas, Chester decided to rent a flat at the Palais Rouaze in Cannes, in order to write.
Soon he complained: "My novel moves all right but it is not swinging.
I like to both read and write novels that swing. . . . So this exercise is
getting slightly on my nerves. The theme is hilarious but the writing
is definitely pedestrian."[21] In the inclement autumn weather Himes
felt lonely and utterly miserable, in spite of visits to the Colemans,
whose marriage was breaking up apace. At this juncture he returned
to Paris and asked Lesley to marry him. They did not leave the city
until June 1965, when they went to Greece and Rhodes. In the fall
they drove to Denmark, this time in a brand-new beige Jaguar, and
stayed for several months near Copenhagen, where Chester worked
on a new Série Noire novel and also on his European reminiscences.
In mid-March 1966 they drove down to La Ciotat and stayed at Daniel
Guérin's Rustique Olivette, where Himes started his autobiography.
The weather was balmy, and they could eat and live outside. Now,
partly thanks to Guérin's hospitality, he could relax. He recorded this:
"I was beginning to enjoy France for the first time."

It was time to go back, but they spent an enjoyable month in Aix-
en-Provence. While looking for a cheap place to rent, they were shown
a big farmhouse at Venelles, a village outside of Aix on the way to
Manosque, where Giono lived. The house belonged to an acquaintance
of Larry Potter, Himes's painter friend: it was for sale, and they could
rent it for a year at a good price. In *My Life of Absurdity* Himes provides an enthusiastic description of the old-time farmhouse of brown
Provençal mud with walls a yard thick. He liked living in seclusion
because he could work at leisure and repair to Aix when he felt like it:

> The whole place was a wonderland. Food in the supermarkets was
> good, plentiful, specializing in lamb from the Alps and good wine from
> all regions. The cafés on Cours Mirabeau were always packed with over-
> flowing terraces.

It was the first time I had really lived as I wanted. . . . My life fell quickly into a pattern so that everything pleased me. (*My Life*, 326)

They had only a few visitors: Edwina Rubinstein; Larry's friend Nicole Toutain, who came from Nice; Jay Clifford, "that fantastic story-teller" from Monte Carlo. Apart from visiting the Luccionis and the Colemans, with whom they enjoyed walking in the spring along the Durance and partying at Christmas, there was little distraction. Yet Himes's writing did not jell. He made many unsuccessful attempts at another detective story. Instead of typing, he would catch himself pottering about the house or garden, exercising his dog or shooting at targets. Was inspiration lacking, or was it subject matter?

I knew so little about the French I couldn't even talk about them, much less write about them. That's why I became obsessed with a house, and not even my house. When it came right down to the facts, I didn't really know anyone but myself. I didn't go to see French movies or plays or read French books, newspapers, or about French wars, or politics. I had never really arrived in France, but the Americans did not want me. But I wrote quick, short vignettes about the way I saw blacks in their country, or even in other countries. I kept writing about myself, the life of my mind, hoping to put these vignettes into a book. And it had become very boring. (*My Life*, 333)

Himes had some financial worries, too; yet they do not explain his attitude toward France, which was strangely contradictory at the time, as is shown by an episode in his autobiography. He went to a dentist in Aix who—accidentally, he said—pulled one of his expensive front crowns. When he went back because the bleeding continued, he was recognized as Chester Himes and greeted warmly, which led him to remark: "That was my entire life in France; I was treated like a nigger until the natives recognized me and I became a celebrity and the natives tried to make up for the damage they had inflicted. I became so angry I went to New York as soon as possible, arriving May 2, 1967" (*My Life*, 337).

But he did not stay in America very long. After a lovely summer at Venelles, he and Lesley rented the Paris apartment of a Swedish friend at 21, Rue de l'Estrapade, close to the picturesque market on Rue Mouffetard and just off the lively Place de la Contrescarpe, which was filled with tourists day and night. They had few visitors, but the crowds in the neighborhood bothered Himes, as did the fact that he did not have a permanent home. He had reached the point of chronicling his affair with Regine but felt he could not write. Consequently, he and Lesley left for Holland in August. They then moved to Spain, down to Moraira near Alicante, where they bought a plot of land to have a house built. They did not return to Paris until the following May, when they stayed in Nicole Toutain's apartment on the Rue Abel-Ferry in the 16th arrondissement. This was far enough from the Latin Quarter when the students started demonstrating.

The couple returned from a week in England just as the rioting was becoming dangerous. When it reached Saint-Germain-des-Prés and the riot police broke down the doors of the Deux Magots and the Café de Flore, they began thinking of another city but found a place near Montparnasse: "Our landlord had a big TV set we could use, and we bought much exotic food from the Chinese stores and fresh French food from Inno-France and always ate well and plentifully. I worked quite hard but did not accomplish much because of distraction. The neighborhood lured us out of doors, the stores and fascination of the station area within walking distance, from Boulevard du Montparnasse to Boulevard Raspail" (*My Life*, 358–59). Thus did Himes live through the historic events of May 1968, thinking of fine food and exploring the city while the whole country was still in turmoil. His last extended stay indeed demonstrated his typical lack of interest and noninvolvement in the political life around him.

In September 1968 the Himeses left for Alicante. They stopped again in Paris only in early May 1969, on their way to London, and their next visits to France were brief. They attended the Nice Book Fair from May 26 to June 2, 1970: this time, it was the Hotel Ruehl, Monte Carlo, champagne at the Negresco with the Targs, a visit to Duhamel and a side visit to Saint-Tropez. This also was Chester's first really leisurely tourist trip, with the Targs, by way of Arles and Van Gogh's bridge, the beach at Sète, with a feast on the shore of Étang de Thau and a picnic at Béziers. They had just arrived in Barcelona when they were called back for five days in Paris because *Blind Man with a Pistol* was being published in French. At the Hotel Pont-Royal journalists and interviewers filed in; there were parties at Gallimard's, an ORTF television program, drinks with acquaintances, and a private showing of the film *Cotton Comes to Harlem*, but too little time for friends like Nicole Toutain, Jean Miotte, Walter Coleman, and George and Davina Troller. And soon Himes had to fly to Germany for another literary round organized by Rowolt. But from then on the Himeses lived in Casa Griot, their house overlooking the sea at Moraira-Teulada in the sun of Spain. They went back to Paris, usually for medical reasons, on only three occasions in the late seventies.

Himes admitted that, even after his most extended sojourns in France, he did not feel enough at ease in European societies to go beyond using them as settings in his fiction. He used Paris as a locale only in *A Case of Rape*, making the most of his Latin Quarter experiences and picturesque acquaintances. In his autobiographical writing, he was clearly more interested in retracing his own growth, hurts, and emotional involvements than in creating any kind of human comedy; consequently, no French character is dealt with in depth. Himes excelled in the witty vignette and in caricature. He thus sketched Wright's imposing concierge, for instance, as "some prehistoric species of the human race. . . . Huge, drooping breasts topping a squarish, big-hipped body" (*Hurt*, 173) or a cantankerous hotel proprietor as a "mean old crone . . . the last of the broomstick witches" (*Hurt*, 295). Such descriptions were akin to the lurid Rabelaisian characters teeming in his Harlem detective stories—i.e., very close to stereotypes. Himes would even use "French" as a descriptive epithet in speaking of a neighbor in Arcachon as a "buxom woman with a rugged French face" (*Hurt*, 225). He often resorted to clichés, taking one instance as representative of the whole group. Not only does he speak of "typical French gallantry" or "inherent French courtesy," but French curiosity has people always stare at an American black "with the lighthearted, wonderfully free interest of watching monkeys at the Zoo, so common to the French" (*My Life*, 87). The autobiography abounds in remarks on European mores—at times accurate, sometimes mere wisecracks. For instance, when Himes claimed he wasn't showing the Negro "as an oppressed downtrodden people, as the French had been taught to believe" (*My Life*, 178), he was making an important point. When he remarked, "At that time if a French father sired enough children, he no longer needed to work; the government would take care of him and his family" (*Hurt*, 231), he exaggerated only slightly since measures existed to encourage population growth. Yet when he extended "French fetishism for pregnancy" to animals—"in strict French tradition, he [the tomcat] was seldom home during Madame's pregnancy" (*My Life*, 231)—he only desired to be witty at all costs. Himes's impressions should be taken strictly for what they are: fleeting, often superficial, reactions. But his emotions also colored his apparently objective descriptions. Dejected and broke as he came back to Paris with Willa near the end of their love affair, he spoke of walking, luggage in hand, along the "dirty fetid stinking Seine" (*My Life*, 341). The Seine is dirty; it could have been stinking that summer, but certainly not near the Pont Neuf on a cold October morning. Yet, because Himes was angry and unhappy, the Seine was "fetid."

Should one conclude that Himes's vignettes of French life are less authentic than those of Claude McKay, the black writer closest to

Himes in his desire not to follow his race brothers unquestioningly and yet not to be deceived by pro-French propaganda? Himes confessed his bias when he remarked: "Maybe all that untrue crap Hemingway wrote about Paris prejudiced me. I thought that all the waiters at Café Select were racist and all the clients racist too" (*My Life*, 126). The "crap" is the "movable feast" image displayed by a literary ancestor. Himes is honest insofar as he makes the reader aware that, when he writes the narrative of his life in Paris, his opinion no longer coincides with what he thought at the time he lived it. Yet the general impression remains that he was in a rather hostile environment, cut off from it and taken advantage of because of the language barrier.

Speaking of literary ancestors, Himes never alluded to more than a half-dozen French authors in his writings. He described Mlle. Cancalen as "an angular spinster who looked as though she came from Zola's novels" (*Hurt*, 233), referring obviously to *Germinal* and *L'Assommoir*, works he appreciated as much as those of Maupassant or Flaubert (the latter's largely because of their value as historical documents). But he spoke of George Sand only because he happened to visit the Valdemosa charterhouse, where she stayed with Chopin. He hinted at Sartre being the *roi de l'existentialisme* and Camus his *dauphin*, yet his single reference to the latter ("Albert Camus once said that racism is absurd. Racism introduces absurdity into the human condition" [*My Life*, 3]) in the opening of the second volume of his autobiography remains untraceable. Did he read many French books other than Rimbaud's *Season in Hell* (in translation) before going to Paris? He mentions very few French writers in his interviews. He associated briefly with writers like Jean Giono and Jean Cocteau because they praised his work publicly, but he did not read their works.

Not that Himes did not like France. Looking back in the seventies, he declared repeatedly that he liked it better than any other country in Europe (he chose to settle in Spain only for financial reasons), although he always remained critical of the French as a nation he saw as chauvinistic, contemptuous of other peoples, preoccupied with material things, and more racist than was generally publicized. But he made little use of France in his books. Above all, Paris became a means for his winning literary appreciation and, eventually, international fame. Indeed, his own judgment of the five-year period when he was starting to write detective stories could be extended to apply to his whole stay in Europe, from 1953 to 1970: "I travelled through Europe trying desperately to find a life into which I would fit; and my determination stemmed from my desire to succeed without America. I received much help, I realized afterwards; . . . I never found a place where I even began to fit, due in great part to my inability to learn any foreign language and my antagonism toward all white people who, I thought, treated me as an inferior" (*My Life*, 153).

NOTES

1. Chester Himes to the author, November 2, 1978.

2. Himes, *The Quality of Hurt* (New York: Doubleday, 1972), 117, hereafter cited in the text as *Hurt*.

3. Himes to John A. Williams, July 9, 1963.

4. Himes, unpublished manuscript, March 1954, 3.

5. Himes to Carl Van Vechten, May 12, 1953, Yale.

6. Himes to Yves and Yvonne Malartic, May 11, 1953.

7. Himes, unpublished manuscript prepared for *Ebony*, May 1954, 4.

8. Ibid., 3.

9. Ibid., 18.

10. Himes to the Malartics, September 9, 1954.

11. Himes to Van Vechten, October 16, 1954.

12. Himes to Yves Malartic, February 18, 1955.

13. Himes, *My Life of Absurdity* (New York: Doubleday, 1976), 30, hereafter cited in the text as *My Life*.

14. Himes to Walter Freeman, September 23, 1956.

15. Himes to Freeman, December 10, 1956.

16. Himes, *A Case of Rape* (Washington, D.C.: Howard University Press, 1984), 54.

17. Himes to Lesley Packard, September 18, 1961.

18. Himes to Van Vechten, October 9, 1962, Yale.

19. Himes to Van Vechten, November 29, 1962, quoted in *My Life*, 252.

20. Himes to the author, September 15, 1971.

21. Himes to Lesley Packard, undated, quoted in *My Life*, 295.

15

William Gardner Smith:
An Eternal Foreigner

Although William Gardner Smith was not a writer of the same magnitude as Richard Wright, James Baldwin, or Chester Himes—his fellow "expatriates"—his French experience is of great interest. Like them, he went to Paris at the end of World War II, but he was the only one to reside there continuously until the black power period.

Spanning two important decades, Smith's reactions can be seen as a synthesis of the other writers' less complete involvement. Like Wright, but unlike Baldwin and Himes, he was able to gauge the new developments in Africa because he spent several years in Ghana. Like Baldwin, but unlike Wright and Himes, he took the measure of the changed racial and political climate in the United States at the height of the black power movement. Finally, he used France as more than a source of inspiration for his fiction; to a large extent he made it his own country. More fluent in French than any other Afro-American of the same generation, he shared the French life-style to the point of marrying a Parisian and raising a family there. As a result, in many respects his responses—close as they are to those of his black contemporaries in France—are often more accurately attuned to the realities of the place. Also, not being such a celebrity himself, he often proved a less self-centered, more objective witness of facts or moods, which his training as a journalist and reporter enabled him to use to good effect.

Like Claude McKay in the 1920s, William Gardner Smith was an Afro-American writer who became, and remained, very much what he had chosen to be: a cosmopolitan, worldly mind, inclined to enjoy the more leisurely pace of European life, if not its luxuries, and capable of adapting to diverse cultural milieus. He chose expatriation because he felt it would be propitious for the development of his sensibilities and the continuance of his freedom, and he managed to preserve these, sometimes at great cost.

Smith was born in south Philadelphia in 1927. When he was seven, his mother married a janitor who treated him like a son but whom he never quite accepted as a father. He managed to be both street-wise and an excellent student at mostly white Barratt Junior High School. At Benjamin Franklin High School he was editor of the school newspaper, an avid reader of Faulkner and Hemingway, and encouraged by his teachers to write fiction. Refusing scholarships to Howard and Lincoln after graduating in 1944, he joined the Pittsburg *Courier*, the important black weekly, as a reporter working with the Philadelphia editor. Early in 1946 he was drafted and assigned to the forces in Germany as a clerk-typist. After serving for eight months in Berlin, he returned home with the material for a first novel. It was published by Farrar and Straus as *Last of the Conquerors*—the story of a love affair between a German girl and a black American GI and an indictment of the way the U.S. Army treated the conquered Nazis better than its own Negro soldiers.

In 1949 he married Mary Sewell, a former schoolmate. They attended Temple University together, but Smith soon dropped out to devote himself to reporting and writing. His second novel, *Anger at Innocence*, appeared in 1950. A local celebrity now, Bill liked to stay up late, writing or enjoying the company of acquaintances who talked politics. He was somewhat lionized by the Left and did not fit in with his wife's middle-class family. Away from home at the Yaddo Writers' Colony in May 1951, he realized that his marriage had been a mistake: he did not want the settled life but preferred freedom to feel, write, and starve without paying a mortgage or an insurance policy or having to invite friends home for a polite evening.

Smith's plan to go to Paris in the fall of 1951 thus resulted from a desire to break away from the conformity of the black bourgeoisie of which he felt he was a prisoner rather than from a need to escape the racial scene. Why did he choose Paris? Possibly because his utter admiration for Hemingway made it easier for him to project himself into the role of the expatriate in search of himself at the "movable feast" of Europe. Possibly because French liberalism was emphasized at the time in such magazines as *Negro Digest*, where Bill's colleague Roi Ottley would write: "To an extent equalled by few cities in the world, Paris is the nearest approach to civilized living for the black man. He unquestionably has personal dignity, freedom of movement, may work at any occupation he is qualified to do."[1] Possibly too because Smith's studies in French in high school and his reading of the French realists from Balzac to Zola made him somewhat familiar with the environment he expected to be his. Last but not least, the example of Richard Wright loomed large in his mind. In June he wrote Wright that he was thinking of settling in France for a while with his wife—one or two years maybe. And he plied him with questions about living there. Could one afford an apartment? Was the heating sufficient in the winter? Must one be cautious about food and water? Were the French easy to get acquainted with? Could one manage without speaking the language? What should he bring with him? And, especially, could one listen to United States–made records on French-made gramophones? He concluded that he would like to see the great republic before "the jackals" started aiming atom bombs at it.[2]

When he crossed the Atlantic on board the *Liberté* in mid-October 1951, Bill was not traveling alone, however. Mary had been enthusiastic about the project and was following him to a new setting where, they hoped, their marriage could have a second chance. Like most newcomers the Smiths first settled in the Hotel des États-Unis, apartments being a rarity at the time. They enjoyed the company of fellow-Philadelphian Harry Goldberg, who was completing an M.A. in library science and who introduced them to Paris.

Bill and Mary spent much time seeing the part of Paris not usually visited by tourists, especially the working-class areas of Barbès and Belleville, the Buttes Chaumont, which appealed to Bill's simple, popular tastes, and getting acquainted with the language. He wrote his mother at the time: "This is the second Christmas I spend in a strange, European city [the first one had been Berlin] and, funny to say, I don't feel like a stranger at all. I feel at home in Paris."[3] The Smiths were consorting with many Americans, though: Canada Lee had been there for two weeks; they had seen the Wrights frequently, even having dinner at their house, and Bill noted that Richard was "very nice, just an ordinary Joe" with two lovely children.[4]

Soon Smith got in touch with his agent, Mrs. Bradley (her deceased husband had been the agent of the lost generation), and met the translator of *Anger at Innocence*, which had been selected by the prestigious Club Français du Livre. This, in his own mind as well as the brothers', conferred much prestige on Bill at a time when Wright's novels had not achieved similar distinction in France. He did not receive the attention bestowed upon Wright but was interviewed by quite a few magazines and hailed as an American writer of stature. He behaved accordingly, going to the cafés down the street from his hotel in the morning to write notes for a new novel. Mary wanted "a real place," however, and they were lucky enough to secure a two-room apartment for a bargain—fifty-five dollars a month. They kept expenses low by eating cheap, though plentiful, meals in restaurants; yet the couple's reserves would not last more than three months at this rate, and they tried to find a source of income.

By December 1951 Smith had managed to make an extra hundred dollars by writing a weekly column for the Pittsburgh *Courier;* the money situation was worrisome, however, and Mary, who spoke next to no French, decided to try her luck at finding employment in London. For several months she desperately searched for a suitable job, her father sending her the funds for a return ticket three times before she finally decided to go back to the United States. Now installed at the Hotel de Tournon in the Latin Quarter, Bill visited her in early March in London before they decided to separate: "The separation was no sudden thing. The things that led to it began, both Mary and I knew, almost from the first day that we were married. . . . Marriage, to her, is not for me; and marriage, to me, should not be for her. We are too utterly different in every conceivable way. . . . Mary needs a home, she needs comfort, affection, to be near her parents, to be settled and steady. I go absolutely crazy in the same situation. I can't stand to be settled for life. I want to move. I want always to live, to discover something new. The *boredom* of marriage drove me nearly crazy."[5] Indeed their trip to Europe had been a vain attempt to save their marriage. There was no talk of divorce, however, until Mary made up her mind about it.

Alone in Paris Smith was almost penniless, and for a while he lived on borrowed money, subsisting on one meal a day that he cooked on a small alcohol burner in his hotel room. Yet he felt cozy in his Spartan setting: a double bed, two closets, a washbowl, a bed table, a larger table on which he typed his novel in front of the window that looked out on the small, lively street. On the walls he had pinned some prints of famous paintings and a large map of Paris. On top of his bookcase he kept a dish always filled with fruit. And he worked; getting up between ten and eleven, he would drink coffee and eat some fruit while typing away until two or three in the afternoon. Then, when he could afford it, he had a seventy-five-cent, three-course meal in a small restaurant; when he could not, he ate bread and cheese before repairing to his favorite café: "The café de Tournon is small, not immaculately clean and kind of noisy. Everyday some Frenchmen, old and young, sit around there playing cards, checkers or chess. They know me and like me, so I sit with them and talk or play chess. They also try to get me to play bridge but I refuse, though I've learned how to play. I don't like that game very much."[6] Around five he would go back to his room and work again for a couple of hours. After dinner he usually visited friends, went to cafés, sometimes saw a movie or attended a concert; only occasionally would he return to his room and read.

There was nothing glamorous about such a routine, but Smith felt free to use his time as he wished. Through eating too little, he lost ten pounds, but he could write his mother: *"And yet I was happy! Because I was living the way I want to live."* [7] The poor writer's bohemian life-style, like Hemingway's in the 1920s, was to his liking, and he could pursue it with excitement because of the freedom of affection and the discoveries it permitted. Later, when he wrote *Return to Black America,* he would remember:

> I had meant to leave only for several months. But the months, like the years, multiplied. At one point, when I was quite broke in Paris the editor [the white editor of a national magazine who had offered Smith a position as associate editor of his publication] came on a visit to the French capital and dropped by to see me. I shall never forget his utterly stupefied look as he stood in the doorway of my little attic room, fresh from his luxurious American apartment, staring at the ugly peeling wallpaper, the lumpy iron bed, the bare lopsided table, the two rickety chairs, the worn linoleum and the washstand attached precariously to the wall.
>
> "My God!" he exclaimed. "Do you mean to tell me it's for *this* that you turned down the job I offered you?"
>
> I was almost amused. I said, "Yes, precisely for this."
>
> He shook his head, aghast. He did not understand. It was all right. He could not be expected to understand. [8]

Living alone in Paris was sometimes hard to take, however, especially after the news came of the sudden death of his friend Canada Lee. Although opposed to marriage, Smith needed women, and in the fall of 1952 he started having numerous affairs. In spite of his pockmarked face, he was handsome, with a lively smile, a quick mind, and a genuine concern for people; consequently, he soon became a great ladies' favorite among the group of black expatriates in the Latin Quarter. For nearly a year he lived with a white Canadian girl who largely supported him while he was writing his third novel. He had chosen *South Street* as the title, since it dealt with the rough, teeming artery of the Philadelphia black district. The many characters also served to raise the problems—desire for advancement, racial loyalty, need for love and culture—that Smith and Mary had confronted.

Although Smith's favorite café was already the nearby Tournon, at that time most of the Afro-American writers and artists in Paris still congregated at the Monaco Bar, down from the Rue Monsieur-le-Prince, where Wright lived. Smith would often join the crowd there for long talks and a few drinks. His relationship with Wright, whom he had visited soon after his arrival in France, dated from the time he had interviewed the nationally acclaimed author of *Black Boy* for *Ebony* in 1945. When Smith managed to become the Paris correspondent for Johnson Publications, he covered Wright's life there, this time in a longer story that appeared in July 1953 as "Black Boy in France." As was his wont, Wright would advise his younger colleague about writing, stressing what he considered the black writer's duty—i.e., that he should address himself to essential problems. More famous and feted than Smith, he was apparently piqued to see that the latter's *Anger at Innocence* had become a Club du Livre selection before his own *Native Son* was awarded the same distinction. According to Chester Himes this may have been one of the reasons why the two men did not really like each other. Another reason was Bill's youthful cocksureness; he was proud in a rather naïve way, which was the source of his charm but which could alienate elders whose attitude he perceived as patronizing. Himes himself met Smith in 1953, when Wright introduced them at the Café Tournon and recalled a "pleasant-looking, brown-skinned young man who talked very rapidly in choppy, broken sentences."[9]

Among the group that gathered, first at the Monaco then increasingly often at the Tournon, there were several black "brothers," including some from Africa, but mostly white American and other English-speaking artists, budding writers and students like Christopher Logue, Jake Beretti, Katia Grotkamp, Heather Chisholm, John Singleton, and Pamela Oline, among those who were closest to Bill. There was the strong personality of bulky LeRoy Haynes, an ex-GI who, with his French wife, had opened his soul food restaurant in Montmartre. There was the beaming and stimulating presence of Pittsburgh *Courier* cartoonist Ollie Harrington. The feeling of being part of "the scene" was exhilarating and sustaining. Paris also provided exciting cultural surroundings, the more so as by then Smith had become fluent in French. He would write his family of his satisfaction: from the point of view of his personal education, his stay had been marvelous, and he found life in France very rich. "No matter what happens afterwards, I'll always have this."[10]

South Street came out in 1954, and its modest commercial success helped Smith manage. More important, he was hired as a desk editor by Agence France Presse, the leading news agency. His job consisted mainly of rewriting and translating into English the dispatches and news stories that came in in French. Working six hours a day, six days a week, he could now support himself with a salary of some 200 dollars a month. And to make time for his busy social life, he requested permission to work at the office from 6 P.M. until midnight.

Completing *South Street,* an angry book steeped in his own past, had amounted to a kind of therapy for Smith, who was then still in the United States emotionally and still involved in a kind of protest that he

discovered was leading him nowhere. His stay in Paris was beginning
to liberate him from deep-seated tensions, and by the end of the fifties
he would appraise his own growth in the following terms: "While I
was writing about the past, I was undergoing what you might call "an
agonizing reappraisal" of myself and what I wanted to write. . . . I'm
coming out of the waiting period, the fallow period. I haven't lost my
anger. I've lost the daily irritations. But I don't want to write out of
anger. I don't want a book to be a cry of anguish. I want it to shed
light [that] will come from the friction of the characters . . . and the
characters will be part of me. Paris has opened up a whole world for
me. This is a beginning. Not an end."[11]

In 1955, after several fallow years during which he was content
with publishing articles and working at Agence France Presse, he had
tasted enough of life in France to write to his mother: "When I think of
the States, it seems to me that I'm thinking of a foreign country. Paris
is more familiar to me, it seems." He had the impression he wanted
nothing else of what he had left in the United States but the pleasure
of seeing his mother again. And he had the feeling that every one of
his acquaintances who had recently returned home to America regretted not having stayed in Europe. He considered himself exceptionally
lucky to have found a job, for they were scarce, and the French did
not like to hire foreigners. He did not pretend he was making it any
more than the expatriates who were almost all living in rooms they
never would have lived in at home. But, he concluded: "Life takes on a
different meaning here, and things like that don't count very much."[12]
Life was more human in Paris and prejudice rare. Bill liked to tell
an anecdote concerning his friend Colette Lacroix, a secretary at the
French League against Racism and Anti-Semitism: wanting to test her
mother's attitude, she had told her she was thinking of marrying an
American Negro musician they both knew. And her mother had answered: "Do you want to marry an *American?*" Smith was not deceived
by French demonstrations of liberalism, but he was convinced that,
provided he did his work well and took care of his own business, he
was free to enjoy French hospitality.

He was happy to have another old friend again in Paris. Richard
Gibson, a fellow Philadelphian of a distinguished family related to
Henry Tanner, had been attending Kenyon College when he and Bill
met in 1949; both were journalists in Philadelphia—Bill for the Pittsburgh *Courier* and Richard for the local edition of the *Afro-American*—
and both were interested in writing fiction. In 1951 Gibson had gone
to Rome on a Whitney fellowship to complete a novel, which was published in 1958 as *A Mirror for Magistrates,* and when his money ran out,

he had worked as a publicist for Italian Film Export and as an assistant to writer and filmmaker Curzio Malaparte. He had visited Paris in 1952 to see the Smiths. In late 1954, after being discharged from the Army, he had come to study at the Sorbonne on the GI Bill. The following summer Smith helped him get a job at Agence France Presse. The two men became close, and Bill was best man when Gibson married Joy Kaye, his English girlfriend, in March 1956. By then Smith was living with ex-actress Musi Haffner, who had long supported him while he was writing. Although Mary got Bill to sign the application for divorce on the grounds of desertion and mutual consent, he did not marry his companion. He felt more attracted to a French student, Solange Royez-Reussner, whom he was to marry five years later.

For a few years Smith wrote mostly for money, though not without talent and humor. In October 1956 *Modern Man,* a girlie magazine, printed his "Master of the Sex Story," which, in spite of its alluring title, dealt with the art of Guy de Maupassant in rather literary fashion. In December the same magazine published his "Europe's Most Naked Boy," a witty piece about the statue of the Manneken-Pis in Brussels. Again, "The World's Most Famous Nudes," which appeared under Smith's name in *Art and Photography* in April 1957, dealt with masterpieces of world painting. He turned to a decidedly lighter, more satirical vein in fiction when he completed a novel, "Ballets Roses," during the period from 1957 to 1960. The title—which like the theme is reminiscent of *Pinktoes* by Chester Himes—hinted at a much-publicized scandal. Important Frenchmen, including members of the government, were involved: old gentlemen, overripe ladies, and teenage girls recruited by a former chauffeur of the Sureté had been having fun in high society clubs and even an official state residence for some ten years when the press got hold of the story. Smith's novel exploited the topical and potentially commercial value of this erotic episode more than it attempted to investigate moral or political corruption. At any rate, the novel never appeared because the typescript got lost at Éditions Plon, which was to publish it, and Smith had kept no copy.

"Ballets Roses" was followed by a much more racially and politically oriented work, *The Stone Face,* which found its source in Smith's Parisian experience and growing concern with the racial situation in France relative to the Algerian war.[13] It deserves close attention as one of the few works of fiction genuinely inspired by Afro-American expatriate experience. It is a fair testimony to the atmosphere of the times. That *The Stone Face* never really attracted the attention it deserved was largely due to its late publication, in 1963, when the scene of racial confrontation had shifted from France and the Algerian war to the United States and the civil rights movement. But it was a timely novel indeed. The title points to the obsessive symbol of American racism confronted by the protagonist, Simeon Brown, a black American artist who has fled to France in order to escape violence. Like Smith, Brown lives in the racially mixed American community in the Latin Quarter. The group comprises a famous self-exiled black novelist, Benson, whose role corresponds closely to that played by Richard Wright; Babe Carter, a jazz musician who is the leader of the group; Maria, a Polish refugee studying to become an artist; and a white American couple—Clyde, a drunkard, and Jinx, a nymphomaniac. The treatment of these characters implies much criticism of the white expatriates' self-indulgent quest for pleasure, but it also questions the effects of exile on the blacks: Benson has achieved psychological composure at the expense of his committed writing; Simeon himself has found in France a haven free of racial violence, but having regained his peace of mind, he runs the risk of being cut off from his roots and never achieving wholeness.

Paris is first perceived as the equivalent of harmony: in the opening paragraph, while looking at his face in the mirror, Simeon meditates on his new expatriate condition. He sees the peace of Europe as a remedy for the harmful effects of racism in America, making possible his rebirth. However, Babe Carter, who has spent over a decade in Paris, sees it mostly as a catalyst, a crucible in which one can either be renewed or sink completely: "Great town, if you don't weaken. If you can stand up under the drinking and the screwin' and the good food and wine." Paris is a place where white American coeds become whores, where some bums can become respectable again, and where even "crackers became negrophiles—at least while they were here." At best, it is a temporary retreat, and Simeon is confronted with the question of the length of his own exile (*Stone Face*, 9).

The French in the novel offer no model of behavior but simply represent an environment in which American expatriates can function naturally and be themselves. Possible models are Maria, with whom Simeon falls in love, and, even better, Ahmed, an Algerian activist with whom he makes friends. Maria wants to become an actress, and her choice amounts to a sort of escape: she has come to Paris to seek "the froth of life," the capacity to dream and to play denied her Jewish childhood under the Nazis. Ahmed is a sensitive, middle-class intellectual whom Simeon considers as a brother, an alter ego. He wants to become a writer, but he feels the urgency of his commitment at a time when his people are fighting in the Algerian resistance. His reponse confronts Simeon with the same question: how can he remain in Europe when he sees the faces of black teenagers confronting white hatred in order to integrate Deep South schools? His place is with them, on the home front.

An urgent plea for solidarity with the Algerians, the novel reveals that the black expatriate's encounter with these brothers in oppression opens his eyes to a new vision of France: the French like American blacks, but the Arabs are to them what the blacks are to American whites. As an Algerian puts it: "We're the niggers here! Know what the French call us—*bicot, melon, raton, nor'af.* That means *nigger* in French" (*Stone Face,* 19). This realization comes during an episode when, believing she is being molested by an Arab, Simeon naïvely sides with a Dutch girl who has stolen money from the man; the protagonist has thus earned the title of "white man" among the Algerians. In order to become a "brother," the black American must first return to his own memories: U.S. police have treated him just the way the Paris *agents* treat the Arabs. As a look of mutual recognition passes between them and him, he perceives the commonality of their plight.

Now Simeon can understand better the sometimes veiled, sometimes open, contempt of the French for what it is. When he takes Arab friends to the exclusive club where he has hitherto been welcome, the manager leads them to a far corner, glaring at them sullenly. He finds himself a "nigger" again in their company, and this sets him apart from the whites. The attitude of the French police—methodically picking up Algerians in the streets during routine identity checks, keeping tabs on them, and jailing or deporting them after two or three such occurrences—is described at length. Smith, as an intruding narrator, even explains this change in attitude as a beefing up of white power in response to growing unrest and independence in the colonies. Simeon becomes the critical observer who watches the image of liberal France (the France of the Revolution, the Commune, and the Resistance) disintegrate as the poison of nationalistic chauvinism penetrates French institutions with the return of embittered settlers and callous soldiers turned torturers and the upsurge of racist organizations like OAS: purged of officers who had shown softness in dealing with Algerians in France, the police are no longer polite and attentive but insolent and rough with everyone. And among the French population few care enough to act or even to protest. Most of them are becoming silent accomplices of the repression, just as the Germans did under Hitler.

The novel forcefully retraces the evolution of a generous and sophisticated black American expatriate from contented appreciation of his newly found peace of mind to an uneasy consciousness of the injustice around him and, finally, to a new commitment. It also provides an accurate evaluation of French attitudes under the stress of the Algerian war. In a conversation with two students in a Latin Quarter café, Simeon has asked about racism in France. His French friends reply that it does not exist and that Africans feel perfectly at home there. But, concerning Arabs, Raoul concedes:

> "That's different. The French don't like the Arabs, but it's not racism. The Arabs don't like us either. We're different. . . . They're a closed people. You can't really get to know them. They scowl when you laugh; you never know what they're thinking. And if you turn your back, they're liable to stick a knife in it."
> "I've heard that kind of argument before."
> "It's different. I assure you it's not racism."
> Henri shook his head: "Cut it out, Raoul. That's nonsense. The French are racists as far as the Algerians are concerned, no doubt about it." (*Stone Face*, 54)

Simeon modifies his own attitudes and makes friends with a number of FLN sympathizers, including Ahmed, who later dies after being beaten up by the French police. With this very autobiographical novel Smith provided a rare example of solidarity with the Algerian liberation cause on the part of black Americans in Paris.

William Gardner Smith had long been racially committed; he had worked with the NAACP at home. Politically, he leaned toward the Trotskyites and denounced the CPUSA's opposition to the Negro slogan "Victory Abroad, Victory at Home" and to the March on Washington organized by A. Philip Randolph during the war. His job at Agence France Presse meant reading daily dispatches telling of atrocities perpetrated by the "outlaws" and the progress of French "pacification" in Algeria. Initially it was hard to realize that the Algerian rebellion was, in fact, a war of liberation and an important anti-imperialist revolution. By 1957, however, the situation had escalated, and the disturbances in the French colony could no longer be quelled. Ugly scenes occurred every day in Paris, where many Algerians lived, and due to the increase in FLN terrorism the French police stopped any swarthy male and searched him for weapons. A silent, nonviolent pro-FLN demonstration had been drenched in blood by police intervention. The dark-skinned expatriates were gradually led to take the side of the Algerian "rebels" with whom the police tended to confuse them when checking papers in the streets, before respectfully glancing at their U.S. passports. Smith refrained from airing his views in interviews. He would have run the risk of losing his job and being expelled from the country for interfering in French politics. Yet his sympathies, like those of Gibson, Wright, Harrington, and many other brothers, were with the Algerians, a colored, colonial people who suffered from police harassment and from the racist behavior of many French people.

Did such pro-Algerian sympathies give rise to what Richard Wright later called "l'affaire Gibson"? Were manifestations of commitment to the Algerian cause used to conceal personal enmity between individual members of the black expatriate group? Was the occasion exploited by the CIA to manipulate them? The episode has never been satisfactorily explained. The Letters to the Editor section of *Life* magazine for October 1957 printed a rebuttal, signed by Ollie Harrington, to an article titled "Hopeful Plan for Algeria" that had appeared in the September 30 issue. The letter concluded: "Any American who thinks that France, of her own will, will grant Algeria, if not independence, at least some liberal status . . . is mad." Similar letters to the editor also appeared in the London *Observer*. The views expressed, all strongly pro-Algerian, were far from inaccurate, but the letters had not been sent by Harrington. When this news leaked out, it created no small disturbance in the black expatriate group. Someone was clearly trying to implicate Harrington, exposing him to the risk of being expelled from France on the spot. Richard Wright and others were quickly persuaded that Richard Gibson had planted those letters to avenge himself. In 1956 Harrington had accused Gibson of refusing to vacate the apartment on the Rue de Seine that Harrington had rented and placed at Gibson's disposal. He had even beaten Gibson up in front of the Café Tournon. Richard Wright sided with Harrington, and his investigation paralleled that of the French police, to whom Smith may have denounced his friend. At any rate, Gibson signed a confession admitting that he had written the letters. But what were his motives?

Gibson later wrote that the whole thing had been the result of a scheme he and Smith had concocted. Gibson, a left-winger, had become involved with the FLN because, being light-skinned, he was often mistaken for a North African by the French police; and treated as such, he had acquired strong pro-Algerian sympathies. Smith had allegedly joined him in doing something to help the Algerians by denouncing French colonialism in English-language publications. Signing the names of others would serve as a protection, and if questioned by French authorities, each in turn could deny having written the letter. Smith was to get the approval of other black Americans and reportedly suggested that the first letter be sent in the name of Ollie Harrington.[14]

Assuming Gibson's guess was right when he thought that Smith had provided the police with proof that he was the forger, Smith's motives for betraying him are unclear. Did he act out of sexual jealousy? Was he under pressure from the French DST or police who were uneasy about anyone meddling with French policy in Algeria? Did he use Gibson as a scapegoat to protect himself? Smith never wanted to discuss what he considered "an ugly occurrence."[15] At any rate, he broke off with Gibson and, the latter claims, personally insisted that he be dismissed from Agence France Presse.[16] He even got up a petition among fellow staff members, and because of the fuss, Gibson was discharged with good compensation because nothing could be said against his professional ability and conduct at AFP. He quickly found a job at CBS News.

The case certainly contributed to splitting up the group of black American expatriates in Paris. It generated suspicion and bitterness, with almost everyone accusing everyone else of being an agent of Moscow or the CIA. But there were other reasons for the group to break up in 1958: the best times of the Tournon were past, mostly because of people's tendency to go their own separate ways.

Although Smith was not moved by the Algerian situation to the point of openly declaring his sympathies for the revolutionaries, he was concerned about anti-Arab racism in France—deeply enough to make it one of the themes of *The Stone Face*. This need for involvement, as well as the necessity of writing in order to exist in his own eyes, was central to Smith's exile. To his friend Joseph Barry, the New York *Post* correspondent in Paris, he confessed that he believed the sociological novel was more important than the psychological because he had a feeling of guilt for running away instead of fighting discrimination in America. He quoted the anecdote about Thoreau and Emerson: Thoreau was in jail for civil disobedience. Emerson passed by and, seeing him behind bars, said: "Henry, what are you doing in there?" And Thoreau answered, "Ralph, what are you doing out there?" He now found himself too far from home to write only about America, yet he felt ill at ease "sitting it out" in Paris, while Chester Himes himself had turned from protest writing to detective fiction. He concluded, "I'll probably always write about social situations but they'll be where I am."[17] Not unlike Richard Wright's still unpublished "Island of Hallucinations," Smith's new novel was a means of reorienting his writing, adapting it to a new, European locale and to a broader world scene of racial confrontation. At the same time he made good use of his French experiences.

Where did he stand in relation to the United States at that time? In the fall of 1958 an unsigned *Time* article called "Amid the Alien Corn" reported that Smith claimed that in Paris one asked for his opinion as a man first, not as a Negro, and that he could forget the color of his skin; but he was also quoted as saying: "I've no intention of writing about France, much as I like it. It's not my homeland. But if I'm going to be writing about the States, something may be wrong, little nuances. I'm very far from home." [18] Considering that Wright's supposed interview, quoted in the same article, had been made up so brazenly that he attempted to sue the magazine, the quotation from Smith may be far from accurate. There is probably more truth about Smith's own motivations as a writer in "The Compensation for the Wound," the homage to Wright that he sent to the little magazine *Two Cities*. Wright's death in late November 1960 was a severe blow to Smith, as it was to Chester Himes. He had sometimes opposed Wright's views and disliked his fatherly advice, but the elder writer's presence was a fixed bearing in his ideological and literary map and an encouragement to delve into socially oriented fiction.

In the early sixties Smith seemed to become even more of a Frenchman: after having known Solange Royez for four years, he married her, allowing himself to become a family man, getting on famously with her own family, utterly delighted when she bore him a daughter, Michelle, in 1963. Meanwhile, the racial conflict in America was making the headlines. The March on Washington, culminating in Martin Luther King's "I Have a Dream" speech, had not achieved more than the various nonviolent strategies of the civil rights movement. Although Smith was specifically in charge of the Far East desk, he followed every new development in the United States at AFP. He sided with the leaders who advocated the more radical positions, even the most revolutionary ones. On February 17, 1964, he wrote his sister Phyllis: "I sometimes feel guilty of living way over here—especially when I read about 'freedom marchers' and the like. Maybe I'll come back eventually. But, sincerely, I can't stand that country [the United States]—not only racially but politically and culturally. I am for Castro and Mao Tse Tung."

Circumstances as well as his own desire soon gave Smith an opportunity to become more actively involved in black liberation. Near the end of 1964 he met Shirley Graham, widow of W. E. B. Du Bois, professionally. She was working for President Kwame Nkrumah and asked Smith to help start Ghanaian television in Accra. At the time he was head of the AFP Far East Section, living in a cozy apartment on the Avenue Gambetta with Solange and six-month-old Michelle. Was it the "boredom of marriage" or the sense of his responsibilities to the Third World? He did not hesitate to forsake comfort for adventure. From September 1964 till February 1966, when Nkrumah was overthrown,

Smith worked in Ghana as assistant editor-in-chief of the Ghana Television Network and as director of the School of Journalism, entrusted
with organizing an African News Service and consorting with many
Afro-Americans then living in Accra. Among them were Maya Angelou, St. Clair Drake, Martin Kilson, Leslie A. Lacey, Julian Mayfield,
and Tom Feelings.

After Nkrumah was ousted, Agence France Presse was happy to
have him back, and the family, including a son born in Accra in 1965,
settled into a two-room apartment on the Rue Geoffroy Saint-Hilaire.
At that time Baldwin was spending most of his time in the United
States, and Smith was encouraged by the French press to assume the
role of black spokesman that Richard Wright had often played in the
1950s. His opinion was sought when violence erupted in the ghettos
during the "hot summers." In 1967 Agence France Presse decided to
send him as a special representative to cover the race riots. He had
not been back for sixteen years, and he was overjoyed at the chance to
revisit his family and also to witness the changes that had taken place.
In an attempt to achieve a balanced picture of the situation, he spent a
couple of months interviewing leaders and grassroots militants. Upon
his return he wrote his mother on September 9, 1967: "The visit was
very important for me psychologically. It reattached me strongly to
my roots—to you and the rest of the family. . . . The trip to the States
made such an impact on me, and seeing you and old friends was so
wonderful and startling, that I am still under the effect. It seems to me
that nothing can be quite the same afterwards. I see Paris and everything else through different eyes." He would repeat the visit soon, he
hoped, as the New York Bureau of Agence France Presse led him to
believe.

When he returned, Smith was asked to comment on his impressions of the United States in an endless round of radio and TV pro-
grams, and he was also invited to speak publicly on a number of
occasions as the guest of various organizations, like the Mouvement
contre le Racisme et l'Antisémitisme and PACS, a movement organized
in France by American protesters against the Vietnam War, in which
long-time expatriate Maria Jolas played a leading role. His trip had
made him the leading expert on the racial situation in America, and
he gladly accepted his new role as an observer: "It was a relief to get
back to Paris, despite my regret at leaving the United States—particularly Philadelphia—earlier than expected. Life seems so much more
human and relaxed here, and there are no racial tensions. . . . I really
enjoy my job: it combines creativity with a sense of liberty. It is nice
to know that, bit by bit, I shall undoubtedly travel all over the world,

gathering material which can eventually serve in books. I doubt that I shall ever live in the States again, though some Black nationalists are pressing me to do so."[19]

In October 1967 Smith spent three weeks in Algiers covering a conference of Third World countries. His experiences in Africa inspired him to write about that part of the world, but by mid-April 1968 he had changed his plans: he would write a book about his return to America and the important changes he had been able to record. The assassination of Martin Luther King made the subject even more timely.

Meanwhile, his marriage to Solange had been slowly disintegrating. Bill "could not find in a single person everything he was looking for; he was looking for the whole world," Solange said later.[20] He adored their children and had a real liking for his in-laws, but this was not enough. They separated, and he moved to a little room, with a nice balcony overlooking the rooftops, at the Hotel du Sénat on the Rue Saint-Sulpice, where he completed *Return to Black America*. Ira Reuben, an Indian from Bombay in her mid-twenties, went to visit him there after the hectic days of 1968, and he soon began to spend more and more time with her, especially when some friends let them have their little flat in the Marais. Smith and Solange were divorced, and he was very responsible about paying alimony.

Return to Black America was published by Prentice-Hall in 1970. By that time the black power movement had peaked and was subsiding: the book did not attract much attention and was a commercial failure in the United States. But it was translated into French as *L'Amérique noire* and signaled the consecration of Smith as a representative black writer in Paris. It contained echoes of his rootlessness at the time; in spite of what he had written to his mother, he felt—and this feeling had possibly been intensified by his recent separation from Solange— that he did not belong anywhere: "The black man who established his home in Europe paid a heavy price . . . in tearing himself from his past, from the things and people he loved or hated but which remained part of him, from which he would never escape despite the miles or the decades separating him from them. He paid for it in guilt. . . . He paid for it, finally, in a sort of rootlessness. . . . The black man, no matter how long he lived in Europe, drifted through those societies an eternal 'foreigner' among eternal strangers."[21]

After *Return to Black America* Smith started work on an essay called "Through Dark Eyes," which was to analyze the black man's experience on three continents—America, Europe, and Africa. He was so dissatisfied with it that he would not allow even Ira to read it.[22] By

that time he was working again on a sequel to *The Stone Face,* of which
he had already completed a version called "Simeon," the name of its
protagonist. His correspondence with Jerry Bryant, a teacher who was
preparing an article on his fiction, provides some information about
the book, which he considered one of his two best novels (the other
being "Ballets Rose," which had been lost by the publisher). "Simeon"
dealt with a black politician who rose quite high on the American
political scene but was destroyed because he ignored his ghetto origins. Also, when working on *The Stone Face,* he had originally planned
to have his hero go back to Africa in the end, but his editor's suggestion made him send Simeon back to America because of the racial
developments there. Now he was returning to his original inclination.

Smith had actually written some ten novels (but had lost several
manuscripts in travel), he said, and he could now see his evolution in
those terms: "As my books shifted from communication to the unag-
gressive affirmation of our worth, I think they became less accessible
to white readers." At the end of five unfruitful years, he had started
doubting himself: "That, I presume, is the reason why without meaning *consciously* to do so, I simply lost the manuscripts."[23] When it came
to the fiction writing that was so essential to his own self-confidence,
Smith had indeed a tortured mind at times. He could never settle for
journalism; he considered himself a creative writer first, but he wanted
his sensibilities to coincide with his criticism of the social scene. It was
not an unconscious gesture, however, that was responsible for the loss
of "Simeon." Smith made no photocopy of the book because he was
more broke than ever: the French income tax bureau had learned that
he had not declared royalties from the States and had begun to demand arbitrary payments based on large sums they assumed had been
brought into France illegally. The manuscript reached Jerry Bryant
but got lost in the end-of-the-year mail when he returned it.

In early 1972 Bill and Ira, now married, moved to Ivry, a working-
class suburb south of Paris. The four-room apartment was large
enough to accommodate a family of three—the baby, Rachel, was now
almost a year old—and also Claude and Michelle when they visited on
weekends. Bill had kept Solange's friendship and her parents' affection; the latter still treated him as a son-in-law, and the children suffered little from the divorce. Bill had been promoted to chief of the
English-language service at Agence France Press. A noted lecturer
on the race question, a committed sympathizer with such progressive
movements as the Black Panthers and PACS, he was becoming, as he
had predicted, a world traveler as a special correspondent for AFP. He
had covered the nonaligned nations' conference in Belgrade, the Arab

summit conference in Morocco, and the important October 1971 economic meeting in Peru, and made a trip to Biafra at the close of the
Nigerian civil war. At the age of forty-five he had become somewhat
settled without losing any of his mettle or his opposition to certain
American policies. He would write his mother on December 30, 1972:
"America is gaining itself the reputation of another Nazi Germany
through its actions in Vietnam. I am ashamed to show an American
passport." Nor did he miss an opportunity to fight for the race: when
William Styron published *The Confessions of Nat Turner,* which pictured
the black rebel Nat as a prey to guilt and various complexes, Smith
appeared on French TV among the critics of Styron's view of black
history.

In 1973 Smith's health suddenly deteriorated. He quit work in
December to be operated on for cancer of the esophagus and undergo
subsequent cobalt treatment. But it was too late. He died on November 5, 1974, after twenty-three years in exile. A memorial service was
held on November 12: Clara Malraux praised his literary work; Maria
Jolas recalled his active opposition to the Vietnam war in PACSW;
New York *Times* correspondent Herbert Lottman read an extract from
The Stone Face in which Simeon, sipping a drink at the Rhumerie
Martiniquaise, discovers French lack of racism when he realizes that
an attractive blonde who has shunned his advances is not prejudiced
against Negroes but is simply waiting for her coal-black African boyfriend. Bernard Redmont probably most accurately evoked what living
in France meant to Smith, when he quoted the passage from *Return
to Black America* that concludes Smith's precise analyses of European
freedom and of European racism:

> A black person could live in greater peace with his environment in
> Copenhagen or Paris than in New York. . . . But he found it at times
> harder to live at peace with himself. The black man who established his
> home in Europe paid a heavy price . . . in guilt for, no matter what the
> rationalization, no matter whether he cooperated with the black move-
> ment from abroad, he could never escape the conviction that the real
> fight was *there,* on the spot, on the battleground. He paid for it, finally, in
> a sort of rootlessness; for, seriously, who were all these peculiar people
> speaking Dutch, Danish, . . . French? What songs had they sung in child-
> hood, what games had they played, what books had they read, what
> "corners" had they hung out on? Above all, what did they know about
> the black Skin's long, bitter, and soon triumphant odyssey? The black
> man, no matter how long he lived in Europe, drifted through those
> societies an eternal "foreigner" among eternal strangers.[24]

NOTES

1. Roi Ottley, "Black Frenchmen," *Negro Digest*, February 1, 1948, 20.
2. William Gardner Smith to Richard Wright, June 14, 1951, Yale.
3. Smith to Edith Earle, December 20, 1951.
4. Smith to Edith Earle, November 1, 1951.
5. Smith to Edith Earle, March 15, 1952.
6. Smith to Edith Earle, February 21, 1953.
7. Smith to Edith Earle, March 15, 1952.
8. Smith, *Return to Black America* (Englewood Cliffs, N.J.: Prentice-Hall, 1970), 4.
9. Chester Himes, interview with the author, June 1970.
10. Smith to Edith Earle, February 21, 1953.
11. Smith, quoted in Joseph Barry, "An American in Paris—II," New York *Post*, March 25, 1959, 36.
12. Smith to Edith Earle, June 17, 1955.
13. Smith, *The Stone Face* (New York: Pocket Books, 1964), hereafter cited in the text.
14. Richard Gibson to LeRoy Hodges, June 26, 1977.
15. Smith, interview with the author, February 1969.
16. Gibson to the author, November 18, 1987.
17. Joseph Barry, "An American in Paris—III," New York *Post*, March 29, 1959, 34.
18. "Amid the Alien Corn," unsigned article in *Time*, November 17, 1958, 28.
19. Smith to Mary Sewell, September 3, 1967.
20. Solange Smith to LeRoy Hodges, July 18, 1977, quoted in his *Portrait of an Expatriate* (Westport, Conn.: Greenwood Press, 1985), 90.
21. Smith, *Return to Black America* (Englewood Cliffs, N.J.: Prentice-Hall, 1970), 71.
22. "Later, he kept his notes with his typewriter and his other papers in their cellar from which, one day, some petty burglar removed everything" (Ira Smith to the author, July 12, 1987).
23. Smith to Jerry Bryant, February 26, 1971.
24. Smith, *Return to Black America*, 71.

16

Literary Coming of Age in Paris

For the older generation going to Paris was the next best thing to going to glory. Their juniors, however, wondered about the desirability of crossing oceans and drinking coffee in smelly cafés. In 1964 black nationalist poet Larry Neal wrote "For Black Writers and Artists in 'Exile.'"

> How many of them die their deaths
> looking for sun, finding darkness in the city of light.
> motherless, whirling in a world of empty words,
> snatching at, and shaping the rubbish
> that is our lives
> until form becomes, or life dances to an incoherent finish.[1]

Despite the doubts, a few did not hesitate. Jamaica-born Lindsay Barrett, who arrived in 1961, used Paris as a base for travels in Europe and North Africa and for the writing of *The State of Black Desire*. His book, one of the first publishing ventures of the press of the new Shakespeare and Company bookshop, was illustrated by St. Kitts painter Larry Potter. Because he suffered from asthma, Potter spent a lot of time in bed and was an omnivorous reader. A dark-skinned black, he was devoted to the "brothers" and universally popular, unlike Berthel, another black artist, whom Chester Himes used in his contemporary *A Case of Rape* as the model for Cesar Gee, the black hero who walked the streets with a snow-white borzoi and once painted his whole room black except for white footprints up the wall and across the ceiling.

At about the same time, George Whitman's Mistral Bookshop, renamed after her death for Sylvia Beach's own venture, had already become a rallying point for young English-speaking writers, black and white, as the Beats had moved the literary scene from the Café Tournon to the Saint-Michel area. Starting with Allen Ginsberg, many a

City Lights writer had crashed in the Hotel Rachou on the Rue Gît-le-Coeur, on the way from San Francisco to Katmandu.

Hart LeRoy Bibbs, not Berthel, should have been the inspiration for Himes's weird character. He was a self-styled jazz poet, a hippy type who was very far from evoking from the new French surrealists—the group of Claude Pélieu, Jean-Jacques Lebel, and *L'Archibras* magazine—the same reverence as Bob Kaufman or the same excitement as Ted Joans.[2] It was Pélieu and Mary Beach, who had translated most of Ginsberg and other luminaries of the Beat movement, who managed to get Bibbs into print. His *Dietbook for Junkies (Camétude),* refused by many U.S. publishers, was brought out by Bourgois in 1969 and, largely because of Pélieu's enthusiastic preface, attracted some attention in Paris. Bibbs claimed that only racism had prevented its publication in the United States. In France his work (a diatribe on violence, drugs, sex, and revolt, written in provocative and frequently obscene slang in the style of Miller or Burroughs) was often mentioned, if not hailed, alongside that of major Beat contemporaries. Bibbs also printed a slim pamphlet, *Polyrhythms to Freedom,* and a book of poems, *Hey Now Hey.* He attracted some attention by producing jazz poetry records with sax player Sonny Murray and by organizing an exhibition of photographs in 1973.

Some considered Bibbs an embodiment of those young blacks, oppressed by the American environment, who tried to express themselves—often in the lurid rhetoric of LeRoi Jones's revolutionary heroes—through jazz music and language alien to the mainstream. Whether or not the Beat and jazz poets partly reflected the influence of such European ancestors as Antonin Artaud, Jean Genet, and Henri Michaux, their use of verbal violence, sex, and drugs prolonged the antibourgeois tradition of dada and the surrealists.

One of Bibbs's most interesting evocations of Paris in the 1960s is to be found not in his poetry but in the texts for his photo album, *Paris Jazz Seen.*[3] He focused on some fifteen musicians in France, from old-timers Count Basie, Memphis Slim, and Kenny Clarke to more recent arrivals like Marion Brown, Sonny Murray, and Alan Silva. He graphically recorded the impact of the Free Jazz movement upon the Latin Quarter, where the streets were yet torn up, as the students in the revolt had used the paving stones as missiles against the police in May 1968. At this juncture Free Jazz musicians began arriving and "with more or less impact, they dropped like a bomb, fizzin' and fartin' and making all kinds of seemingly senseless noises, like all death-dealing devices do" (*Paris Jazz Seen,* 8). Most of them were in their thirties, unknown even at home, dressed in colorful costumes, talking of black power and Panthers, and supposedly escaping the black struggle in order to create their own music now. Bibbs describes them as a "terrifying horde" bearing down on the French as though to replace the recently expelled NATO forces: "They came to Europe for the same pilgrim-politic reasons: pilgrims are prophets who are never loved at home. . . . It is no more strange that they should invade France to do this. Why not? She is an old slave trail teaching a slave language that the roots of these men reached for a recount" (*Paris Jazz Seen,* 9).

Under the revolutionary slogan of Free Jazz, such musicians often had to fight their way into acceptance—even physically. Bibbs recalled a Homeric battle involving musicians Muhammad Ali, Frank Wright, Alan Silva, and Noah Howard at the Hotel de Buci, in an appropriate setting:

> Notre Dame is the great heart of Paris but Rue de Seine, in the Latin Quarter, is its bowels; tight passages like a duodenum make a few dips and dives and suddenly after a serpentine curve dump you out into the river Seine. The street is well travelled by dogs and artists, tourists, and anyone else who has bowel business to take care of in one of the small shops, galleries, or restaurants. On one corner heading towards the Boulevard Saint-Germain sits the famous Louisiana Hotel where the great bluesman Curtis Jones kept his guitar and music business hopping. . . . For most musicians the price of rooms at the Louisiana was out of sight; but just across the street are the equally famous markets of rue de Buci, where even the cincher can find the most succulent exotic food in all of Paris. Across the market is a small hotel. (*Paris Jazz Seen,* 19)

It all started with the owner refusing to understand Frank Wright saying "Buci" with a heavy southern accent until the word became "some monster like Pussy." Raving at the misunderstanding, the musician was ordered out by the hotel-keeper, who soon found himself downed, sagging against his desk, while, on the street again, the quartet disbanded: "Ali accused Rev of being too fast with his hands. Bell struck out to the market saying nothing, and Noah stepped on the curb to scrape some dogshit off his boots. The last ray of sun flashed in the rivulets of Seine water rushing down the gutters. A homemade brush-broom pushed and hurried the garbage along, a tired-looking African behind it all" (*Paris Jazz Seen,* 20).

Another vignette evokes Allen Shorter swinging a golf club in the middle of the Rue de Seine, stopping the traffic—horns tooting wildly and drivers swearing at the nuisance—until Muhammad Ali whispered something into his ear and he picked up a racing bike on the curb and wheeled it down toward the Seine. And while Rev and Bell were having trouble in a café, which luckily had two entrances, Noah discovered a Benin bronze head in a nearby gallery and ended by accusing Europe of having stolen all the art objects of Africa.

The whole gang would sit at the Café Palette, in front of the Beaux-Arts school, in the company of Marion Brown, who downed superb Côtes du Rhône and told wild stories of his getting lost at the corner of the Boulevard Saint-Michel, shouting at the top of his voice while the surrounding crowd yelled, "He is mad! Oh, là là! Stop your jive!" in their incomprehensible tongue!

In his unpublished "Saxophone Diary, 1974–1981," Frank Wright himself noted some of his experiences in Paris: the police patrolling the streets and asking for identification, stopping mostly Algerians and Africans; his playing the "Loto" and calling New York from the corner café whose owner treated most people like dirt but thought he had money and was someone different; blacks sweeping the streets after the market at Belleville; his playing the saxophone so loudly that the walls shook and a neighbor asked him to stop so his daughter could study her lessons; an occasional party with Santana's band who often had dinner at the Coupole at 5 A.M.: "The people were amazed at the musicians but I am used to that; and the Rosebud was another crowd of people—the same shit as usual. Everybody loves everybody or everybody is still telling that lie . . . more booze everybody wants." It was a hard and lonely life, and the sax player commented: "After returning from my work and looking at the Seine of Paris and the bums that are sleeping on the sidewalks, they seem to be happy—at least they had a bottle of wine . . . and I don't have anything to eat and no money in my pocket to buy food . . . but I am the music man."[4]

Yet there were good times. Hart LeRoy Bibbs tells of the success of Sonny Murray, who would introduce French people to the style of Albert Ayler and to his own at the Vieille Grille cabaret. Ambrose Jackson was also there; in fact, there were enough black American musicians to form a group. The regulations of the French musicians' union forbade it, however; there had to be one Frenchman to every foreigner. Murray was to perform while Bibbs read, and he shouted at the MC, André Francis, who hastily brought a microphone for the poet to chant "The Stroller": "Ambrose was beside me and Sonny unmercifully directed the horns. He for a moment seemed to love to be playing overly loud but only for a moment, and then my voice shifted gears to more or less follow his guidance. I had chosen my side, feeling more at ease in all manner with these young musicians than I had ever felt with those more my age" (*Paris Jazz Seen*, 34).

In spite of the ideological differences and conflicts of the late sixties, a good deal of understanding existed between black and white artists. However, for the Free Jazz musicians or for a Beat poet like Bibbs, Paris was no haven: they tended to treat the city as conquered territory, as the scene to which they brought their "thing." But occasionally they caught the nostalgia of the sun glimmering on age-old walls or the suffering contained in the tired gesture of an African hand pushing all the garbage along the gutters . . .

Not all younger black American writers who came to visit or sojourned for a while were associated with Free Jazz or the Black Power movement—far from it, although French reporters and critics were eager to interpret their works and sayings as political statements.

One of those who stayed longest was Melvin Van Peebles, who came in 1959. Partly of Dutch origin, and Chicago-born, he had been a navigator on an air force bomber, a trolley conductor, and a portrait painter and had first gone to Holland to study astronomy. But his real vocation was filmmaking. This elegant, light-skinned youth, with his cap and his lost appearance, quickly learned to speak French and did not have much difficulty adapting to Paris. Friendly and reliable, he led a very secluded life, made many helpful friends in French progressive circles, and, apart from Chester Himes, seldom associated with Americans. He soon was making a living as a journalist; from 1962 onwards he worked for the provocative left-wing illustrated tabloid *Hara-Kiri*, writing a column called "L'Homme qui rit" ("The Laughing Man") and also supplying the words for their serial adaptation of Himes's famous story of black detectives, "La Reine des pommes" ("For Love of Imabelle"), while Wolinski did the cartoons. Van Peebles thus became integrated into the group of avant-garde radical French cartoonists that included Topor, Cavanna, and Wolinski. Around the same time he wrote free-lance for *France-Soir* and more frequently for the *Nouvel-Observateur*, where Patrick Levino soon gave him a column. He specialized in literary and artistic events, with a definitely progressive slant, and was not relegated to "the racial problem."

But he was determined to pursue filmmaking. In 1961 he collaborated with Pierre Braunberger on his first "court métrage," *Les Cinq Cents Balles*, which was awarded the Jean Vigo prize. Yet, in order to be considered a real scriptwriter and be eligible for funding from the Centre National du Cinéma (this consisted of an advance on potential sales), a filmmaker needed to be a published author. A story has it that it was only for this reason that Van Peebles started writing. He began with a novel, *Un ours pour le FBI (A Bear for the FBI)*, which was first published by Buchet-Chastel in 1964 and got very encouraging reviews. His second attempt, a semiautobiographical satirical story, *Un américain en enfer (An American in Hell)*, was published the following year by Denoël, and Van Peebles acquired a deserved reputation for fantasy: his philosophical tale took a resourceful black protagonist, Abe Carver, to the court of God the Father, but it was also a sly denunciation of racism and segregation and was often hailed as such in Paris.

Meanwhile, Van Peebles was working on a movie, *La Fête à Harlem*, the story of a groovy Harlem house-rent party where the Devil could not find his way out and where Negro humor and fantasy triumphed. This was shown in 1964 at the Liège film festival. He then started a full-length film on a French-American theme—*La Permission*, which he wrote and directed and which his friend Michel Kelber filmed at Étretat. It was the story of a brief idyll on a Normandy beach between a French girl and a black GI on weekend leave, told in moving, beautiful scenes. Shot on a limited budget, this venture was successful enough for Van Peebles to be sent by La Cinémathèque Française to a film festival in San Francisco in 1967. Around that time he became a kind of star of the counterculture in the United States, where his political outlook did not correspond to the views of the silent majority. By then "Black Is Beautiful" had become fashionable, and he took advantage of that to make a few authentically black and provocative films: his *Sweet Sweetback Baaadass Song* was a commercial success, but the U.S. film selection committee refused to send it to the Cannes Festival because it was considered too un-American. Later, *Ain't Supposed to Die a Natural Death* and *Don't Play Us Cheap* enjoyed long runs as musical plays.

In many ways, then, Melvin Van Peebles's career was greatly helped, if not determined, by his stay in Paris. There he started making films, there he started publishing books, there he found supportive and devoted friends. When he first arrived, he was with his American wife and two young children, but they soon separated, and after 1963 he established a lasting relationship with Janine Euvrard, herself a writer with an interest in film, whose support was all-important to him. So was that of Colette Lacroix (of the French-American Fellowship, which her friend Richard Wright had organized in the early 1950s), at whose place in the Cévennes, Luziers, Melvin wrote *La Fête à Harlem*. Living with Janine at 31, Rue d'Assas, he was perfectly integrated into the French way of life, so much so that he used it as a basis for his fiction, not only in *La Permission* but also in *Le Chinois du XIVe*, an intriguing collection of short stories, illustrated by his friend Topor, which Jérome Martineau published in 1966. The mythical Chinese of the

14th arrondissement ("chinois" may also mean "hodgepodge") is a pretext for very ordinary Parisians to swap tales around a kerosene lamp in a typical bistro when a power failure deprives them of TV. Van Peebles delights in chronicling the deep-seated obsessions and glowing memories of the French man and woman in the street: concierges, park sweepers, small shopkeepers, and petty civil servants, who praise the abilities of their dogs, complain about the traffic, thrill at royal love affairs, remember the Resistance and the black market, and derive from this experiential bric-à-brac some kind of day-to-day philosophy of existence. In *La Quinzaine Littéraire* Geneviève Serreau, who reviewed the volume, very earnestly compared his tenderness and humor to Salinger's in *The Catcher in the Rye,* and praised him for being one of the first to take black literature out of the ghetto. His story "The Tale of the Black American" was one of the best: in it he tells of riding in a train across the whole state of Virginia, with the head of an unknown white woman resting on his shoulder as she slept, and of the irrepressible fear that he might be lynched for that.

But he told revealing stories about the French too. There is the Maupassant-like fate of the maid-of-all-work whom innkeepers hire to care for the illegitimate offspring of their own daughter, having made her play the role of the pregnant girl by wearing well-placed cushions. There is the very sly strategy of quickly inheriting from an embarrassingly healthy old man by making him sit in an icy draft. There is the nightwatchman whose wife makes money on the side by sleeping with other men, and the prisoner who can see (but only see) a girl undressing every night for three whole years. The situations are always intriguing and extraordinary—exactly the stuff a good yarn is made of—but people are keenly observed in their cultural differences and their common humanity, with tremendous humor and respect.

Besides Van Peeble's *Le Chinois du XIVe* two other books were reviewed under the heading "Three Black Novelists" in the first 1967 issue of *La Quinzaine Littéraire.* None of those novels had previously appeared in English. One was *Un Sang mal mêlé (Badly Mixed Blood)* by Granby Blackwood. The author was described as an American mulatto; whether he lived long in Paris is not known. The novel did not do well. This "well-made and well-written book," which could have been "a powerful and tragic work," explored the theme of the tragic mulatto through two brothers, one darker, one lighter—their conflicts, attraction, hatred, and reconciliation.[5]

The third book was also a first novel, as yet unpublished in the United States: *Les Flagellants* by Carlene Polite. In this case, in contrast to Granby Blackwood's, the reviewers were able to make much of the author's background. Polite was an attractive thirty-four-year-old dancer who had once worked as a bunny in a Playboy club; indeed, she had done specialty dancing in *The Boyfriend* and *The King and I*. She had not only studied at Sarah Lawrence under Martha Graham and Alvin Ailey, but she had also lived with the Beats in Greenwich Village and gotten involved with Zen Buddhism. In 1963 she had been the major organizer of the Northern Negro Leadership Conference and a follower of Martin Luther King. When the Detroit Council on Human Rights closed down in 1964, Carlene Polite decided to go to Paris to fulfill her lifelong ambition to become a writer: at twelve she had already been composing overwritten prose poems, by candlelight in order to be more romantic, and had given herself a French pen name. The opportunity came when a French visitor who had asked her to write down all the things she liked was so impressed by the vitality of her style that he wrote a publisher friend of his that he "had found a writer." Dominique De Roux, the energetic editor of *L'Herne* magazine and an adviser to the Presses de la Cité, thus encouraged Carlene to go to Paris.

The writing of the novel took a couple of years, during which she lived on almost nothing but soup and chocolate but also discovered Paris. By that time De Roux had become editor-in-chief at the new Presses de la Cité subsidiary, Éditions Christian Bourgois, and the novel enjoyed the honor of marking the birth of the new publishing house, thus benefiting from more than ordinary publicity.[6] The novel recorded the stormy relationship of a couple, Jimson and Ideal, and their daily flagellations by tongue-lashing in a Greenwich Village setting, where the pressures of prejudice and racism were present but "ever-present blackness was no longer a sociological plague."[7] The book was generally hailed for its style and as proof that an American Negro need not write only protest literature. "Hysterical with Carlene Polite . . . the narrative comes close to poetry," wrote Pierre Descargues; Charles de Richter spoke of Polite as "a poet of the weird, an angel of the bizarre and the decrepit in an unknown world"; while René Vigo noted "terrible visions of the black ghetto" conveying the everlasting quest for the absolute in this pitiless fight between reality and imagination; it was "a book so haunting, so rich in thoughts, sensations, so well located in a poetic chiaroscuro that one [could] savor its ineffaceable harshness."[8]

Reviewers spoke of the cruel exchanges of Edward Albee's dramas and the free-flowing rhapsodies of Henry Miller, but Polite herself maintained that she preferred Céline and wrote out of the fire-and-brimstone brand of religion in which she had been brought up. She was attempting to liberate black Americans from the feeling that crucifixion and suffering had an exemplary, redemptive value. Had she been influenced by French writing? Everyone wanted to know. She had only been in Paris for about a year and still spoke little French, but she had begun to read it: "My friends say that my own book is the first work in French I shall have read to the end. And now as I wonder how Pierre Alien did translate such or such sentence and I rise from my bed or my chair to read whole passages, I feel as though I had written in French."[9]

Polite was quite conscious of belonging to a new generation, in many ways close to Ralph Ellison's preoccupations with writing first. She did not feel she had to perform as a Negro writer to be accepted. She was committed, however, and aware that France was no haven as far as racism was concerned, especially for Arabs. But she preferred to divide up her writing so as to do creative literature and editorial protest at separate times: "Simone de Beauvoir says in *The Second Sex* that the problem of women is similar to the problem of the Negro. No woman can create literature until she is freed of the cross of second-class citizenship. The French tell me there can't be a real American Negro writer until racism has disappeared."[10]

Polite did not live a hectic café life but enjoyed her modern Left Bank apartment, which she shared with her two daughters. She usually went out only when invited, unless it was to LeRoy Haynes's soul food restaurant. Shortly after Farrar, Straus and Giroux accepted *The Flagellants* for U.S. publication in 1967, she started a second novel, which was supposed to deal with Playboy bunnies and be directed mainly at her French audience. It appeared in 1975 under the title *Sister X and the Victims of Foul Play* and takes place largely on the fringes of the artistic world of Paris, as Black Will, a "travelin' man" back from a recent stint in Zambia, learns about the end of Sister X, alias Arista Prolo, from her costume designer, Abyssinia.[11] Written in the style of Ishmael Reed's fantasies, the book does not try to recreate the French setting: Abyssinia limits herself to sarcastic rremarks about French ways, like "A French telephone can ring so loud that it blasts not only the watermark off the page but all the print too" (*Sister X*, 65) or "Although France is by no sense the most devoutly Catholic country . . . these people have themselves a saint for every day the Good Lawd sends" (29). She describes high-rise apartment buildings as "cold complex cement compoundedly non-Communist consumptive constrictive communes consisting of plasterboard-lined, human-size file cabinets. . . . Luckily the African, Arab, Immigrant Workers (who the French begrudgingly

allow entry into their beautiful country . . .) had the foresight to name
the hallucinating constructions 'Bâtiments, A, B, C.' . . . 'Contemporary Catacombs' would have been more like it" (10).

There may be a hint at Polite's own life in Paris in Abyssinia's remarks about her environment: "after months of looking out of her
fishbowl-style windows, tripping on the Paris skies, predicting, blessing, cursing the weather, seeing the neighbors come and go, open and
close their shutters" (*Sister X*, 38). Yet this is only used to introduce the
funny story of a husband who, as his wife became more and more pregnant, took to disrobing more and more in front of the windows and was
watched by scores of neighbors who were saved the trouble of using
clocks and watches by the couple's regular habits. Likewise, the caricature of a sixty-ish French beau welcoming Arista, whom he had seen
in a Detroit cabaret, to his luxurious apartment in the fanciest quarter
of Paris borders on the unbelievable. He showers her "with Gallic hospitality, normally reserved for visiting dignitaries, chieftains, kings,
potentates, diplomatic representatives of 'underdeveloped' countries"
(58), finally offering anything she may desire, including "another man,
two men, a beautiful woman, a dog" (59). Similarly, the final scene
about Ann, the British burlesque queen literally dancing her ass off
along a pole at the Jacques de Diamants Club, is too beautiful to be in
any way realistic, even though the narrator suggests that anything can
happen with the French: "Dear Reader, if I'm lyin', I'm flyin'. If you
have been to Paris, you know that I'm not" (143). In search of real-
ism, one finds remarks like the one about "those awful black tobacco
French cigarettes": "The French defend the things by saying that they
are better for your health than American ones, which they call 'blond.'
And expatriates say that you get used to them, then prefer them, once
your American dollars are all gone" (123).

Clearly, *Sister X* capitalized on the black power and soul fashion,
wittily proclaiming the innovation and vitality of the black nationalist
bias while making fun of Europe, seen as a kind of antiquated monumental graveyard, and indicting Western exploitation of black talent.
It was in no way directed at a French audience but made constant
cartoon-like use of American stereotypes about the French.

Another, more talented, black woman who moved to Paris to create
around that time was Barbara Chase. A former Philadelphian and a
Yale arts graduate, she was a sculptor when she married French photographer Marc Riboud, then famous for his reporting in Vietnam,
and settled in France. While her compositions in metal or cloth were
being exhibited in Paris galleries, notably at the Cadran Solaire and

the French National Center for Contemporary Arts, Barbara Chase-Riboud started her literary career in 1974 with a fine volume of poetry, *From Memphis and Peking*. She gave a few readings from it, mostly at the American Cultural Center.

In 1969 she had been quoted as saying, "I could easily go back to America and find my place politically because black people are fighting. When I left in 1961 it seemed that if you were a militant you were all alone."[12] Some ten years later, she did return for a while to do historical research on Thomas Jefferson and his slave mistress Sally Hemings. She had been struck by the fact that the earliest Afro-American women to visit Paris were either maidservants to white mistresses or the quadroon daughters of parents who wished them to receive the education and culture they were denied in America. Also, according to early Afro-American fiction, many of these light-skinned women went as mistresses of wealthy whites: once in Paris, they could be acknowledged as their lovers' wives. In *Iola Leroy* by Frances Ellen Harper, Paris is the destination of a southern gentleman who wishes to take his mulatto wife and children there to escape the evils of slavery.

Chase-Riboud's best-selling novel *Sally Hemings* evokes Paris as a romantic city, but mostly as an architecturally beautiful one in which Sally's memories of the cities of Virginia pale by comparison and in which she feels so free that she forgets her position as a slave. Her brother James makes the point, a couple of times, that they have been emancipated by touching French soil, where slavery is outlawed. Sally, a gifted student, also acquires culture and education; Jefferson notes that since her arrival "her training and tutoring was beginning to show, her musical education as well . . . and her French was perfect."[13] The French people she meets verbally espouse the liberty their country stands for; upon hearing that Sally Hemings is bearing Jefferson's baby, Madame Duprée advises her to remain in France since she and the child will be free there. In spite of the utter absence of racial prejudice and the friendly disposition of her freedom-loving acquaintances, Sally Hemings, unlike her brother, does not engage in any revolutionary activity. The only thing that prevents her from gaining freedom and social dignity is her love for Jefferson, from whom she cannot bear to be separated and who, she hopes, will eventually emancipate her. History has shown that she waited in vain. Chase-Riboud's patient research in the French national archives and in the Jefferson papers and her investigation of the history of the French and American revolutions, plus her residence in Paris for several years, allowed her to present a convincing, albeit romantic, picture of a black female protagonist. Since then, she has chosen to live in Paris, spending more time on writing than on sculpture, with notable success, as the prize awarded to her volume of poetry, *Portrait of a Nude Woman as Cleopatra* (1987), testifies. *Validé, a Tale of the Harem* (1986) retraces the career of a sultan's favorite. *Echoes of Lions* (1989) is a superbly crafted historical novel based on the well-known *Amistad* mutiny and trial.

NOTES

1. Larry Neal, "For Black Writers and Artists in 'Exile,'" *Hoodoo Hollerin' Bebop Ghosts* (Washington, D.C.: Howard University Press, 1974), 68.

2. Although black San Franciscan Bob Kaufman never set foot in France, he was held in high esteem in avant-garde Paris circles, and his "Abomunist Manifesto" was quoted in the same breath as texts by Ginsberg, Corso, Kerouac, or Ferlinghetti. *Golden Sardine* and *Solitudes Crowded with Loneliness* appeared in bilingual editions in Paris in the mid-1960s, and the prestigious review *L'Herne* devoted a big issue to Kaufman and Pélieu in 1967.

3. Hart LeRoy Bibbs, *Paris Jazz Seen* (n.p., 1980), hereafter cited in the text.

4. Frank Wright, "Saxophone Diary," October 14, 1975, unpublished manuscript.

5. Jean Wagner, "Trois écrivains noirs," *La Quinzaine Littéraire*, January 1, 1967, 6.

6. See Herbert Lottman, "Authors and Editors," *Time*, June 12, 1967, 20–21.

7. Wagner, "Trois écrivains noirs," 6.

8. Pierre Descarques, "Du nouveau dans le jeune roman," *Tribune de Lausanne*, October 9, 1968, 7; Charles de Richter, "Chronique littéraire," *La République du Centre*, undated clipping; René Vigo, "Les Franges du romanesque," *Est Éclair*, July 31, 1967.

9. Julia Hervé, "Portrait: Carlene Polite ou l'école du feu et du soufre," *Jeune Afrique*, November 20, 1966, 75.

10. Carlene Polite, quoted by Herbert Lottman in "The Action Is Everywhere the Black Man Goes," *New York Times Book Review*, April 21, 1968, 9.

11. Carlene Polite, *Sister X and the Victims of Foul Play* (New York: Farrar, Straus and Giroux, 1975), hereafter cited in the text as *Sister X*.

12. Chase-Riboud, quoted in Thomas A. Johnson, "Paris: Negroes' Way Station," *New York Times*, March 19, 1969.

13. Barbara Chase-Riboud, *Sally Hemings* (New York: Avon, 1980), 110.

17

A New Mood:
Black Power in Paris

In November 1961 *Negro Digest* printed "What Paris Means to Me" by Hazel Scott, the famed pianist who had gone to Paris for a single engagement and stretched her three-week vacation into a three-year stay. True to form, at the end of the 1950s the artist enjoyed fun-filled and work-filled years, a large apartment in Paris, and occasional visits to friends on the Riviera. She appeared in two French movies with top stars, consorted with Billie Holiday shortly before the Lady died, entertained at many clubs all over the Continent and North Africa, and "absorbed the healthy, restful atmosphere of Paris," which she defined thus: "My Paris is not the city of champagne and caviar. My Paris is a pot full of red beans and rice and an apartment full of old friends and glasses tinkling . . . the warmth of the big Thanksgiving dinners I had every year for my old and dear friends. My Paris is the enchantment of wandering through an old museum, hand in hand with an old friend from Hollywood, lost in the wonder of Rodin. My Paris is the magic of looking up the Champs Élysées from the Place de la Concorde and being warmed by the merry madness of the lights." She conceded: "Whenever I encountered racism in any form, it was so rare that it was an exception rather than the rule and it stuck out as an incident. I'm not going to say that France is paradise but I will say this: 'You can live anywhere if you've got the money to live. You can go anywhere if you've got the money to go and whomever you marry or date is your business.'"[1]

It is worthwhile to contrast Hazel Scott's impressions with those that poet and autobiographer Maya Angelou had of France around the same time. Angelou came to very different conclusions. Before becoming a writer, she had visited Paris as an actress in the role of Ruby when Gershwin's *Porgy and Bess*, produced by Robert Breen, had been taken on a European tour. The all-black troupe was booked for three weeks at the Théâtre Wagram in Paris, but they were held over for several months because of their tremendous success. In order to save money, Angelou moved from her hotel to a tiny pension near the Place des Ternes and was forced to speak French in this noninternational atmosphere. Yet she met a number of black entertainers in Paris, notably dancer Bernard Hassell from the Folies Bergères and Nancy Holloway, who sang at the Colisée. They all visited the Left Bank of the expatriate generation and also L'Abbaye cabaret, whose owner, Gordon Heath, provided his own entertainment as a singer. They went to the Mars Club, where Angelou was welcomed as a star of *Porgy and Bess;* there she got an engagement as a singer in the midnight show, and she also worked at La Rose Rouge as a typical Parisian entertainer.

In her autobiography Angelou noted revealing details, such as the partial acculturation of the black American entertainers in Paris, evidenced by their fluttering their hands and raising their eyebrows "in typical Gallic fashion."[2] She was surprised by the cordial way her Mars Club pianist, a white southerner, treated her. She was happy to find economic opportunity as well as social freedom. She was so delighted that she considered starting a career there, largely because she wanted her son brought up in an egalitarian atmosphere: "I could rent an apartment and send for Clyde. He was bright and would learn the language quickly. He would be freed from racial prejudice that occasionally made every black childhood sunless. He would be obliged to be good for his own sake rather than prove to a disbelieving society that he was not a brute" (*Singin'*, 187). One incident, however, revealed ingrained French attitudes toward blacks. Angelou had been quick to note the sense of exoticism with which her audience appreciated her singing: she was good enough, and different—"not African, but nearly, not American, but nearly" (*Singin'*, 181). But one day a high-society Parisian asked her to sing at a reception. The woman insisted upon speaking English (badly) and imitated a rendition of "St. Louis Blues," clearly bringing out her idea of a "négresse" and her negative stereotypes of blacks. What was more, on the day of the reception Angelou was escorted by two handsome, impeccably dressed, Senegalese friends; the woman greeted them warmly and began to flirt with the men until Maya introduced them: they were not members of the *Porgy and Bess* troupe, but Africans. 'D'Afrique? D'Afrique?' stuttered the woman. She looked at me as if I had betrayed her" (*Singin'*, 184). Her African acquaintances themselves had occasionally told Angelou that France was a civilized country where no discrimination existed. But she could now see between white French and black Africans the same kind of racism that prevailed in the United States. She drew her own conclusions: "Paris was not the place for my son. The French could entertain the idea of me because they were not immersed in guilt about a mutual history—just as white Americans found it easier to accept Africans, Cubans, or South American Blacks than Blacks who had lived with them foot to neck for two hundred years. I saw no benefit in exchanging one kind of prejudice for another" (*Singin'*, 184–85).To Angelou this condescension, which other black writers also documented, was sufficient reason not to settle in France, and she significantly ended the chapter with an emphatic "Adieu, Paris."

Still more interesting was Hazel Scott's remark that after her return to America she had been reproached for running away from "the problem." Even a room-service waiter in a hotel told her she had fallen in his estimation because she had left America, where the fight was. That the fight was not confined to America, that one needed to counter the image of the Negro propagated overseas by armed service personnel—most of whom were white southerners—was unimportant. Clearly, by the time of Richard Wright's death in exile, the civil rights movement had changed the situation in America to the extent that leaving the scene was considered a kind of betrayal. James Baldwin had already felt guilty about being away in 1956, when the police unleashed German shepherds against little black girls in the South. But Wright had died, assured by the visit of Martin Luther King that black militancy was only timidly gathering momentum.

When Wright's collection of short stories, *Eight Men*, appeared posthumously in 1961, however, both Jay Saunders Redding and Arna Bontemps expressed the view that he had been away too long. And the same implication was to be found in the poems of Conrad Kent Rivers, to whom Wright was a literary god for his poetry alone. In his "To Richard Wright," Rivers wrote that the new black generation needed him back, needed his strong voice for the sit-ins. Had not his sailing to France been a way of giving up the fight in order to sleep soundly? There was more than a hint of reproach in the statement:

> A boat leaves for France every evening,
> but Sartre wants to come here. I hope that you bask on the Riviera
> and teach your children the non-sensitivity of caviar.[3]

At Rivers's request, Langston Hughes had sent Wright a copy of the poem, which reached him shortly before his death.

Rivers felt only reverence for the City of Light; even in childhood he had already roamed its streets in his mind, as he claimed in "Four sheets to the wind and a one-way ticket to France, 1933":

> As a black child I was a dreamer
> I bought a red scarf and women told me how
> beautiful it looked

Wandering through the heart of France
As France wandered through me

. . . .

I read in two languages, not really caring
which one belonged to me
I liked to watch the bohemians gaze at the
paintings along Gauguin's bewildered paradise.
Braque once passed me in front of the Cafe musique

. . . .

I read Gide
and tried to
translate Proust (now nothing is real except French wine)
For absurdity is reality, my loneliness unreal
And I shall die an old Parisian with much honor[4]

After Wright's death Rivers undertook a pilgrimage to his Paris in the summer of 1963. He registered, along with his disappointment about Paris, the distance between his dream of the city and the reality of Western Europe imitating the United States, while "France embraces greed and mediocrity."[5] The bright white city stirred discontent in the young black because she had sold "her soul for symbols"; she was no longer true to the liberal image he had of her, and he felt Europe was too far removed from the aching scenes of black protest. In "Night-letter from Paris" he reiterated how little could be expected from the ideological Parisian scene where Afro-Americans were lost:

I found French-speaking bigots and sterile blacks
polished Americans and very little of the chosen few . . .
I found Africans scattered all over the place,
an occasional Harlem boy in need of chops and grits,
a few men of color seeking a final identity.
I saw little pride or God in their disgrace.[6]

Thus Rivers registered the changes that had occurred since the lively Paris of the fifties that he had imagined, the Paris of the Latin Quarter expatriates. Yielding to the spreading influence of American values, Paris was now filled with Coca Cola and "bright African lads forgetting their ancestral robes," a place where the garçons "come and go counting old-fashioned American dough."[7] Not only did Paris no longer fulfill humanistic expectations or seem adapted to the militant spirit of Afro-Americans, but as a backlash against the loss of Algeria and a consequence of increased African and West Indian immigration, the French were becoming more racist.

A few years later Herbert Lottman, himself an old-timer in the city and a close associate of Afro-Americans there, noted that the Paris scene was no longer the same: Wright was gone, Baldwin now hovered across the Atlantic, but mostly the days of the Café Tournon, where one observed the events at home from exile, were over. Lottman quoted Wright's own daughter, Julia Hervé, a left-wing journalist who had worked in Ghana during the Nkrumah regime, as saying, "We just can't sit around tables speculating about a brave new world."[8] The number of black Americans residing in Paris had dwindled to some 1,500—half as many as there used to be during the preceding decade—and their situation was different in many ways.[9] When they were not siding with black and Third-World liberation movements, long-time residents were often challenged to justify remaining abroad. Jazz pianist Art Simmons, of the Living Room nightclub, had the distinct feeling that the young blacks were no longer impressed that he lived in Paris but were asking what he was doing for the cause. There were black entertainers, artists, writers, ex-servicemen, and employees of the U.S. government, the United Nations, and a few major American business concerns. Many had married Europeans. A few had become French citizens, like LeRoy Haynes, who still catered to soul brothers and Parisians alike in his restaurant on the Rue Clauzel. Aaron Bridgers, who had come with the United Nations in 1948, was pursuing his career as a pianist. Ollie Stewart, who had arrived as a foreign correspondent with the Free French, was still writing free-lance for the American press.

Not that they lacked commitment or even militancy. When Americans in Paris created an organization against repressive American policy and the war in Vietnam, none other than the dean of American expatriate writers, Maria Jolas, was at its head, and William Gardner Smith himself—who had become the dean of expatriate Afro-American writers—was active in it. He claimed that if black Americans met now, it was more likely to be to work out concrete support for black power or oppose the war in Vietnam than to talk about literature. And he alluded to the setting up of an organization in France to raise money for SNCC while more radical movements like the Revolutionary Armed Movement also had their supporters in France.

This by no means proved that all black Americans had turned revolutionaries, but it demonstrated that even the word "expatriate" had become something of a misnomer. The writers of the preceding generation had often fled from home as a gesture of repudiation and defiance, political or racial, or they had embarked on an isolated, solitary search for identity. The newcomers were not really leaving America: for one thing American influence had become so pervasive and immediate that it could not be escaped in France. America's problems, including the racial situation, had become the problems of the world.

The newcomers who left America because of the war in Vietnam or because their economic status now made it easier came not to repeat the quest of a James Baldwin or a Chester Himes but to experience a change of scene. Admittedly, they wanted to flee from the outrage of racism and the oppression of "Babylon" (in the terminology of the Black Panthers) but also to look at it from a distance and test whatever bonds existed between them and the Third World. A sense of black nationalism made Paris no longer a place in which one settled but a way-station on the journey to other European countries, especially Holland and Scandinavia, and, most important of all, to newly freed and recovered Mother Africa.

How could the French setting help under such circumstances? For one thing, French youth were moving toward more liberal perspectives that culminated in the May 1968 student revolution, and they, and French progressive and leftist parties, provided some support for civil rights and black power militants at the time when the ghetto revolts were making headlines. Significant numbers of students, misguidedly believing that all Afro-Americans were becoming Black Panthers, sincerely but naïvely identified with their cause: exposure in the media helped, at a time when the books of Martin Luther King, *The Autobiography of Malcolm X*, and Eldridge Cleaver's *Soul on Ice* were not only critical but popular successes in France. Malcolm X visited Paris several times on his way to and from Africa, each time gathering huge crowds at the Mutualité. When, on his last trip, he was not admitted by the airport police, angry protest filled the newspapers.

In a similar way, after visiting several African countries, Stokely Carmichael flew from Copenhagen to Paris in December 1967 to address a mass rally at the Salle de la Mutualité organized by the Vietnam National Committee, a French organization in support of the Liberation Front. At Orly airport the police detained him as "undesirable in France." It took the intervention of influential members of the Vietnam Committee and a government minister to have the order rescinded by President De Gaulle, who knew nothing about the decision. Carmichael remained in Paris for several weeks, giving interviews, making speeches, addressing African organizations and student groups. During that trip the radical black-power leader was cheered wildly when he said, under a huge portrait of Che Guevara at the Mutualité: "We do not simply want peace in Vietnam. We want the Vietnamese people to defeat the United States of America."

Four months later SNCC leader James Forman also spoke in Paris, reminding his audience that it was not enough to cheer the Vietnamese people or the black people of America from afar. They had a job to do in France, where injustice and racism flourished. The students who attended such rallies and who had adopted Che and Ho Chi Minh as heroes were among those who later went out into the streets in May 1968.

In 1964, in the heyday of the civil rights movement, most black Americans in Paris had signed a petition that they solemnly delivered to the American Embassy during a march led by James Baldwin, with the full support of the American Church in Paris. On May 12, 1969, when a few black militants interrupted a service at the American Church to demand reparations for past exploitation of American Negroes, the Reverend Emerson Hangen let them speak, although some of the congregation shouted "Blackmail!" However, an usher quickly called the police. The group, friends of SNCC, was led by Julia Wright Hervé. They gave the congregation two days to comply with their demand for a "token payment" of five thousand dollars toward the fund sought by James Forman's National Black Economic Development Conference: no money was given. Although French left-wingers viewed such attempts favorably, it appeared that Paris was not the place for a meaningful confrontation.

It is, moreover, impossible to claim that France was responsible for making Angela Davis into a revolutionary, although her stay there probably contributed to it. She had found French her most difficult subject in high school, yet when she was admitted to Brandeis University in 1961, she chose it as her major. She concentrated on literature, from Balzac to Sartre. Later she wrote her honors thesis on the novels of Robbe-Grillet. As the "nouveau roman" as well as the existentialists were then being widely taught in U.S. colleges, this did not indicate any special liking for the avant garde. Her stay in Paris from 1963 to 1964, when she studied at the Sorbonne during her junior year, was more significant.

In her sophomore year she had met a German exchange student who was majoring in philosophy. Manfred Clemens introduced her to the works of Nietzsche and Herbert Marcuse, helping her grow from a middle-class coed into a politically conscious black American. By the end of the year they had fallen in love, but Manfred's proposal was met with a no by the Davises, and the Clemenses were also opposed to the marriage. Manfred established himself in Paris, and the two spent much time together, studying, exploring the city, enjoying the Christmas vacation in the Alps. But the events taking place in France and the impact of Marxism were the major influences that led to the radicalization of Angela Davis. According to an interview she granted

Ebony magazine: "It was there, at twenty, hearing, seeing, thinking, that she began achieving psychological distance from the kind of 'educated Negro middle class' identity for which so much had fitted her. In Paris, Angela began extending her interests beyond Rabelais, Montaigne, Balzac and other maîtres of French literature. She began delving into philosophical thought. Phenomenology interested her; existential truths became even more clear. Kant and Hegel offered much, but a favorite was the political philosopher Karl Marx." [10]

The writings of Sartre and Camus certainly played a part in convincing Davis of the necessity of "engagement." But her own everyday experiences also counted. In her *Autobiography* she recalled that when she first explored Paris she was horrified by the racist slogans on the walls threatening death to the Algerians. Some of her first contacts with French-speaking students were with Africans, Haitians, and West Indians. From them she learned of the daily difficulties and humiliations inflicted by racism in France and started with a view of the country that was more politically aware than that of the average college junior. She dined in working-class Arab restaurants near la Goutte d'Or; she went to cafés run and frequented by North Africans, where police raids and bombings were not infrequent. These were also the times of civil rights activism in the United States. Angela learned of the death of four of her childhood friends, killed by a racist bomb in a Birmingham church. With her fellow students she attended rallies protesting racial violence: "One afternoon I attended a demonstration for the Algerian people in the square in front of the Sorbonne. When the *flics* broke it up with their high-power water hoses they were as vicious as the redneck cops in Birmingham who met the Freedom Riders with their dogs and hoses." [11]

Davis could easily draw a parallel between the situation of blacks in America and that of Arabs in France. Like Claude McKay thirty years before but unlike most black Americans who first became aware of the black diaspora through its cultural manifestations, she saw France with the eyes of a left-winger for whom the class struggle was a key to understanding the situation. Her attraction to Marxism as an explanatory theory and a basis for action soon prevailed. Color extended beyond blackness; the Third World extended beyond color. She began to realize this when she accompanied a friend who had been invited to attend a Vietnamese Tet celebration. There she discovered world reactions to the Americans fighting in Vietnam, and she understood the reasons for the recurring criticism of her country.

At the Sorbonne Davis was an eager and competent student of French literature, mostly drama and contemporary ideas. Yet her response to the Sorbonne milieu is indicative of her attitude toward European cultural institutions. Culture attracted her because of its far-ranging principles and liberating currents, but she was put off by its solemn trappings: "In the Sorbonne, I always felt as if I were in church—it was centuries old, with tremendous pillars holding up uncommonly high ceilings which displayed faded old paintings. The sacredness exuded by the place forced thousands of students inside to observe the silence" (*Autobiography,* 132). Such could have been the atmosphere of any lecture hall, especially the Grand Amphithéâtre, which seats over a thousand, with its imposing frescoes by Puvis de Chavanne, or the Amphithéâtre Richelieu with its wood paneling and mythological scene above the blackboard.

In Europe Angela Davis managed to meet Herbert Marcuse, and partly upon his advice, she decided to pursue a degree in philosophy at the University of Frankfurt, Germany. But she soon became convinced, like James Baldwin a few years before, that she should play her own part in the civil rights movement. She was now certain of the universality of racist oppression, but like many blacks abroad she "felt pained when reading about some new crisis in the struggle at home, to be hearing about it second hand" (*Autobiography,* 145). In Paris, she believed, she could not contribute anything concrete to the struggle; she therefore decided to return home.

If the academic year that Angela Davis spent in Paris did not alter the course of her existence or reveal a special interest in the city's international scene, other black students underwent significant changes there. One of them was Faith Berry, whose stay in Paris at age twenty-five became, she says, a turning point in her career. Not only did she meet many Africans at a time when independence was still recent in the former African colonies; she was also exposed to a new culture and decided to launch into a career in French literature.[12] She came in September 1964 to do research on literature written in French by blacks and Algerians like Kateb Yacine. She lived at the Cité Universitaire and in a shared apartment on Avenue de Suffren, improved her knowledge of the language at the Institute for the Teaching of French Abroad, followed courses in comparative literature, and on the whole kept away from Americans in Paris.

Because of her light skin she was defined in France not as a Negro but as a *métisse,* a surprising new, intermediate, category for her. In an essay titled "Le nègre, le négro et le noir," which she wrote for *Jeune Afrique,* the leading Paris-based weekly dealing with African politics and culture, she illustrated the nuances implied by such definitions as early as July 1965—i.e., years before Afro hairstyles and black power slogans were in vogue. The piece evokes what might have turned into a racial incident in a Left Bank café: an American coed discussing politics with an African student called him a *nègre* and he erupted, vociferating: "I'm not a Negro, I am an African. Negro is the word you white people used to call us by when we were slaves." Berry remarked that she herself could have made the same mistake: Africans called themselves black (*noir*), not Negro (*nègre*), and whatever her skin color, she had better call herself *Américaine noire* too. She perspicaciously analyzed the reciprocal images between Afro-Americans and Africans, noting that the former were persuaded the Africans liked them.

That same year, shortly before Helen Gurley turned *Cosmopolitan* into a *Playgirl* format for dimwits, the magazine printed Berry's well-documented article "American Working Girls in Paris." Not only did she discuss work permits and au pair girls, low-paid typing jobs and hookers on Rue Saint-Denis, or the high cost of living expenses, but she also focused on many individual cases, including long-haired and chestnut-skinned Marpessa Dawn. This medical secretary from the suburbs of Pittsburgh had spent three years in Paris before a chance meeting with a film director led her to a role in his new movie, then to play Eurydice in Marcel Camus's *Black Orpheus*, which was shot in Rio and won both an Oscar and a Golden Palm award at Cannes in 1959. Berry also recalled how Nancy Holloway had been hired and fired nearly simultaneously at the Club Mars because she could sing "Hip-Shaking Mama" and nothing else, yet after touring the Middle East with the USO she had returned to Paris and opened her own club in 1961.

Faith Berry herself did some free-lance reporting for *Jeune Afrique,* notably on the Watts riots and on Marian Anderson. For *Harper's Bazaar* she wrote a tongue-in-cheek satirical piece about the new Paris scene: the miniskirt was everywhere, together with girl-boy types, yéyé music, and the horrendous mixture of French and English known as "franglais," while it was now "in" to hang out at the Hilton's Western Bar or at the Drugstore across the boulevard from Les Deux Magots. She was witnessing fast Americanization, heralded by the invasion of supermarkets, quick lunches, and gadgets, not excluding discothèques where one could, as in Les Zoros, sample octopus and Beaujolais between two frug sessions. Faith Berry concluded: "Almost everyone is keeping late hours all over the place. Cutting Up. Letting their hair grow long. Showing their kneecaps. Bring your cameras and binoculars. You may not believe your eyes." [13]

Berry was a keen observer of Europeans as well as Americans, white and black, and Africans in Europe. She collected her essays for publication under the title *Between Two Worlds,* but Viking Press turned the book down in 1972. Probably more important to her was a novel based upon her life in France; she took many notes but its writing was interrupted by her completion of an anthology and a biography of Langston Hughes, her work as staff writer for public TV, and her academic career. Meanwhile, she has completed another novel that is set in New York City and Key West, Florida—*The Kingdom of the Shore,* to be published shortly.

Paris was not likely to lose its prestige in the eyes of old-timers like Arna Bontemps, one of the foremost propagandists of the New Negro movement, who had to wait thirty-five years before visiting France. He was a francophile from the start, in part due to the prestige attached by his own family to his French ancestors. His mother's father was a Jacques Laurent from Louisiana who had played an important part in the civil rights struggle in 1867; on his father's side Bontemps was descended from early French settlers in the New Orleans area, and as a boy Arna heard French patois spoken. His early education included not only black Alexandre Dumas but writers like Balzac, Stendhal, and Hugo, and in the 1920s René Maran's *Batouala* was his first stunning discovery of contemporary black literature in French. When he worked on *Black Thunder,* a novel based on the Denmark Vesey rebellion, and *Drums at Dusk,* a story of the Haitian revolution, Bontemps declared he was inspired by André Malraux, who blended compelling form with social consciousness. While most of his friends managed to sail to Paris in the 1920s, Bontemps was starting a family and too poor to follow them. But he kept in close touch with French writing, especially by blacks; he was one of the first American readers of Aimé Césaire's *Cahier d'un retour au pays natal* in the early 1940s and collaborated with Langston Hughes on a monumental anthology of Negro poetry.

At long last, in 1960 Arna and his wife spent most of August and September in the City of Light. "I sat at my first sidewalk café last night and fell in love with Paris on the corner of Place de l'Opéra and Boulevard des Capucines," he wrote Langston Hughes as triumphantly as he might have done in 1925. As luck would have it, Richard Wright often guided them through the city, although his health was none too good. They had become friends in Chicago in the 1930s; Arna had lent Richard, who needed change for tram fare, one of the "lucky pennies" he had retrieved in a purse long lost by his father. And Richard had become known as a writer shortly after. Was it superstition? Now Arna came to France and luck seemed to desert Richard. . . . The Bontempes visited Paris in detail, also in the company of cartoonist Ollie Harrington, before heading for Kampala and Nairobi in early October. Arna's second visit, in 1965, on his way to a P.E.N. conference in Central Europe was even briefer, but throughout his life Paris remained his dream city. As proud of being able to understand Louisiana patois as of enjoying Césaire's elaborate French, he was busy researching his French ancestry in order to complete his autobiography when he died.[14]

When he was "Richard Wright's last guest at home" in November 1960, Langston Hughes himself had not seen France since 1938. He had remained in touch with French cultural life, however, especially with the literary production of French-speaking blacks, while his autobiography *The Big Sea* and many of his poems appeared in translation, and "Mulatto" was broadcast on French radio in 1957.

Finally, when he was invited to Nigeria to attend President Ben Azikiwe's inauguration in 1960, Hughes made a point of stopping in Paris on the way back. At the Hotel Logos, where he stayed in the Latin Quarter, he met a young Senegalese, Diallo Alpha, with whom he spent three wonderful days; but he spent most of his time with Jimmy "Lover Man" Davis, the Afro-American expatriate singer he had befriended in 1947, and Richard Wright, ready to go for his final checkup at the Clinique Eugène Gibez. Upon his return to the United States, Hughes wrote Carl Van Vechten: "Paris seemed to me as lovely as ever. I want to go right back." [15]

He did not return when his musical *Black Nativity* ran for several weeks at the Théâtre des Champs-Élysées in January 1961, but the following summer, on his way home from Israel, he stopped briefly in Nice and longer in Paris. It was rainy and cold, but Hughes was in the right mood to enjoy the city, thinking of old memories after visiting Bricktop in Rome. He wrote Arna Bontemps: "Paris is still as lovely as ever and I've had a week of complete peace, nobody knowing I'm in town. . . . Last night was the fêtes de la Libération de Paris from the Nazis and Josephine Baker in her French uniform was the star and sang 'Mon Paris' and 'J'ai deux amours' before what looked like half a million people in the square of the Hôtel de Ville. She had all her medals on and without makeup—quite thrilling. And the crowd was made up of all the races in this very cosmopolitan (more than ever) city—many, many Africans, Algerians, Indo-Chinese, Moroccans, Americans." Hughes had done no work at all and was staying

in a small "real French hotel full of African students," run by a wonderful massive lady named Madame Tina, who "mothers everybody
and shouts all over the place when they get too loud."[16] He remarked
that Paris was getting expensive and tourists were bypassing it on their
way to Spain or Italy, but for him it remained the place to enjoy life.
He tarried there until October.

The following year Hughes was invited to the Berlin Poetry Festival
organized on the theme Poetry in a Changing World. After serving as
a sort of moderator in the Africa vs. the West and French-speaking vs.
English-speaking poets' "confrontation" at the festival in late September, Hughes again spent several weeks in Paris, staying at the Hotel
California. François Dodat had been entrusted with preparing a volume on him for the prestigious Poètes d'aujourd'hui series run by
Éditions Seghers, in which he would be the fourth American poet
represented, after Whitman, Poe, and Emily Dickinson. On the occasion of its publication, Seghers gave a party with Aragon, Elsa Triolet,
and other old-time left-wing intellectuals. Hughes was then honored
with a reception given by the Comité National des Écrivains on October 29, 1964, at the Hotel Lutétia. The next day he gave a reading at
the American Cultural Center. After Hughes's difficulties with the Un-
American Activities Committee in the days of McCarthyism, he was
being made into a sort of unofficial cultural ambassador by the U.S.
Information Service, which surprised him, since he had found almost
no books by Afro-Americans in their libraries overseas. He made this
remark to Jean Wagner, the French professor of American studies
who was then completing *Black Poets in the United States,* which Hughes
considered "the first really comprehensive criticism of my poetry as
yet in print, done with great sympathy and an over-all understanding
on the whole."[17]

During those eight weeks in France Hughes became the friend of a
young African, Blanchard Kekeh, who was established in a suburban
immigrant hostel at Chevilly-Larue. He later helped him by sending
him books and small sums of money over a period of several years.
He expected to see him again at the opening of his *Prodigal Son* at the
Théâtre des Champs-Élysées in September but did not return until
the following year. This time he came on a USIS-sponsored trip for a
seminar on Negro literature that had been suggested by Jean Wagner.
This took place in late May 1965 with Hughes, William Melvin Kelley,
and Paule Marshall reading, lecturing, and speaking with over a score
of teachers and research students. The recent political developments
of the civil rights struggle had given black literature a new visibility:
at a roundtable at the Centre d'Études Américaines, racial and politi-

cal issues were debated vigorously. Later, at Royaumont and a couple
of private parties, Hughes read his works and spoke of the relationship between art and politics: he had felt offended by the obscenity
of LeRoi Jones's *The Toilet* and believed less in antagonizing the bourgeoisie than in the effects of example and persuasion.

In June 1966, after attending the Dakar Festival of Negro Arts and
lecturing all over Africa for USIS, he stopped in Paris again and was
feted by many young black writers, especially after the reading he
gave, with Ted Joans playing solo trumpet, at the new Shakespeare
and Company bookstore near Notre-Dame: "Paris seems to be full of
young cullud writers and artists and actors from the States," Hughes
reported to Bontemps on July 7. By then he was seriously considering
taking up residence in Paris, at least part of the year, the way James
Baldwin was doing. He alluded to it in his letters to Kekeh and Jimmy
Davis, and even asked a French friend to find him a small apartment.
For a few months he rented one on the Boulevard Raspail, not far
from Denfert-Rochereau, but gave it up in 1967 for lack of money.
To his plans to settle in France, Arna Bontemps had replied: "If you
plan to go to Paris for always, as you say, we will visit you now and
then. . . . In any case I think one whose career has reached the point of
warm reflection and the reading of biographies in writing of himself
has earned residence in Paris, prior to residence in glory. It would be
the ideal place for you to write volume III of your own *autobiography*
for instance. Moreover, Harlem's problems seem to have reached a
certain plateau and can probably be viewed just as well from a certain
distance."[18] Hughes died shortly after, on May 22, before he could
realize his wish.

During the black power period black American writers were, more
forcibly than ever, compelled to come to terms with their commitment
and their identity, and the pressure was often such that, even when
they were enjoying the relatively free and culturally stimulating atmosphere of Paris, they knew they would soon have to face the problem of
readjusting to the normal course of things in the United States, since
few of them could think of staying away from home permanently.

The attitudes of two writers separated by a generation and their reactions to France at roughly the same period—1970—illuminate the
range of possible responses. One was Horace Cayton, the sociologist
and co-author of *Black Metropolis,* who went to Paris to complete research for a biography of his old friend Richard Wright. Cayton had
not visited Paris since the 1930s. At that time he had attended a conference against war and fascism and become acquainted with progressive

French intellectuals while sampling the pleasures and leisure of the city. When he came again, he had only two French contacts, journalist Georges Baguet of *La Croix* and me, and he was curious about the new feeling created by the May 1968 "revolution" among my students, with whom I arranged a couple of seminars for him. Although several African students openly told him of the discrimination they often met with, clearly in his eyes Paris was still the symbol of liberty and racial equality. One evening, having dinner with us in our Antony apartment, from which one could see the skyline lit up by a brilliant line of arc-lights as well as the last reflections of the setting sun against the clouds, he exclaimed in awe: "Paris, what a beautiful, peaceful city! This is the place where I could die." Was it a premonition? Ironically, Horace Cayton did die of a heart attack in his Montparnasse hotel room about a week later.

Literary critic Addison Gayle—author of *Wayward Child* (1971), *The Black Situation* (1970), and also a biography of Richard Wright—was a not-infrequent traveler to Europe and Paris around that time. In an essay called "The Expatriate," which was published by *Black World* in May 1970 at the time of Cayton's death, he evoked the atmosphere of Paris in a scene contrasting the ambiance in the TWA jumbo jet returning home and reminiscences of a friend who had suddenly left for Europe in 1958: Roland could no longer take the tough life reserved for blacks in South Carolina and had settled in Paris. He had written once, "The French don't bother me, don't get into my hair. Not because they are so damn moral. But you see they have their niggers in the Algerians, so they don't annoy me." [19] Yet one day, while waiting for a train in a bar in Chartres, Roland had undergone an "American" experience: the waitress had tripped over his bag, which lay close to his table, and had shouted at him in bad English: "You, damn neegar!" Roland had not heard those words for so long that he had turned around to see if perhaps she was addressing someone else, and then he had burst out laughing.

On his recent trip, Gayle's narrator had met Roland again: "We stood in Paris on the Right Bank. Behind us was the Louvre. Directly below, between the parapet and the water, was a narrow road which the French motorists use as a freeway. In the distance the Eiffel Tower stood like an Egyptian princess, vying with the golden stars for majesty and glory. The waters of the Seine were peaceful and calm, stirred only by the double-deckered *bateaux-mouches* loaded with Germans, Spaniards and Americans" ("Expatriate," 58). But now the expatriate had lost his job as an interpreter for a foreign newspaper; he was forced to live on his African wife's earnings, and he dwelt in the Algerian quarter at la Goutte d'Or. His race brother conjured up in his mind only another well-to-do American, someone who hesitated to sever all ties with his mother country, although he hesitated to call her that. Such was probably the tragedy of expatriation, but returning to the United States meant readjusting to a code of behavior. Addison Gayle's narrator had by no means been won over by French customs, but he concluded: "I would go back where I would have to readjust my whole life style, pay attention to insignificant acts of protocol which I had not needed during my whole stay in Paris, redevelop strategies simply to stay alive" ("Expatriate," 65).

NOTES

1. Hazel Scott, "What Paris Means to Me," *Negro Digest*, November 1961, 61.

2. Maya Angelou, *Singin' and Swingin' and Gettin' Merry like Christmas* (New York: Random House, 1976), 171, hereafter cited in the text as *Singin'*.

3. Conrad Kent Rivers, "To Richard Wright," *Antioch Review* (Winter 1960–61), 464.

4. Conrad Kent Rivers, "Four sheets to the wind and a one-way ticket to France, 1933," *These Black Bodies and This Sunburnt Face* (Cleveland, Ohio: Freelance Press, 1962), 1–2.

5. Conrad Kent Rivers, "For Richard Wright," *The Wright Poems* (London: Paul Breman, 1972), 15, hereafter cited in the text.

6. Conrad Kent Rivers, "Night-letter from Paris," *The Wright Poems*, 16

7. Ibid., 18.

8. Julia Hervé, quoted by Herbert Lottman, "The Action Is Everywhere the Black Man Goes," *New York Times Book Review*, April 21, 1968, 6.

9. The change in the number of Americans in Paris was due in part to passage of a labor law stating that at least half of the musicians in any jazz orchestra must be French.

10. Angela Davis, interview in *Ebony*, quoted by J. A. Parker in *Angela Davis* (New Rochelle, N.Y.: Arlington House, 1973), 85.

11. Angela Davis, *Autobiography* (New York: Random House, 1974), 122, hereafter cited in the text.

12. Faith Berry, interview with the author, March 1988.

13. Faith Berry, "Paris Reoccupied," *Harper's Bazaar*, September 1966, 156.

14. Arna Bontemps, interview with the author, March 1972.

15. Langston Hughes to Carl Van Vechten, December 12, 1960, Yale University Library, JWJ, Hughes Archive.

16. Hughes to Arna Bontemps, August 25, 1963, Yale University Library.

17. Hughes to Bontemps, April 13, 1963, Yale University Library.

18. Bontemps to Hughes, May 7, 1967, Yale.

19. Addison Gayle, "The Expatriate," *Black World*, May 1970, 58, hereafter cited in the text.

Countee Cullen and Harold Jackman on a Paris boulevard in the 1930s

Claude McKay on the Seine embankments, 1929 (photo from *Back to Montparnasse* by Sisley Huddleston [London: Harrap, 1931])

Richard Wright in front of the English bookstore on Rue de Seine in the late 1940s

Richard Wright and Léopold Senghor at the conference of Negro writers and intellectuals at the Sorbonne, September 1956

James Baldwin and Beauford Delaney at an exhibition of Delaney's paintings at the American Cultural Center in the 1970s (photo from the United States Information Service)

Chester Himes, seated next to Lesley Packard, with friends including Nicole Barclay of Barclay Records (center facing) in the 1960s

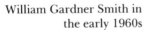
William Gardner Smith in the early 1960s

Afro-American literature conference, spring 1965, at Royaumont: above, left to right, Langston Hughes, Paule Marshall, Sim Copans, and William Melvin Kelley; below, Kelley (photos from the United States Information Service)

Ronald Fair in the early 1970s

Melvin Dixon, 1973

Melvin Van Peebles, 1968

Carlene Polite in the late 1960s

Left to right, LeRoi Jones, Michel Fabre, and Ted Joans in front of Shake-speare and Company in 1979

Barbara Chase-Riboud on a French television panel discussion of the TV adaptation of Alex Haley's *Roots* in 1978

James Emanuel in the Pyrénées mountains in the mid-1970s

18

Visitors All, or Nearly

In spite of changed expectations, most of the new black writers took to visiting Paris as their predecessors had done. Charles Wright went even before his novel, *The Messenger,* was translated, and so did Cecil Brown and Alston Anderson in the 1970s. In addition to the artists, entertainers, and authors already mentioned, a sizable number of people went mostly for business purposes. Maya Angelou visited again in 1980, when a bilingual edition of her poems *And Still I Rise* followed the translation of her autobiography. Ishmael Reed attended a conference on postmodernism at the Sorbonne Nouvelle in 1977, after Éditions du Seuil had put out *Mumbo Jumbo.* LeRoi Jones went to Paris several times in the 1970s, well after his black revolutionary plays, especially *The Slave* and *Dutchman,* had stirred up heated controversies among the French as early as 1965; there was talk of the Opéra de Paris producing his musical *Money* in 1979, but the project was dropped, whether for lack of funding or because of pressure from U.S. officials who did not like Jones/Baraka's move from black cultural nationalism to Marxist-Leninist ideology. Although most were only visiting, a few came to stay in Europe, either for good, like novelist Ronald Fair and poet James Emanuel, or to use Paris as a base or port of call in a sort of international commuting, like poets Ted Joans and Melvin Dixon.

An Afro-American best-seller was written partly in France—namely, *Roots* by Alex Haley. In 1968 Haley was reportedly working on a book for Doubleday called *After This Anger,* for which he already had a paperback contract and a movie sale to Elia Kazan. In this project, begun when he was a teenager in Tennessee, he was tracing his roots to Africa, having done research in Gambia, at the Public Records Office in London, and in other places. A rather recent arrival on the Riviera on magazine assignments for *Reader's Digest* and *Playboy,* he had come to interview Richard Burton during the filming of *The Comedians.* He discovered the Hauts de Cagnes and established residence there because, like James Baldwin, he felt that the atmosphere of the Midi was propitious for writing. However, he often went back to the States to lecture at universities or see his publishers. According to Herbert Lottman, "Alex Haley didn't feel that he was tied down by living abroad: London, Paris, Rome, Amsterdam are each but two hours away and the U.S. is also an airplane ticket removed from Nice airport. Paris itself is never more than a stopover. . . . Nor does absence from the American scene diminish commitment. 'From where I sit now, in a perspective sense,' he comments, 'I'd say that the rest of my life's writings invariably will treat one or another aspect of truth regarding the Negro.' That is his mission, not as an expatriate but with at least half of each year in the United States."[1]

Haley's feelings and situation, like Baldwin's at the time, reflected a choice made by some of the more affluent black American writers: they established residence in Europe and commuted to and from the United States when it was required by the business side of their careers. This was a new development in the late sixties, largely made possible by the fact that a few black writers now could "make it." Most of them, however, would still go to Paris on a sort of cultural pilgrimage or in quest of an atmosphere conducive to writing, always eager to seize upon any opportunity provided by fellowships, conferences, or lecture tours to which, due to the greater visibility of black Americans in the media, they were now more often invited. Most of the black writers who spent time in Paris during the last two decades—William Melvin Kelley, Paule Marshall, John A. Williams, Ronald Fair, William Demby, Cyrus Colter, Addison Gayle, Ishmael Reed, Maya Angelou, Toni Morrison, Charles Johnson especially—often took advantage of publishers' invitations and international writers' conferences. They went more as visitors eager to reach new readers or as tourists curious about the French milieu than as pilgrims hoping to derive inspiration from their stay.

William Melvin Kelley had already published three volumes of fiction and Paule Marshall two when they were both invited, with Langston Hughes, to participate in the black literature seminar at Royaumont in May 1965. At the time they represented new black voices. Both of them felt quite attracted to France. Since then Paule Marshall has returned a number of times, visiting France during European tours or vacations or at the invitation of her French publisher when *Brown Girl, Brownstones* came out in Paris in 1983. She has friends in France and likes to stay at the Hotel California on the Rue des Écoles—the favorite haunt of Hughes, who introduced her to the place in 1965. William Melvin Kelley spent several months in Paris in 1967 and 1968, preparing for a trip to Africa. As he devoted most of his time to writing the elaborate prose of *dunfords travels everywheres,* he did not really become part of "the scene," although he could hardly escape the agitated atmosphere of the Latin Quarter during the May 1968 student uprising.

Other writers, however, were prompt to make use of the dramatic events of the May "revolution" in their fiction, at least as a setting— not only white American James Jones, comfortably established on the Ile Saint-Louis, where he completed *The Merry Month of May,* but also black Frank Yerby, then living in Madrid and no witness to the events. Shortly after repairing to Europe in the 1950s, Yerby had lived on the French Riviera; then, convinced that racism was as bad in France as anywhere in spite of his expectations, he had settled in Spain, the country of his second wife. In 1967 he decided to explore Paris again, but when the Israel war broke out, he thought it more prudent to remain in the Midi, closer to the Spanish border, and so sojourned in Aix-en-Provence.

In his novel *Speak Now* Yerby used Paris as a backdrop only, as a couple of young Americans, a spirited blonde and a self-confident black, meet and fall in love amid the clashes between students and antiriot squads that do not detract too much from the romantic atmosphere of the City of Light. As was his wont, Yerby did extensive and serious research but felt free to use his imagination: "If you find some exoticism in the novel, this had nothing to do with my sources; only with the way my own brains work."[2] Another, recently reprinted, novel by Yerby, *Voyage Unplanned,* takes place partly in France under the German occupation. Just like *Speak Now,* it reveals a writer fascinated by, and at times finely attuned to, French habits and culture.

Just like Yerby, John A. Williams knew enough of Europe to make the Paris and Amsterdam scenes of his memorable *The Man Who Cried I Am* (1967) credible to a native. Also like Yerby, he chose to settle for a while in Spain after visiting a few other European countries. Speaking a serviceable Spanish and having sojourned at length in Barcelona, he loved the little fishing villages that he used as a locale for the adventures of an established American novelist in Europe, the protagonist of his more recent novel, *¡Click Song!* Williams's own French experience, however, was largely limited to driving across the country twice, in 1964 and 1965, stopping in Paris both times. As for Paris, he researched there at the War Documentation museum material for his novel *Captain Blackman,* met with Ellen Wright and the editor Jean Rosenthal, and ate at LeRoy Haynes's restaurant. He was there when *Ebony* opened its office temporarily on Avenue Georges V, and he visited Chester Himes when Himes and Lesley lived in the Latin Quarter.

Cyrus Colter had already visited Paris when he decided to return in September 1973 to do research for the French scenes in his novel *Night Studies*.[3] Colter had enjoyed the city as a well-off tourist, and he remembered the terrace of Fouquet's on the Champs-Élysées—but not well enough to be sure his memories were accurate, as he wrote a French acquaintance: "I hope you won't hesitate to mark the story up and point out as many gaucheries as you have time for. The café Clouet is of course Fouquet's but I couldn't remember the latter well enough to use it so I faked Clouet's. Do the other settings also seem so faked as to make the story implausible and/or of an unpublishable quality?"[4] Colter sketches picturesque views of the city in a couple of accurate phrases: St. Germain's church, its thirteenth-century stone and mortar scaling and decaying, becomes "the romanesque tower a dunce cap in the drizzle"; the Rue Bonaparte is reduced to a "one-way traffic, slender strip of sidewalk" (*Night Studies*, 40). The documentary minutiae of Colter's novel manage, indeed, to create verisimilitude in terms of both locale and French characters.

Clearly, Colter associated French culture with refinement and elegance: he sent his talented black protagonist, Mary Dee Atkins, to take courses at the Beaux-Arts school. In Paris Mary Dee meets the son of a wealthy white American family, Philip Morgan Wilcox, who has come to study architecture, and she falls in love with him. One of their mutual friends, Raoul, is the one who really introduces Mary Dee to the city. Colter places his characters in likely surroundings while providing tactful explanations for the non-French reader: he mentions the narrow, crooked streets of the St. Germain-des-Prés area, where natives wend their way oblivious of others: "They went about their chores, menial, academic or business with the Parisian's usual aplomb, ironic exuberance and nonchalance" (*Night Studies*, 38). He describes the Fouquet's terrace with even greater precision: "The great awning was blood red with a straight golden trim, the chairs honey-yellow wicker, the tables circular and tiny. Correct black-coated waiters with their long white aprons moved about outside among the patrons bringing them food and drinks of a wide variety (*Night Studies*, 48–49). A French couple happens to be sitting there; they are about sixty, and the husband whispers, "Regarde la belle négresse," while his wife tactfully refrains from speaking, content to admire Mary Dee in silence.

Colter even ventures to recreate a "typically French" exchange between Raoul and his friend Adrienne. The scene takes place at Regent's, near the Avenue Matignon, where four of the characters are having lunch: "three of them had poached eggs, sweetbread and a sea-food terrine. Raoul roast woodcock; the wines were first a Sancerre, then a claret of great character" (*Night Studies*, 53). During the meal Raoul and Adrienne quarrel about their assessment of President Pompidou. To her claims that Pompidou is a French Nixon, he retorts: "Can you imagine Nixon as a president living in a house once the home of a courtesan—Madame de Pompadour? . . . French politics has always been romantic, emotional, theatrical. . . . France wept even as it executed its king. It has manned revolutionary barricades that brought tyrants to power. Adrienne, I will not allow you to render us so prosaic" (*Night Studies*, 53).

This image of the French for American readers at times comes close to the more flattering clichés. Enjoying the pleasures and refinement of Paris as a distinguished man of letters and a tourist, Colter perpetuates the tradition that pays tribute to French culture; he is content with noting the features of French behavior and education that account for appreciation of the beauty of a Negro, but he does not grapple with racial tensions in France. When it becomes apparent that, because of racism in America, Philip cannot possibly marry Mary Dee, she finds solace in French culture and in the company of brotherly Raoul in much the same way black male protagonists in James Baldwin's novels are allowed to blossom, spiritually and sentimentally, in their new Paris environment.

It is interesting to compare Colter's treatment of Paris with the contemporary image provided by Toni Morrison in *Tar Baby*.[5] Morrison's black protagonist comes from a fictional West Indian island named after the Queen of France, and even her name—Jadine—sounds somewhat French. She goes to Paris, not on a pilgrimage or quest for European roots but only to get an education. In France she discovers that her beauty is appreciated: her face is even selected to grace the cover of *Elle*, a fashion magazine. This could lead to easy acceptance: several men soon want to "marry, live with, support, fund and promote her" while smart and beautiful women want "to be her friend, confidante, lover, neighbor, guest, playmate or simply near" (*Tar Baby*, 47). Paris appears as a social paradise in which a black woman is welcome and desired and loved, especially when she is fair-skinned and European-looking. But Jadine increasingly wonders whether her French lover is attracted to her because of a supposedly exotic quality in her or because of her real self: "I wonder whether the person he wants to marry is me or a black girl? . . . What will happen when he finds out that I hate ear hoops, that I don't have to straighten my hair, that Mingus puts me to sleep, that sometimes I want to get out of my skin and be the only person inside?" (*Tar Baby*, 48).

She will eventually run away, not only from her French companion but from Paris, because of an incident that causes her to discover another side of her personality. In a Paris supermarket she comes into contact with an African woman, with "too much hip . . . too much bust" under her canary yellow dress, but regally beautiful in her dignity: "The woman walked down the aisle as though her many-colored sandals were pressing gold tracks on the floor. Two upside-down V's were scored into each of her cheeks, her hair wrapped in a gelée as yellow as her dress. The people in the aisles watched her without embarrassment, with full glances instead of shy ones" (*Tar Baby*, 45). Jadine then realizes that such confident elegance is not acquired through French universities or haute couture; she starts feeling unauthentic and lonely, a sort of hybrid, whose Sorbonne degree and photograph on the cover of *Elle* in no way make her superior to the unforgettable African woman whose image now haunts her so much that she feels compelled to reconcile herself with that "black dimension" of her identity.

It would be misleading to interpret Morrison's symbolic episode in autobiographical terms. Jadine remains fictional, even though her author occasionally visited Paris, first as a tourist, then on business (for instance, when *Song of Solomon* came out in French in 1984), or to attend literary seminars, starting with the 1982 conference on the contemporary American novel, with William Styron, James Baldwin, Paul Theroux, Francine du Plessix Gray, and others, where Morrison was by far the most forceful and meaningful speaker.

There is certainly more autobiography in the experiences of Sarah Phillips, the protagonist of a novel of the same name by Afro-American writer Andrea Lee. Lee herself spent years in Paris, and her fair-skinned, middle-class, well-educated heroine largely reflects her own experience: in the opening section, "In France," Sarah goes to Paris after graduating from Harvard in very much the same way as the typical American coed tries to flee her safe, puritan, middle-class upbringing. Sarah encounters many reflections of herself in white fellow citizens, mostly in Kate, who seems to her like an alter ego; how is she to deal with her Negroness, with her class? Fearing that she may come across wealthy black Americans who know her family, she would like to repudiate her entire past. But France cannot let her forget America: America is all over the place, and her French friends, Alain and Roger, and her lover, Henri, are obsessed with westerns, fast food, and Coca Cola.

What is more, while Sarah attempts to keep the African part of her background at an emotionally safe distance, the very racism of her French lover compels her to reclaim that part of herself: in a fit of anger, Henri once launches into an explanation of Sarah's beauty— pale skin but kinky hair—by recalling her ancestors, her Irish mother who was also part Jew and part Indian and who was raped by a black American musician "as big and black as King Kong with sexual equipment to match."[6] The offensive stereotypes here serve to disprove any mythical image of nonracist Europeans, and they also compel Sarah to come to terms with what she is: the silly tale illuminates for her "with blinding clarity the hopeless presumption of trying to disregard my portion of America" (*Sarah Phillips*, 12). One is again reminded of the Baldwin of the 1950s, who wrote essays about "What It Means to Be an American," as Sarah muses, some thirty years after him: "How wonderfully simple it had seemed to be ruthless, to cut off ties with griefs, embarrassments and constraints of a country, a family; what an awful joke it was to find as I had found that nothing could be dissolved or thrown away. I had hoped to join the ranks of dreaming expatriates for whom Paris had become a self-sufficient universe but my life there had been no more than a slight hysteria, filled with the experimental naughtiness of children reacting against their training. It was clear much as I did not want to know that my days in France had a number, that for me the bright, frank, endlessly beckoning horizon of the runaway had been, at some point, transformed into a complicated return" (*Sarah Phillips*, 14–15).

Novelist Ronald Fair had already published *Many Thousand Gone* and *World of Nothing* and had just completed *We Can't Breathe* by the time he visited Chester Himes, who had praised his work, in his Spanish residence in Moraira in December 1971. He had plans to spend a year or so in Sweden with his wife, Neva, a budding writer herself, and only stopped in Paris on his way, barely long enough to find the city beautiful. In spite of the generous offer of the Swedish Institute of Letters to assist in their relocation, Fair refused to spend more than a few weeks in "cold, cold Sweden." *We Can't Breathe* was selling well, and he hoped to be able to settle in France. In order to get acquainted with the country, the Fairs accepted the offer of French academics who were spending a semester in the United States to use their country house, only sixty miles from Paris, between Fontainebleau and Sens.

Born in Chicago, Ronald Fair had lived mostly in large cities, and he appreciated the seclusion propitious to writing more than the pleasures of the countryside. The house was adequate but not luxurious;

taking care of the lawn and the yard and shopping in nearby towns became a not-unpleasant routine; the neighbors were helpful to Americans whose French was nearly nonexistent. Ronald spent afternoons, and often nights, on successive versions of an ambitious novel, "The Migrants," and he soon preferred to drive his Fiat 124 to pick up his mail at the post office in the nearby village to being awakened by a 9 A.M. delivery. By mid-May Neva was pregnant, and although the sales of Ronald's novels were dwindling, they hoped they would be able to remain in France. He certainly was daydreaming when he wrote that he planned to go back to the United States and make enough money to "buy a house over here and return HOME to France."[7] Even though this was nothing more than thinking out loud, he was sincere. His enthusiasm about France was indicative at least of the pleasure of being able to write far from racial tensions. Living in France and living in the country seemed to go hand in hand: they were experimenting with a return to authenticity after the "plastic" civilization of America. Ronald even invited his mother and his children by his first wife to spend the summer at Les Bergeries. While they were there, he nearly completed "The Migrants," the 800-page saga of a black family in which he attempted to retrace the huge changes brought to America by the Great Migration that drew the black masses from the rural South to northern cities from the 1870s to the 1940s. But as American interest in soul literature declined, his earlier novels were not selling any more; talks about a French publication by Flammarion of *We Can't Breathe* resulted in nothing. When his friends returned, Ronald Fair moved again to Switzerland; later he established himself in Finland.

Fair's stay in France was an attempt at living abroad in the old style of American writers. He was not leaving the United States for political reasons or only fleeing the pressure of racism, but he (who had long earned his living as a court reporter) was trying to subsist by writing, in a milieu where relative poverty would be neither a stigma nor a hindrance to writing. Encouraged by the example of Chester Himes, he had resolved to establish himself in Europe, far from the civilization that did not allow the ghetto dwellers to breathe in a "world of nothing." He was not looking for contacts with "colorful" Africans, he did not entertain romantic notions about Paris as a cradle of culture; but like many young black American writers of his generation, he had to stake much upon his personal growth, both spiritual and artistic, not to be left in a void as public interest in blackness flagged. That he faded away from the literary scene and took up sculpture, then "gave his life to Jesus" in 1980 was due only in part to his expatriation. What is remarkable is that he was unwilling to try his hand at non-American scenes and situations. "The Migrants" (never published) and the poems in *Rufus* are rooted in Afro-American history and the blues, the soil that nourished Fair at his best.

Clarence Major was already an established writer when he came to France, first as a lecturer and a tourist, then in 1983 and 1984 for a whole year as an associate professor at the University of Nice. His fiction is decidedly postmodernistic and so little referential that it is hard to find in it echoes of his own experience. He is more topical, sometimes autobiographical, in *Inside Diameter,* a volume of verse subtitled "The France Poems."[8] Almost every piece was inspired by an incident at a specific place, Paris or the Midi. A woman sitting on a rock looking upon the sea at "Pointe de Rompe Talon" becomes a metaphor for peace. Beaulieu-sur-Mer is the setting for a careful disquisition on the strategy of eating red mullet. Near the ancient fort at Montalban, the proximity of the blazing forest fires and the shuttling back and forth of the Canadair planes conjures a vision of danger:

> Flames pour from the cottage window.
> Hurry! the plane goes down to the sea,
> scoops up a beak full of water,
> like a pelican, returns
> to the burning vision
> of the crucifixion which smells of the artist's linseed oil
> and the trapped mistress,
> his muse.
>
> (*Diameter*, 11)

"Revelation at Cap Ferrat" contrasts the elements of secular and religious sense with the "rising and lifting / falling and / catching of the spirit / before it crashes" (*Diameter*, 12), while "Dancing under the Stars at Nice" is a pretext to analyze the "motion of biochemistry" in the effortless movement of the dancers and to counterpoint it with the mood of a friend who has just learned that he has cancer. "On Promenade des Anglais" is more a meditation on the changing forms of Woman—"Call her Bardot . . . Lena Horne, Lauren Bacall, The Duchess of Alba or Gabrielle Chanel" (*Diameter*, 24)—than an evocation of the sea-front boulevard. There are very personal pieces, like "Towards the Old Roman Road," with Jacqueline bearing flowers near the Route de Bellet, where the poet feels "doomed here at Saint Isidore / in front of the little post / office across from our butcher /shop" to attempt to express adequately the music in his head (*Diame-*

ter, 25). Or "Drinks at Café au Charbonnage" serves to admonish the artist (as painter) to get closer to the people in the village instead of keeping at a distance, the better to sketch them.

Major's stay in Paris inspired a couple of bleak pieces: "Seine Split" embodies a sense of dissociation of the self into a kind of twin personality, while " 'Home' on Rue du Bourg Tibourg," far from vaunting the beauty of the Marais, evokes a nightmarish symphony in gray after a kaleidoscopic haze of sensations:

> You are lying flat on your back in Paris
> without knowing you are inside your own
> air-conditioned skull, cross-sectioned
> *(Diameter,* 15)

Decidedly, Major's best poems are those set on the Riviera, where he lived longest. In "Absence of the Sefirotic Fire," the towns of Éze, Cap Roux, and Beaulieu become landmarks in a sort of spiritual Jacob's ladder, while allusions to the French *poètes damnés* close the meditation:

> Read Rimbaud ("des vertiges,
> des silences, des nuits") to me.
> Decorate my house with black
> flags, with Baudelaire's dead
> flowers.
> *(Diameter,* 18)

The kinship with French writers and artists is emphasized in the two beautiful vignettes of "Atelier Cézanne," in which a visit to the nearly sacred place is made in hushed reverence, detailing each commonplace object, until the view of Montagne Sainte-Victoire erupts out on the path. And in the second section, in the "frozen garden," the poet is reunited with the dead painter and with Vincent Van Gogh. The final poem in the volume, "Last Days in France," is a nostalgic enumeration of lyrical moments and soon-to-be-forgotten impressions of Nice—the beach, bins of tripe in the Old Town, coffee on Cours Saleya—clouded with sadness. As "Selected Moments in France—*in memory of my illusions*" makes clear, the France of Clarence Major is one of disrupted continuity, of separate moments when the setting itself is not so important: such things could happen anywhere and the narrator could be any writer preoccupied with himself:

> I ate a Gervais
> from a stick. University students
> lined up in front of the Sorbonne.
> Blood? Still on the tip of my toe

> from kicking a wino sleeping
> in Place Wilson: he'd pretended to be me.
> The snot of moules was deep
> in my diet; curse of living
> by the sea. Winter was now vanishing!
>   (*Diameter*, 30–31)

In *My Amputations,* one of Major's more recent novels, his one-year stay in Nice and on the Riviera served him in good stead as the story takes Mason Ellis (an American novelist out to compensate, or take revenge, for the wrongs done to him) from Chicago to Europe and Africa.[9] For the audacious burglar, fleeing to Europe means not only running away but also seeking himself. His encounters with an Italian swordsman, a violent German secret society, and a group doing an old-fashioned dance in rural Greece may make the wonders of the Riviera seem pale by comparison. A whole section, though, celebrates the idiosyncratic charm of old Nice: "In Nice you can get through the winter. It won't run into you like a boy on a skateboard. At the corner of avenue de Suède and rue Halévy is a bar–pizza joint that sells Sicilienne pizza for twenty-five francs and you can even get dinner there for thirty-eight. If you're feeling rich you can drink at the swank bar of the Negresco Hotel which faces the sea. You might even bump into James Baldwin. The doorman, by the way, is a sight in his red and blue livery" (*Amputations,* 79).

And the enumeration goes on with the Grand Café de Turin, the Jok Club at Casino Ruhl, the café on Cours Saleya, the Bar de la Dégustation across from the Palais de Justice: "There, just beside the entrance of the tiny café-bar a fisherman sells his freshly caught fish out of a wobbly old pushcart usually on Thursdays and Fridays. When you buy from him he talks nice to you and wraps your fish quickly in old sheets of *Nice-Matin*" (*Amputations,* 80). The description then focuses on Square Dominique Durandy, in front of the old library, where on Sunday mornings philatelists gather to trade, carrying on business while holding umbrellas over their heads when it rains, fingering stamps of the République Française. And at carnival time Mason meets an exchange student at the university: "He was made deeply lonely by the arrival of carnival time in Nice. Too many full moons, too much promise of spring. Place Masséna with its giant cartoon figures of Saint Nick and his nicky helpers, Popeye, Snoopy, Clark Gable, Roy Rogers, were a bit much. The New Moon had him by the balls. Ash Wednesday got his goat. He had the howling Quadragesima blues. Lent let him down" (*Amputations,* 82).

There are echoes of Major's own art historian's enjoyment of Aix and the Provence landscape as the hero tours the area in his blue Simca on his leisurely way to a lecture at the American College in Paris: "Spring was a gentle wrestler holding the body of Nice in an agonizing embrace. Then he made her kiss the canvas. . . . Then just north of the view of Mont Sainte Victoire, as he felt the geometry of Cézanne's landscape. . . . He stopped at Arles. The outlying areas, farmland; hadn't changed since that strange tormented painter cut off his ear here in, was it, 1888. The city itself was strictly tourist. Roman ruins in the old center. The postman and his wife were not in sight. The lamp-lighted café? The glare of the lighted billiards table?" (*Amputations,* 87–88). The shade of Vincent Van Gogh still haunts the place.

In Paris, after visiting the IHICE headquarters across from Père Lachaise, Mason walks through the cemetery like an inspired pilgrim, in search of Richard Wright's ashes: "He entered the cemetery's profusion of gravestones and leaf and although he didn't find Wright hidden at the foot of a stairway to vaults, he found the lonely graves of Stein and Modigliani and, yes, Balzac and Roussel and one big, blunt tomb marked simply, 'Family Radiguet.' Bewildered, he came out at a brisk pace" (*Amputations,* 50). But Mason is not ready for Paris. He enters one bookstore on the Left Bank and complains that it is full of giddy young Americans. Self-centered, he looks for his own works but cannot "find his own name . . . on any spine on the shelves. Pigalle was a flesh hustle that bored him. The lines were too long at the museums. Night life was more expensive than it was worth" (*Amputations,* 91).

By contrast, Nice seems a beautiful haven, in the house on the labyrinthine estate of the Rosatis, "the villa itself an altar to the sun overlooking the sea" (*Amputations,* 92) at the northern end of the estate, where an Italian family takes care of the carnation fields, harvests the fruit in season, and flays rabbits expertly. The protagonist goes happily back to a seminar on detective fiction and talks with French colleagues on the beach, remembering why they were out in the streets in 1968. Eventually his quest takes him to England and Germany, and out of France.

NOTES

1. Herbert Lottman, "The Action Is Everywhere the Black Man Goes," *New York Times Book Review,* April 21, 1968, 9.

2. Frank Yerby to the author, March 12, 1979.

3. Cyrus Colter, *Night Studies* (Chicago: Swallow Press, 1979), hereafter cited in the text.

4. Cyrus Colter to the author, April 12, 1972.

5. Toni Morrison, *Tar Baby* (New York: Knopf, 1981), hereafter cited in the text.

6. Andrea Lee, *Sarah Phillips* (New York: Random House, 1984), 11, hereafter cited in the text.

7. Ronald Fair to Michel and Geneviève Fabre, May 17, 1972.

8. Clarence Major, *Inside Diameter* (New York: Permanent Press, 1985), hereafter cited in the text.

9. Clarence Major, *My Amputations* (New York: Fiction Collective, 1986), hereafter cited in the text.

19

William Melvin Kelley and Melvin Dixon: Change of Territory

For younger writers like William Melvin Kelley and Melvin Dixon, going to France embodied the new double itinerary of Afro-American imagination in the black power era. By then Paris was mainly a way station for fresh incursions into the world of the French-speaking black diaspora, which already included Africa and the Antilles. For Dixon a trip to Paris still amounted to a cultural pilgrimage. But unlike Countee Cullen or James Baldwin, who searched for the European roots of their Americanness, the younger generation was mostly interested in the setting in which the Afro-American expatriates of the Wright and Himes generation had lived and expanded their vision. These earlier expatriates were now considered the literary pioneers and ancestors whose heritage had to be claimed, whose message had to be understood.

When William Melvin Kelley attended the 1965 Royaumont seminar on black literature, he was a newcomer to France, although not to Europe. He had lived in Italy with his family for a few months and, if one is to believe his 1965 *Mademoiselle* article, "An American in Rome," had greatly enjoyed the Latin way of life. In 1966 he decided to spend a year or two in France. After the fine reception of his first novel *A Different Drummer,* his books were selling well enough, and he conceived of a stay in Paris as a kind of introduction to French-speaking Africa, where he contemplated taking a long trip in search of his roots, after having been struck by the resemblance between his own facial features and those of a pygmy on a record jacket. Kelley had studied at Harvard and taken John Hawkes's creative writing course. He had proved he could write well and even emulate Faulkner. At the time he was concerned not with establishing his reputation in mainstream America but with discovering and exploring the hidden dimensions of his African heritage: "In the year since I was in Paris, a year in which I did a great deal of thinking and very little writing, I came to the realization that . . . the Black man in America is less American than anyone else because of segregation. It kept him apart and forced him to keep alive his African culture in very subtle ways."[1]

Bill, his wife, Karen (a painter), and two-year-old Jessica thus arrived in Europe on April 24, 1967. They stayed first at Ibiza, then in Barcelona, before being able to settle in the two-room sublet a friend managed to secure for them in Paris. The apartment was located on the top floor of the very house in which Richard Wright had occupied a ground-floor studio, at 4 Rue Régis near the Bon Marché department store. Kelley saw this as a good omen. He had finished polishing the final version of his fourth book, *Dem,* a satire on the effects of the Vietnam War on the American psyche and the suspenseful story of a black trickster. Karen had begun to paint again.

Soon Kelley was working on a new, very experimental novel in the style of *Finnegan's Wake.* Although he was keen to revisit Joyce's old haunts and the site of Sylvia Beach's and Adrienne Monnier's bookshops on the Rue de l'Odéon, Kelley had decided, well before coming, to write a daringly experimental narrative that would present a parable of the duality of the Afro-American soul. Like Joyce's Shem and Shaun, Kelley's protagonist is double, consisting of Carlyle Bedlow, a trickster perfectly aware of the rules of the racial game, and Chig Dunford, little conscious as yet of the African dimension of his cultural makeup.

When relating the adventures of Chig in an imaginary Mediterranean country, Kelley kept to standard English, but he resorted to ghetto slang when dealing with Carlyle. He recorded his protagonist's dreams and half-conscious ramblings in an innovative Joyce-like mixture of phonetic transcriptions and word creations in which homophony and punning predominate. Yet at that stage Kelley experimented less with language than with sounds; he tended to keep away from other black American writers, but he mixed with musicians, especially sax players Marion Brown and Steve Potts and, later, Clement Marshall. He would spend hours attempting to modulate vowel sounds without interruption, sometimes inspired by the recordings of pygmy music he kept buying, or to transcribe the rhythms of the horn in a sort of phonetic language. He learned just enough current French to get by with shopkeepers and with students when he occasionally lectured at Nanterre University, but he delighted in exploring the semantics of little-used and obsolete words and phrases in order to launch into ever more recondite translinguistic puns.

In many ways France was too close to his experience for him to step back and make use of it. The more realistic scenes of *dunfords travels everywheres,* located in Smepriroa in the Great Republic of Reupeo, de-

rive from the atmosphere and cafés of Rome, not Paris, even though
the custom of obliging half the inhabitants to wear blue or yellow
every other day in order to allow a clear state of segregation is purely
imaginary.

dunfords travels everywheres (the lack of capitals was deliberate and
the title hinted at Joyce's *Haveth Childers Everywheres*) was written at a
time when Kelley occasionally associated with a few French academics,
including novelist and Joyce specialist Hélène Cixous. Due to them,
an extract from the novel in progress was published under the title
"Oswhole'stalking" in an issue of *L'Arc* magazine devoted to Joyce.

Although they lived on a tight budget, the Kelley family loved
Paris, but they had not gone to stay. Their next step was to be
French-speaking Africa, since Bill felt that in the United States he had
"already been in English-speaking Africa." He felt that "the action" was
wherever black people were, and he intended to learn things for the
future. He felt that much of him could not be explained in terms
of Western civilization and that the oral tradition of Africa was calling him across the seas: "The experience of a man who grows up in
Harlem and never leaves it is not different from the experience of
another black man who has always lived somewhere else."[2]

Kelley was very conscious that there were many race brothers
around and was glad of it, but he kept much to himself and did not
haunt the cafés of the Latin Quarter with other Americans. His second
daughter, Cira, was born in Paris in the spring of 1968. That was the
spring of the student revolution, and Bill lived it day after day. I recall
taking him across the torn-up barricades, through gutted streets, and
by burned shells of cars, the morning air still pungent with tear gas,
from the Luxembourg Métro station to the Odéon Cultural Center,
to participate in a roundtable on new American writing. Yet William
Melvin Kelley, like Chester Himes, did not realize the importance of
what was taking place at that moment. He was already somewhere else,
in his African dream. After de Gaulle had restored order, he would
simply write: "It's been a very strange summer here, for us. And Paris
too. There was nobody here, fewer people than last year. There were
lots of tourists, but they weren't having any fun. And the weather was
bad. I worked up to the end of July, I guess, got to a point where I
could stop."[3] Later he remembered more vividly street scenes at the
markets around the Rue Régis, housewives at the launderette where
he took the family's clothes, or meeting Jean Seberg on the Rue de
la Paix while on his way to the Chase Manhattan bank. Jokingly, he
told of Catherine Deneuve driving up in a red roadster to the corner
of the Rue du Cherche-Midi where he was seated on a café terrace,

stopping, and looking at him deeply, their eyes meeting for ten unforgettable seconds: "Man, then I knew I had to split, with all those
beautiful women around!"

William Melvin Kelley never saw Africa, because the Rockefeller
Foundation grant he was awarded had to be spent in the New World.
In order to abide by that condition, he picked Jamaica, the next best
thing to Africa. So in the fall the family packed and left France.
Although their Paris interlude had been a satisfactory experience in
the lives of the Kelleys, whatever use of it the novelist made in fiction
is difficult to assess since his subsequent fiction never saw print.

Connecticut-born Wesleyan University graduate Melvin Dixon had
already completed and co-produced two plays and published drama
and film criticism when he went to Paris for five days in the summer
of 1971 during a European tour. He wanted to be a creative writer as
well as a scholar and "fell absolutely in love with the city": "Returning to it with the ambition of continuing my research and perhaps
doing more creative writing myself links me with the adventures of
Langston Hughes and Wright himself. Even if I am not successful in
obtaining a Fulbright I may come to France on whatever little money I
can gather together. I feel the cultural experience of France is important for any writer's development. To the list of the 'lost generation'
expatriates Stein and Hemingway and then Baldwin and Wright, perhaps the name of Melvin Dixon can be included in about another fifty
years (SMILE)."[4]

Dixon was a Ph.D. student at Brown University, and failing to obtain
a Fulbright, he was awarded a French government grant and the
André Istel Fellowship of the Alliance Française to study in Paris. He
wanted to do independent research on Richard Wright's exile and his
response to negritude and pan-Africanism and to work on a novel,
already entitled "Let the River Answer." By July 1972 he was ready
to leave in the fall, working on his French and "re-reading Chester
Himes's *Quality of Hurt* to gather together the flavor of the times and
the literary intrigues of Wright and Himes's generation."[5]

Shortly after his arrival Dixon had looked for a student room
through the Paris University housing office, but it was already late in
the academic year, and he had to go through the newspaper ads. On
the phone a landlady readily accepted the young American's application, but upon seeing his color when he arrived at her door one hour
later she hastened to tell him the room was already rented. Such discrimination was to be expected in the United States, not in France,
and Dixon's enthusiasm cooled considerably. "Wood and Rain," prob-

ably his first Paris poem, inspired by a walk in the Bois de Boulogne, told of finding oneself as a black American abroad:

> I am a black man
> in woods weeping where
> old trees stand like men rooted
> and hollering in this wind
> for lost children.[6]

Dixon finally stayed with the family of French friends for a couple of months, near Denfert-Rochereau. Then, for the cost of utilities he lived in the house that those friends had just acquired in the city and that was being remodeled. Despite the inconvenience of having to change rooms as the repairs proceeded and the occasional banging of the carpenters, he found the place propitious to writing: it was close to the Parc Montsouris, about a block from the former Rue du Douanier, where Countee Cullen had once resided. A good omen!

He quickly made friends, mostly with French, African, and West Indian students. It was also the beginning of a long-lasting companionship with a law student about his age; this was the occasion of many visits to Didier's family and several trips to the French provinces and to Spain. Paris, with the thrills of love and the pains of loneliness, provided inspiration, as in "Métro: correspondances":

> 1.
> The gypsy woman
> hides her child from coins people
> throw to make her go,
> 2.
> The one-legged man
> with torn guitar sings that he
> has not yet been paid,
> 3.
> The man with no eyes
> shakes a cup so they hear and
> fear the dark he knows,
> 4.
> And forward people
> push in one fat train on these
> broken human tracks.[7]

This haiku-like sequence, written in 1973, registered the everyday tragedies and unconcern of a cruel city. Another contemporary piece, "Climbing Montmartre," expressed the inside knowledge of a foreigner who also was, by choice but inescapably, the spokesman of the black diaspora and the downtrodden people of the Third World. The poem superimposed three successive images of Paris—the city of tourists, the city of ordinary people, the city of colored immigrants. The tourists were seen rushing up the steps leading to the Sacré-Coeur, ready to click cameras, buy postcards, and throw francs into the fountains. Among those vistors, many American blacks were to be counted:

> Langston in the twenties and old Locke too
> Cullen from the Hotel Saint Pierre
> Wright from rue Monsieur le Prince, even
> Martin came to climb Montmartre.[8]

But beyond the glamour the poet saw the lives of ordinary people: the commuters at Gare du Nord, the old women feeding pigeons, the street vendors and beggars, the "jazz in / twisted TV antennas and wire clotheslines." What is more, he saw the hill of Montmartre as representative of Europe in its lack of pity for the colored underdogs: "your green eyes / don't see this body drop on angry gargoyles." The symbolic body of the black man, his "primitive feet danced out" or re-enacting a modern tragedy of *The Hunchback of Notre-Dame*, served to question the stereotype of Paris as a "movable feast."[9] Indeed, "Getting Directions" begins with the famous quote from Hemingway to celebrate not the poetry of bohemianism but the fraternity between black Americans and Africans:

> Entering Paris
> on a moveable feast of clouds
> thick as an old man's beard,
> I walk the streets kept clean
> by the sweep of black
> and Arab hands. . . .
> One Senegalese face
> studies mine.
> His scarifications
> of work and clan
> point. . . .
> to feet far from ceremonial dance
> when sewer water claimed him,
> and to both of us
> standing in the flow
> leaving Paris [10]

Paris was not for Dixon the city of Hemingway but that of Wright, Baldwin, and countless literary and racial ancestors and predecessors

who had found sustenance there. "Kin of Crossroads" mentioned a
November 1973 visit to the grounds of the Gurdjieff Institute, where
Jean Toomer had come to follow the teachings of the guru:

> November drive through Fontainebleau
> past Napoleon's house and into Prieuré d'Avon
> where the pines thin out and tufts
> of mistletoe make nests in distant treetops.
> We see the farmyard, the white house
> fenced in, the wintering field
> deserted of silent reaping.
> "It was the Gurdjieff Institute"
> you point smiling . . .[11]

In March 1974 Dixon went to Saint Étienne and Lyons for a conference, and there he met Richmond Barthe, the black sculptor of the
Harlem Renaissance, who was visiting Louis Achille, himself a fellow
student of Senghor at the time when the negritude movement started.
"Richmond Barthe: Meeting in Lyons" superimposes the image of the
capital of the Gauls at the confluence of two rivers and the coming
together of two generations of black creative artists:

> Lyon is a city of two rivers and Roman aqueducts
> two thousand years old. I come by snake-roads
> through the faces of three mountains, following
> butterflies and the tracks of old bones.
>
> I find you in the hour of molding and the time
> of two rivers running there. Old fingers press
> into clay. *The old ones touch the young
> and help them to believe.*[12]

By the time he prepared to leave, the young poet had also greatly
expanded his acquaintance with francophone black writing. He knew
the language adequately, probably better than any black American
visitor except Mercer Cook and Jessie Fauset. Dixon read African and
West Indian poetry in French, from Senghor to Aimé Césaire, from
Jean-F. Brièrre to Jacques Roumain. He even thought of writing about
the U.S. occupation of Haiti and the works of Roumain, and set about
translating Roumain's poetry.

On July 6, 1974, Dixon left Paris for a month in Senegal which
proved "an incredible experience."[13] There he met Félix Morrisseau-
Leroy and Jean Brièrre, who spoke to him about Roumain and read
some of their own poems for him to tape. On his return he spent a
few days in the Midi at La Grande Motte seaside resort, and was back

in New York by mid-August, having completed the novel on which he had been working assiduously in the meantime. He was planning to return to Europe in the fall but was required to stay at Brown to complete his course of doctoral studies. On October 17, 1974, he wrote: "Still in my mind is a long poem on Richard Wright and Paris and me. How crucial to my development as a writer/thinker was last year in Paris. It wasn't just an 'experience' of an American abroad, it was a deep part of my life, and one that I plan to see grow into something lasting and solid. . . . How terribly I miss Paris and the working tranquility of Square Montsouris."[14]

By December he was back in Paris for several months. The poem on Wright and Paris probably took another form when Dixon was asked to help sort some of the Wright manuscripts, which were being acquired by Yale University. Later, in 1979, "Richard, Richard: American Fuel" would contrast Wright's craving for freedom as he exiled himself in 1947 with his suspicious death and ominous cremation. But "Richard, Richard: An American Hunger" was a reverent tribute and a meditation upon the meaning of exile for the writer:

> We peel your pages one
> by one to the skeleton
> of travel. We hold
> this exile which is meat,
> these words of warning
> offered as food.[15]

In 1976 Dixon joined the faculty at Williams College, which made it possible for him to spend some time in Haiti to do research on Roumain. He went back to Paris in December 1977 to read from his poetry and lecture at the Sorbonne. In May 1978 he traveled to Martinique, resisting the urge to return to Europe in order to learn more about the Caribbean: "This notion of comparative black literature is building and building inside. . . . I should be so busy this summer that I'd forget all about croissants and delicious wine and cool breezes along the Champs-Élysées."[16] Yet he could not resist the urge to go and find solace in Paris after Houghton-Mifflin rejected "Let the River Answer."[17] He spent three weeks there in August, revising the novel. And he was in Paris again in January 1979, visiting Didier and lecturing at universities.

In June 1980 he was off to West Africa again for several weeks, stopping first in Casablanca with the purpose of writing a series of articles on West African arts and literature for Encore magazine. The trip left echoes in many lines of the poem "Hemispheres":

Mint tea in Marrakech in a storm of sun
. . . .
Bamako, Dakar, Abidjan, Lagos, Ife, Ibadan.
Crossing the Sahara by Boeing jet,
everywhere the red-orange glow of sandstorm.
. . . .
Itinerant weaver in Grand Bassam,
left Ghana in the uncertainty of cowries
. . . Fingers gnarled
from pulling, pulling, pulling for a price,
anxious for English and broad smiles,
"For family back home," I said.[18]

But Senegal, especially Dakar, had inspired several poems already:
"Going to Africa," "Tour Guide: La Maison des Esclaves," prompted
by a visit to Gorée, and "Sandaga Market Women." There he felt very
much at home. When Dixon returned to Paris in December 1983, he
was on his way to Dakar on an invitation to read poetry and lecture at
the University. The following year he spent several months in Dakar
before taking an appointment for a year at the University on the Fulbright exchange program. His reason for going to Dakar was a desire
to return to the motherland of Léopold Senghor and negritude. While
in Dakar he put together a short second volume of poetry, *Six Poems
for Senegal* (1986), which opens with a quotation from Jean Toomer:
"When one is on the soil of one's ancestors, most anything can come
to one."

Dixon's first volume, *Change of Territory*, had recorded his spiritual,
as well as geographical, itinerary from the eastern seaboard to the
Deep South, then to Africa—with France serving as a transitional,
although most important, stage in his initiation. Echoes of Richard
Wright and other black American writers in exile had drawn him
to Paris when he was still in his early twenties. There he discovered
new inclinations and new aspects of his personality. Dixon's residence
in France was a shaping, though not a determining, influence in his
development as a writer.

NOTES

1. William Melvin Kelley to the author, August 25, 1968.
2. Kelley, quoted by Herbert Lottman, "The Action Is Everywhere the
Black Man Goes," *New York Times Book Review*, April 21, 1968, 9.
3. Kelley to the author, September 6, 1968.
4. Melvin Dixon to the author, December 7, 1972.
5. Dixon to the author, July 23, 1973.

6. Dixon, "Wood and Rain," to Michel and Geneviève Fabre, December 9, 1973.

7. Dixon, "Métro: correspondances," unpublished poem quoted by permission of the author.

8. Dixon, "Climbing Montmartre," *Change of Territory*, Callaloo Poetry Series (Lexington: University Press of Kentucky, 1983), 24.

9. Ibid., 25.

10. Dixon, "Getting Directions," *Change of Territory*, 18.

11. Dixon, "Kin of Crossroads," *Change of Territory*, 17.

12. Dixon, "Richmond Barthe: Meeting in Lyons," *Change of Territory*, 22

13. Dixon to the author, August 22, 1974.

14. Dixon to the author, October 17, 1974.

15. Dixon, "Richard, Richard: An American Hunger," *Change of Territory*, 21

16. Dixon to Michel and Geneviève Fabre, June 13, 1978.

17. "Let the River Answer" was an early version of the novel *Trouble the Water*, which won a literary prize when it was published by the University of Colorado Press in 1989.

18. Dixon, "Hemispheres," *Change of Territory*, 60.

20

Ted Joans:
"The Surrealist Griot"

The poetry of Melvin Dixon and James Emanuel does not attempt to discard the traditions of the American mainstream. That of Ted Joans is closer to achieving the jazz polyrhythms that Hart LeRoy Bibbs prided himself upon writing, and it finds its inspiration not only in Afro-American music but in the avant-garde experiments of the French surrealists.

In "I, Black Surrealist," Ted Joans claimed that surrealism existed before Guillaume Apollinaire coined the word to describe *Les Mamelles de Tirésias*, his 1918 play in which huge breasts were seen floating like a pair of balloons.[1] For surrealism is not art but a way of looking at things that goes together with a certain approach to life. By defining himself as a black surrealist, Joans emphasized the link between the open, creative weltanschauung proclaimed by the French avant-garde of the 1920s and the soul-expanding force of black power that reached its peak in the United States in the mid-1960s. But he refused to restrict black surrealism to those historical avatars of a trend that went back to "the Olduvai Gorge on the continent of Africa," thousands of years before Apollinaire. Surrealism as a literary and artistic movement, however, was for Joans an early incentive to create; from his childhood onward it made France an exciting place in his eyes.

"Where I got turned onto surrealism consciously was back in Indiana and my old Kentucky home where my aunt worked for a wealthy WASP family as a housemaid" ("Black Surrealist," 36). Indeed, the aunt often brought home discarded items given her by her cosmopolitan employers, who knew Nancy Cunard and haunted art exhibitions. There were European articles of clothing and travel pamphlets and magazines. Among those throwaways Ted found a copy of the November 1933 issue of *Vogue*, with an article about Salvador Dali discussing surrealism, the special number of *L'Illustration* on the 1931 Paris Colonial Exhibition, copies of *Le Minotaure*, *Der Querschnitt*, *Arts et Métiers Graphiques*, *This Quarter*, and *Révolution Surréaliste*. In 1938 Ted's aunt even brought back, among many books, a real treasure—the *Diction-naire abrégé du surréalisme*—and, later, David Gascoyne's *Short Story of Surrealism*—a better introduction, since it was in English. But at age thirteen Ted Joans was so fascinated, and so upset because he could not read French, that he went to mow the white folks' lawn to be able to buy a dictionary and start translating word by word some of the texts he had collected. By that time he already imitated the surrealist pictures he saw, including African sculptures that seemed strangely familiar to him. What he saw liberated him from the representational orientation of popular painting; he also started doing collages. Joans was mostly under the influence of Dali, and he even wrote poems in Dali's style after his sister presented him with *The Secret Life of Salvador Dali.*

As a teenager Ted also fell madly in love with a beautiful school-mistress, Frances Parrish, who married a doctor and left for Paris, Tennessee. He grew to associate her with France, and among the burning Dali-like poems he wrote for her was "The Enigma of Frances Parrish of Paris, France," already surrealistic in its associations:

> Under the hot frosted bed I saw
> a mangled trumpet that Dizz never blew
> and never wished to
>   the sound of a crushed baby filled the
> ears of all horses and toothpicks
> happy as I shall be to see this . . .[2]

But Joans was already becoming a "black" poet, his first really sought-after influence being not Dali but Langston Hughes, who caused him to write "poor hymns to poor me," using a much simpler vocabulary and jazz rhythms.

From the University of Indiana Joans went straight to New York's bohemia. He lived on 14th Street, close to the big storefront studio of expressionist painter Frank Kline, a jazz fan who helped him like a friend. He started mixing with artists and musicians, haunting—all eyes and ears—the Cedar Bar, where avant-garde artists congregated. Shortly after his arrival in New York, Sally Southern, an art major with surrealistic tastes in her writing and paintings, became the first companion of this New York period: with her he met Yves Tanguy, who did a "cadavre exquis" with them and gave them *Paroles* by Jacques Prévert. With gusto, Sally and Ted at once translated "Au hasard des oiseaux" by "the Langston Hughes of Paris."

At that time Joans lived in a Cooper Square studio and liked to give parties to which people would come masked or costumed: the actress

Vicki Dugan was seen as a marvelous personification of "la femme surréaliste" and poet Jean Billard would read Breton, Prévert, Péret, and
others in French next to American poets reading in English. Joans was
keenly interested in "the American Rimbaud," Philip Lamantia; he
participated in surrealist "happenings," and he was popular in the Village, where French Cuban Armand Díaz hailed him as "Ted Joans, oeil
naïf du surréalisme." Joans was painting and writing in the surrealist
style, creating "poems-objects" that he exhibited in cigar boxes. He was
part of a small active group with Ralph Gladstone, a classical jazz cor-
net player called Jim Heanue, and Marsha and Joe Axelrod, but they
had next to no contact with Europe. Joans had counted on Village creativity to further his aesthetics, but he was disappointed. The fashion
was abstract expressionism, and Joans was invited to participate in the
activities of the expressionists' select group, but he preferred partying
with the Beats and associating with writers like Kerouac, Sorrentino,
Corso, Ginsberg, Di Prima, and LeRoi Jones.

He then started a small, African-decorated place with Serge Kling
in an East 6th Street basement, showing art and selling food at Bwana's
Table, soon renamed Port Afrique. It became a success after some
African official patronized it. This allowed Joans and others to start a
photo gallery on St. Mark's Place—Galerie Fantastique, whose emblem
was a rhinoceros, where Ted did a "new-new" surrealist painting exhibition. He was reading more books on surrealism, including Ferdinand
Alquié's *The Philosophy of Surrealism,* and he attended classes at the
New School for Social Research under Kurt Seligman, who taught surrealistic techniques and introduced him to Urs Graf and tarot cards.
Joans also became acquainted with new French surrealists like Alain
Jouffroy and Jean-Jacques Lebel. With Jean-"Shock" he did surrealist
acts, like traveling the city by subway in the winter of 1960, carrying
an awesome U.S. Air Force practice bomb they had bought for five
dollars, clearing whole cars without saying a word.

In 1958 Jean Billard had told Joans that in spite of Europe being
quiet, one could still find intellectual activity there and most people in
big cities in those circles would not be hostile to surrealism and would
surely appreciate jazz music. In February of that year Joans had acted
as MC for a Beat poets' reading, and most of the poets had become his
friends; he was invited to present his own work and sold many copies
of his *Funky Jazz Poems,* a pamphlet with collages and an enthusiastic
introduction by George Reisner. He could now earn a living by reading
at private parties or in Manhattan coffee houses, mainly the Gaslight,
as well as by file-clerking at the United Nations. Yet he was intent on
moving, not only to Europe but to Africa, and by March 1960 he de-

scribed his going as an attempt to become a "surrealist missionary with [his] natural Black Magic from America and Africa."

When he reached Paris, Joans headed for the "Beat hotel" at 9, Rue Gît-le-Coeur, which, since Ginsberg had discovered it in the mid-fifties, had become the stopping place for most Americans on their way from San Francisco to Katmandu. There he met Brion Gysin, the cosmopolitan writer and painter who, with William Burroughs, was inventing the cut-up technique. Fate also wanted Joans to come across André Breton in the street so that he could say, "I am a man. I kissed André Breton on Rue Bonaparte in Paris."[3] Chance also had him literally run into his "amour de France," Christine Gondre, as he was hurrying across the Odéon toward Café de Seine; he knocked her down. She was twenty-one, cute and intelligent, and she detested Americans. For him, Nadja suddenly became reincarnated in this daughter of the mayor of a large French city, himself an avid reader of Chester Himes's thrillers. Ted took her to meet his Beat friends, and they drank cheap wine, smoked Turkish hash, and made love.

Later they traveled all around Europe on a still-valid Eurailpass given them by a couple of West Coast Americans, changing their appearance to match the photographs. A whole section of "Travelin'" is called "Travelin' with Christine" and tells of their two quick weeks ending in Monaco and the Riviera. They slept in the open near the Léger Museum, because black American painter Walter Coleman had not offered to put them up, and they were broke:

> and the Antibes
> scene with food
> and Grimaldi musée, where once Picasso did stay
> talking endless to international beats—one from
> S. Africa way
> watching southern pétanque players
> bang iron balls together[4]

After Jean-Jacques Lebel's aunt supplied them with food and money, they hastened to Paris, only to discover that M. Gondre had set the police searching for his daughter. She went back home, and Ted returned to the Beat hotel, to Corso and South African writer Sinclair Beiles, and to other laymates and playmates who helped him through a couple of months.

But Christine came back and wanted to take him to her parents' chateau to have him propose to her before her father. Marriage was out of the question for Ted; he had not yet divorced his first wife, Detroit-born Joyce Smith, who had borne him four children, but he used his last two days on the Eurailpass to visit the Gondres. This was his first encounter with traditional France, and it was like a caricature: the father could not prevent his adult daughter from marrying him, but he insisted that he become a Catholic, accept a position in an import-export firm, and take up French citizenship. After a long dinner with lots of servants and full cutlery—a cultural ordeal—Ted fled to Paris, where, a month or so later, Christine joined him again. This time she had money and initiated him into the art of haute cuisine by lunching at La Tour d'Argent, Lapérouse, and other fancy restaurants. But soon Joans was summoned to the U.S. Embassy and asked to hand in his passport, which was returned stamped "Not good for travel outside France unless for direct return to the United States." This was the mayor's attempt to get rid of him. He gladly accepted Christine's father's offer to pay for his transportation on the *Queen Elizabeth,* since he had been waiting to go back to New York.

Joans was going back to his Astor Place studio and poetry readings at the Gaslight, the Bizarre Café, and the Rafiot, where the waitresses would pass mugs for collections. He now legally separated from Joyce. He saved his money for his trip to Africa. Christine had written that she would join him in Timbuktu and live there with him. His collection of poems and collages, *All of Ted Joans and No More,* which he published in April 1961, was dedicated to "mon amour in France, Mlle. Christine Gondre," and the introduction mentioned that he was "in love and engaged . . . to a French fiancée." Some poems, like "Travelin'" and "Je suis un homme," bore traces of his French experience; others, like "Confession mais jamais sur Dimanche," simply incorporated French terms; while "The Enigma of Frances Parrish of Paris, France" used pieces of a Paris map for a collage. The book was selling well in the Village, but Joans was bent upon leaving the country "until the President of the USA was a black woman."

He crossed the Atlantic again, to Tangiers. Christine was supposed to wait for him at the Hotel George V in Casablanca. Instead, he was instructed to move on to Dakar. There a letter finally came: Christine had had dinner with de Gaulle and had succumbed to the argument that France needed all of its youth to build a greater Europe. Very blue and sad, Ted took the old Niger railway line to Bamako, Mali, and finally settled in Timbuktu. A decade later he reflected: "It was there alone that I came to realize my miraculous destiny of living this long automatic poem, a long poem to be written across warm suntanned pages of winter Africa and subversive cornbread and butter spring/summer pages in Europe where some active Euro tribes poets/hipsters live as active revolutionaries; these autumn embers glow big and bright among the impotent ashes of this vast antique cemetery" ("Black Surrealist," 200).

Born again, he crossed the Sahara back to Tangiers, where he lived with a colony of Western intellectuals and hipsters, also staying for a time with painter Ahmed Yacoubi. There he met his Norwegian "wife," Grete. Later, after she had left, pregnant with his son, Joans wrote to the surrealist group in Paris: "Qui suis-je? . . . I am an Afro-American and my name is Ted Joans. . . . Without surrealism I would have been incapable of surviving the abject vicissitudes and racial violence which the white man in America imposed upon me every day. Surrealism became the weapon I used to defend myself, and it has been and always will be my own style of life" ("Black Surrealist," translation mine). This was his first letter to Breton and the first time he actually wanted to be part of the movement—he who had never been a joiner or a card-carrying member of any group. But he felt tired of being "just another isolated active surrealist doing his bit" and wished to be part of a common effort.

He had come across André Breton by chance in 1960 as Breton, clad in gray and wearing gray suede shoes to set off a distinguished head of gray hair, was waiting for a bus. Breton was for him the absolute surrealist, just as W. E. B. Du Bois was Afro-America's first international intellectual. And he saw surrealism as the ultimate liberation enterprise. His poem "Nadja Rendezvous" succinctly evoked the stages of the relationship between the two men:

> I first read his works in June 1942
> I met him in June 1960
> I last saw him in June 1966
> I was going to see him again in 1967 June
> but the Glass of Water in the Storm (1713)
> of 4–2 rue Fontaine kept an almost forgotten
> rendezvous with Nadja in the Magnetic Fields . . .[5]

They talked about the international dimensions of the movement, all more or less triggered by Breton's famous manifesto. Joans believed that automatism was surrealism's most liberating invention and saw the black jazz musicians as the pacesetters in America; he thought that Senghor had been too preoccupied with correct French to make surrealism more than a spice in his negritude poetry. He was investigating all the links between blackness and surrealism: Aimé Césaire, of course, but also Malagasy poet Jean-Joseph Rabearivelo, who, as he committed suicide in 1937, continued writing his impressions until it was all over. Joans believed, however, that Étienne Léro was the greatest, since this Martinique-born black, inspired by such Harlem Renaissance poets as Langston Hughes, had participated in launching *Légitime Défense* in 1932. Joans was happy to learn that, during the 1931 Exposition Coloniale, the Paris surrealists had opened an anticolonialist exhibit displaying European "tribal fetishes" like Bibles, crucifixes, and stereotyped images of blacks of the kind found on Banania cocoa boxes. Although Léon-Gontran Damas, the "wayward child of the exciting thirties," had come close to joining surrealism, the only black in Breton's group had been Léro.

Joans went several times to 42, Rue Fontaine, where Breton's canary, the Flying Piranha, inspired him with the title of a later volume. The walls of the poet's study were covered with marvelous photographs, objects, and drawings; Joans described the littered desk as "a living surrealistic collage." Shortly after Breton's death Joans was riding the elevated Métro line across the Seine when he saw Paris's small Statue of Liberty lying on its side on the Left Bank, on its way to a new location. He considered it an omen and wrote a poem on "The Statue of 1713," the magic number suggested by the way Breton used to sign his initials.

In the fall of 1966 he wrote one of the most moving tributes to the poet:

> Oh André, you father of everything
> You who prepared me and the others
> for anything, anywhere, any time!
> . . . .
> Monsieur Breton you played no god, no pope,
> no king, no dictator to us
> We who offer our very best in your trust.
> I chose le merveilleux without knowing,
> at the tender age of fourteen.
> Your lightning strikes everywhere,
> bringing its spiritual funnel of revolution.
> . . . .
> Your point of view liberated us.
> How can I thank you for the exquisite encounter
> on rue Bonaparte in Paris (June 1960)
> of a giant in grey and an Afroamerican sunbeam?[6]

Joans attended many of the frequent surrealist meetings at the Promenade de Vénus, at the corner of the Rue Coquillère and the Rue du Louvre, near the Halles, from 1962 to 1969. There he met Gérard Legrand, who wrote him up in his French art journal in 1964 under the title "Peut-on être surréaliste aujourd'hui?" and also Jean Schuster, the editor of *L'Archibras* magazine, and Vincent Bonoure, the founder of the *Bulletin de Liaison Surréaliste,* to which Joans also contributed. Joans defined Schuster and Bonoure as "the Clifford Brown and the Don Cherry of surrealism who have split the group in opposite directions."

In galleries, at vernissages, and even in the streets, Joans had many encounters in which he liked to see the hand of "objective chance." In the early 1960s he met Jacques Prévert at a vernissage for Dorothy Tanning's exhibition; the place was crowded, but Prévert complimented Ted and Grete on their appearance in the street in stunning red, white, and blue matching attire. "He told me," Joans remembered, "that I had the sun in my belly and that my smile was the sunbeams."[7] Joans acknowledged the influence of Prévert's poetry on his own, especially upon "Why Try?" inspired by Diahann Carroll. There he met other surrealists, like Maria Toyen and Gabriel de Kervorkian. And he met Jean-Claude Silbermann at a surrealist gathering, while, at a vernissage, a tired-faced man introduced himself as André Pieyre de Mandiargues. However, Ted Joans's closest surrealist friends remained Alain Jouffroy, Jean-Jacques Lebel, and Robert Benayoum.

Year after year Paris was becoming the field of "fate-ordained encounters" for Joans, a world traveler who, already in 1962, could recite like a litany the names of the cities he had visited in Europe and Africa. He could soon enumerate likewise the streets and cafés of Paris where such chance meetings had taken place:

> on this sunnyside street in Paris
> a black flower first saw Man Ray
> and last saw Le Verre d'Eau dans la Tempête
> the naked beard makes sounds of dogs barking
> on the rue Jacques Callot
> on the rue Jacques Callot in Europe
> where exquisite corpses drink no wines
> the moon is pregnant with old poems
> and young whores' knees lock against fever
> on the rue Jacques Callot in France[8]

Like Henry Miller, Ted Joans came to know places no tourist, not even the average Parisian, was aware of, such as the gargoyle near the porch of Hotel de Cluny, "where the greatest water-drain in the entire world hangs its monk's bare ass over the heads of millions yearly while the holding monk frowns due to no one ever looking up" ("Black Surrealist," 123).

He could sing of cafés:

> The Cinq Billards café on Place de la Contrescarpe
> Place Maubert-Mutualité the café Métro where
> I retire after reading poetry in
> public—and there is a secret
> one near Notre Dame where one
> can still see a painting being
> burned, and hear a poem
> being erased . . .

For him La Coupole remained the café where he met Giacometti. And second meetings would take place under a new star: he had once met Max Ernst in New York, and he saw him again "twelve years later walking behind a doll-like hippie girl on Boulevard Saint-Germain, he like his Loplop bird seeming ready to pounce" ("Black Surrealist," 93). There were even multiple chance encounters. One day, sitting at the Café Palette, he met expatriate American surrealist Man Ray with his shoestring tie and black cane. Man Ray invited him to his Rue Férou studio, and later Joans attended a "Salute to Man Ray" session at the American Artists and Students Center, where sat old but still youthful Marcel Duchamp, "the coolest cat on that discussion panel." In the Village Joans lived just a block away from Duchamp on 14th Street, and he had noticed the names "Duchamp-Villon-Matisse" on the mailbox and doorbell, but he had been too full of awe to ring the bell and disturb the master. Now was his first (and last) opportunity to talk with him of his art idols.

Increasingly, Joans used French terms in his poetic language and gave French titles to his poems. "The Overloaded Horse" is a straight surrealist composition based on a phrase overheard in the Métro, which sounded like "On a battu le cheval au mois de mai" ("They flogged the horse in the month of May"). "The Pieds Noirs"—which applies to French colonists born in North Africa—celebrated the colonizer's retreat from it. Before Josephine Baker's death, he wrote "La Grande Granny" in her honor:

> she fled to France and bared her black soul
> international fame was her royal role
> Europe recognized her / made images of
> her / adored her / gave her medals / and even
> married her but none gave her gold
>
> . . . .
>
> she is now old / struggling but still
> beautiful and black
> when we get black power lets bring
> our Granny Jo back[9]

"Louvre Afrique," dedicated to James Baldwin, criticized black lack of interest in African art:

> Dimanche novembre white onlookers admire
> Louvre lookers gaze at black art
> & some even feel their fire
> Dimanche grey Paris uncrowded
> & sunday Français toujours whisper mute
> où est mes frères noirs?
> (in their tight shirt collars & looking cute)
> . . . . the truth is
> they are all
> on St. Michel
> chasing tail! [10]

Dedicated to Joyce Mansour, "Promenade de Vénus" celebrates Joans's encounter with the surrealist also born in Cairo (Egypt, not Illinois) with whom he later collaborated on publishing ventures:

> I the traveller who crossed les Halles at summer's end admiring the nude
>   rear of a fur flower from Egypt
> I walked with desperate steps looking for the café PROMENADE DE VENUS
> She a dark slit of beauty having escaped from a large sphinx's paws
> admired the power of griot in Army overcoats from Norway. . . .
> She a fur flower agonized by taxi-message-machine-music ignores my
>   meter. . . . [11]

Joans was fully satisfied with becoming a member of the Paris surrealist group. Of them he said: "I wonder where I would be if I had been greeted by such a group of good people when I first arrived in New York, instead of those jiveass and basically racist abstract expressionists" ("Black Surrealist," 155). As the sixties wore on, however, the black American scene changed from the civil rights struggle to the black power era. In the late fifties Joans had heralded the trends of black power cultural nationalism with his "jazzaction painting" and the Port Afrique exhibitions of African art. Now fashion was catching up with him, and he was even solicited by politically involved brothers whose attempts at black liberation interested him. There again, he could see the European surrealists as natural allies of black liberation. In the 1920s they had started to subvert, within their own milieu, the rational, money-making, dehumanizing bent of Western civilization; Léopold Senghor had called them sharpshooters and infiltrators behind the enemy lines as he proposed the antidote of negritude. André Breton had promoted Aimé Césaire, to whom Benayoum and Jouffroy were now close. The former helped publish Joans's *Proposition pour un manifeste (Black Power) Pouvoir Noir* because he felt that "being surrealists they sincerely believed that the only cause worth serving is the emancipation of humankind" ("Black Surrealist," 10).

In Paris Joans had met scores of West Indians and Africans, including the Congolese poet Tchicaya U'Tamsi; the Ethiopian painter Skunder, who had changed from his native Coptic style to "African surrealism"; Alioune Diop; and Léon-Gontran Damas. Césaire himself he saw at the Salle de la Mutualité when Malcolm X, back from Africa, came to speak in Paris in 1964. Césaire and Diop were on stage at the meeting, which had been organized by the Society of African Culture and turned out to be a triumph, the too-small room upstairs overflowing with enthusiastic supporters. In 1967 a similar meeting was held in the large hall of La Mutualité to raise funds for black power. On that occasion Joans was to read poetry, and he sat on stage with James Forman, Julia Wright Hervé, Trotskyite historian Daniel Guérin, Césaire, and Sartre.

Around that time he became acquainted with Cuban surrealist painter Jorge Camacho, and he quickly grew fond of his "brown, black and red vision, a beautiful haze hovering above the greatest jungle in the world" ("Black Surrealist," 126). In 1965 the "afrospanishjewish-moroccan musician/hipster" Marcel Muyall had introduced him to the works and person of Cuban surrealist sculptor Agustín Cárdenas. Among other black artists, he also got to know Haitian painter Hervé Télémaque and the work of the late Hector Hippolyte, whom he considered one of the world's greatest primitives. Thus surrealism and black power gradually converged in Joans's aesthetic while Paris became a crossroads, a lively meeting place between annual winter trips to Africa: "Summers . . . I come to Europe to do my safari-for-bread (the only reason why I come to this antique dull cemetery) and for chance encounters of my tribe, the Afro-American, and to obtain some Western-manufactured supplies" ("Black Surrealist," 91).

In spite of the lyrics of "April in Paris," the city was often "a real drag for lovers." There he often stayed with friends, sometimes at Colette Lacroix's, whose apartment was a wonderful setting for Left Bank living. Then he repeatedly stayed at the Hotel Stella, where he enjoyed the largest room he ever had in Paris, shared at times with fashion models and other playmates. But when *Jazz Hot* printed his address in the course of an exchange of letters on the music of Albert Ayler, he had to move out for privacy and settled at the Grand Hotel du Midi.

He had separated from Grete, and he was now ready to encounter and live with his "greatest femme fatale of Belle France." Olivia

Formissuy of Bougival, a teacher at the Sorbonne, was a real surrealist who did creative work with Joans, helping him with frottages, collages, and pressages. He even devised a combination of these techniques, called "re-pressage," by placing some ridged or raised material beneath the magazine page as he transferred the image. In 1960 he put together a book of collages called *The Hipsters.* Ted and Olivia visited scores of exhibitions, and he introduced her to Langston Hughes and most of the free jazz musicians in Paris, who were all his friends. She went with him to see Stokely Carmichael the second time he spoke at La Mutualité, in 1967. She was a devoted companion, and when needed she helped him with money, paying his fare back to Timbuktu. More important, it was a mutual shaping of tastes and personalities, and she accepted his decision "not to allow any temptation to separate [him] from Africa for Europe." He made her the occasion and subject of many poems, like "It Is Ours" (to my angel, Olivia).

In 1966 Langston Hughes, Joans's mentor of the 1950s who had published his "It Is Time" (although cutting many "offensive" lines) in his anthology *New Negro American Poetry,* came to Paris and read at Shakespeare and Company. He insisted that Ted play obbligato solo trumpet as he read. This was their last meeting. Joans also participated in the first "black power reading" that year, again in George Whitman's bookstore, with Jamaican writer and singer Fritz Gore; Arthur Peebles, a young free jazz musician who invented his own instruments; and Abbey Lincoln, who recited her poems and sang some original songs. Joans chanted his latest "black pow-wow" pieces to an overflow crowd that included Max Roach. The meeting was reported in the Paris-based *New York Herald Tribune,* which branded it an example of "reverse racism." In August 1967 a jazz event—this time at the American Center on the Boulevard Raspail—attracted many and turned into a small fete. Several surrealists who attended praised Joans's new writings, especially his long poem enumerating his favorite jazz musicians, "Jazz Must Be a Woman."

Joans had always wanted to exhibit his works in Paris and was able to do so at the Galerie Maya, Rue Mazarine. He organized an exhibition of "Afro-American fetishes" to be traded, rather than sold, for "Euro-tribal creations." For example, a small oil painting with objects hanging from it, "Des cheveux noirs entourant le volcan (cuntinent)" was offered for one trench coat; "Open Wide Your Legs" went for a pair of Clark's desert boots size 11/12; "Timbuktu Rush Hour" was worth one mask from the Congo. Other items were to be exchanged for twenty-five switchblade knives, one .45-caliber pistol, or an Ostend-London round-trip ticket. Most of Joans's friends attended, including

Elisa Breton, Bonoure, Isvic, Camacho, and musicians Albert Nicholas and Eddie Barnett. Ted "read" the fetishes, which were mostly collages of bones, hair, cowries, and linen, while two African drummers beat on tom-toms in honor of "le griot surréaliste," as Michel Le Bris called him in his *Jazz Hot* article. This was April 24, 1968. On a night just before the May 1968 student revolt (which Joans preferred to call a "revelation"), he invited the whole surrealist group to the American Center for Students and Artists for an evening of music and poetry: he performed, punctuating his poetry by beating time with two human bones—one French, one American—as he read a dozen pieces, including "Jazz Must Be a Woman" and "Exquisite Encounter," about his meetings with Breton.

One of the high points of Joans's black power period was his participation in the Algiers Pan-African Arts Festival in 1969, along with the poet Don Lee, the playwright Ed Bullins, and singers Miriam Makeba, Marion Williams, and Nina Simone. When he spoke in Algiers, he vehemently attacked the theft of African art pieces and their "imprisonment" in European museums, including the former Musée des Colonies at Porte Dorée, where he had studied the African and South Pacific masks, and the Musée de l'Homme, where Michel Leiris worked. Leiris had been in the audience at Joans's 1967 reading with Césaire, but they had not actually met before his diatribe at the Algiers Festival, to which Leiris took no exception. Soon Joans liked "that unselfish old man . . . who shines like the soft glow of candlelight through the grey antiquity of Paris" ("Black Surrealist," 157). He saw him again in Paris, where Joans's companion was now a southern white anthropologist and SNCC militant, Joan: Ted "married" her at a luncheon with Leiris, who inscribed his *Afrique Fantôme* for them in the shadow of the Eiffel Tower. Joans made special use of the surrealist glossary of the book and learned much from his new-found friend.

After Joan another femme-enfant companion important to Ted was Anna B., an English girl, whom his imagination characterized as his Mona Lisa muse and associated with the city as he walked her out of Shakespeare and Company into the churchyard of Saint-Julien-le-Pauvre, then to the Pont Neuf:

> Jean-Pierre . . . picked us up later at the foot of the equestrian statue of Henri IV on the little isle of Vert Galant where the river Seine opens its legs to be fucked by Notre Dame, that old lesbian whore that fucks tourists for centimes. Annab and I dined in Art Nouveau and Marché aux Puces cluttered apartment in the 16ème. The three of us dined and wined, his thin El Greco wife and enfant gâté child being absent. We said goodbyes and thank-yous and walked to the Place de Barcelone and it is

there where my love for Annab [came out] and she got hold of what was
really Surreally me, before the Guimard métro entrance a pissoir of tall
trees the river Seine curing all and curving around the old middle-sized
statue of so-called Liberty, she and me sat sipping black café until a flash
of warm rain ran us away on that beginners' Sunday. . . . No sex but
unhappy poems were born, for she made me pregnant with them. . . .
Annab whose initials were the same as André Breton who had long gone
from the human scene. ("Black Surrealist," 40–41)

During Breton's life he and Joans had become inseparable, and
Joans's devotion to Elisa Breton continued their friendship. Elisa introduced Ted to Bucharest-born poet Gherasim Luca, in whose company
he met Afro-Chinese painter Wilfredo Lam at a signing party for a
book on Lam's paintings in 1975. Matta and Cogollo he could admire
in May 1972 at an exhibition to which he hastened to take Elisa—an
occasion he recalled in "Straight Croissants":

> Elisa again with me enter gallery-of-everything / ready for anything
> exhibit polluted with déjà vu fantasy
> only Cogollo Cárdenas Charvez Dedicova Peclard and Matta
> say a fresh bon jour to Elisa and me
> Ms Illa Errus in black hands now [12]

The following year he visited Elisa at the Bretons' summer home
in the Lot Valley, and he met Adrien Dax, whose poetry suggested
"the marvellous web of beauty that he lives." St. Cirq Lapopie inspired
Joans to write one of his rare poems on France:

> Stone woman called village
> Towering lady of cliff thighs
> Cool sister to moss family
> Ignorant to confitures of traffic jams
> River caresses your green field breasts
> Quilts of vegetable patches are your buttocks
>
> . . . .
>
> Instant mirror of Tombouctou
> Every breeze here is a new poem [13]

With time Joans became convinced that surrealism was coming into
black hands, and not only his own. Matta he had met during the May
1968 "revelation," and the painter had helped him fly back to Harlem
that summer. In 1975 Joans took the initiative of gathering Camacho,
Cárdenas, young Afro-Colombian painter Herberto Cogollo, Lam,
Matta, and Télémaque so that they, "the seven black sons of Lautréamont," could make the longest exquisite corpse he could think of.
That year the publication of a collection of collages and poems, *Spetro-*

philia, followed his better-publicized *Afrodisia* (1971), whose themes were Africa and black culture on the one hand and erotica on the other. In 1977 Joans and Joyce Mansour contributed a long poem each to *Cogollo Caniculaire,* a series of eight lithographs by the painter Joans had discovered in the 1972 group exhibition "25 Ways to Be (or Not to Be) a Surrealist"—excruciating pictures that attempted to restore the original African vision blurred by modern European art.

Joans's own project now consisted of effecting a "new Negro step," of which *Flying Piranha*—in collaboration with Joyce Mansour—is an example. This volume of poetry and collages in honor of Breton's famous canary came out at a time (1978) when Joans claimed: "Now that I have graduated from that vast old academia called Europe, I have attended all her history classes, which is nothing but the past with no future outlooks on the marvellous, I wish it were possible that I could print here in this book some of the letters I received from André Breton in which he gave me personal information about the future of surrealism" ("Black Surrealist," 172). He was persuaded that Breton had foreseen the importance and future prevalence of blackness in surrealism when he had written in *Anthologie de l'humour noir* that "the Black Sphinx of Objective Humor cannot fail to meet on the dusty road, the road of the future, the White Sphinx of Objective Chance, and all ulterior human creations will be the fruit of their embrace."[14]

Ted Joans keeps moving between Europe and Africa and, increasingly, the United States, and his feelings have not changed much. As early as 1961 he had written to Rosey Pool that he would never give up his American citizenship, even after traveling in twenty-eight countries and liking it abroad; he wanted to be "free as the white American that is involved in the arts. Man, it's a big drag to have to create under a false flag. That's my first reason for splitting and my second reason is Africa. . . . I don't want too much: just to be a free human and treated as such."[15]

When completing "I, Black Surrealist" more than a decade later, he concluded that he would never live in the United States again, nor "set up shop" in Europe: "For me those two, too white places are mere meeting places for humankind to do technological and monetary jive. But I do have some good friends in and out of these two places" ("Black Surrealist," 110). Remaining an outsider to the "Amerikkkan" way of life, he also remained an outsider to the traditional French way of life, and he did so out of choice, having sampled the fare of the middle class as well as of the intellectual circles. An artist and writer "on the margin," although by no means marginal, he embodies a latter-day avatar of negritude, which Senghor has defined as a synthesis of the values of Africa and the West, but he is at the same time a surrealist. He has learned French well enough to write a few poems in this language and make surrealist puns. He has become acquainted with Paris in the way Henry Miller was, enjoying it as a city filled with inexpensive means of survival, with out-of-the-way places of beauty, and original, authentic people of all races and nationalities. But he has remained true to his vow not to allow any temptation to separate him from Africa in favor of Europe.

NOTES

1. Ted Joans, "I, Black Surrealist," typescript of unpublished autobiography, hereafter cited in the text.

2. Joans, "The Enigma of Frances Parrish of Paris, France," *All of Ted Joans and No More* (New York: Excelsior Press, 1961), 38.

3. Joans, "Je suis un homme," *All of Ted Joans and No More*, 3.

4. Joans, "Travelin' with Christine," *All of Ted Joans and No More*, 70.

5. Joans, "Nadja Rendezvous," *Black Pow-Wow* (New York: Hill and Wang, 1969), 113.

6. Joans, *Spetrophilia* (Amsterdam: Het Cafe "De Engelbewaarder," 1973), 21–23.

7. Joans, interview with the author, September 12, 1973.

8. Joans, *Black Pow-Wow*, 47.

9. Joans, "La Grande Granny," *Black Pow-Wow*, 27.

10. Joans, "Louvre Afrique," *Afrodisia* (New York: Hill and Wang, 1971), 67.

11. Joans, "Promenade de Vénus," Ibid., 98.

12. Ted Joans, "Straight Croissants," *Spetrophilia*, 6. "Ms Illus Errus" means surrealism.

13. Joans, in *Flying Piranha*, by Ted Joans and Joyce Mansour (New York: Bola Press, 1978), 30.

14. André Breton, quoted in Joans, *Flying Piranha*, 5.

15. Joans, quoted in *Beyond the Blues*, ed. Rosey Pool (Lympne: Hand and Flower Press, 1962), 131.

21

James Emanuel:
A Poet in Exile

When contrasted with the near-dissolution of Ronald Fair in the limbo of expatriation, the example of poet James Emanuel strikingly reveals how expatriation and the French environment could be used to renew and reorient creative energies that the American setting, familial and national, had nearly silenced. A professor of English at the City College of the City University of New York, James Emanuel was already known as the author of the critical study *Langston Hughes* when Broadside Press published his first volume of poetry, *The Treehouse and Other Poems* (1968), a gathering of reflective, intimate pieces, soon followed by the more militant poems of *Panther Man* (1970), which included his widely publicized homage to the slain Black Muslim leader, "For Malcolm."

When Emanuel first came to France, in October 1968, as a Fulbright exchange professor, he had not specifically chosen France from several possible European countries: that he taught in Grenoble was due to the request of Jean Wagner, himself the author of a monumental study of black poets in the United States, published in 1964. Yet in the back of Emanuel's mind the image of France as a kind of haven had lingered ever since he had read the sonnets of Countee Cullen. He thus gladly took up residence for a year in the little village of Seyssins, not far from the campus. This was an exciting occasion: not only his first sabbatical but the stimulating prospect of breaking away from the debilitating memories of years of struggle and setbacks, typified by troubles encountered in early 1966 after he had run for a seat on the Mount Vernon Board of Education in a black community–inspired campaign for integration.

France was a discovery—the joy of driving amid the splendid mountain landscapes of Isère and also the welcome and literary friendship of Jean Wagner. And in the attic room of the chalet the poet in him had been moved to write, less about the towering Three Sisters peak or the majesty of the Belledonne range than about home scenes: in

"Fourteen" about the energy of his son James shaking the frail banisters when running down the stairs; in "Black Humor in France" about his wife, Etha, shouting "Boo!" with her face covered by a white mask of soapsuds.

The family took to traveling, driving as far as Toledo, Capri, and Copenhagen, and James attended a conference in Skanderborg, Denmark. In Isère, however, he was rather restricted in his social ambiance, living outside the city, seeing few faculty members, not daring to ski, learning little about the French political and social situation. As they were about to leave, most of his memories were related to the chalet, the mountainside, and the increasing number of occurrences when Etha had behaved strangely, thinking herself the target of invisible enemies.

In June 1969 he enjoyed revisiting Paris; he read and lectured at the new University Center at Vincennes, where left-wing students and teachers had been accommodated after the May 1968 uprisings. He could note that many a French student there saw each black American as a potential revolutionary. This discovery led him to ponder the images of blackness that were being projected; and this was reflected in the organization of *Panther Man,* which amounted to a sensitive chronicling of the poet's reactions vis-à-vis the traumas of racism.

Back in the United States in the fall, Emanuel missed the atmosphere of France: "I find myself remembering with some nostalgia the view from your windows, together with those from windows in our chalet at Seyssins. Adjustment to conditions in America is not easy." [1] But he was sustained by the hope of returning the summer after next, if not earlier. Later, in "Snowflakes and Steel: My Life as a Poet," he recalled: "Actually, since my return to New York . . . America's uncivil racial atmosphere resumed the blighting effect that it had always exerted upon my adult life—this time with an intensity which, combined with worsening marital troubles, left me devoid of the creative strength necessary for writing poetry." [2] When he sailed from New York on the SS *France* in August 1971, James Emanuel was persuaded that his mother-country would never treat black people as citizens; except for a handful of relatives, he did not care intimately for anybody there; he was thus leaving nearly everything of his previous life behind.

He drove his Volkswagen from Le Havre to Toulouse, where he was to spend the academic year as visiting professor in the English department. A colleague had arranged for him to rent a villa at 10, Rue Marie. "My awareness of differences, of contrasts between my opening life in Toulouse and the Seyssins experiences, was perhaps comparable to the springtime ventilation of a room that has been closed all winter" ("Snowflakes," 36). He enjoyed the comfortable villa, the regular friendly outings of the English department in the scenic countryside, the dinner invitations from colleagues, the multiplying friendships. Mostly, he was away from the increasing mental unbalance and relentless tongue-lashings of his wife.

During the vacation around All Saints' Day he was invited to spend a few days in Corrèze. This visit was not the occasion for a poem, but he retained happy memories: "As the weeks pass, I know that my mind will go back to the chestnut-picking, fireplace-sitting, and strolls and visits experienced at L'Anglade."[3] When snow came in December, he joined a busload of colleagues to go skiing at Mont d'Olmes and experienced his first day on the slopes, mostly falling and rising with the beginners' group. He later skied a lot, and even had an accident at Pas de la Case, near the Spanish border, while going down a steep slope with his friends the Lozès. Although he later recorded the event in a poem, "My Animal: Pas de la Case," at that time "some poetic knack in [him] had not yet recovered. [He] was not yet fit" ("Snowflakes, 42).

It took a little French girl to spur Emanuel to writing poetry again. While having dinner at the home of his friends the Cordesses, James was again given the key to inspiration by their three-year-old daughter, who taught him the French names of animals and things in her picture-book:

> The genuinely lively talk at the table; the food, tasting as only the French can make it; the undependable ceremonies of putting the children to bed (there was also a younger brother)—all were ordinary in comparison with the childlike echo of the word *clé*.
>
> In the late afternoon of 4 June, I wrote the poem in fifty-five minutes . . . "For Alix, Who Is Three":

>> Foreign country of her eyes
>> picture-book blue
>> as lakes she fingered while she read
>> and taught me simple words
>>
>> . . . .
>> And there again was Alix,
>> who was three,
>> who in foreign country
>> of her eyes and chocolate smile
>> gave me the key
>> the *clé*
>> I will throw away
>> if ever I want
>> to lock my doors again.[4]

Another visit to the Cordesses in mid-June 1972 inspired "It Was Me Did These Things," its title hinting that "a desire for self-expressive freedom lay behind my presence in France" ("Snowflakes," 45).

Around that time James had become the friend of Marie-France Plassard, a librarian who not only initiated him into the quaint and lovely places around Toulouse but served as a travel guide when they went to London at Easter, attended the summer festivals at Orange and Avignon, and visited a Bonnard exhibition at Albi. "During the noon hour of August 15, I was comfortably settled in the largest room of "Le Barry," the beautiful summer home of Madame Christine Plassard-Naples, a well-known lawyer in the province of Gers. It was one of my early visits there with Marie-France, her daughter. Shortly after twelve the spacious calm of the green-walled room and the orderly expanse of lush flowers and trees visible through the open shutters moved me to the activity that was to become constantly characteristic of my visits: poetry writing" ("Snowflakes," 53).

In this elaborate evocation of the friendly, though stately, atmosphere, the poet stresses his ability, for the first time, to write love poetry—an untitled fragment that, with the added distance of a visit to the Lake District and Scotland, the country of Wordsworth and Burns, became "Lovelock Back," a piece ending perfectly with

> Leave-taking now is tender part of you
> I dare not
> touch
> but with this hand that once waved
> to the hills.[5]

Another poem followed in October, hinting of meals taken on a balcony and of Saint-Sernin, the romanesque cathedral at Toulouse, illuminated by a night of light and music. A dinner at the Petit Bedon restaurant, where his friend Albert Poyer had invited him, and the somewhat unheeded singing of Maya Biasio performing with her guitar as the meal reached its high point inspired "Chanteuse de Restaurant, Toulouse." "Clothesline, Rue Marie" was less a description of a neighbor's yard with drying linen than a meditation on himself in his "skinthings" close to his heart. "For Madame Plassard, a Thanks," again inspired by staying at his friend's country place, nicely recreated the peace and composure of the French milieu:

> A bed of rest and quiet, simple thing
> and high enough for me to reach and pull aside
> far-other drapes that catch all light and shade:
> for when I pushed the actual shutters

out into the dawn
the words that might have floated in the night
grew plain on barrelled plants, red tile
stuck in the grass,
a vine-sucked wall of stone and scores of
outlived wooden things
that, leaning, huddled one another,
awaiting shaping hands to make them new.[6]

In late January 1973 a story told by Alix Cordesse's parents gave birth to "French Child, Buying Bread," about the disappointment of the little girl who expected to receive a hoard of golden pennies in return for a nickel five-franc piece but got no change at all when buying a baguette at the baker's.

With summer came the necessity of going back to the United States; stopping in Paris, Emanuel attempted his last poetic effort of substance in France in "Sidewalk Café, Rue des Pyramides":

Her back to me,
sweetstanding at the curb,
imagination gave her to my arms,

. . . .

and she was French, with grace
a changing wind could never change—

when Middleamerika
pink in slacks so fat
they wobbled on the street
drew rows of X's across my sight . . .

("Snowflakes," 89)

This fragment pictured the elegant French girl and her flashy American opposite in unambiguous terms: it is obvious where Emanuel's heart lay.

On August 31, 1973, he sailed on the *France* back to the United States and to five excruciating years during which his increasingly paranoid wife made his life miserable until divorce was pronounced: "I had reached the nadir of my struggle with the dragon," as he put it ("Snowflakes," 262). By July 1978 deliverance was finally in sight; he had received confirmation of his second sabbatical leave. He planned a year of creative work in London and Paris, but in mid-September he was back in Toulouse to join Marie-France for an auto trip to southern Spain, and he went to Toulouse again to spend the 1978 Christmas vacation, prepared for another Yuletide celebration at Le Barry: "And soon I was in that country place, in the largest bedroom always given me, arranging my clothes in the spacious wardrobe and pleasurably anticipating the champagne and fresh oysters, country-made foie gras, pink and green candies, truffles, and other chocolates that always made the winter holidays seem memorable" ("Snowflakes," 319). A small bird accidentally flying into the large room inspired "Robin Redbreast in the House," a Christmas Day fragment that would need enlargement.

Robert Tricoire, a music critic, translator, and American Embassy employee, let Emanuel use his lodgings until he found two small rooms separated by an entrance hallway from the larger apartment of painter Françoise Estachy at 14, Avenue du Maine—just a few minutes from the Tour Montparnasse and the lively 15th arrondissement: "My third-floor Paris hideaway promised only a modest amount of comfort, but seemed to offer what I needed for another long period of continual creativity: within my own walls, quiet and solitude; on the streets, jostling crowds and at least a peripheral contact with humanity" ("Snowflakes," 321). There one of his first poetic efforts of 1979 transformed the "Robin Redbreast" piece into "The Birds," which would finally become the seventy-two-line "The Birdpeople."

In January, as he strolled in the Tuileries, a visual gift from chance and the city inspired him to write another poem:

> Mounting to the northern terrace from rue de Rivoli, I felt the white steps transporting me slowly into a retrospective, icy corridor of time where a decade (I had first walked through the Tuileries over ten years earlier) was being dissolved into present sensations. A black and white dog was sniffing the frozen ground; workers near a truck pointed at the Jeu de Paume Museum had momentarily stopped their tree cutting; and I found myself walking precisely in ready-made footprints, slightly melted, drawing a trail through the sparse snow that took me, with unaccountable surprise, to some downward steps. The bust of the garden designer Le Nôtre claimed my momentary attention; but my gaze was drawn unwaveringly towards various figures sitting on benches below me, motionless as if frozen in different attitudes of expectancy. Then, lifting my glance, as with a conscious effort, towards the Orangery Museum and the hidden Seine River just beyond it, I knew that my thoughts were dropping into the intervening space, into the huge boat basin that had so refreshed my flagging spirits in the autumn of 1968.
>
> Like a dream halting its movement as the waking sleeper reclaims his latest identity, the octagonal pool stood still for my approach—only to present me with an unbelievable sight as I drew near. I stared, unmoving, at the strewn-around jumble of overturned iron chairs jutting out of the ice that formed the interior of the basin. With feigned casualness, I sought to verify my sense of reality by looking around the pool for other observers. I was apparently alone. ("Snowflakes," 324–25)

Emanuel's poetic prose in his autobiographical narrative almost equals
the balance of what became "The Boat Basin, Years Later," in January 1979:

> It was in front of me somewhere, the Boat Basin,
> floating up,—no, I was stepping downward—
> more disappearing footprints fitting mine,
> loosening beneath the sun, stopping.
> Looking up, I saw them scattered around me, people,
> sitting bent and curved like deep-freeze packages
> slow thawing in some drafty door propped open,
> their scarves poked out for breathing,
> their bones all angles gloved and padded,
> positioned as if for a vigil.
> .   .   .   .
> recoiling from the frozen scene
> I inward saw, and outward woke to like a dream:
> the ice spread calmly near its heart,
> but turbulently strained to its extremities,
> in every middle zone still trapping arms and legs
> (portions of metal chair half visible,
> reaching through the ice, thrust up and down,
> depending on the drama that had played).
>
> No face approached me, not a hint,
> no shudder in the ground; and yet
> a memory of peopled autumn chairs came by:
> poolside sponsors doting on their sailboat tenders
> when suddenly midwinter came . . .[7]

The treatment of unreality in that poem, where untruth was only
"the guise of pedestrian normality" ("Snowflakes," 329), reminds one
of Malaparte's evocation of horses frozen in a Russian lake in *Kaputt*.
Yet this surrealistic trend characterized some of Emanuel's writing at
the time, like the pieces on the theme of a floor that danced, which he
started in London and reworked into "Worksheets, Flat No. 9."

Living in Paris meant many things besides writing poetry. Apart
from talks with Robert Tricoire and a few French academics and
friends, or seeing *Bubbling Brown Sugar* at the Théâtre de Paris,
Emanuel had little social life. He had deliberately isolated himself. At
Tricoire's apartment a painting of the exiled black American painter
Beauford Delaney inspired his notes on "Art for the People." On January 30, he gave a poetry reading at the Sorbonne, sharing the event
with Melvin Dixon, who read excerpts from a novel in progress.

Poetry also served to allay anguish and fight fears concerning the fate of Emanuel's prized literary documents, which his wife had managed to have stolen from his Mount Vernon file cabinet for her lawyer, Mrs. DuBroff: "By early February 1979, the dragon had come to Montparnasse and . . . I had to face at last, in poetry, the creature that I had been unable to oppose in court" ("Snowflakes," 341). It took Emanuel more than a month to complete the final version of "White Belly Justice: A New York Souvenir." Couching his grievances and pain on paper had some therapeutic effect, and he then broke his habit of generally avoiding Americans. He visited the American Center for Students and Artists on Boulevard Raspail and sat in on a poetry workshop at La Pensée Sauvage bookstore on the Rue de l'Odéon. On March 6, he visited Shakespeare and Company on the Rue de la Bûcherie, where a poetry reading had been scheduled, and he participated ex tempore. His reading of "Eric, at the Blythe Road Post Office" and "White Belly Justice" aroused such interest that he thought of submitting a new volume of poetry to Lotus Press, which had printed *Black Man Abroad: The Toulouse Poems* in 1978. He also gave a reading at the University of Toulouse, where the pieces inspired by his previous experiences there evoked much interest. He read again, on April 3, at Shakespeare and Company, to a crowded room in which many of the listeners had to stand, and enjoyed a very heartening reception.

The Easter vacation was spent with Marie-France in Burgundy and Morvan, famed for ancient cathedrals as well as prestigious wines: Autun, Châlon-sur-Saône, Beaune. There, walking through the Paupers' Ward of the Hôtel Dieu, he found that the Grande Salle reminded him of two works of Black American literature. "A church nave in reality, its Gothic interior resembling a ship turned bottom-up, the 'Grande Salle' was reminiscent of settings used by Jean Toomer near the end of the long 'Kabnis' chapter of *Cane,* and by LeRoi Jones/ Baraka in *The Slave Ship*" ("Snowflakes," 261).

In early May Emanuel was back in Toulouse, and by the beginning of the summer he had accepted an invitation to serve as a visiting professor at the university in 1980 and 1981. He did not wish to return to New York, since, without explanation, City College had stopped paying him: "So I cast my lot for the next two years with a foreign bureaucracy that owed me nothing but the rights of an alien, rather than with a city whose legal arm had recently flung me nothing but the rights left to Dred Scott in 1857" ("Snowflakes," 370).

In the fall of 1979 Emanuel enjoyed a unique experience: he was asked to teach a one-semester course in his own poetry. "November, which began with a holiday auto trip along some of the awesome roads high above the Tarn River and down to the strange limestone rocks of Montpellier-le-Vieux, quickly revealed itself as the month in which university obligations multiplied" ("Snowflakes," 381). On top of regular courses, he had to tutor students working on M.A.s and to evaluate a doctoral dissertation—all written in French—on the works of Gwendolyn Brooks, which took him over a month's assiduous labor. He derived from this experiment the idea of writing his "poetic autobiography," focusing on events only insofar as they were the occasions and sources of his verse.

Two winter trips took Emanuel to Russia and to Dublin, the latter in connection with a reading. In the spring of 1980 a hernia in the left groin was especially worrisome, as after a previous hernia operation the doctors had warned him that another one might be dangerous. Prepared for the worst, he put his last will on tape, specifying that he wished to be buried not in America but in Europe, preferably in France: "The manner in which I have been treated by the court system in New York, and thus in America, during the past several years makes me entirely indisposed to be buried in what is supposed to be my country" ("Snowflakes," 398). Everything went fine. At about that time his second collection of poems with Lotus Press, *A Chisel in the Dark,* came out in the United States.

A vacation in Bulgaria inspired more poems, but the beautiful "Scarecrow: The Road to Toulouse" stemmed from a familiar French sight harking back to unforgettable memories of American lynchings:

> A man, hanging stiffly from the roadside tree,
> smeared my eyes awake with sunlight dyes,
> and after-luncheon calm burst against the rolling scream
> our tires must have sucked into the road,
> twisting out of sight that dangling arm.[8]

Emanuel claims that the completion of "Scarecrow," together with the recovery of his physical strength after the operation, helped him decide to enter into another long period of writing as he had done in isolation in 1978 and 1979. He looked for a room in Paris until he found a seventh-floor studio at 201, Rue de Vaugirard in early September 1980. On a year's leave of absence without pay from City College, he had to live sparingly.

The literary work that kept him busy was not poetry but autobiographical prose, "Snowflakes and Steel," about the composition of his poems written in Europe and their connection with his life. Going through documents, correspondence, diaries, old tickets and stubs was time-consuming spadework for autobiography, "but it sufficed that I was in Paris, where I knew only several people, none of whom I contacted. I was a writer once again, so I spent my time writing. . . . It was unlikely that I would subsist for a year on my own sounds testing sotto voce the rhythms of my prose" ("Snowflakes," 407–8). He therefore allowed himself some evenings at the Opera, hearing recitals by Jessye Norman, Janet Baker, Martti Talvela, and Barbara Hendricks, and attended a conference on black writing at the University of Créteil, before the now customary Christmas celebrations at Le Barry and a New Year's Eve performance of *Notre Faust*.

According to the preface of *Black Man Abroad*, significantly subtitled *The Toulouse Poems*, his first residence in Toulouse had corresponded for James Emanuel to "two years of revival and reorientation in a foreign land" after a barren period in the late 1960s. He visited many other European countries and was inspired to write about or in them, but "the hub of the wheel of influence was Toulouse, where I restored my life and my will to write."[9] In Toulouse he made lasting and faithful friends, not only with the Plassards but also among university colleagues, like the Cordesses, the Poyets, Marvin Holdt, Anthony Suter, the Rocards, Maurice Lévy, and the department chairman whose death in an accident prompted Emanuel to write the tribute "For Fernand Lagarde (died April 13, 1982)." Through his experiences in Toulouse, the French ambiance played a revitalizing role in the poet's creative career, and he found a kind of haven there.

Not that he stopped caring about his responsibilities as a black American writer. "After the Poetry Reading, Black," implicitly an answer to those Western whites who were arrogant enough to define how a "black" poet should behave, indicated what their real motives and fears were. It translated into a series of clichés what a student must have meant when he exclaimed, at a reading by Emanuel at the University of Toulouse: "He is not black enough!" On the contrary, in the introduction to *The Broken Bowl*, he alludes to his "recurrent treatments, after 1968, of personal and racial injustice."[10] What is more, the dedication of that volume to the memory of his son James, "who in his purest light will long outlive three cowardly cops in San Diego," marks the poet's lasting alienation from the United States after a terrible tragedy: his only child, the beloved son about whom he had written numerous early poems and to whom he had dedicated *The Treehouse and Other Poems*, killed himself in 1983 after having been jailed for racist reasons and repeatedly harassed both before and after suffering a brain concussion from police beating. Happening in the country where the New York courts had already deprived him of his rights in his divorce case, this shattering loss pushed James Emanuel into definitive self-exile. He thus decided to accept an early retirement scheme offered by City College and live frugally and freely in France. In the summer of 1984 France increasingly became his home, and one cannot but think of Countee Cullen's sonnets to "la belle, la douce, la bonne" when considering James Emanuel's choice half a century later.

Since Paris provided both a retreat where he could write in peace and stimulation from the cultural life he could share and the contacts he could choose to make, Emanuel decided to live there. He established himself first in the Latin Quarter, at 28 bis, Rue du Cardinal Lemoine, until 1986. Then he moved to a small walk-up apartment on the Boulevard Montparnasse.

Paris continued to inspire significant poems. "Crossing the Square, Montparnasse" already contained all the associations of an old habitué of city street scenes, with its vignette-like accuracy: "Pigeons almost fly into an old man's face / senselessly, unbirdlike in their beggary." A familiar sight—a couple of young people, drowsy and tramp-like in their rumpled jeans—stretch and stare when the unexpected changes the whole atmosphere as music breaks across the chilly square:

> a long-haired, bearded trumpeter
> tilts back his head and cracks the sky
> with a silver beam unchanging in its cry.
> . . . .
> He blows, a gathering crowd is warmed,
> and one-franc pieces tinkle in his cap.[11]

"Daniel in Paris" goes further and tries to suggest the gifts of the French way of life. The piece begins ominously as an American angrily damns the French thieves after his wife's jewelry has been burglarized from their apartment. He startles their son Daniel from his sleep, and the couple remark that at least the little boy may have been preserved from the deleterious influence of the city, since after several months in a nursery school he still has not spoken a single word of French. Yet, as his father takes him in his arms to put him to bed again, the boy "timed it right / to say / *'Je t'aime, Papa, je t'aime.'*"[12] There is violence in the city, but it can also bring unexpected spiritual gifts.

James Emanuel is well aware that there is racism in France, but he sees it in perspective and makes a distinction that can shed light upon the way some black Americans feel about it: such racism comes from people from whom he considers he has no right to expect any special sympathy, being a foreigner and a kind of uninvited guest. He is inclined to tolerate it—at least rationalize it—because his status as a foreigner deprives him, so to speak, of his expectations as a citizen.

On the contrary, racism in the United States hurts him as badly as the rejection of a mother who, unjustifiably, relegates to a marginal, second-rate existence some of the children she should treat with love.

Such is roughly the message of "Racism in France," the interesting poem that concludes *The Broken Bowl*. At the end of a friendly luncheon the narrator answers a question of his hostess by implying that in the United States racism is more like the machinations of parents slyly attempting to do away with one of their children. How would her daughter Jacqueline, for instance, feel if she saw her putting some kind of poison into her food?

> ". . . something to contaminate her tongue,
> so that, forever, the taste of home-things
> would sicken her, make her remember
> you despised her without cause,
> planned her destruction."
>
> .   .   .   .
>
> The vision clanked in iron shoes around them
> till I stopped it:
> "Jacqueline would read the headlines *her* way:
> 'HOME-GROWN POISON KILLS EIGHT, WOUNDS THIRTY: FOREIGNERS
>   NOT INVOLVED.'"
> I paused. They could not taste it,
> could not know,
> not feel some family arrow
> turning, burning through the night.[13]

It is likely that James Emanuel will remain in Paris, pursuing his career as a poet (in 1987 he published *Deadly James*, a new volume of poems written in his Paris abode) and that he will continue his search as both "Negro author and earth citizen," as one of his critics called him. In his case, Cullen's wish (in his sonnet "To France") of finding "some ship" that might beach him, "glad, though on their sharpest stones, / Among a fair and kindly foreign folk," will perhaps have been realized.

NOTES

1. James Emanuel to the author, September 17, 1969.

2. Emanuel, "Snowflakes and Steel: My Life as a Poet," 1981 typescript deposited at the Jay B. Hubbell Center for American Literary Historiography, Duke University, quoted by permission of James Emanuel, who allowed me to read it and take notes in October 1985. Further references to "Snowflakes" are cited in the text.

3. Emanuel to the author, November 2, 1971.

4. Emanuel, "For Alix, Who Is Three," *Black Man Abroad: The Toulouse Poems* (Detroit: Lotus Press, 1978), 14.

5. Emanuel, "Lovelock Back," *Black Man Abroad*, 21.

6. Emanuel, "For Madame Plassard, a Thanks," *Black Man Abroad*, 25.

7. Emanuel, "The Boar Basin, Years Later," *A Chisel in the Dark* (Detroit: Lotus Press, 1980), 62–63.

8. Emanuel, "Scarecrow: The Road to Toulouse," *The Broken Bowl* (Detroit: Lotus Press, 1983), 47.

9. Emanuel, *Black Man Abroad*, 7.

10. Emanuel, *The Broken Bowl*, ix.

11. Emanuel, "Crossing the Square, Montparnasse," *The Broken Bowl*, 75.

12. Emanuel, "Daniel in Paris," *The Broken Bowl*, 62.

13. Emanuel, "Racism in France," *The Broken Bowl*, 84–85.

Conclusion

Is it at all possible, at the end of this panoramic view, to formulate a general conclusion concerning the expectations and experiences of so many black American writers, artists, and visitors over a period of a century and a half? Is there a common factor in the changing, but enduring, image of liberal France that may attract them, or do we witness, with time and changing political social circumstances in the United States and the world generally, a decline in the attraction exerted on those writers by Paris.

If figures and statistics provide a reliable indication, the following remarks should be made. In the 1850s a dozen artists, all free men of color from the New Orleans area, were sojourning, studying, or living in France; the best-known among the writers were Victor Séjour, Camille Thierry, Armand Lanusse, and P. Valcour. In the 1980s one can hardly count many more: Barbara Chase-Riboud, James Emanuel, Ted Joans, Hart LeRoi Bibbs are the only ones who come to mind. The recent death of James Baldwin, coming a few years after those of William Gardner Smith, Beauford Delaney, Memphis Slim, and Chester Himes, seems to put an end to the generation of the expatriates. For years Richard Gibson has been living in London; and Ollie Harrington, in East Germany. Herb Gentry, Joshua Leslie, and others who were associated with those writers are back in the United States. Only Jimmy "Lover Man" Davis and Gordon Heath remain in Paris to evoke the good old days of the café Tournon and of the Abbaye cabaret in the 1950s.

Times and places have changed. Haynes's soul food restaurant on rue Clauzel looks very much the same, but it caters to a more exclusive clientèle. The cheap Left Bank hotels have been closed or modernized. Indeed, many landmarks still remain, sometimes intact. Some cafés like the Monaco bar, still painted acid yellow; the Tournon, whose long bar where Madame Alazard presided has been preserved; the Café du Départ, where *Pinktoes* was written. A few hotels like the Saint Pierre on Rue de l'Ecole de Médecine, where Countee Cullen stayed nearly every summer throughout the 1930s; like the Delavigne, where Himes found by sheer chance the room reserved for him by Richard Wright on his first night in the city; or Hotel California, now upgraded, where Langston Hughes liked to stay toward the end of his life. But many places are gone, like the "beat hotel" on rue Git-le-Coeur, whose proprietor, Monsieur Rachou, extended credit to many a budding but broke black genius; or hotel Jeanne d'Arc, where Himes subsisted on red wine and discarded vegetables from the nearby Buci market. And what about the houses and apartments, occupied for a few weeks or many years: the places on rue des Trois Frêres and rue Nollet on the Right Bank where Hughes stayed in 1924 when he washed dishes as le Grand Duc; the friendly house on Rue du Douanier in the 14th arrondissement where Cullen, just married, tried to understand his wife and consoled himself by composing *The Black Christ;* the small room of Jacques Vollet, Baldwin's friend, near Porte de Vincennes, which served as a model for the one in *Giovanni's Room.* Rue Bourbon-le-Château, probably the shortest street in the city, is also the street where Malcolm X visited Himes in his fifth-floor walk-up with clochards snoring on the terrace next door. On the walls of the ornate brick and stone house at 14, rue Monsieur le Prince, a plaque commemorates composer Saint-Saens as a resident; perhaps someday a second plaque will honor Richard Wright, who spent some twelve years there. Another might mark the house on 4 rue Regis, where William Melvin Kelley occupied a top-floor sublet eight years after Wright had lived his last days in his ground-floor studio.

A special guidebook points out places linked with American presence in France, but out of ignorance born of indifference it hardly includes blacks. However, one could easily be devoted to the Afro-American presence in the city. Guidebooks are keys to museums and monuments of the past more than to living places where everything is in constant change, and with time Paris has become a vast monument that new generations of black visitors come to sample. They are often ignorant of the black American presence mutely inscribed in its stones, but those who know can read it, as Melvin Dixon did in "Climbing Montmartre," as a palimpsest of black freedom and hunger, and of French racism and celebration of blackness. The fact is that, as a place of shelter from "the American madness," as Baldwin called it, France has largely served its purpose and, no longer a haven, is no longer needed.

How many among the some two million American tourists who visited France last year are Afro-Americans? How many Americans are aware of that black history and presence? It is impossible to guess. It is just as difficult to evaluate how many of the newcomers take away with them something unforgettable from their stay in France. Students mostly, sometimes young writers, express a desire to come back and live there. Few do pursue it, in fact. Fiction writer Davida Kilgore, who came in the spring of 1989 from Minnesota on a writer's fellowship, got on so well with people, despite the language barrier, that she swore she would spend another year. But can one say the charm of Paris has remained as powerful as it used to be?

The main reason for France's lessening attraction is that the black situation in the United States has changed so much during the last century. It is now quite unnecessary for black artists like the painters Ed Clark and Sam Middleton to follow the footsteps of Henry Ossawa Tanner in order to get recognition; rather, the trend has been inverted and European artists often go to the United States to start a career. The political situation is also different from the tense days of the cold war and the McCarthy witch-hunts;left-wingers no longer need to seek shelter abroad. Finally, self-imposed exile by blacks is rarely now a gesture of anger or defiance against a racist mother country; it is mostly a matter of convenience and personal taste.

As a consequence, the motives and expectations of black American writers and artists who come to France approximate those of their white fellow citizens. James Baldwin often remarked that by seeing in Europe many people who were not American and whose sense of reality was different from his own the writer gradually discovered that he was an American. And he like to speak of the romantic legend of Paris, in order to debunk it, and claimed that he had never been fooled by it. Yet from "This Morning, This Evening, So Soon" to *Just above My Head,* his fiction is filled with idylls that, precisely, can take place only in France and are celebrated as peerless experiences. In his last novel he wrote: "If, in addition to being young and seeing the Champs-Elysées for the first time at night with a lover, that lover, furthermore, happens to be French, one is in a rare and exalted category indeed."[1]

As early as the 1920s, when Langston Hughes fell in love with Ann Coussey in the Luxembourg Gardens, he raved about April and romance in the City of Light. To a large extent the myth of romantic Paris, where Frank Yerby set the idyll of *Speak Now* among the 1968 barricades, is still working. And it is still duplicated by that of Hemingway's "moveable feast," the notion that the city is a hothouse propitious to the blossoming of literary talent. Quite naturally, black writers are attracted to it like any others.

But does any special link still exist between French people and black Americans, as there used to be in the era of World War I? Or do any historical reasons explain why the latter are generally treated better, not only than other blacks but also than white Americans? The answers are difficult and bound to be too general. Yet there are special circumstances that explain converging sets of attitudes on the part of the French.

Historically, racism has always existed on either side of the Channel, but it has taken different forms, especially in the colonies. The Anglo-Saxons were convinced they were the superior race; they implicitly assumed that the natives were so radically inferior that they could never become like their masters. As a result, under a system of indirect rule they left native cultures somewhat to themselves. The French were just as convinced that they were a superior people—in fact, entrusted with the mission of enlightening the world. Their implicit assumption, however, was that, given the basic features common to all peoples, all mankind could become like the French. Therefore, they granted full or partial citizenship to a few colonial subjects and forced assimilation on the native cultures. Roughly speaking, the first type of racism is exclusive and keeps the Other at a distance; the second type is assimilationist and wants to make the Other like oneself. To black Americans, excluded for so long from the benefits of citizenship in their home country, such assimilationist policy understandably seemed attractive, at least until the time of black power and the resurgence of black cultural nationalism.

For reasons having partly to do with colonial resistance to cultural assimilation, those among the French who are racists harbor the most inimical feelings toward North Africans (considered dangerous, possibly because of the cohesion of Muslim culture, long before the Algerian liberation war), then in decreasing order toward Africans, West Indians, and finally black Americans. The Americans are, to a degree, exonerated from their blackness because of the prestige of their country—a powerful, patriotic, economically successful nation where law and order are supposed to prevail.

Those among the French who dislike Americans, for whatever reason, will tend to consider black Americans victims of the American racist system, even to the detriment of their real social and economic advancement. In 1956 Chester Himes remarked that "the French don't have too much liking for that type of propaganda which involves cases of actual Negro advancement. The Emmett Till case is more to their liking, something 'bloody . . . terrible . . . inhuman' that brings out all the good grim gristly French adjectives." These French people do not necessarily harbor a special liking for blacks but want to spite white Americans, so they may go out of their way to make up for the sufferings the blacks are all supposed to have undergone.

Dislike of Americans may have many sources. It may be a reaction against the hordes of noisy, loud, unfeeling tourists who complain about not finding what they are used to at home and cannot appreciate native culture and art. It may be rooted in a political opposition to U.S. capitalism and politics, as was often the case during the cold war; then the racial problem in America was invariably used to serve anti-American propaganda. Whatever the reason for anti-Americanism, in this case the black American is exonerated from being American because he is black. Implicitly he is perceived as alienated in America, therefore not responsible for its evils; he is considered as not quite an American.

Another, quite different, response to black Americans, rather common among French people, often disconcerts black visitors. Because in France recognition was granted early to jazz as "highbrow" music and to the blues and spirituals as authentic cultural productions and not only entertainment, the French often see a black American as a member of the group that gave the world a superior kind of music, just as in the mind of a foreigner a French person can be associated with the generous principles of the French Revolution. When asked by a group of French acquaintances to sing or play an instrument, the black American visitor may first believe he is being submitted to the familiar routine of the "natural entertainer." In Ollie Harrington's wonderful cartoon about this subtle way of "putting the Negro back where he belongs," academics at a learned societies meeting ask their black colleague, "Now, Professor Jones, before lecturing on relativity, would you mind singing a spiritual?" The French attitude is often diametrically opposed, the visitor discovers with surprise and relief; it is the manifestation of a possibly naive but sincere regard for the sophisticated cultural gifts of black Americans to the whole world.

One could say that the old stereotypes still persist; as a result, the analyses of French prejudice, chauvinism, and discrimination which Claude McKay offered in *Banjo* before World War II are still valid to a large extent. However, James Baldwin—generally, with Claude McKay, the most perspicacious analyst of French reactions to black Americans—may be somewhat mistaken when he blends these two attitudes in the same sentence: he writes that French people "consider that all Negroes arrive from America, trumpet-laden and twinkle-toed, bearing scars so unutterably painful that all the glories of the French Republic may not suffice to heal them."[2]

Another cultural feature that many black Americans and French people seem to share is their sense of belonging, of roots and the soil. Although France early became industrialized, it is still so rural and, comparatively, so small that people have generally kept close links not only with their families but with their birthplaces and the homes of their ancestors. And black Americans, especially those who have migrated to urban areas, are well known for periodically going "down home"—to the rural South, for instance—for large family reunions. Another common manifestation of this "rural" mentality could be found in an unashamed, earthy enjoyment of food, of meals lovingly prepared. Apart from that, resemblances are more often a matter of familial history, personal upbringing, education, and tastes. This applies to all black visitors; writers come with additional, specific expectations. Here, Americans of all races and ethnic groups are very much in the same situation, and over the decades hundreds of writers have supplied the same answers, which have a common denominator.

Why do writers often find a sustaining atmosphere in Paris today? First, because being a writer, even an as-yet unknown and unpublished writer, still carries more prestige than it does in the United States. Writing to his editor at the New American Library, Chester Himes remarked that unlike the lost generation he was not attracted to Paris by a cheaper cost of living. Actually, he could live on much less money in New York but would not be as well amused: "Here one can walk the streets and be entertained by both the architecture and the characters and it costs nothing, and one can sit in a café and spend only a dollar." The essential difference, however, was the mental attitude and the enormous pressure in New York. Then there was the problem of writing: "Just as in Spain everyone· paints, here in Paris everyone writes, and no one thinks it strange. Every screwball in the world come to Paris trying to write a book. . . . So for me who want to write books and never make enough money doing it to escape the various forms of pressure in the U.S., this is at least a better city than New York."[3]

Second, in the specific case of black writers Paris may seem more welcoming because the French may be more willing than their fellow Americans to listen to their version of the American story, which is what they usually write about. Precisely because Afro-Americans are not "of the mainstream," they tell the story of America from a distance—a view they share to some extent with the French. Although the former are very central to American culture and the latter increasingly imitate its features and adopt its customs, both stand outside of it. The French are obliged to, as foreigners little eager to become assimilated. The black American is blessed, or afflicted, with the double perspective—what Du Bois called "that twoness," being inside and outside. Accordingly, his vision of America may seem more critical, hence more congenial, to the French reader. As for black American writers, if their common expectation was to find a congenial setting in which to work, protected from Philistinism and prejudice, their widely varied personalities, economic status, and previous experiences and the different durations and circumstances of their stays in France produced uncommon responses. They might be critical about it, like Claude McKay and Maya Angelou, or enthusiastic, like Mary Church Terrell and Countee Cullen; they might use France as a shelter, like James Emanuel, or as a temporary way station, like Melvin Dixon or Ted Joans. However, even if they did not fall in love with France, they were all more or less enriched and changed by their stay there.

This does not mean that they will ever give up their American passports. Although for a while Chester Himes considered doing so, he often proclaimed his Americanism and his true relationship to America. It appeared to be very close to that of Wright, McKay, and Emanuel, among others, when he claimed that many people seemed to miss the point about him, that he was simply "an American just like any other American. I like the U.S. and respect its racial attitudes and moral mores more than I do those of any white nation on earth. But because I am an American, I take it is my right to criticize America to whatever extent I wish. It is just the same as I might criticize my mother and father. America is my country and any time it treats me in a way I feel to be unjust I become violently angry."[4]

A final metaphor sums up the authenticity, as well as the many ambiguities, of the love story between black American writers and artists and France. Watching the Bastille Day parade celebrating the bicentennial of the 1789 Revolution, broadcast to millions over the world, one was entranced by the stunning performance of the Florida A&T marching band. But the most memorable image is that of Jessye Norman, magnificently draped in the tricolor, singing "La Marseillaise" on Place de la Concorde—which she had volunteered to do. Beyond the greatness of Norman as an artist and her popularity among French audiences, one could perceive the symbolic meanings of the choice of a black American opera singer to embody the spirit of French freedom—the recognition of black American talent in a musical field other than "black" music, and the will of the French government to make a national commemoration into an international celebration via a member of the "colored" majority of the world, to give the principles of "liberté, égalité, fraternité" their fullest meaning. Was this clever propaganda? It certainly was. But a propaganda in keeping with a long history of similar public stands, similar flamboyant reaffirmations of racial equality, similar instances of recognition of black talent and merit—a tradition that amounts to more than propaganda and myth.

There is enough truth in the myth of liberal France, just as in the myth of democratic America, to keep these myths alive, propagate them, and help them provide living inspiration for the new generations.

NOTES

1. James Baldwin, *Just above My Head* (New York: Dial Press, 1979), 468.
2. James Baldwin, *Notes of a Native Son* (New York: Bantam, 1971), 101.
3. Chester Himes to Walter Freeman, March 3, 1956.
4. Himes to Freeman, December 10, 1953.

Bibliography

Adam, Paul. *Vues d'Amérique.* Paris: Ollendorf, 1906.

"African Art at the Barnes Foundation." *Opportunity,* May 1924, 139–40.

Angelou, Maya. *Singing' and Swingin' and Gettin' Merry like Christmas.* New York: Random House, 1976.

Baldwin, James. *Just above My Head.* New York: Dial Press, 1979.

———. "The Negro in Paris." *Reporter,* June 6, 1950, 34–36.

———. "The New Lost Generation." *Esquire,* July 1960, 113–15.

———. *Nobody Knows My Name.* New York: Dell, 1963.

———. *No Name in the Street.* New York: Dial Press, 1972.

———. *Notes of a Native Son.* Boston: Beacon Press, 1955; rpt. New York: Bantam Books, 1971.

Bennett, Gwendolyn. "Tokens." In *Ebony and Topaz,* edited by Charles S. Johnson, 147–49. Freeport, N.Y.: Books for Libraries Press, 1971.

———. "Wedding Day." *Fire* 1 (November 1926), 26–28.

Berry, Faith. *Langston Hughes: Before and after Harlem.* Westport, Conn.: Laurence Hill, 1983.

Bibbs, Hart LeRoy. *Paris Jazz Seen.* N.p., 1980.

Blackwood, Granby. *Un sang mal mêlé.* Paris: Denoël/Lettres Nouvelles, 1966.

Bontemps, Arna. Obituary of Countee Cullen. *Saturday Review of Literature,* March 22, 1947, 13.

Brown, William Wells. *The Black Man, His Antecedents, His Genius, His Achievements.* New York: Thomas Hamilton, 1863; rpt. New York: Johnson Reprint Co., 1968.

———. *Sketches of Places and People Abroad.* Boston: John P. Jewett, 1855.

Carter, Vincent. *The Bern Book.* New York: John Day, 1970.

Cayton, Horace. *Long Old Road.* New York: Trident Press, 1965.

Chase-Riboud, Barbara. *Sally Hemings.* New York: Viking, 1979; rpt. New York: Avon, 1980.

Coleman, Edward Maceo. *Creole Voices.* Washington, D.C.: Associated Publishers, 1945.

Colter, Cyrus. *Night Studies.* Chicago: Swallow Press, 1979.

Cook, Mercer. "Booker T. Washington and the French." *Journal of Negro History* 40 (1955), 318–40.

Cooper, Wayne. *Claude McKay.* Baton Rouge: Louisiana State University Press, 1988.

———, ed. *The Passion of Claude McKay.* New York: Schocken, 1973.

Cullen, Countee. *The Black Christ.* New York: Harper, 1929.

———. "Countee Cullen on French Courtesy." *Crisis,* June 1929, 193.

———. "Countee Cullen to His Friends." *Crisis,* April 1929, 119.

———. "Letter from Paris." *Opportunity,* September 1928, 271–73.

———. *On These I Stand.* New York: Harper, 1947.

Cullen, Frederic. *From Barefoot Town to Jerusalem.* N.p., n.d. [post 1944].

Cunard, Nancy. "Does Anyone Know Any Negroes?" *Crisis,* September 1931, 300.

Davis, Angela. *Autobiography.* New York: Random House, 1974.

Desdunes, Rodolphe. *Nos hommes et notre histoire.* Montreal, Canada: Arbour and Dupont, 1911.

Dixon, Melvin. *Change of Territory.* Callaloo Poetry Series. Lexington: University Press of Kentucky, 1983.

Douglass, Frederick. *The Life and Times of Frederick Douglass.* 1892; New York: Macmillan, 1962.

Du Bois. W. E. B., *Against Racism: Unpublished Essays, Papers, and Addresses, 1887–1961,* edited by Herbert Aptheker. Amherst: University of Massachusetts Press, 1985.

———. "The American Negro in Paris." *American Monthly Review of Reviews,* November 1900, 575–78.

———. *The Autobiography of W. E. Burghardt Du Bois.* New York: International Publishers, 1968.

———. "The Colored American in France." *Crisis,* February 1919, 167–69.

———. Editorial. *Crisis,* March 1919, 216–17.

———. "Opinions." *Crisis,* May 1919, 13.

Emanuel, James. *Black Man Abroad: The Toulouse Poems.* Detroit: Lotus Press, 1978.

———. *The Broken Bowl.* Detroit: Lotus Press, 1983.

———. *A Chisel in the Dark.* Detroit: Lotus Press, 1980.

Fauset, Jessie. *Comedy: American Style.* New York: Frederick Stokes, 1937.

———. *There Is Confusion.* New York: Boni and Liveright, 1934.

Fox, Stephen R. *The Guardian of Boston: William Monroe Trotter.* New York: Atheneum, 1971.

Garrison, William E. *William Wells Brown, Author and Reformer.* Chicago: University of Chicago Press, 1969.

Gayle, Addison. "The Expatriate." *Black World,* May 1970, 58–65.

Good, Charles Hamlin. "The First American Negro Literary Movement." *Opportunity,* March 1932, 76–79.

Harlan, Louis, et al., eds. *The Booker T. Washington Papers.* Vol. 5. Urbana: University of Illinois Press, 1976.

Harper, Frances Ellen. *Iola Leroy; or, Shadows Uplifted.* 1892; rpt. Salem, N.H.: McGrath, 1969.

Himes, Chester. *A Case of Rape.* Washington, D.C.: Howard University Press, 1984.

———. *My Life of Absurdity.* New York: Doubleday, 1976.

———. *The Quality of Hurt.* New York: Doubleday, 1972.

Hughes, Langston. *The Big Sea.* 1940; New York: Hill and Wang, 1963.

Hunton, Addie, and Kathryn Johnson. *Two Colored Women with the American Expeditionary Forces.* New York: Brooklyn Eagle Press, n.d.

Huret, Jules. *De New York à la Nouvelle Orléans.* Paris: Fasquelle, 1904.

Joans, Ted. *Afrodisia.* New York: Hill and Wang, 1969.

———. *All of Ted Joans and No More.* New York: Excelsior Press, 1961.

———. *Black Pow-Wow.* New York: Hill and Wang, 1969.

———. *Spetrophilia.* Amsterdam: Het Café "De Englebewaarder," 1978.

Joans, Ted, and Joyce Mansour. *Flying Piranha.* New York: Bola Press, 1978.

Johnson, James Weldon. *Along This Way.* New York: Viking, 1933.

Lee, Andrea. *Sarah Phillips.* New York: Random House, 1984.

Logan, Rayford W., and Michael R. Winston, eds. *Dictionary of American Negro Biography.* New York: Norton, 1982.

Lottman, Herbert. "The Action Is Everywhere the Black Man Goes." *New York Times Book Review,* April 21, 1968, 6.

McKay, Claude. *Banjo.* New York: Harper and Brothers, 1929.

———. *A Long Way from Home.* New York: Lee Furman, 1937.

———. *The Negro in America.* Port Washington, N.Y.: Kennikat Press, 1979.

———. "Once More the Germans Face Black Troops." *Opportunity,* November 1929, 324.

Major, Clarence. *Inside Diameter: The French Poems.* Sag Harbor, N.Y.: Permanent Press, 1985.

———. *My Amputations.* Brooklyn, N.Y.: Fiction Collective, 1986.

Marshall, Herbert, and Mildred Stock. *Ira Aldridge, the Negro Tragedian.* London: Rockcliff, 1958.

Mason, Monroe. "With the American Legion in France." New York *Amsterdam News,* September 28, 1927.

Morrison, Toni. *Tar Baby.* New York: Knopf, 1981.

Mulzac, Hugh. *A Star to Steer By.* East Berlin, DDR: Seven Seas Books, 1965.

O'Neill, Charles. "Theatrical Censorship in France, 1844–1875: The Experience of Victor Séjour." *Harvard Library Bulletin* 26 (1978), 425–26.

Payne, Daniel. *Recollections of Seventy Years.* Nashville, Tenn.: AME Sunday School Union, 1888.

Paynter, John. *Fifty Years After.* New York: Margent Press, 1940.

Pickens, William. "How Colored Soldiers Defeated the Real Enemy at Granvillars." *Crisis,* November 1919, 200–203.

Polite, Carlene. *Les Flagellants.* Paris: Christian Bourgois, 1966.

———. *Sister X and the Victims of Foul Play.* New York: Farrar, Straus and Giroux, 1975.

Proctor, Henry Hugh. *Between Black and White.* Boston: Pilgrim Press, 1925.

Reed, John, and Clive Wake, eds. *Selected Poems of Léopold Senghor.* New York: Oxford University Press, 1954.

Rivers, Conrad Kent. *Those Black Bodies and This Sunburnt Face.* Cleveland, Ohio: Freelance Press, 1962.

———. *The Wright Poems.* London: Paul Breman, 1972.

Rivers, W. Napoleon. "Gautier on Aldridge." *Crisis,* January 1932, 460.

Rogers, Joel A. "The Second AEF Invasion of France." New York *Amsterdam News,* October 21, 1927.

Scott, Hazel. "What Paris Means to Me." *Negro Digest,* November 1961, 61–63.

Simmons, William J. *Men of Mark.* 1887; New York: Arno Press, 1968.

Smith Amanda. *The Story of the Lord's Dealings with Mrs. Amanda Smith.* Chicago: Meyer and Brother, 1893.

Smith, William Gardner. *Return to Black America.* Englewood Cliffs, N.J.: Prentice-Hall, 1970.

———. *The Stone Face.* New York: Farrar Straus, 1963; Pocket Books, 1964.

Terrell, Mary Church. *A Colored Woman in a White World.* Washington, D.C.: Ransdell, 1940.

———. "Mary Church Terrell's Letters from Europe to Her Father." *Negro History Bulletin* 38 (September 1976), 615–16.

Thierry, Camille. *Les Vagabondes, poésies américaines.* Paris: Lemerre; Bordeaux: De Laporte, 1874.

Tilton, Theodore. "Frederick Douglass in Paris." *Open Court* 2 (April 28, 1887), 151.

Van Peebles, Melvin. *Le Chinois de XIVieme.* Paris: Jérome Maartineau, 1966.

———. *La Permission/La Fête à Harlem.* Paris: Jérome Martineau, 1967.

Washington, Booker T. *Up from Slavery* (1901). In *Three Negro Classics.* New York: Avon, 1965.

White, Walter. *A Man Called White.* New York: Viking, 1948.

Wright, Bruce McMarion. *Repetitions.* New York: Third Press, 1980.

Wright, Richard. *American Hunger.* New York: Harper and Row, 1978.

———. *Black Boy.* New York: Harper and Row, 1945.

———. *The Outsider.* New York: Harper and Row, 1953.

Index